Willmington's

COMPLETE GUIDE TO BIBLE KNOWLEDGE

New Testament People

New Testament People

Willmington's Complete GUIDE to BIBLE KNOWLEDGE

HAROLD L. WILLMINGTON

Tyndale House Publishers, Inc.
WHEATON, ILLINOIS

This book, the second in the series
Willmington's Complete Guide to Bible Knowledge,
is affectionately dedicated
to my faithful office associates and staff:

REVA ARNOLD
RICK BUCK
VICTOR GOSNELL
MELANIE CRAWFORD
KIM BLACK
HELEN TERRELL
KELLEY LYLE

Scriptures, unless otherwise noted, are from the King James Version of the Bible.

Library of Congress Catalog Card Number: 90-70187
ISBN 0-8423-8162-7

Printed in the United States of America

97 96 95 94 93 92 91
7 6 5 4 3 2 1

PART ONE

CHRONOLOGICAL, THEOLOGICAL, AND STATISTICAL SUMMARIES OF NEW TESTAMENT PEOPLE

Aeneas

CHRONOLOGICAL SUMMARY

I. The misery involved—"And it came to pass, as Peter passed throughout all quarters, he came down also to the saints which dwelt at Lydda. And there he found a certain man named Aeneas, which had kept his bed eight years, and was sick of the palsy" (Acts 9:32-33).

II. The miracle involved

A. In the physical realm—"And Peter said unto him, Aeneas, Jesus Christ maketh thee whole: arise, and make thy bed. And he arose immediately" (Acts 9:34).

B. In the spiritual realm—"And all that dwelt at Lydda and Saron saw him, and turned to the Lord" (Acts 9:35).

STATISTICS

First mention: Acts 9:33
Final mention: Acts 9:34
Meaning of his name: "Praise"
Frequency of his name: Referred to two times
Biblical books mentioning him: One book (Acts)
Occupation: Probably a beggar
Important fact about his life: He was healed of the palsy by Peter.

Agabus

CHRONOLOGICAL SUMMARY

I. Predicting the absence of food in Jerusalem—"And in these days came prophets from Jerusalem unto Antioch. And there stood up one of them named Agabus, and signified by the Spirit that there should be great dearth throughout all the world: which came to pass in the days of Claudius Caesar" (Acts 11:27-28).

II. Predicting the arrest of Paul in Jerusalem—"And as we tarried there many days, there came down from Judaea a certain prophet, named Agabus. And when he was come unto us, he took Paul's girdle, and bound his own hands and feet, and said, Thus saith the Holy Ghost, So shall the Jews at Jerusalem bind the man that owneth this girdle, and shall deliver him into the hands of the Gentiles" (Acts 21:10-11).

STATISTICS

First mention: Acts 11:28
Final mention: Acts 21:10
Meaning of his name: "To love"
Frequency of his name: Referred to two times
Biblical books mentioning him: One book (Acts)
Occupation: Prophet
Important fact about his life: He was a Jerusalem prophet in the days of Paul.

Ananias (1)

CHRONOLOGICAL SUMMARY

I. His deception—"But a certain man named Ananias, with Sapphira his wife, sold a possession, and kept back part of the price, his wife also being privy to it, and brought a certain part, and laid it at the apostles' feet" (Acts 5:1-2).

II. His discovery—"But Peter said, Ananias, why hath Satan filled thine heart to lie to the Holy Ghost, and to keep back part of the price of the land? Whiles it remained, was it not thine own? and after it was sold, was it not in thine own power? why hast thou conceived this thing in thine heart? thou hast not lied unto men, but unto God" (Acts 5:3-4).

III. His death—"And Ananias hearing these words fell down, and gave up the ghost: and great fear came on all them that heard these things" (Acts 5:5).

STATISTICS

Spouse: Sapphira (Acts 5:1)
First mention: Acts 5:1
Final mention: Acts 5:5
Meaning of his name: "God has been gracious."
Frequency of his name: Referred to three times
Biblical books mentioning him: One book (Acts)
Place of death: Jerusalem
Circumstances of death: He was killed by God (Acts 5:5).
Important fact about his life: He lost his life by lying to the Holy Spirit (Acts 5:3).

Ananias (2)

CHRONOLOGICAL SUMMARY

I. Ananias and God
  A. The revelation to Ananias—"And there was a certain disciple at Damascus, named Ananias; and to him said the Lord in a vision, Ananias. And he said, Behold, I am here, Lord. And the Lord said unto him, Arise, and go into the street which is called Straight, and enquire in the house of Judas for one called Saul of Tarsus: for, behold, he prayeth, and hath seen in a vision a man named Ananias coming in, and putting his hand on him, that he might receive his sight" (Acts 9:10-12).
  B. The reluctance of Ananias—"Then Ananias answered, Lord, I have heard by many of this man, how much evil he hath done to thy saints at Jerusalem: And here he hath authority from the chief priests to bind all that call on thy name" (Acts 9:13-14).
  C. The reassurance to Ananias—"But the Lord said unto him, Go thy way: for he is a chosen vessel unto me, to bear my name before the Gentiles, and kings, and the children of Israel: For I will shew him how great things he must suffer for my name's sake" (Acts 9:15-16).

II. Ananias and Saul
  A. His message for Saul—"And Ananias went his way, and entered into the house; and putting his hands on him said, Brother Saul, the Lord, even Jesus, that appeared unto thee in the way as thou camest, hath sent me, that thou mightest receive thy sight, and be filled with the Holy Ghost" (Acts 9:17).
  B. His ministry to Saul—"And immediately there fell from his eyes as it had been scales: and he received sight forthwith, and arose, and was baptized" (Acts 9:18).
    1. Pastoring (Acts 9:18)
    2. Predicting—"And he said, The God of our fathers hath chosen thee, that thou shouldest know his will, and see that Just One, and shouldest hear the voice of his mouth. For thou shalt be his witness unto all men of what thou hast seen and heard" (Acts 22:14-15).

STATISTICS

First mention: Acts 9:10
Final mention: Acts 22:12
Meaning of his name: "God has been gracious."
Frequency of his name: Referred to six times
Biblical books mentioning him: One book (Acts)
Important fact about his life: He ministered to Saul of Tarsus following his Damascus Road conversion.

Ananias (3)

CHRONOLOGICAL SUMMARY

I. Striking Paul in Jerusalem—"And Paul, earnestly beholding the council, said, Men and brethren, I have lived in all good conscience before God unto this day. And the high priest Ananias commanded them that stood by him to smite him on the mouth" (Acts 23:1-2).

II. Slandering Paul in Caesarea—"And after five days Ananias the high priest descended with the elders, and with a certain orator named Tertullus, who informed the governor against Paul" (Acts 24:1).

STATISTICS

First mention: Acts 23:2
Final mention: Acts 24:1
Meaning of his name: "God has been gracious."
Frequency of his name: Referred to two times
Biblical books mentioning him: One book (Acts)
Occupation: Jewish high priest (Acts 23:2)
Important fact about his life: He was the religious leader who persecuted Paul.

Andrew

CHRONOLOGICAL SUMMARY

I. Andrew's first meeting with Christ
  A. The seeker
    1. Andrew was originally a disciple of John the Baptist.
    2. He was introduced to Christ by John—"Again the next day after John stood, and two of his disciples; and looking upon Jesus as he walked, he saith, Behold the Lamb of God! And the two disciples heard him speak, and they followed Jesus. Then Jesus turned, and saw them following, and saith unto them, What seek ye? They said unto him, Rabbi, (which is to say, being interpreted, Master,) where dwellest thou? He saith unto them, Come and see. They came and saw where he dwelt, and abode with him that day: for it was about the tenth hour. One of the two which heard John speak, and followed him, was Andrew, Simon Peter's brother" (John 1:35-40).
  B. The soul winner—"He first findeth his own brother Simon, and saith unto him, We have found the Messias, which is, being interpreted, the Christ. And he brought him to Jesus. And when Jesus beheld him, he said, Thou art Simon the son of Jona: thou shalt be called Cephas, which is by interpretation, A stone" (John 1:41-42).

II. Andrew's full-time ministry for Christ
  A. His dedication—"And Jesus, walking by the sea of Galilee, saw two brethren, Simon called Peter, and Andrew his brother, casting a net into the sea: for they were fishers. And he saith unto them, Follow me, and I will make you fishers of men. And they straightway left their nets, and followed him" (Matt. 4:18-20).
  B. His doubts—"One of his disciples, Andrew, Simon Peter's brother, saith unto him, There is a lad here, which hath five barley loaves, and two small fishes: but what are they among so many?" (John 6:8-9).

STATISTICS

Father: Jonah (John 1:42)
Brother: Peter (John 1:40; Matt. 4:18)
First mention: Matthew 4:18
Final mention: Acts 1:13
Meaning of his name: "Manly"
Frequency of his name: Referred to 12 times
Biblical books mentioning him: Five books (Matthew, Mark, Luke, John, Acts)
Occupation: Fisherman before becoming an apostle (Mark 1:16)
Place of birth: Probably Bethsaida in Galilee (John 1:44)
Place of death: Tradition says he was martyred in Greece.
Circumstances of death: Tradition says he was crucified on an X-shaped cross.
Important fact about his life: He brought his brother Peter to Christ (John 1:40-42).

Anna

CHRONOLOGICAL SUMMARY

I. Her widowhood—"And there was one Anna, a prophetess, the daughter of Phanuel, of the tribe of Aser: she was of a great age, and had lived with an husband seven years from her virginity" (Luke 2:36).

II. Her worship—"And she was a widow of about fourscore and four years, which departed not from the temple, but served God with fastings and prayers night and day" (Luke 2:37).

III. Her witness—"And she coming in that instant gave thanks likewise unto the Lord, and spake of him to all them that looked for redemption in Jerusalem" (Luke 2:38).

STATISTICS

Father: Phanuel (Luke 2:36)
First mention: Luke 2:36
Final mention: Luke 2:36
Meaning of her name: "Grace"
Frequency of her name: Referred to one time
Biblical books mentioning her: One book (Luke)
Important fact about her life: She gave thanks to God at the dedication of the infant Jesus.

Annas

CHRONOLOGICAL SUMMARY

I. Annas and Jesus
  A. He browbeat the Savior—"And led him away to Annas first; for he was father in law to Caiaphas, which was the high priest that same year. The high priest then asked Jesus of his disciples, and of his doctrine" (John 18:13, 19).
  B. He bound the Savior—"Now Annas had sent him bound unto Caiaphas the high priest" (John 18:24).

II. Annas and Peter
  A. The demand of the high priest—"And when they had set them in the midst, they asked, By what power, or by what name, have ye done this?" (Acts 4:7).
  B. The declaration of the apostle—"Be it known unto you all, and to all the people of Israel, that by the name of Jesus Christ of Nazareth, whom ye crucified, whom God raised from the dead, even by him doth this man stand here before you whole" (Acts 4:10).

STATISTICS

Son-in-law: Caiaphas (John 18:13)
First mention: Luke 3:2
Final mention: Acts 4:6
Meaning of his name: "Grace of Jehovah"
Frequency of his name: Referred to six times
Biblical books mentioning him: Three books (Luke, John Acts)
Occupation: Former Jewish high priest
Important fact about his life: He was a wicked religious leader before whom Jesus stood trial.

Apollos

CHRONOLOGICAL SUMMARY

I. His ministry in Ephesus
  A. The instruction rendered by Apollos
    1. The messenger—"And a certain Jew named Apollos, born at Alexandria, an eloquent man, and mighty in the scriptures, came to Ephesus" (Acts 18:24).
    2. The message—"This man was instructed in the way of the Lord; and being fervent in the spirit, he spake and taught diligently the things of the Lord, knowing only the baptism of John" (Acts 18:25).
  B. The instruction received by Apollos—"And he began to speak boldly in the synagogue: whom when Aquila and Priscilla had heard, they took him unto them, and expounded unto him the way of God more perfectly" (Acts 18:26).

II. His ministry in Greece—"And when he was disposed to pass into Achaia, the brethren wrote, exhorting the disciples to receive him: who, when he was come, helped them much which had believed through grace: For he mightily convinced the Jews, and that publickly, shewing by the scriptures that Jesus was Christ" (Acts 18:27-28).

III. His ministry in Corinth
   A. He had ministered in Corinth (1 Cor. 1:12; 3:6).
   B. He was on one occasion urged by Paul to revisit Corinth, but felt it was not God's will at the time (1 Cor. 16:12).

STATISTICS

First mention: Acts 18:24
Final mention: Titus 3:13
Meaning of his name: "Destroyer"
Frequency of his name: Referred to 10 times
Biblical books mentioning him: Three books (Acts, 1 Corinthians, Titus)
Occupation: Evangelist and preacher
Place of birth: Alexandria, Egypt (Acts 18:24)
Important fact about his life: He was probably the most gifted preacher in the New Testament.

Aquila

CHRONOLOGICAL SUMMARY

I. The tentmaker—"After these things Paul departed from Athens, and came to Corinth; and found a certain Jew named Aquila, born in Pontus, lately come from Italy, with his wife Priscilla; (because that Claudius had commanded all Jews to depart from Rome:) and came unto them. And because he was of the same craft, he abode with them, and wrought: for by their occupation they were tentmakers" (Acts 18:1-3).

II. The traveler—Both Aquila and Priscilla accompanied Paul on one occasion from Corinth to Ephesus (Acts 18:18-19).

III. The teacher—"And a certain Jew named Apollos, born at Alexandria, an eloquent man, and mighty in the scriptures, came to Ephesus. This man was instructed in the way of the Lord; and being fervent in the spirit, he spake and taught diligently the things of the Lord, knowing only the baptism of John. And he began to speak boldly in the synagogue: whom when Aquila and Priscilla had heard, they took him unto them, and expounded unto him the way of God more perfectly" (Acts 18:24-26).

IV. The trustee (Rom. 16:3-5; 1 Cor. 16:19)—"Greet Priscilla and Aquila my helpers in Christ Jesus: Who have for my life laid down their own necks: unto whom not only I give thanks, but also all the churches of the Gentiles" (Rom. 16:3-4).

STATISTICS

Spouse: Priscilla (Acts 18:2)
First mention: Acts 18:2
Final mention: 2 Timothy 4:19
Meaning of his name: "Eagle"
Frequency of his name: Referred to six times
Biblical books mentioning him: Four books (Acts, Romans, 1 Corinthians, 2 Timothy)
Occupation: Tentmaker (Acts 18:3)
Place of birth: Rome, Italy (Acts 18:2)
Important fact about his life: He and his godly wife greatly assisted and encouraged the Apostle Paul.

Aristarchus

CHRONOLOGICAL SUMMARY

I. A fellow preacher with Paul
   A. He was roughed up in Ephesus (Acts 19:29).
   B. He traveled with Paul from Ephesus to Turkey (Acts 20:4).
   C. He then accompanied the apostle from Caesarea to Rome (Acts 27:2).

II. A fellow prisoner with Paul (Col. 4:10; Philem. 24). He was also incarcerated with the apostle during Paul's first Roman imprisonment.

STATISTICS

First mention: Acts 19:29
Final mention: Philemon 24
Meaning of his name: "The best ruler"
Frequency of his name: Referred to five times
Biblical books mentioning him: Three books (Acts, Colossians, Philemon)
Occupation: Missionary

Place of birth: Thessalonica (Acts 20:4)
Important fact about his life: He was one of Paul's faithful missionary associates.

Barabbas

CHRONOLOGICAL SUMMARY

I. Barabbas, the prisoner
- A. He was an anarchist (Mark 15:7; Luke 23:19).
- B. He was a murderer (Mark 15:7; Luke 23:19).
- C. He was a robber (John 18:40).

II. Barabbas, the pardoned
- A. The invitation by Pilate—"Therefore when they were gathered together, Pilate said unto them, Whom will ye that I release unto you? Barabbas, or Jesus which is called Christ? . . . But the chief priests and elders persuaded the multitude that they should ask Barabbas, and destroy Jesus. The governor answered and said unto them, Whether of the twain will ye that I release unto you? They said, Barabbas" (Matt. 27:17, 20-21).
- B. The injustice by Pilate—"Then released he Barabbas unto them: and when he had scourged Jesus, he delivered him to be crucified" (Matt. 27:26).

STATISTICS

First mention: Matthew 27:16
Final mention: Acts 3:14
Meaning of his name: "Son of Father"
Frequency of his name: Referred to 11 times
Biblical books mentioning him: Five books (Matthew, Mark, Luke, John, Acts)
Occupation: Outlaw
Important fact about his life: This criminal was selected by the Jewish leaders to be set free in place of the innocent Jesus.

Bar-Jesus/Elymas

CHRONOLOGICAL SUMMARY

I. The perverted—"And when they had gone through the isle unto Paphos, they found a certain sorcerer, a false prophet, a Jew, whose name was Bar-jesus" (Acts 13:6).

II. The punished
- A. Elymas's blasphemy—"Which was with the deputy of the country, Sergius Paulus, a prudent man; who called for Barnabas and Saul, and desired to hear the word of God. But Elymas the sorcerer (for so is his name by interpretation) withstood them, seeking to turn away the deputy from the faith" (Acts 13:7-8).
- B. Elymas's blindness—"Then Saul, (who also is called Paul,) filled with the Holy Ghost, set his eyes on him, and said, O full of all subtilty and all mischief, thou child of the devil, thou enemy of all righteousness, wilt thou not cease to pervert the right ways of the Lord? And now, behold, the hand of the Lord is upon thee, and thou shalt be blind, not seeing the sun for a season. And immediately there fell on him a mist and a darkness; and he went about seeking some to lead him by the hand" (Acts 13:9-11).

STATISTICS

Father: Jesus (not the Christ)
First mention: Acts 13:6
Final mention: Acts 13:8
Meaning of his name: Elymas means "powerful"; Bar-jesus means "son of Jesus."
Frequency of his name: Referred to two times
Biblical books mentioning him: One book (Acts)
Occupation: False prophet and sorcerer
Important fact about his life: He was temporarily blinded by Paul for his sin.

Barnabas

CHRONOLOGICAL SUMMARY

I. Sacrificing (Acts 4:36-37)—"Having land, sold it, and brought the money, and laid it at the apostles' feet" (Acts 4:37).

II. Sponsoring—"And when Saul was come to Jerusalem, he assayed to join himself to the disciples: but they were all afraid of him, and believed not that he was a disciple. But Barnabas took him, and brought him to the apostles, and declared unto them how he had seen the Lord in the way, and that he had spoken to him, and how he had preached boldly at Damascus in the name of Jesus" (Acts 9:26-27).

III. Shepherding (Acts 11:21-24)—The church at Jerusalem received news concerning a great revival occurring in the city of Antioch.
  A. Barnabas, the mission for God—"Then tidings of these things came unto the ears of the church which was in Jerusalem: and they sent forth Barnabas, that he should go as far as Antioch" (Acts 11:22).
  B. Barnabas, the message from God—"Who, when he came, and had seen the grace of God, was glad, and exhorted them all, that with purpose of heart they would cleave unto the Lord" (Acts 11:23).
  C. Barnabas, the man of God—"For he was a good man, and full of the Holy Ghost and of faith: and much people was added unto the Lord" (Acts 11:24).

IV. Selecting—"Then departed Barnabas to Tarsus, for to seek Saul: And when he had found him, he brought him unto Antioch. And it came to pass, that a whole year they assembled themselves with the church, and taught much people. And the disciples were called Christians first in Antioch" (Acts 11:25-26).

V. Sowing (Acts 13–14)—Barnabas and Saul were called by the Holy Spirit to conduct the first official missionary journey to the Gentiles in the New Testament. "As they ministered to the Lord, and fasted, the Holy Ghost said, Separate me Barnabas and Saul for the work whereunto I have called them. So they, being sent forth by the Holy Ghost, departed unto Seleucia; and from thence they sailed to Cyprus" (Acts 13:2, 4).
  A. He met Sergius Paulus, governor of the Isle of Cyprus in the capital city of Paphos (Acts 13:7).
  B. He encouraged Jewish and Gentile converts at Antioch of Pisidia (Acts 13:43).
  C. He rebuked some troublemaking Jews at Antioch of Pisidia (Acts 13:46).
  D. He was expelled from Antioch of Pisidia by the unbelieving Jews (Acts 13:50).
  E. He was mistaken for the pagan god Jupiter at the city of Lystra (Acts 14:12).
  F. He forbade the natives of Lystra to worship him as a god (Acts 14:14-15).

VI. Summarizing (Acts 15)—Barnabas and Paul testified before the Jerusalem Council how God's grace had been poured out upon the Gentiles, as witnessed during their first missionary journey.
  A. The dissension—"And certain men which came down from Judaea taught the brethren, and said, Except ye be circumcised after the manner of Moses, ye cannot be saved. When therefore Paul and Barnabas had no small dissension and disputation with them, they determined that Paul and Barnabas, and certain other of them, should go up to Jerusalem unto the apostles and elders about this question" (Acts 15:1-2).
  B. The declaration—"Then all the multitude kept silence, and gave audience to Barnabas and Paul, declaring what miracles and wonders God had wrought among the Gentiles by them" (Acts 15:12).
  C. The decision
    1. That Paul and Barnabas report to the Gentiles—The Jerusalem church selected these men to relate the decision of the council. "It seemed good unto us, being assembled with one accord, to send chosen men unto you with our beloved Barnabas and Paul, men that have hazarded their lives for the name of our Lord Jesus Christ. . . . For it seemed good to the Holy Ghost, and to us, to lay upon you no greater burden than these necessary things; that ye abstain from meats offered to idols, and from blood, and from things strangled, and from fornication: from which if ye keep yourselves, ye shall do well, Fare ye well" (Acts 15:25-26, 28-29).
    2. That Paul and Barnabas return to the Gentiles—"And when James, Cephas, and John, who seemed to be pillars, perceived the grace that

was given unto me, they gave to me and Barnabas the right hands of fellowship; that we should go unto the heathen, and they unto the circumcision" (Gal. 2:9).

VII. Separating—Paul and Barnabas parted company.
  A. The reason for their disagreement—"And some days after Paul said unto Barnabas, Let us go again and visit our brethren in every city where we have preached the word of the Lord, and see how they do. And Barnabas determined to take with them John, whose surname was Mark. But Paul thought not good to take him with them, who departed from them from Pamphylia, and went not with them to the work" (Acts 15:36-38).
  B. The results of their disagreement—"And the contention was so sharp between them, that they departed asunder one from the other: and so Barnabas took Mark, and sailed unto Cyprus; and Paul chose Silas, and departed, being recommended by the brethren unto the grace of God" (Acts 15:39-40).

VIII. Sinning—On one occasion Barnabas allowed himself to be briefly corrupted by the legalistic Judaizers (Gal. 2:13).

STATISTICS

First mention: Acts 4:36
Final mention: Colossians 4:10
Meaning of his name: Joses means "increaser"; Barnabas means "son of encouragement."
Frequency of his name: Referred to 30 times
Biblical books mentioning him: Four books (Acts, 1 Corinthians, Galatians, Colossians)
Place of birth: The Isle of Cyprus (Acts 4:36)

Bartimaeus

CHRONOLOGICAL SUMMARY

I. The beggar
  A. His cry—"And they came to Jericho: and as he went out of Jericho with his disciples and a great number of people, blind Bartimaeus, the son of Timaeus, sat by the highway side begging. And when he heard that it was Jesus of Nazareth, he began to cry out, and say, Jesus, thou Son of David, have mercy on me" (Mark 10:46-47).
  B. His critics—"And many charged him that he should hold his peace: but he cried the more a great deal, Thou Son of David, have mercy on me" (Mark 10:48).
  C. His call—"And Jesus stood still, and commanded him to be called. And they call the blind man, saying unto him, Be of good comfort, rise; he calleth thee" (Mark 10:49).

II. The believer
  A. Requesting—"And he, casting away his garment, rose, and came to Jesus. And Jesus answered and said unto him, What wilt thou that I should do unto thee? The blind man said unto him, Lord, that I might receive my sight" (Mark 10:50-51).
  B. Receiving—"And Jesus said unto him, Go thy way; thy faith hath made thee whole. And immediately he received his sight, and followed Jesus in the way" (Mark 10:52).

STATISTICS

Father: Timaeus (Mark 10:46)
First mention: Mark 10:46
Final mention: Mark 10:46
Meaning of his name: "Son of Timaeus"
Frequency of his name: Referred to one time
Biblical books mentioning him: One book (Mark)
Occupation: Blind beggar
Place of birth: Probably Jericho
Important fact about his life: He received his sight at the hand of Jesus.

Bernice

CHRONOLOGICAL SUMMARY

I. Her encounter with Paul (Acts 25:13, 23)—"And on the morrow, when Agrippa was come, and Bernice, with great pomp, and was entered into the place of hearing, with the chief captains, and principal men of the city, at Festus' commandment Paul was brought forth" (Acts 25:23).

II. Her evaluation of Paul—"And when he had thus spoken, the king rose up, and the governor, and Bernice, and they that sat with them: And when they were gone aside, they talked between themselves, saying, This man doeth nothing worthy of death or of bonds" (Acts 26:30-31).

STATISTICS

Father: Herod Agrippa I
Brother: Agrippa II
First mention: Acts 25:13
Final mention: Acts 26:30
Frequency of her name: Referred to three times
Biblical books mentioning her: One book (Acts)
Occupation: Queen
Important fact about her life: She heard the imprisoned Paul preach in Caesarea.

Caiaphas

CHRONOLOGICAL SUMMARY

I. Caiaphas and Christ
- A. The plotter—"Then assembled together the chief priests, and the scribes, and the elders of the people, unto the palace of the high priest, who was called Caiaphas, and consulted that they might take Jesus by subtilty, and kill him. But they said, Not on the feast day, lest there be an uproar among the people" (Matt. 26:3-5).
- B. The persecutor
  1. The harassment by Caiaphas—"And the high priest arose, and said unto him, Answerest thou nothing? what is it which these witness against thee?" (Matt. 26:62).
  2. The hypocrisy of Caiaphas—"Then the high priest rent his clothes, saying, He hath spoken blasphemy; what further need have we of witnesses? behold, now ye have heard his blasphemy" (Matt. 26:65).
- C. The prophet
  1. The stating of his prophecy—"And one of them, named Caiaphas, being the high priest that same year, said unto them, Ye know nothing at all, nor consider that it is expedient for us, that one man should die for the people, and that the whole nation perish not" (John 11:49-50).
  2. The source behind his prophecy—It was the Holy Spirit himself who put the words into the mouth of this wicked high priest. "And this spake he not of himself: but being high priest that year, he prophesied that Jesus should die for that nation" (John 11:51).
  3. The salvation resulting from his prophecy—"And not for that nation only, but that also he should gather together in one the children of God that were scattered abroad" (John 11:52).

II. Caiaphas and Peter
- A. The demand by Caiaphas—"And Annas the high priest, and Caiaphas, and John, and Alexander, and as many as were of the kindred of the high priest, were gathered together at Jerusalem. And when they had set them in the midst, they asked, By what power, or by what name, have ye done this?" (Acts 4:6-7).
- B. The declaration by Peter—"Be it known unto you all, and to all the people of Israel, that by the name of Jesus Christ of Nazareth, whom ye crucified, whom God raised from the dead, even by him doth this man stand here before you whole" (Acts 4:10).

STATISTICS

First mention: Matthew 26:3
Final mention: Acts 4:6
Meaning of his name: "Depression"
Frequency of his name: Referred to nine times
Biblical books mentioning him: Four books (Matthew, Luke, John, Acts)
Occupation: High priest

Important fact about his life: He was the wicked Jewish high priest who plotted the death of Christ.

Christ *(see Jesus Christ)*

Claudius Lysias

CHRONOLOGICAL SUMMARY

I. He rescued Paul in Jerusalem.
  A. First occasion: From a Jewish mob (Acts 21:31–22:39)
    1. He saved Paul from certain death just outside the temple—"And all the city was moved, and the people ran together: and they took Paul, and drew him out of the temple: and forthwith the doors were shut. And as they went about to kill him, tidings came unto the chief captain of the band, that all Jerusalem was in an uproar. Who immediately took soldiers and centurions, and ran down unto them: and when they saw the chief captain and the soldiers, they left beating of Paul" (Acts 21:30-32).
    2. He questioned Paul—"Art not thou that Egyptian, which before these days madest an uproar, and leddest out into the wilderness four thousand men that were murderers? But Paul said, I am a man which am a Jew of Tarsus, a city in Cilicia, a citizen of no mean city: and, I beseech thee, suffer me to speak unto the people" (Acts 21:38-39).
    3. He allowed Paul to address the Jewish mob (Acts 21:40–22:21).
    4. He ordered Paul to be scourged—"The chief captain commanded him to be brought into the castle, and bade that he should be examined by scourging; that he might know wherefore they cried so against him" (Acts 22:24).
    5. He quickly reversed the command, however, upon learning that Paul was a Roman citizen (Acts 22:25-29).
  B. Second occasion: From the Jewish Sanhedrin (Acts 22:30–23:11)—"And when there arose a great dissension, the chief captain, fearing lest Paul should have been pulled in pieces of them, commanded the soldiers to go down, and to take him by force from among them, and to bring him into the castle" (Acts 23:10).
  C. Third occasion: From a conspiracy consisting of 40 men (Acts 23:12-22)
    1. The fanaticism of the plotters—"And when it was day, certain of the Jews banded together, and bound themselves under a curse, saying that they would neither eat nor drink till they had killed Paul" (Acts 23:12).
    2. The failure of the plotters (Acts 23:16-22)—The plot was discovered by Paul's nephew, who reported it to both the apostle and Claudius.

II. He removed Paul from Jerusalem (Acts 23:23-31).
  A. The men he assigned—"And he called unto him two centurions, saying, Make ready two hundred soldiers to go to Caesarea, and horsemen threescore and ten, and spearmen two hundred, at the third hour of the night; and provide them beasts, that they may set Paul on, and bring him safe unto Felix the governor" (Acts 23:23-24).
  B. The message he sent—"And he wrote a letter after this manner: Claudius Lysias unto the most excellent governor Felix sendeth greeting. This man was taken of the Jews, and should have been killed of them: then came I with an army, and rescued him, having understood that he was a Roman. . . . And when it was told me how that the Jews laid wait for the man, I sent straightway to thee, and gave commandment to his accusers also to say before thee what they had against him. Farewell" (Acts 23:25-27, 30).

STATISTICS
First mention: Acts 23:26
Final mention: Acts 24:22
Frequency of his name: Referred to two times
Biblical books mentioning him: One book (Acts)
Occupation: Roman military officer
Important fact about his life: He saved Paul from a murderous Jewish mob at Jerusalem.

Cleopas

CHRONOLOGICAL SUMMARY

I. His reunion with Jesus—"And it came to pass, that, while they communed together and reasoned, Jesus himself drew near, and went with them. But their eyes were holden that they should not know him" (Luke 24:15-16).

II. His request from Jesus—"And he said unto them, What manner of communications are these that ye have one to another, as ye walk, and are sad?" (Luke 24:17).

III. His reply to Jesus—"And the one of them, whose name was Cleopas, answering said unto him, Art thou only a stranger in Jerusalem, and hast not known the things which are come to pass there in these days? And he said unto them, What things? And they said unto him, Concerning Jesus of Nazareth, which was a prophet mighty in deed and word before God and all the people: And how the chief priests and our rulers delivered him to be condemned to death, and have crucified him" (Luke 24:18-20).

IV. His rebuke by Jesus—"Then he said unto them, O fools, and slow of heart to believe all that the prophets have spoken: Ought not Christ to have suffered these things, and to enter into his glory? And beginning at Moses and all the prophets, he expounded unto them in all the scriptures the things concerning himself" (Luke 24:25-27).

V. His recognition of Jesus—"And it came to pass, as he sat at meat with them, he took bread, and blessed it, and brake, and gave to them. And their eyes were opened, and they knew him; and he vanished out of their sight. And they said one to another, Did not our heart burn within us, while he talked with us by the way, and while he opened to us the scriptures?" (Luke 24:30-32).

VI. His report concerning Jesus—"And they rose up the same hour, and returned to Jerusalem, and found the eleven gathered together, and them that were with them, Saying, The Lord is risen indeed, and hath appeared to Simon. And they told what things were done in the way, and how he was known of them in breaking of bread" (Luke 24:33-35).

STATISTICS
First mention: Luke 24:18
Final mention: Luke 24:18
Frequency of his name: Referred to one time
Biblical books mentioning him: One book (Luke)
Place of birth: Probably Emmaus
Important fact about his life: He was joined by the resurrected Christ on the first Easter Sunday en route to Emmaus.

Cornelius

CHRONOLOGICAL SUMMARY

I. A religious sinner in Caesarea
  A. His veneration for God—"There was a certain man in Caesarea called Cornelius, a centurion of the band called the Italian band, a devout man, and one that feared God with all his house, which gave much alms to the people, and prayed to God alway" (Acts 10:1-2).
  B. His visit from God
    1. The messenger—"He saw in a vision evidently about the ninth hour of the day an angel of God coming in to him, and saying unto him, Cornelius" (Acts 10:3).
    2. The message—"And when he looked on him, he was afraid, and said, What is it, Lord? And he said unto him, Thy prayers and thine alms are come up for a memorial

before God. And now send men to Joppa, and call for one Simon, whose surname is Peter: He lodgeth with one Simon a tanner, whose house is by the sea side: he shall tell thee what thou oughtest to do" (Acts 10:4-6).

3. The mission—"And when the angel which spake unto Cornelius was departed, he called two of his household servants, and a devout soldier of them that waited on him continually; and when he had declared all these things unto them, he sent them to Joppa" (Acts 10:7-8).

II. A redeemed sinner in Caesarea
- A. The conversation with Cornelius
  1. The reception
     a. The reaction by the sinner—"And as Peter was coming in, Cornelius met him, and fell down at his feet, and worshipped him" (Acts 10:25).
     b. The rebuke by the soul winner—"But Peter took him up, saying, Stand up; I myself also am a man" (Acts 10:26).
  2. The perception—"Then Peter opened his mouth, and said, Of a truth I perceive that God is no respecter of persons: But in every nation he that feareth him, and worketh righteousness, is accepted with him" (Acts 10:34-35).
- B. The clarification to Cornelius
  1. Peter explained the person of Jesus—"How God anointed Jesus of Nazareth with the Holy Ghost and with power: who went about doing good, and healing all that were oppressed of the devil; for God was with him" (Acts 10:38).
  2. Peter explained the promise of Jesus—"To him give all the prophets witness, that through his name whosoever believeth in him shall receive remission of sins" (Acts 10:43).
- C. The conversion of Cornelius
  1. His belief in Christ (Acts 10:44-45)
  2. His baptism in Christ (Acts 10:46-48)

STATISTICS

First mention: Acts 10:1
Final mention: Acts 10:31
Meaning of his name: "A horn"
Frequency of his name: Referred to 10 times
Biblical books mentioning him: One book (Acts)
Occupation: Roman military officer
Important fact about his life: He sent for and was led to Christ by the Apostle Peter at Caesarea.

Crispus

CHRONOLOGICAL SUMMARY

I. Crispus, the ruler—He was the chief ruler of the Jewish synagogue in the city of Ephesus (Acts 18:8).

II. Crispus, the redeemed—He was led to Christ by Paul during the apostle's second missionary journey (Acts 18:8).
- A. The record of his belief—"And Crispus, the chief ruler of the synagogue, believed on the Lord with all his house . . ." (Acts 18:8).
- B. The record of his baptism (1 Cor. 1:14)

STATISTICS

First mention: Acts 18:8
Final mention: 1 Corinthians 1:14
Meaning of his name: "Curled"
Frequency of his name: Referred to two times
Biblical books mentioning him: Two books (Acts, 1 Corinthians)
Occupation: Jewish religious leader
Important fact about his life: He was Paul's first recorded convert in Corinth.

Demas

CHRONOLOGICAL SUMMARY

I. He assisted Paul during the apostle's first Roman imprisonment (Col. 4:14; Philem. 24).

II. He abandoned Paul during the apostle's second Roman imprisonment.

A. Why he did it—"For Demas hath forsaken me, having loved this present world" (2 Tim. 4:10a).
B. Where he went—"Departed unto Thessalonica" (2 Tim. 4:10b).

STATISTICS

First mention: Colossians 4:14
Final mention: 2 Timothy 4:10
Meaning of his name: "Popular"
Frequency of his name: Referred to three times
Biblical books mentioning him: Three books (Colossians, Philemon, 2 Timothy)
Occupation: Missionary
Important fact about his life: He left Paul during the apostle's final Roman imprisonment.

Demetrius

CHRONOLOGICAL SUMMARY

I. The tradesman—"For a certain man named Demetrius, a silversmith, which made silver shrines for Diana, brought no small gain unto the craftsmen" (Acts 19:24).
II. The troublemaker
A. He warned the craftsmen that their gold was in danger—"Whom he called together with the workmen of like occupation, and said, Sirs, ye know that by this craft we have our wealth. Moreover ye see and hear, that not alone at Ephesus, but almost throughout all Asia, this Paul hath persuaded and turned away much people, saying that they be no gods, which are made with hands" (Acts 19:25-26).
B. He warned the craftsmen that their goddess was in danger—"So that not only this our craft is in danger to be set at nought; but also that the temple of the great goddess Diana should be despised, and her magnificence should be destroyed, whom all Asia and the world worshippeth" (Acts 19:27).

STATISTICS

First mention: Acts 19:24
Final mention: Acts 19:38
Meaning of his name: "Belonging to Demeter"
Frequency of his name: Referred to two times
Biblical books mentioning him: One book (Acts)
Occupation: Silversmith (Acts 19:24)
Place of birth: Probably Ephesus
Important fact about his life: He instigated a riot against Paul at Ephesus.

Diotrephes

CHRONOLOGICAL SUMMARY

I. The wicked attitude of Diotrephes—He was a proud and arrogant dictator who had forced his way into power (3 John 9).
II. The wicked actions of Diotrephes (3 John 10)
A. His sin against the elder of God (the Apostle John)—Diotrephes had gossiped maliciously about John, slandering the apostle at every opportunity (3 John 10).
B. His sin against the elect of God (the missionaries and members associated with the church)
1. Concerning the missionaries—He had refused to welcome them into the local church fellowship.
2. Concerning the members—He had removed them from the local church fellowship.

STATISTICS

First mention: 3 John 9
Final mention: 3 John 9
Meaning of his name: "Nurtured by Zeus"
Frequency of his name: Referred to one time
Biblical books mentioning him: One book (3 John)
Important fact about his life: He was a godless church leader condemned by the Apostle John.

Dorcas/Tabitha

CHRONOLOGICAL SUMMARY

I. Her deeds—"Now there was at Joppa a certain disciple named Tabitha, which by interpretation is called Dorcas: this woman was full of good works and almsdeeds which she did" (Acts 9:36).

II. Her death—"And it came to pass in those days, that she was sick, and died: whom when they had washed, they laid her in an upper chamber" (Acts 9:37).

III. Her deliverance

A. The call for Peter—"And forasmuch as Lydda was nigh to Joppa, and the disciples had heard that Peter was there, they sent unto him two men, desiring him that he would not delay to come to them. Then Peter arose and went with them. When he was come, they brought him into the upper chamber: and all the widows stood by him weeping, and shewing the coats and garments which Dorcas made, while she was with them" (Acts 9:38-39).

B. The command by Peter—"But Peter put them all forth, and kneeled down, and prayed; and turning him to the body said, Tabitha, arise. And she opened her eyes: and when she saw Peter, she sat up. And he gave her his hand, and lifted her up, and when he had called the saints and widows, presented her alive" (Acts 9:40-41).

STATISTICS

First mention: Acts 9:36
Final mention: Acts 9:40
Meaning of her name: "Gazelle, roe"
Frequency of her name: Referred to four times
Biblical books mentioning her: One book (Acts)
Place of death: Joppa
Important fact about her life: She was raised from the dead by Peter at Joppa.

Elisabeth

CHRONOLOGICAL SUMMARY

I. Elisabeth, the faithful—Both she and her husband Zacharias loved and served God. "And they were both righteous before God, walking in all the commandments and ordinances of the Lord blameless" (Luke 1:6).

II. Elisabeth, the sorrowful—"And they had no child, because that Elisabeth was barren, and they both were now well stricken in years" (Luke 1:7).

III. Elisabeth, the thankful—"And after those days his wife Elisabeth conceived, and hid herself five months, saying, Thus hath the Lord dealt with me in the days wherein he looked on me, to take away my reproach among men" (Luke 1:24-25).

IV. Elisabeth, the joyful

A. The babe of Elisabeth—"And it came to pass, that, when Elisabeth heard the salutation of Mary, the babe leaped in her womb; and Elisabeth was filled with the Holy Ghost" (Luke 1:41).

B. The blessing by Elisabeth—"And she spake out with a loud voice, and said, Blessed art thou among women, and blessed is the fruit of thy womb. And whence is this to me, that the mother of my Lord should come to me? For, lo, as soon as the voice of thy salutation sounded in mine ears, the babe leaped in my womb for joy. And blessed is she that believed: for there shall be a performance of those things which were told her from the Lord" (Luke 1:42-45).

V. Elisabeth, the fruitful—She gave birth to John.

A. The neighbors and her son— "Now Elisabeth's full time came that she should be delivered; and she brought forth a son. And her neighbours and her cousins heard how the Lord had shewed great mercy upon her; and they rejoiced with her" (Luke 1:57-58).

B. The naming of her son—"And it came to pass, that on the eighth day they came to circumcise the child; and they called him Zacharias, after the name of his father. And his mother answered and said, Not so; but he shall be called John" (Luke 1:59-60).

STATISTICS

Spouse: Zacharias (Luke 1:5)
Son: John the Baptist (Luke 1:57-60)
First mention: Luke 1:5
Final mention: Luke 1:57

Meaning of her name: "God's oath"
Frequency of her name: Referred to nine times
Biblical books mentioning her: One book (Luke)
Important fact about her life: She miraculously gave birth to John in her old age.

Epaphras

CHRONOLOGICAL SUMMARY

I. The fellow servant (Philem. 23)
II. The faithful servant (Col. 1:7)
III. The fervent servant (Col. 4:12)

STATISTICS

First mention: Colossians 1:7
Final mention: Philemon 23
Frequency of his name: Referred to three times
Biblical books mentioning him: Two books (Colossians, Philemon)
Occupation: Missionary
Important fact about his life: He was a faithful missionary associate of the Apostle Paul.

Epaphroditus

CHRONOLOGICAL SUMMARY

I. The messenger of Philippi
- A. His mission from the Philippians to Paul— "But I have all, and abound: I am full, having received of Epaphroditus the things which were sent from you, an odour of a sweet smell, a sacrifice acceptable, well-pleasing to God" (Phil. 4:18).
- B. His mission from Paul to the Philippians—"Yet I supposed it necessary to send to you Epaphroditus, my brother, and companion in labour, and fellow-soldier, but your messenger" (Phil. 2:25a). "I sent him therefore the more carefully, that, when ye see him again, ye may rejoice, and that I may be the less sorrowful. Receive him therefore in the Lord with all gladness; and hold such in reputation" (Phil. 2:28-29).

II. The minister to Paul
- A. His service—"Yet I supposed it necessary to send to you Epaphroditus, my brother, and companion in labour, and fellowsoldier, but your messenger, and he that ministered to my wants" (Phil. 2:25). "But I have all, and abound: I am full, having received of Epaphroditus the things which were sent from you, an odour of a sweet smell, a sacrifice acceptable, well-pleasing to God" (Phil. 4:18).
- B. His sickness—"For he longed after you all, and was full of heaviness, because that ye had heard that he had been sick. For indeed he was sick nigh unto death: but God had mercy on him; and not on him only, but on me also, lest I should have sorrow upon sorrow. I sent him therefore the more carefully, that, when ye see him again, ye may rejoice, and that I may be the less sorrowful. Receive him therefore in the Lord with all gladness; and hold such in reputation: Because for the work of Christ he was nigh unto death, not regarding his life, to supply your lack of service toward me" (Phil. 2:26-30).

STATISTICS

First mention: Philippians 2:25
Final mention: Philippians 4:18
Meaning of his name: "Lovely"
Frequency of his name: Referred to two times
Biblical books mentioning him: One book (Philippians)
Occupation: Missionary
Important fact about his life: He was a faithful missionary associate of Paul whom God healed of a critical illness.

Erastus

CHRONOLOGICAL SUMMARY

I. Erastus: The sacred account—He served under Paul as an associate (along with Timothy) during the apostle's third missionary journey (Acts 19:22).

II. Erastus: The secular account—He served as city treasurer at Corinth (Rom. 16:23; 2 Tim. 4:20).

STATISTICS

First mention: Acts 19:22
Final mention: 2 Timothy 4:20
Meaning of his name: "Beloved"
Frequency of his name: Referred to three times
Biblical books mentioning him: Three books (Acts, Romans, 2 Timothy)
Occupation: City treasurer
Important fact about his life: He was one of Paul's missionary associates who later became the city treasurer in Corinth.

Eunice

CHRONOLOGICAL SUMMARY

I. The family of Eunice
  A. She was married to an ungodly spouse (Acts 16:1).
  B. She was the mother of a godly son—"Then came he to Derbe and Lystra: and, behold, a certain disciple was there, named Timotheus, the son of a certain woman, which was a Jewess, and believed; but his father was a Greek" (Acts 16:1).
II. The faith of Eunice—Paul attested to this faith. "When I call to remembrance the unfeigned faith that is in thee, which dwelt first in thy grandmother Lois, and thy mother Eunice; and I am persuaded that in thee also" (2 Tim. 1:5).

STATISTICS

Son: Timothy (Acts 16:1; 2 Tim. 1:5)
First mention: Acts 16:1
Final mention: 2 Timothy 1:5
Meaning of her name: "Conquering well"
Frequency of her name: Referred to two times
Biblical books mentioning her: Two books (Acts, 2 Timothy)
Important fact about her life: She was the godly mother of Timothy.

Euodias

CHRONOLOGICAL SUMMARY

I. Her faithfulness—She had rendered great assistance to the Apostle Paul. "Which laboured with me in the gospel" (Phil. 4:3b).
II. Her feud—She was at odds with another woman in the Philippian church. "I beseech Euodias, and beseech Syntyche, that they be of the same mind in the Lord" (Phil. 4:2).
III. Her friend—Paul requested that a mutual friend of these two women attempt to reconcile them. "And I entreat thee also, true yokefellow, help those women" (Phil. 4:3a).

STATISTICS

First mention: Philippians 4:2
Final mention: Philippians 4:2
Meaning of her name: "Fragrance"
Frequency of her name: Referred to one time
Biblical books mentioning her: One book (Philippians)
Important fact about her life: She had rendered great service to Paul.

Eutychus

CHRONOLOGICAL SUMMARY

I. The death of Eutychus
  A. Sleeping—"And there sat in a window a certain young man named Eutychus, being fallen into a deep sleep " (Acts 20:9a).
  B. Sliding—"As Paul was long preaching, he sunk down with sleep, and fell down from the third loft, and was taken up dead" (Acts 20:9b).
II. The deliverance of Eutychus—"And Paul went down, and fell on him, and embracing him said, Trouble not yourselves; for his life is in him. When he therefore was come up again, and had broken bread, and eaten, and talked a long while, even till break of day, so he departed" (Acts 20:10-11).

STATISTICS
First mention: Acts 20:9
Final mention: Acts 20:9
Meaning of his name: "Fortunate"
Frequency of his name: Referred to one time
Biblical books mentioning him: One book (Acts)
Place of death: Troas
Important fact about his life: He was raised from the dead by Paul.

Felix

CHRONOLOGICAL SUMMARY

I. Receiving a letter about Paul—The Roman commander in Jerusalem, Claudius Lysias, sent his prisoner Paul to Governor Felix in Caesarea along with a letter of introduction and explanation (Acts 23:25-30).

II. Reviewing a lawsuit against Paul—"Who, when they came to Caesarea, and delivered the epistle to the governor, presented Paul also before him. And when the governor had read the letter, he asked of what province he was. And when he understood that he was of Cilicia; I will hear thee, said he, when thine accusers are also come. And he commanded him to be kept in Herod's judgment hall" (Acts 23:33-35).

A. The defamation (Acts 24:1-9)—"And after five days Ananias the high priest descended with the elders, and with a certain orator named Tertullus, who informed the governor against Paul" (Acts 24:1).

B. The defense (Acts 24:10-21)—"Then Paul, after that the governor had beckoned unto him to speak, answered, Forasmuch as I know that thou hast been of many years a judge unto this nation, I do the more cheerfully answer for myself" (Acts 24:10).

C. The decision—"And when Felix heard these things, having more perfect knowledge of that way, he deferred them, and said, When Lysias the chief captain shall come down, I will know the uttermost of your matter. And he commanded a centurion to keep Paul, and to let him have liberty, and that he should forbid none of his acquaintance to minister or come unto him" (Acts 24:22-23).

III. Refusing a lecture delivered by Paul—"And after certain days, when Felix came with his wife Drusilla, which was a Jewess, he sent for Paul, and heard him concerning the faith in Christ. And as he reasoned of righteousness, temperance, and judgment to come, Felix trembled, and answered, Go thy way for this time; when I have a convenient season, I will call for thee" (Acts 24:24-25).

IV. Requesting some money from Paul—"He hoped also that money should have been given him of Paul, that he might loose him: wherefore he sent for him the oftener, and communed with him" (Acts 24:26).

STATISTICS
First mention: Acts 23:24
Final mention: Acts 25:14
Meaning of his name: "Happy"
Frequency of his name: Referred to eight times
Biblical books mentioning him: One book (Acts)
Occupation: Roman governor

Festus

CHRONOLOGICAL SUMMARY

I. Festus and the plotters

A. Their ungodly plan—"Now when Festus was come into the province, after three days he ascended from Caesarea to Jerusalem. Then the high priest and the chief of the Jews informed him against Paul, and besought him, and desired favour against him, that he would send for him to Jerusalem, laying wait in the way to kill him" (Acts 25:1-3).

B. Their unsuccessful plan—"But Festus answered, that Paul should be kept at Caesarea, and that he himself would depart shortly thither. Let them therefore, said he, which among you are able, go down with me, and accuse this man, if there be any wickedness in him" (Acts 25:4-5).

II. Festus and the prisoner
   A. The accusations—"And when he was come, the Jews which came down from Jerusalem stood round about, and laid many and grievous complaints against Paul, which they could not prove" (Acts 25:7).
   B. The answers—"While he answered for himself, Neither against the law of the Jews, neither against the temple, nor yet against Caesar, have I offended any thing at all" (Acts 25:8).
   C. The appeasement—"But Festus, willing to do the Jews a pleasure, answered Paul, and said, Wilt thou go up to Jerusalem, and there be judged of these things before me?" (Acts 25:9).
   D. The appeal—"Then said Paul, I stand at Caesar's judgment seat, where I ought to be judged: to the Jews have I done no wrong, as thou very well knowest. For if I be an offender, or have committed any thing worthy of death, I refuse not to die: but if there be none of these things whereof these accuse me, no man may deliver me unto them. I appeal unto Caesar" (Acts 25:10-11).
   E. The agreement—"Then Festus, when he had conferred with the council, answered, Hast thou appealed unto Caesar? unto Caesar shalt thou go" (Acts 25:12).

III. Festus and the potentate—"And after certain days king Agrippa and Bernice came unto Caesarea to salute Festus" (Acts 25:13).
   A. He introduced Paul to the king (Acts 25:14-21)—"And when they had been there many days, Festus declared Paul's cause unto the king, saying, There is a certain man left in bonds by Felix" (Acts 25:14).
   B. He interrupted Paul before the king.
      1. The falsehood—"And as he thus spake for himself, Festus said with a loud voice, Paul, thou art beside thyself; much learning doth make thee mad" (Acts 26:24).
      2. The facts—"But he said, I am not mad, most noble Festus; but I speak forth the words of truth and soberness" (Acts 26:25).

STATISTICS

First mention: Acts 24:27
Final mention: Acts 26:32
Meaning of his name: "Joyful"
Frequency of his name: Referred to 13 times
Biblical books mentioning him: One book (Acts)
Occupation: Roman governor
Important fact about his life: He accused Paul of allowing his vast knowledge to render him insane.

Gaius (1)

CHRONOLOGICAL SUMMARY

I. The ministry he received from Paul—Gaius was led to Christ and baptized by the apostle in the city of Corinth (1 Cor. 1:14).

II. The ministry he rendered to Paul—During a later visit to Corinth Paul stayed in the home of Gaius and wrote the Epistle to the Romans from there (Rom. 16:23).

STATISTICS

First mention: Romans 16:23
Final mention: 1 Corinthians 1:14
Meaning of his name: "Name of a Christian"
Frequency of his name: Referred to two times
Biblical books mentioning him: Two books (Romans, 1 Corinthians)
Important fact about his life: He was a convert of Paul from the city of Corinth.

Gaius (2)

CHRONOLOGICAL SUMMARY

I. John's prayer for him—"The elder unto the wellbeloved Gaius, whom I love in the truth. Beloved, I wish above all things that thou mayest prosper and be in health, even as thy soul prospereth" (3 John 1-2).

II. John's praise of him
   A. Because of his faithfulness to the message of God—"For I rejoiced greatly, when the brethren came and testified of the truth that is in thee, even as thou walkest in the truth. I have no greater joy than to hear that my children walk in truth" (3 John 3-4).
   B. Because of his faithfulness to the messengers of God—"Beloved, thou doest faithfully whatsoever thou doest to the brethren, and to strangers; which have borne witness of thy charity before the church: whom if thou bring forward on their journey after a godly sort, thou shalt do well: because that for his name's sake they went forth, taking nothing of the Gentiles. We therefore ought to receive such, that we might be fellow-helpers to the truth" (3 John 5-8).

STATISTICS
First mention: 3 John 1
Final mention: 3 John 1
Meaning of his name: "Name of a Christian"
Frequency of his name: Referred to one time
Biblical books mentioning him: One book (3 John)
Important fact about his life: He was a faithful church member, highly praised by John.

Gallio

CHRONOLOGICAL SUMMARY

I. The distortion by the Jews
   A. Their victim—"And when Gallio was the deputy of Achaia, the Jews made insurrection with one accord against Paul, and brought him to the judgment seat" (Acts 18:12).
   B. Their venom—"Saying, This fellow persuadeth men to worship God contrary to the law" (Acts 18:13).

II. The dismissal by the judge
   A. What he would do—"And when Paul was now about to open his mouth, Gallio said unto the Jews, If it were a matter of wrong or wicked lewdness, O ye Jews, reason would that I should bear with you" (Acts 18:14).
   B. What he wouldn't do—"But if it be a question of words and names, and of your law, look ye to it; for I will be no judge of such matters" (Acts 18:15).
   C. What he did do—"And he drave them from the judgment seat" (Acts 18:16).

STATISTICS
First mention: Acts 18:12
Final mention: Acts 18:17
Frequency of his name: Referred to three times
Biblical books mentioning him: One book (Acts)
Occupation: Roman deputy of Corinth
Important fact about his life: He refused the demands of a Jewish mob to punish Paul.

Gamaliel

CHRONOLOGICAL SUMMARY

I. The student and Gamaliel—The Apostle Paul related his testimony to an angry Jewish mob in Jerusalem, beginning with the following words: "I am verily a man which am a Jew, born in Tarsus, a city in Cilicia, yet brought up in this city at the feet of Gamaliel, and taught according to the perfect manner of the law of the fathers, and was zealous toward God, as ye all are this day" (Acts 22:3).

II. The Sanhedrin and Gamaliel—The leaders in the early church were brought before the Jewish Sanhedrin and forbidden to preach the name of Christ (Acts 5:27-28).
   A. The answer of the apostles—"Then Peter and the other apostles answered and said, We ought to obey God rather than men. The God of our fathers raised up Jesus, whom ye slew and hanged on a tree. Him hath God exalted with his right hand to be a Prince and a Saviour, for to give repentance to Israel, and forgiveness of sins. And we are his witnesses of these things; and so is also the Holy

Ghost, whom God hath given to them that obey him" (Acts 5:29-32).

B. The anger of the Sanhedrin—"When they heard that, they were cut to the heart, and took counsel to slay them" (Acts 5:33).

C. The advice of the lawyer—"Then stood there up one in the council, a Pharisee, named Gamaliel, a doctor of the law, had in reputation among all the people, and commanded to put the apostles forth a little space" (Acts 5:34).

1. His warning—"And said unto them, Ye men of Israel, take heed to yourselves what ye intend to do as touching these men" (Acts 5:35).
   a. The first illustration—"For before these days rose up Theudas, boasting himself to be somebody; to whom a number of men, about four hundred, joined themselves: who was slain; and all, as many as obeyed him, were scattered, and brought to nought" (Acts 5:36).
   b. The second illustration—"After this man rose up Judas of Galilee in the days of the taxing, and drew away much people after him: he also perished; and all, even as many as obeyed him, were dispersed" (Acts 5:37).
2. His wisdom—"And now I say unto you, Refrain from these men, and let them alone: for if this counsel or this work be of men, it will come to nought: But if it be of God, ye cannot overthrow it; lest haply ye be found even to fight against God" (Acts 5:38-39).

STATISTICS

First mention: Acts 5:34
Final mention: Acts 22:3
Meaning of his name: "Reward of God"
Frequency of his name: Referred to two times
Biblical books mentioning him: One book (Acts)
Occupation: Famous Jewish lawyer and teacher
Important fact about his life: He advised the wicked Jewish religious leaders not to persecute the early Christian leaders.

Herod Agrippa I

CHRONOLOGICAL SUMMARY

I. Herod Agrippa and the apostles of God

A. He murdered the Apostle James—"Now about that time Herod the king stretched forth his hands to vex certain of the church. And he killed James the brother of John with the sword" (Acts 12:1-2).

B. He attempted to murder the Apostle Peter.

1. The reason for his failure—"Peter therefore was kept in prison: but prayer was made without ceasing of the church unto God for him. . . . And, behold, the angel of the Lord came upon him, and a light shined in the prison: and he smote Peter on the side, and raised him up, saying, Arise up quickly. And his chains fell off from his hands" (Acts 12:5, 7).
2. The retaliation following his failure—"And when Herod had sought for him, and found him not, he examined the keepers, and commanded that they should be put to death. And he went down from Judaea to Caesarea, and there abode" (Acts 12:19).

II. Herod Agrippa and the angel of God

A. The pride of the king—"And Herod was highly displeased with them of Tyre and Sidon: but they came with one accord to him, and, having made Blastus the king's chamberlain their friend, desired peace; because their country was nourished by the king's country. And upon a set day Herod, arrayed in royal apparel, sat upon his throne, and made an oration unto them. And the people gave a shout, saying, It is the voice of a god, and not of a man" (Acts 12:20-22).

B. The punishment of the king—"And immediately the angel of the Lord smote him, because he gave not God the glory: and he was eaten of worms, and gave up the ghost" (Acts 12:23).

STATISTICS

Father: Aristobulus
Mother: Bernice
Grandfather: Herod the Great
First mention: Acts 12:1
Final mention: Acts 12:21
Meaning of his name: "Seed of a hero"
Frequency of his name: Referred to seven times
Biblical books mentioning him: One book (Acts)
Occupation: King over Galilee and Perea
Place of death: Jerusalem
Circumstances of death: He was executed by God.
Important fact about his life: He murdered the Apostle James.

Herod Agrippa II

CHRONOLOGICAL SUMMARY

I. Learning about Paul—"And after certain days king Agrippa and Bernice came unto Caesarea to salute Festus. And when they had been there many days, Festus declared Paul's cause unto the king, saying, There is a certain man left in bonds by Felix: About whom, when I was at Jerusalem, the chief priests and the elders of the Jews informed me, desiring to have judgment against him" (Acts 25:13-15).

II. Listening to Paul

A. The pomp—"And on the morrow, when Agrippa was come, and Bernice, with great pomp, and was entered into the place of hearing, with the chief captains, and principal men of the city, at Festus' commandment Paul was brought forth" (Acts 25:23).

B. The permission—"Then Agrippa said unto Paul, Thou art permitted to speak for thyself. Then Paul stretched forth the hand, and answered for himself" (Acts 26:1).

C. The preaching—"I think myself happy, king Agrippa, because I shall answer for myself this day before thee touching all the things whereof I am accused of the Jews" (Acts 26:2).

D. The persuasion—"King Agrippa, believest thou the prophets? I know that thou believest. Then Agrippa said unto Paul, Almost thou persuadest me to be a Christian. And Paul said, I would to God, that not only thou, but also all that hear me this day, were both almost, and altogether such as I am, except these bonds" (Acts 26:27-29).

E. The postscript—Agrippa offered a twofold conclusion following his meeting with Paul.

1. First conclusion—"And when he had thus spoken, the king rose up, and the governor, and Bernice, and they that sat with them: And when they were gone aside, they talked between themselves, saying, This man doeth nothing worthy of death or of bonds" (Acts 26:30-31).
2. Second conclusion—"Then said Agrippa unto Festus, This man might have been set at liberty, if he had not appealed unto Caesar" (Acts 26:32).

STATISTICS

Father: Herod Agrippa I
Sister: Bernice (Acts 25:13)
Great-grandfather: Herod the Great
First mention: Acts 25:13
Final mention: Acts 26:32
Meaning of his name: "Seed of a hero"
Frequency of his name: Referred to 11 times
Biblical books mentioning him: One book (Acts)
Occupation: King over Galilee
Important fact about his life: He was the king whom the imprisoned Paul attempted to lead to Christ at Caesarea.

Herod Antipas

CHRONOLOGICAL SUMMARY

I. Herod Antipas and John, the messenger of God
  A. Herod (at first) believed John—"For Herod feared John, knowing that he was a just man and an holy, and observed him; and when he heard him, he did many things, and heard him gladly" (Mark 6:20).
  B. Herod (later) bound John—"For Herod himself had sent forth and laid hold upon John, and bound him in prison for Herodias' sake, his brother Philip's wife: for he had married her. For John had said unto Herod, It is not lawful for thee to have thy brother's wife. Therefore Herodias had a quarrel against him, and would have killed him; but she could not" (Mark 6:17-19).
  C. Herod (finally) beheaded John.
    1. The supper—"But when Herod's birthday was kept, the daughter of Herodias danced before them, and pleased Herod" (Matt. 14:6).
    2. The subtlety—"Whereupon he promised with an oath to give her whatsoever she would ask" (Matt. 14:7).
    3. The spite—"And she, being before instructed of her mother, said, Give me here John Baptist's head in a charger" (Matt. 14:8).
    4. The sorrow—"And the king was sorry: nevertheless for the oath's sake, and them which sat with him at meat, he commanded it to be given her" (Matt. 14:9).
    5. The slaughter—"And he sent, and beheaded John in the prison. And his head was brought in a charger, and given to the damsel: and she brought it to her mother" (Matt. 14:10-11).

II. Herod Antipas and Jesus, the Messiah of God
  A. The craftiness of Herod—Jesus himself referred to this characteristic of Herod. "The same day there came certain of the Pharisees, saying unto him, Get thee out, and depart hence: for Herod will kill thee. And he said unto them, Go ye, and tell that fox, Behold, I cast out devils, and I do cures to day and to morrow, and the third day I shall be perfected" (Luke 13:31-32).
  B. The confusion of Herod—"At that time Herod the tetrarch heard of the fame of Jesus" (Matt. 14:1). "And king Herod heard of him; (for his name was spread abroad:) and he said, That John the Baptist was risen from the dead, and therefore mighty works do shew forth themselves in him. Others said, That it is Elias. And others said, That it is a prophet, or as one of the prophets. But when Herod heard thereof, he said, It is John, whom I beheaded: he is risen from the dead" (Mark 6:14-16).
  C. The curiosity of Herod—Jesus was sent by Pilate to stand trial before Herod. "And as soon as he knew that he belonged unto Herod's jurisdiction, he sent him to Herod, who himself also was at Jerusalem at that time. And when Herod saw Jesus, he was exceeding glad: for he was desirous to see him of a long season, because he had heard many things of him; and he hoped to have seen some miracle done by him. Then he questioned with him in many words; but he answered him nothing" (Luke 23:7-9).
  D. The contempt of Herod—"And the chief priests and scribes stood and vehemently accused him. And Herod with his men of war set him at nought, and mocked him, and arrayed him in a gorgeous robe, and sent him again to Pilate" (Luke 23:10-11).
  E. The conciliation of Herod—"And the same day Pilate and Herod were made friends together: for before they were at enmity between themselves" (Luke 23:12).

STATISTICS

Father: Herod the Great
Spouse: Herodias

Brother: Philip
First mention: Matthew 14:1
Final mention: Acts 13:1
Meaning of his name: "Seed of a hero"
Frequency of his name: Referred to 27 times
Biblical books mentioning him: Four books (Matthew, Mark, Luke, Acts)
Occupation: King over Galilee
Important fact about his life: He ordered the beheading of John the Baptist.

Herod the Great

CHRONOLOGICAL SUMMARY

I. The distress of Herod—"Now when Jesus was born in Bethlehem of Judaea in the days of Herod the king, behold, there came wise men from the east to Jerusalem, Saying, Where is he that is born King of the Jews? for we have seen his star in the east, and are come to worship him. When Herod the king had heard these things, he was troubled, and all Jerusalem with him" (Matt. 2:1-3).

II. The demand of Herod
  A. Requesting information from the chief priests—"And when he had gathered all the chief priests and scribes of the people together, he demanded of them where Christ should be born" (Matt. 2:4).
  B. Receiving information from the chief priests—"And they said unto him, In Bethlehem of Judaea: for thus it is written by the prophet, And thou Bethlehem, in the land of Juda, art not least among the princes of Juda: for out of thee shall come a Governor, that shall rule my people Israel" (Matt. 2:5-6).

III. The deception of Herod—"Then Herod, when he had privily called the wise men, enquired of them diligently what time the star appeared. And he sent them to Bethlehem, and said, Go and search diligently for the young child; and when ye have found him, bring me word again, that I may come and worship him also" (Matt. 2:7-8).

IV. The destruction by Herod—"Then Herod, when he saw that he was mocked of the wise men, was exceeding wroth, and sent forth, and slew all the children that were in Beth-lehem, and in all the coasts thereof, from two years old and under, according to the time which he had diligently enquired of the wise men" (Matt. 2:16).

V. The death of Herod—"But when Herod was dead, behold, an angel of the Lord appeareth in a dream to Joseph in Egypt, saying, Arise, and take the young child and his mother, and go into the land of Israel: for they are dead which sought the young child's life" (Matt. 2:19-20).

STATISTICS

Father: Herod Antipater
Spouses: Doris, Mariamne I, Mariamne II, Malthace, Cleopatria
Sons: Herod Archelaus (Matt. 2:22), Herod Antipas (Matt. 14:1-12), Herod Philip (Matt. 14:3)
First mention: Matthew 2:1
Final mention: Matthew 2:19
Meaning of his name: "Seed of a hero"
Frequency of his name: Referred to nine times
Biblical books mentioning him: One book (Matthew)
Occupation: King over Israel
Important fact about his life: He was the king who attempted to murder the infant Jesus.

Herodias

CHRONOLOGICAL SUMMARY

I. Her hatred for John—"For John had said unto Herod, It is not lawful for thee to have thy brother's wife. Therefore Herodias had a quarrel against him, and would have killed him; but she could not" (Mark 6:18-19).

II. Her hostility against John
  A. She had him arrested—"For Herod had laid hold on John, and bound him, and put him in prison for Herodias' sake, his brother Philip's wife" (Matt. 14:3).

B. She (eventually) had him assassinated.
1. The supper—"But when Herod's birthday was kept, the daughter of Herodias danced before them, and pleased Herod" (Matt. 14:6).
2. The subtlety—"Whereupon he promised with an oath to give her whatsoever she would ask" (Matt. 14:7).
3. The spite—"And she, being before instructed of her mother, said, Give me here John Baptist's head in a charger" (Matt. 14:8).
4. The sorrow—"And the king was sorry: nevertheless for the oath's sake, and them which sat with him at meat, he commanded it to be given her" (Matt. 14:9).
5. The slaughter—"And he sent, and beheaded John in the prison. And his head was brought in a charger, and given to the damsel: and she brought it to her mother" (Matt. 14:10-11).

STATISTICS
Father: Aristobulus
Spouses: Philip and Herod Antipas
Daughter: Salome
First mention: Matthew 14:3
Final mention: Luke 3:19
Meaning of her name: "Seed of a hero"
Frequency of her name: Referred to six times
Biblical books mentioning her: Three books (Matthew, Mark, Luke)
Occupation: Queen
Important fact about her life: She persuaded her husband Herod Antipas to behead John the Baptist.

Hymenaeus

CHRONOLOGICAL SUMMARY
I. The perversion of Hymenaeus
A. The heresy Hymenaeus was circulating—"Holding faith, and a good conscience; which some having put away concerning faith have made shipwreck" (1 Tim 1:19). "Of who is Hymenaeus and Alexander" (1 Tim. 1:20a). "and Philetus" (2 Tim. 2:17b). "Who concerning the truth have erred, saying that the resurrection is past already" (2 Tim. 2:18a).
B. The harm Hymenaeus was causing—"And overthrow the faith of some" (2 Tim. 2:18b).
II. The punishment of Hymenaeus (and his companions)—"Whom I have delivered unto Satan, that they may learn not to blaspheme" (1 Tim. 1:20b).

STATISTICS
First mention: 1 Timothy 1:20
Final mention: 2 Timothy 2:17
Meaning of his name: "Nuptial, marriage"
Frequency of his name: Referred to two times
Biblical books mentioning him: Two books (1 Timothy, 2 Timothy)
Occupation: False teacher
Important fact about his life: He was a heretic who denied the doctrine of the resurrection.

Jairus

CHRONOLOGICAL SUMMARY
I. The agony of Jairus (Mark 5:22-24, 35-43; Luke 8:41-42, 49-56)
A. His dying daughter
1. Jairus's report to Jesus—"And, behold, there cometh one of the rulers of the synagogue, Jairus by name; and when he saw him, he fell at his feet. And besought him greatly, saying, my little daughter lieth at the point of death" (Mark 5:22-23a). "For he had one only daughter, about twelve years of age" (Luke 8:42a).
2. Jairus's request from Jesus—"I pray thee, Come and lay thy hands on her, that she may be healed: and she shall live" (Mark 5:23b).
B. His dead daughter
1. The terrible message—"While he yet spake, there came from the ruler

of the synagogue's house certain which said, Thy daughter is dead: why troublest thou the Master any further?" (Mark 5:35).

2. The tender message—"As soon as Jesus heard the word that was spoken, he saith unto the ruler of the synagogue, Be not afraid, only believe" (Mark 5:36).

II. The amazement of Jairus—Upon reaching Jarius's home, Jesus went into the room where the dead girl lay. "And he put them all out, and took her by the hand, and called, saying, Maid, arise. And her spirit came again, and she arose straightway: and he commanded to give her meat. And her parents were astonished: but he charged them that they should tell no man what was done" (Luke 8:54-56).

STATISTICS

First mention: Mark 5:22
Final mention: Luke 8:41
Meaning of his name: "Enlightened by God"
Frequency of his name: Referred to two times
Biblical books mentioning him: Two books (Mark, Luke)
Important fact about his life: Jesus raised his daughter from the dead.

James the Apostle

CHRONOLOGICAL SUMMARY

I. The ministry of James
  A. His call
    1. James's first contact with Jesus (Matt. 4:21-22; Mark 1:19-20; Luke 5:10-11)—"And going on from thence, he saw other two brethren, James the son of Zebedee, and John his brother, in a ship with Zebedee their father, mending their nets; and he called them. And they immediately left the ship and their father, and followed him" (Matt. 4:21-22).
    2. James's formal call by Jesus (Matt. 10:2; Mark 3:17; Luke 6:14)
  B. His companions—James was especially close to his brother and to Simon Peter. These three alone:
    1. Saw the transfiguration of Christ (Matt. 17:1; Mark 9:2; Luke 9:28)
    2. Were present at the resurrection of Jairus's daughter (Mark 5:37; Luke 8:51)
    3. Were asked by Christ to watch and pray in Gethsemane (Mark 14:33)
  C. His carnality—On at least three occasions, the fleshly nature of James was displayed.
    1. As seen by a sectarian event (Mark 9:38-41; Luke 9:49-50)—"And John answered and said, Master, we saw one casting out devils in thy name; and we forbad him, because he followeth not with us. And Jesus said unto him, Forbid him not: for he that is not against us is for us" (Luke 9:49-50). Note: It is assumed John's personal pronoun "we" as used here was a reference to his brother James.
    2. As seen by a selfish event (Matt. 20:20-28; Mark 10:35-45)
      a. The request of the two—"And James and John, the sons of Zebedee, come unto him, saying, Master, we would that thou shouldest do for us whatsoever we shall desire. And he said unto them, What would ye that I should do for you? They said unto him, Grant unto us that we may sit, one on thy right hand, and the other on thy left hand, in thy glory" (Mark 10:35-37).
      b. The resentment of the ten—"And when the ten heard it, they began to be much displeased with James and John" (Mark 10:41).
      c. The response of the Lord
        (1) Toward the two—"And he saith unto them, Ye shall drink indeed of my cup, and be baptized with the baptism that I am baptized with: but to sit on my right hand, and

on my left, is not mine to give, but it shall be given to them for whom it is prepared of my Father" (Matt. 20:23).

(2) Toward the ten—"But Jesus called them unto him, and said, Ye know that the princes of the Gentiles exercise dominion over them, and they that are great exercise authority upon them. But it shall not be so among you: but whosoever will be great among you, let him be your minister; and whosoever will be chief among you, let him be your servant: Even as the Son of man came not to be ministered unto, but to minister, and to give his life a ransom for many" (Matt. 20:25-28).

3. As seen by a spiteful event
   a. The refusal demonstrated by the Samaritans—"And it came to pass, when the time was come that he should be received up, he stedfastly set his face to go to Jerusalem, and sent messengers before his face: and they went, and entered into a village of the Samaritans, to make ready for him. And they did not receive him, because his face was as though he would go to Jerusalem" (Luke 9:51-53).
   b. The retaliation demanded by the brothers—"And when his disciples James and John saw this, they said, Lord, wilt thou that we command fire to come down from heaven, and consume them, even as Elias did?" (Luke 9:54).
   c. The rebuke delivered by the Lord—"But he turned, and rebuked them, and said, Ye know not what manner of spirit ye are of. For the Son of man is not come to destroy men's lives, but to save them. And they went to another village" (Luke 9:55-56).

II. The martyrdom of James
   A. The monarch—"Now about that time Herod the king stretched forth his hands to vex certain of the church" (Acts 12:1).
   B. The method—"And he killed James the brother of John with the sword" (Acts 12:2).

STATISTICS

Father: Zebedee (Matt. 4:21)
Mother: Salome (Mark 15:40)
Brother: John (Matt. 4:21)
First mention: Matthew 4:21
Final mention: Acts 12:2
Meaning of his name: "Heel catcher, suplanter"
Note: Both he and his brother John were nicknamed "Boanerges" by Christ, meaning, "Sons of thunder" (Mark 3:17).
Frequency of his name: Referred to 19 times
Biblical books mentioning him: Four books (Matthew, Mark, Luke, Acts)
Occupation: Fisherman before becoming one of Christ's three key apostles
Place of birth: Probably Bethsaida in Galilee
Method of death: He was killed by the sword (Acts 12:2).
Important fact about his life: He was the first apostle to be martyred for Christ.

James, the half brother of Christ

CHRONOLOGICAL SUMMARY

I. James, the skeptic—Prior to the resurrection of Christ, James, along with his brothers and sisters, were apparently unbelievers.
   A. Their rebuke—"His brethren therefore said unto him, Depart hence, and go into Judaea, that thy disciples also may see the works that thou doest. For there is no man that doeth any thing in secret, and he himself seeketh to be known openly. If thou do these things, shew thyself to the world.

For neither did his brethren believe in him" (John 7:3-5).

B. Jesus' reply—"Then Jesus said unto them, My time is not yet come: but your time is alway ready. The world cannot hate you; but me it hateth, because I testify of it, that the works thereof are evil. Go ye up unto this feast: I go not up yet unto this feast; for my time is not yet full come" (John 7:6-8).

II. James, the saved (1 Cor. 15:7)—Our Lord appeared to James after his glorious resurrection, at which time James became a believer.

III. James, the shepherd—It is believed that James became the first pastor of the church at Jerusalem. Three events in Acts suggest this:

A. The angel's command to Peter—Following his freedom from prison Peter visited the house of Mary, where many had assembled to pray for his release. "But Peter continued knocking: and when they had opened the door, and saw him, they were astonished" (Acts 12:16-17).

B. James's words to the Jerusalem council—"And after they had held their peace, James answered, saying, Men and brethren, hearken unto me: Simeon hath declared how God at the first did visit the Gentiles, to take out of them a people for his name. . . . Wherefore my sentence is, that we trouble not them, which from among the Gentiles are turned to God" (Acts 15:13-14, 19).

C. Paul's final visit with James—"And when we were come to Jerusalem, the brethren received us gladly. And the day following Paul went in with us unto James; and all the elders were present" (Acts 21:17-18).

IV. James, the segregated—Unfortunately, on at least two occasions, James slipped back (temporarily) into the bond of legalism.

A. First occasion—His influence upon Peter:"But when Peter was come to Antioch, I withstood him to the face, because he was to be blamed. For before that certain came from James, he did eat with the Gentiles: but when they were come, he withdrew and separated himself, fearing them which were of the circumcision" (Gal. 2:11-12).

B. Second occasion—His influence upon Paul: During his final visit to Jerusalem, Paul was persuaded by James to briefly place himself back under the Law to appease certain Jewish legalizers (Acts 21:17-18, 21-24).

V. James, the supporter

A. He encouraged Paul during the apostle's first visit to Jerusalem following his conversion—"Then after three years I went up to Jerusalem to see Peter, and abode with him fifteen days. But other of the apostles saw I none, save James the Lord's brother" (Gal. 1:18-19).

B. He endorsed Paul during the apostle's second visit to Jerusalem following his conversion—"Then fourteen years after I went up again to Jerusalem with Barnabas, and took Titus with me also. . . . And when James, Cephas, and John, who seemed to be pillars, perceived the grace that was given unto me, they gave to me and Barnabas the right hands of fellowship; that we should go unto the heathen, and they unto the circumcision" (Gal. 2:1, 9).

VI. James, the scribe—He was the author of the New Testament epistle that bears his name.

THE EPISTLE OF JAMES

The word "perfect" (a reference to maturity) is found many times in James. Thus the term maturity will be used in outlining this book.

I. Suffering makes a mature man (James 1:1-15).

A. The background of sufferings—Both God and Satan are usually involved in the sufferings of a Christian.

1. God's purpose is to purify and strengthen us. He wants to make us better (James 1:2, 12).
2. Satan's purpose is to pervert and weaken us. He wants to make us bitter (James 1:13-15).

B. The purpose of suffering
1. It produces endurance down here (James 1:3-4).
2. It promises rewards up there (James 1:12).
C. The response to suffering
1. Positive:
a. We are to praise God for it (James 1:2).
b. We are to pray while in it (James 1:5).
c. We are to persevere through it (James 1:12).
2. Negative:
a. We are not to become as tossed waves (James 1:6-8).
b. We are not to become as wilted flowers (James 1:9-11).
II. Scripture study makes a mature man (James 1:16-25).
A. Its author—The Father (James 1:17)
B. Its accomplishments (James 1:18)
C. Its admonitions (James 1:19-22)
1. Our talk is to be pure (James 1:19).
2. Our walk is to be pure (James 1:21-22).
D. Its analogy (James 1:23-24)
E. Its assurance (James 1:25)
III. Sincerity makes a mature man (James 2:1-13).
A. Commands against partiality (James 2:1-8)—An earthly example (James 2:5)
B. Consequences of partiality (James 2:9-13)
1. To be guilty of the Law (James 2:9-11)
2. To be judged by the Law (James 2:12-13)
IV. Christian service makes a mature man (James 2:14-26).
A. The problem—Some have imagined a contradiction between James and Paul. Note:
1. Paul's words—"For by grace are ye saved through faith; and that not of yourselves: it is the gift of God: Not of works, lest any man should boast" (Eph. 2:8-9).
2. James's words—"What doth it profit, my brethren, though a man say he hath faith, and have not works? can faith save him? . . . Ye see then how that by works a man is justified, and not by faith only" (James 2:14, 24).
B. The particulars
1. Paul spoke about vertical justification before God.
2. James spoke about horizontal justification before man.
C. The pattern
1. Two examples of head faith only
a. Concerning the destitute (James 2:15-16)
b. Concerning the devil (James 2:19)
2. Two examples of head and heart faith
a. Abraham (James 2:21-23)
b. Rahab (James 2:25)
D. The principle—"Even so faith, if it hath not works, is dead, being alone" (James 2:17).
V. Sound speech makes a mature man (James 3:1-18; 1:26-27).
A. Importance of the tongue (James 3:2)
B. Illustration of the tongue
1. How it can control
a. It is as a bridle to a horse (James 3:3).
b. It is as a rudder to a ship (James 3:4).
c. It is as a fire to a forest (James 3:5).
2. How it can consume (James 3:5)
C. Iniquity of the tongue (James 3:5-6; 1:26)
1. It can destroy our witness for God (James 1:26).
2. It can defile our walk with God (James 3:6).
D. Incorrigibility of the tongue (James 3:7-8)
E. Inconsistency of the tongue (James 3:9-12)
1. The contradiction (James 3:9-12)
2. The conclusion—"Doth a fountain send forth at the same place sweet water and bitter? Can the fig tree, my brethren, bear olive berries? either a vine, figs? so can no fountain both yield salt water and fresh" (James 3:11-12).

F. Instructions for the tongue
1. Seek and speak the wisdom of God (James 3:13, 17-18).
2. Refuse and renounce the slander of Satan (James 3:14-16).

VI. Submission to God makes a mature man (James 4:1-17).
A. What we escape when we do this
1. The flesh (James 4:1-3, 11-12, 16-17)
2. The world (James 4:4-5)
3. The devil (James 4:7)
B. What we enjoy when we do this
1. God's grace (James 4:6)
2. God's guarantee
a. Of his presence (James 4:8)
b. Of his promotion (James 4:10)
3. God's guidance (James 4:13-15)

VII. Self-sacrifice makes a mature man (James 5:1-6).
A. The consternation of the selfish rich (James 5:1)
B. The corruption of the selfish rich (James 5:2, 5)
C. The cruelty of the selfish rich (James 5:4, 6)
D. The condemnation of the selfish rich (James 5:3)

VIII. Steadfastness makes a mature man (James 5:7-11).
A. A past example—Job and his trials (James 5:10-11)
B. A present example—A farmer and his crops (James 5:7)
C. A future example—The Savior and his return (James 5:8-9)

IX. Supplication makes a mature man (James 5:12-18).
A. The seasons of prayer: When one should pray
1. In times of trouble (James 5:13-14)
2. In times of triumph (James 5:13)
B. The reasons for prayer: Why one should pray
1. Prayer can heal the sick (James 5:14-15).
2. Prayer can restore the carnal (James 5:16).
3. Prayer can accomplish the impossible (James 5:17-18).

X. Soul-winning makes a mature man (James 5:19-20)—"Let him know, that he which converteth the sinner from the error of his way shall save a soul from death, and shall hide a multitude of sins" (James 5:20).

STATISTICS

Father: Joseph (Matt. 13:55)
Mother: Mary
Brothers: Joseph, Simon, Judas (Matt. 13:55)
First mention: Matthew 13:55
Final mention: Jude 1
Meaning of his name: "Supplanter"
Frequency of his name: Referred to 11 times
Biblical books mentioning him: Seven books (Matthew, Mark, Acts, 1 Corinthians, Galatians, James, Jude)
Occupation: Apostle and pastor
Place of birth: Probably Nazareth
Place of death: Tradition says he was martyred in the Kidron Valley outside of Jerusalem.
Circumstances of death: Tradition says he was cast down from the temple pinnacle and stoned as he lay dying.
Important fact about his life: He pastored the church at Jerusalem and authored the New Testament book of James.

James the Less

CHRONOLOGICAL SUMMARY

I. The son of Alpheus (Matt. 10:3; Mark 3:18; Luke 6:15; Acts 1:13)
II. The servant of Jesus

STATISTICS

Father: Alpheus
First mention: Matthew 10:3
Final mention: Acts 1:13
Meaning of his name: "Supplanter"
Frequency of his name: Referred to four times
Biblical books mentioning him: Four books (Matthew, Mark, Luke, Acts)
Occupation: Apostle
Important fact about his life: He was one of the 12 apostles.

Jason

CHRONOLOGICAL SUMMARY

I. The reprisal against Jason
 A. The criminals involved—"But the Jews which believed not, moved with envy, took unto them certain lewd fellows of the baser sort, and gathered a company, and set all the city on an uproar, and assaulted the house of Jason, and sought to bring them out to the people" (Acts 17:5).
 B. The charges involved—"And when they found them not, they drew Jason and certain brethren unto the rulers of the city, crying, These that have turned the world upside down are come hither also; whom Jason hath received: and these all do contrary to the decrees of Caesar, saying that there is another king, one Jesus. And they troubled the people and the rulers of the city, when they heard these things" (Acts 17:6-8).
II. The release of Jason—"And when they had taken security of Jason, and of the other, they let them go" (Acts 17:9).

STATISTICS

First mention: Acts 17:5
Final mention: Acts 17:9
Meaning of his name: "Healing"
Frequency of his name: Referred to four times
Biblical books mentioning him: One book (Acts)
Important fact about his life: He was a convert of Paul, living in Thessalonica, whom the Jews persecuted.

Jesus Christ

(See also Part Two, Observations from the Life of Christ)

CHRONOLOGICAL SUMMARY

I. Overview—A *broad* overview of the life of Christ, featuring one harmony outline on his life as presented collectively by Matthew, Mark, Luke, and John (each biographer presents a different aspect of the Savior)
 A. The introduction to the earthly life of Christ
  1. The two genealogies (Matt. 1:1-17; Luke 3:23-38)
  2. The two prefaces (Luke 1:1-4; John 1:1-5)
  3. The three announcements
   a. To Zacharias (Luke 1:5-25)
   b. To Mary (Luke 1:26-38)
   c. To Joseph (Matt. 1:18-25)
  4. The three songs of praise:
   a. That of Elisabeth (Luke 1:39-45)
   b. That of Mary (Luke 1:46-55)
   c. That of Zacharias (Luke 1:67-79)
 B. The manifestation of the earthly life of Christ
  1. Christ's birth (Luke 2:1-20)
  2. Christ's circumcision (Luke 2:21)
  3. Christ's dedication (Luke 2:22-39)
  4. Christ's visit by the wisemen (Matt. 2:1-12)
  5. Christ's flight into Egypt (Matt. 2:13-20)
  6. Christ's early years in Nazareth (Matt. 2:21, 23; Luke 2:40, 52)
  7. Christ's temple visit at age 12 (Luke 2:41-51)
  8. Christ's forerunner—the ministry of John the Baptist (Matt. 3:1-12; Mark 1:1-8; Luke 1:80; 3:1-18; John 1:6-34; 3:25-30)
  9. Christ's baptism (Matt. 3:13-17; Mark 1:9-11; Luke 3:21-22; John 1:32-34)
  10. Christ's temptation (Matt. 4:1-11; Mark 1:12-13; Luke 4:1-13)
  11. Christ is presented as the Lamb of God (John 1:29).
  12. Christ meets his first five disciples.
   a. John, Andrew, and Peter (John 1:35-42)
   b. Philip and Nathanael (John 1:43-51)
  13. Christ performs the first temple cleansing (John 2:13-25).
  14. Christ meets with Nicodemus (John 3:1-21).

15. Christ meets with the Samaritan woman (John 4:1-42).
16. Christ's first preaching tour of Galilee (Matt. 4:17; Mark 1:14-15; Luke 4:14-15)
17. Christ's first return trip to Nazareth (Luke 4:16-30)
18. Christ moves into Capernaum and makes this city his northern headquarters (Matt. 4:13-16).
19. Christ extends a call to four fishermen (Matt. 4:18-22; Mark 1:16-20; Luke 5:1-11).
20. Christ's second preaching tour of Galilee (Matt. 4:23-25; Mark 1:35-39; Luke 4:42-44)
21. Christ extends a call to Matthew (Matt. 9:9-13; Mark 2:13-17; Luke 5:27-32).
22. Christ's first meeting with John's disciples (Matt. 9:14-17; Mark 2:18-22)
23. Christ's first Sabbath controversy with the Pharisees (Matt. 12:1-8; Mark 2:23-28; Luke 6:1-5)
24. Christ officially selects the 12 apostles (Matt. 10:2-4; Mark 3:13-19; Luke 6:12-16).
25. Christ's third preaching tour of Galilee (Matt. 9:35-38)
26. Christ sends out the 12 apostles (Matt. 10:1-42; Mark 6:7-13; Luke 9:1-6).
27. Christ's fourth preaching tour of Galilee (Matt. 11:1)
28. Christ denounces some key cities in Galilee (Matt. 11:20-24).
29. Christ issues a universal invitation (Matt. 11:28-30).
30. Christ is anointed in Simon's house (Luke 7:36-50).
31. Christ's fifth preaching tour of Galilee (Luke 8:1-3)
32. Christ refuses on two occasions to show the Pharisees a sign.
    a. First occasion (Matt. 12:39-41)
    b. Second occasion (Matt. 16:1-4; Mark 8:11-12)
33. Christ explains who his real family is (Matt. 12:46-50: Mark 3:31-35; Luke 8:19-21).
34. Christ's second return trip to Nazareth (Matt. 13:54-58; Mark 6:1-6)
35. Christ's forerunner is murdered by Herod (Matt. 14:1-12; Mark 6:14-29; Luke 9:7-9).
36. Christ refuses the offer of the Galileans to crown him king (John 6:14-15).
37. Christ hears Peter's confession and promises to build his church (Matt. 16:13-21; Mark 8:27-31; Luke 9:18-22).
38. Christ rebukes Peter (Matt. 16:22-23).
39. Christ is transfigured (Matt. 17:1-8; Mark 9:2-8; Luke 9:28-36).
40. Christ rebukes James and John on three occasions.
    a. First occasion (Mark 9:38-41; Luke 9:49-50)
    b. Second occasion (Luke 9:51-56)
    c. Third occasion (Matt. 20:20-28; Mark 10:35-45)
41. Christ answers the apostles' argument concerning who was the greatest among them (Matt. 18:1-5; Mark 9:33-37; Luke 9:46-48).
42. Christ warns about mistreating a little child (Matt. 18:6, 10; Mark 9:42).
43. Christ is approached by three would-be disciples.
    a. First candidate (Luke 9:57-58)
    b. Second candidate (Luke 9:59-60)
    c. Third candidate (Luke 9:61-62)
44. Christ is rebuked by his own unbelieving half brothers (John 7:2-9).
45. Christ forgives a woman taken in the act of adultery (John 8:1-11).
46. Christ sends out the 70 disciples (Luke 10:1-24).
47. Christ visits with Mary and Martha (Luke 10:38-42).
48. Christ commands people to repent (Luke 13:1-5).
49. Christ teaches on the subject of discipleship (Matt. 16:24-27; Mark 8:34-38; Luke 9:23-26; 14:25-33).
50. Christ teaches on the subject of forgiveness (Matt. 18:21-22).

51. Christ teaches on the subject of hell (Matt. 18:8-9; Mark 9:43-48; Luke 12:4-5).
52. Christ teaches on the subject of church discipline (Matt. 18:15-20).
53. Christ teaches on the subject of divorce (Matt. 5:31-32; 19:3-12; Mark 10:2-12).
54. Christ teaches on the subject of rewards (Matt. 19:27-30; Mark 10:28-31; Luke 18:28-30).
55. Christ teaches on the subject of faith (Matt. 21:21-22; Mark 11:22-24).
56. Christ attends the feast of tabernacles (John 7:14-39).
57. Christ attends the feast of dedication (John 10:22-23).
58. Christ states his overall purpose for coming to earth (Matt. 20:28; Mark 10:45; John 10:10).
59. Christ blesses some little children (Matt. 19:13-15; Mark 10:13-17; Luke 18:15-17).
60. Christ is approached by a rich young ruler (Matt. 19:16-26; Mark 10:17-27; Luke 18:18-27).
61. Christ meets Zacchaeus (Luke 19:1-10).

C. The completion of the earthly life of Christ
   1. The eight-day period
      a. Day one: Saturday
         (1) Christ is plotted against by Caiaphas, the high priest (Matt. 26:3-5; Mark 14:1-2; Luke 22:2).
         (2) Christ is anointed by Mary in the home of Simon the leper (Matt. 26:6-13; Mark 14:3-9; John 12:1-8).
      b. Day two: Sunday—Christ makes his triumphal entry into Jerusalem (Matt. 21:1-11, 14-17; Mark 11:1-11; Luke 19:29-44).
      c. Day three: Monday
         (1) Christ pronounces judgment upon a fruitless fig tree (Matt. 21:18-19; Mark 11:12-14)
         (2) Christ performs the second temple cleansing (Matt. 21:12-13; Mark 11:15-17; Luke 19:45-46).
         (3) Christ is sought after by some Gentile Greeks (John 12:20-29).
      d. Day four: Tuesday
         (1) Christ confronts the Pharisees and Sadducees (Matt. 21:23-27; 22:15-46; Mark 11:27-33; 12:13-37; Luke 20:1-8, 20-44).
         (2) Christ condemns the Pharisees and Sadducees (Matt. 23:1-36; Mark 12:38-40; Luke 20:45-47).
         (3) Christ observes the widow and her mite (Mark 12:41-44; Luke 21:1-4).
         (4) Christ weeps over Jerusalem for the final time (Matt. 23:37-39).
         (5) Christ preaches the Olivet Discourse (Matt. 24; Mark 13; Luke 21:5-36).
         (6) Christ relates the parables of the ten virgins, the talents, and the sheep and goats (Matt. 25:1-46).
      e. Day five: Wednesday—Christ is secretly betrayed by Judas (Matt. 26:14-16; Mark 14:10-11; Luke 22:3-6).
      f. Day six: Thursday
         (1) Christ sends Peter and John from Bethany into Jerusalem (Matt. 26:17-19; Mark 14:12-16; Luke 22:7-13).
         (2) Christ meets with his disciples in the upper room (Matt. 26:20-29; Mark 14:17-25; Luke 22:14-38: John 13:1-30).
         (3) Christ preaches his sermon on the Father's house (John 14:1-31).
      g. Day seven: Friday
         (1) Christ preaches his sermon on fruitbearing en route to the Mount of Olives (John 15–16).
         (2) Christ prays his great high priestly prayer at the Mount of Olives (John 17).

(3) Christ arrives in the garden of Gethsemane and is arrested (Matt. 26:36-56; Mark 14:32-52; Luke 22:39-53; John 18:1-12).
(4) Christ suffers his first unfair trial—the appearance before Annas (John 18:13-14, 19-23).
(5) Christ suffers his second unfair trial—the appearance before Caiaphas (Matt. 26:57, 59-68; Mark 14:53-65; John 18:24).
(6) Christ is denied by Simon Peter (Matt. 26:58, 69-75; Mark 14:54, 66-72; Luke 22:54-62; John 18:15-18, 25-27).
(7) Christ suffers his third unfair trial—the appearance before the Sanhedrin (Matt. 27:1; Mark 15:1; Luke 22:66-71).
(8) Christ's betrayer shows remorse and commits suicide (Matt. 27:3-10; Acts 1:18).
(9) Christ suffers his fourth unfair trial—the first appearance before Pilate (Matt. 27:2, 11-14; Mark 15:1-5; Luke 23:1-5; John 18:28-38).
(10) Christ suffers his fifth unfair trial—the appearance before Herod Antipas (Luke 23:6-12).
(11) Christ suffers his sixth unfair trial—the final appearance before Pilate (Matt. 27:15-26; Mark 15:6-15; Luke 23:13-25; John 18:39–19:16).
(12) Christ suffers his seventh unfair trial—the appearance before the Roman soldiers (Matt. 27:27-30; Mark 15:16-19; John 19:2-3).
(13) Christ walks the road to Calvary (Matt. 27:31-32; Mark 15:20-21; Luke 23:26-32; John 19:16).
(14) Christ is crucified (Matt. 27:33-50; Mark 15:22-37; Luke 23:33-46; John 19:17-30).
(15) Christ's death introduces some supernatural events (Matt. 27:51-54; Mark 15:33, 38; Luke 23:45).
(16) Christ's body is removed from the cross and placed in a tomb (Matt. 27:57-61; Mark 15:42-47; Luke 23:50-56; John 19:31-42).

h. Day eight: Saturday—Christ's tomb is officially sealed (Matt. 27:62-66).

2. The forty-day period
   a. Day one: Sunday—Christ is risen from the dead (Matt. 28; Mark 16; Luke 24; John 20–21).
      (1) The appearance to Mary Magdalene (Mark 16:9-11; John 20:11-18)
      (2) The appearance to some women (Matt. 28:5-10)
      (3) The appearance to Simon Peter (Luke 24:34; 1 Cor. 15:5)
      (4) The appearance to two disciples en route to Emmaus (Mark 16:12-13; Luke 24:13-35)
      (5) The appearance to the apostles in the upper room (Mark 16:14; Luke 24:36-48; John 20:19-23)
   b. Days two through forty—"To whom also he shewed himself alive after his passion by many infallible proofs, being seen by them forty days, and speaking of the things pertaining to the kingdom of God" (Acts 1:3). During this period of time the resurrected Christ made five final appearances:
      (1) The appearance to Thomas and the apostles (John 20:24-31)
      (2) The appearance to seven apostles (John 21)
      (3) The appearance to the apostles and 500 disciples (Matt. 28:16-20; Mark 16:15-18; 1 Cor. 15:6)

(4) The appearance to James, the half brother of Christ (1 Cor. 15:7)

(5) The appearance to the eleven on the Mount of Olives (Luke 24:49-53; Acts 1:3-11) "And while they looked stedfastly toward heaven as he went up, behold, two men stood by them in white apparel; which also said, Ye men of Galilee, why stand ye gazing up into heaven? this same Jesus, which is taken up from you into heaven, shall so come in like manner as ye have seen him go into heaven" (Acts 1:10-11).

II. Topical overview

A. The miracles performed by Christ

1. Turning water into wine (John 2:1-11)
2. Healing a nobleman's son (John 4:46-54)
3. Healing a Capernaum demonic (Mark 1:21-28; Luke 4:31-37)
4. Healing Peter's mother-in-law (Matt. 8:14-17; Mark 1:29-34; Luke 4:38-41)
5. The first great catch of fish (Luke 5:1-11)
6. Healing a leper (Matt. 8:2-4; Mark 1:20-25; Luke 5:12-15)
7. Healing a paralytic (Matt. 9:1-8; Mark 2:1-12; Luke 5:17-26)
8. Healing a withered hand (Matt. 12:9-14; Mark 3:1-6; Luke 6:6-11)
9. Healing a centurion's servant (Matt. 8:5-13; Luke 7:1-10)
10. Raising a widow's son (Luke 7:11-17)
11. Calming the stormy sea (Matt. 8:18, 23-27; Mark 4:35-41; Luke 8:22-25)
12. Healing the maniac of Gadara (Matt. 8:28-34; Mark 5:1-20; Luke 8:26-39)
13. Healing the woman of a bloody flux (Matt. 9:20-22; Mark 5:25-34; Luke 8:43-48)
14. Raising Jarius's daughter (Matt. 9:18-19, 23-26; Mark 5:22-24, 35-43; Luke 8:41-42, 49-56)
15. Healing two blind men (Matt. 9:27-31)
16. Healing a dumb demonic (Matt. 9:32-33)
17. Healing a cripple of 38 years (John 5:1-16)
18. Feeding the 5,000 (Matt. 14:14-21; Mark 6:31-44; Luke 9:10-17; John 6:1-13)
19. Walking on water (Matt. 14:24-33; Mark 6:47-51; John 6:16-21)
20. Healing a demonic girl (Matt. 15:21-28; Mark 7:24-30)
21. Healing a deaf man with a speech impediment (Mark 7:31-37)
22. Feeding the 4,000 (Matt. 15:32-38; Mark 8:1-9)
23. Healing a blind man in Bethsaida (Mark 8:22-26)
24. Healing of a man born blind in Jerusalem (John 9:1-41)
25. Healing of a demonic boy (Matt. 17:14-21; Mark 9:14-29; Luke 9:37-42)
26. The miracle of the tribute money (Matt. 17:24-27)
27. Healing of a blind and mute demonic (Matt. 12:22; Luke 11:14)
28. Healing of a crippled woman of 18 years (Luke 13:10-17)
29. Healing of the man with dropsy (Luke 14:1-6)
30. Healing of ten lepers (Luke 17:11-19)
31. Raising of Lazarus (John 11:1-46)
32. Healing of blind Bartimaeus (Matt. 20:29-34; Mark 10:46-52; Luke 18:35-43)
33. Destroying a fig tree (Matt. 21:17-20; Mark 11:12-14, 20-21)
34. Restoring a severed ear (Luke 22:49-51)
35. The second great catch of fish (John 21:1-14)

B. The parables related by Christ

1. Two houses in a hurricane (Matt. 7:24-27; Luke 6:47-49)
2. Forgiving a large and small debt (Luke 7:36-50)
3. Subduing the strong man (Matt. 12:22-37; Mark 3:22-30)

4. The sovereign sower (Matt. 13:1-9, 18-23; Mark 4:1-9, 13-20; Luke 8:4-15)
5. The secret of the seed (Mark 4:26-29)
6. Satan's tares in the Savior's field (Matt. 13:24-30)
7. The mighty mustard seed (Matt. 13:31-32; Mark 4:30-32; Luke 13:18-19)
8. The cook's leaven and the kingdom of heaven (Matt. 13:33)
9. Finding a fortune in a field (Matt. 13:44)
10. The price of a pearl (Matt. 13:45-46)
11. Sorting out a sea catch (Matt. 13:47-50)
12. A trained man and his treasure (Matt. 13:52)
13. Feasting friends of the bridegroom (Matt.9:14-15; Mark 2:18-20; Luke 5:33-35)
14. A new cloth on an old cloth (Matt. 9:16; Mark 2:21; Luke 5:36)
15. Fresh fruit and broken bottles (Matt. 9:17; Mark 2:22; Luke 5:37-39)
16. A generation of gripers (Matt. 11:16-19; Luke 7:29-35)
17. The forgiven who wouldn't forgive (Matt. 18:21-37)
18. How to know your neighbor (Luke 10:30-37)
19. The spirits and the swept house (Matt. 12:43-45; Luke 11:24-26)
20. A fool in a fix (Luke 12:13-21)
21. Readiness as opposed to careless-ness (Matt. 24:42-51; Luke 12:35-48)
22. The fruitless fig tree (Luke 13:6-9)
23. On being a winner at the banquet dinner (Luke 14:7-14)
24. Two fools and a hen-pecked hus-band (Luke 14:15-24)
25. The missing sheep, the misplaced silver, and the miserable son (Luke 15:1-32)
26. The stewing of a steward (Luke 16:1-13)
27. When Hades petitioned paradise (Luke 16:19-31)
28. When our best is but the least (Luke 17:7-10)
29. A widow and a weary judge (Luke 18:1-8)
30. A haughty Pharisee and a humble publican (Luke 18:9-14)
31. A diagnosis of defilement (Matt. 15:10-20; Mark 7:14-23)
32. Hourly workers and daily wages (Matt. 20:1-16)
33. Two sons who reversed their roles (Matt. 21:28-32)
34. Vicious vine keepers (Matt. 21:33-46; Mark 12:1-12; Luke 20:9-19)
35. A wedding guest with no wedding garment (Matt. 22:1-14)
36. The fig tree and the future (Matt. 24:32-35; Mark 13:28-31; Luke 21:29-33)
37. Virgins, vessels, and vigilance (Matt. 25:1-13)
38. A nobleman, ten servants, and ten pounds (Luke 19:11-27)
39. A traveler, three stewards, and eight talents (Matt. 25:14-30)
40. Separating the sheep from the goats (Matt. 25:31-46)

C. The sermons preached by Christ
   1. The sermon in Nazareth from the scroll of Isaiah (Luke 4:16-30)
   2. The Sermon on the Mount (Matt. 5–7)
   3. The Source of Life sermon (John 5:17-47)
   4. The Bread of Life sermon (John 6:22-71)
   5. The Water of Life sermon (John 7:1-53)
   6. The Light of Life sermon (John 8:12-59)
   7. The Shepherd of Life sermon (John 10:1-39)
   8. The Olivet Discourse (Matt. 24–25)
   9. The Way and the Truth and the Life sermon (John 14:1-31)
   10. The Abundance of Life sermon (John 15–16)

D. The prayers uttered by Christ
   1. At his baptism (Luke 3:21)
   2. Before his first preaching tour of Galilee (Mark 1:35)
   3. After healing a leper (Luke 5:16)

4. Before choosing his twelve disciples (Luke 6:12)
5. After the feeding of the 5,000 (Matt. 14:23; Mark 6:46)
6. Before hearing Peter's great confession (Luke 9:18)
7. During his transfiguration (Luke 9:28-29)
8. Upon hearing the report of the returning seventy (Matt. 11:25-27; Luke 10:21-22)
9. After visiting Mary and Martha (Luke 11:1)
10. After receiving some small children (Matt. 19:13-15; Mark 10:13-16)
11. Before raising Lazarus (John 11:41-42)
12. When some Greeks desired to see him (John 12:27-28)
13. After leaving the upper room (John 17:1-26)
14. In the garden (first prayer) (Matt. 26:39; Mark 14:35, 36; Luke 22:41-42)
15. In the garden (second prayer) (Matt. 26:42; Mark 14:39; Luke 22:44-45)
16. In the garden (third prayer) (Matt. 26:44)
17. On the cross (first prayer) (Luke 23:34)
18. On the cross (second prayer) (Matt. 27:46-47; Mark 15:34-35)
19. On the cross (third prayer) (Luke 23:46)

STATISTICS

Father: His heavenly Father: The first person in the Trinity (Luke 2:49); His earthly Father: The Holy Spirit (Matt. 1:20; Luke 1:35)

Mother: Mary (Luke 2:7)

Half brothers: James, Joseph, Simon, and Judas (Matt. 13:55)

Half sisters: Several unnamed (Matt. 13:56)

Famous ancestors: Abraham and David (Matt. 1:1)

First mention: The Seed of the Woman (Gen. 3:15)

Final mention: The Lord Jesus Christ (Rev. 22:21)

Meaning of his name: Jesus means "Savior"; Christ means "the Anointed One."

Frequency of his name: These three key names and titles, "Jesus," "Christ," and "Lord" appear nearly 2,000 times in the New Testament. In addition, there are literally hundreds of other names and titles found throughout the entire Bible.

Biblical books mentioning him: He is referred to in every one of the 66 books of the Bible.

Occupation: Creator (John 1:3); Redeemer (1 Pet. 1:18-19); Prophet (Matt. 13:57); Priest (Heb. 3:1; 4:14); King (Rev. 19:16); Shepherd (John 10:11); Judge (John 5:22)

Place of birth: Bethlehem (Luke 2:4-7)

Place of death: Outside Jerusalem, on a hill (Matt. 27:33)

Circumstances of death: He was crucified (John 19:18).

Important fact about his life: He was (and is) the Son of God who became the sinless Son of Man that sinful sons of men might become the sons of God.

Jezebel

CHRONOLOGICAL SUMMARY

I. The perversion of Jezebel
   A. She was unrighteous—"Notwithstanding I have a few things against thee, because thou sufferest that woman Jezebel, which calleth herself a prophetess, to teach and to seduce my servants to commit fornication, and to eat things sacrificed unto idols" (Rev. 2:20).
   B. She was unrepentant—"And I gave her space to repent of her fornication; and she repented not" (Rev. 2:21).
II. The punishment of Jezebel
   A. What God would do—"Behold, I will cast her into a bed, and them that commit adultery with her into great tribulation, except they repent of their deeds" (Rev. 2:22).
   B. Why God would do it—"And I will kill her children with death; and all the churches shall know that I am he

which searcheth the reins and hearts: and I will give unto every one of you according to your works" (Rev. 2:23).

STATISTICS
First mention: Revelation 2:20
Final mention: Revelation 2:20
Meaning of her name: "Without cohabitation"
Frequency of her name: Referred to one time
Biblical books mentioning her: One book (Revelation)
Occupation: False prophetess
Important fact about her life: She was a demon-inspired member of the local church at Thyatira.

Joanna

CHRONOLOGICAL SUMMARY

I. Rendering assistance to Christ—"And Joanna the wife of Chuza Herod's steward, and Susanna, and many others, which ministered unto him of their substance" (Luke 8:3).

II. Receiving assurance from Christ—Joanna was one of the women visiting the tomb of Christ on Sunday to finish his burial preparation (Luke 24:1, 10).

A. The mystery which awaited them—"And they found the stone rolled away from the sepulchre. And they entered in, and found not the body of the Lord Jesus" (Luke 24:2-3).

B. The message that awaited them—"And it came to pass, as they were much perplexed thereabout, behold, two men stood by them in shining garments: And as they were afraid, and bowed down their faces to the earth, they said unto them, Why seek ye the living among the dead?" (Luke 24:4-5).

C. The miracle that awaited them—"He is not here, but is risen: remember how he spake unto you when he was yet in Galilee, Saying, The Son of man must be delivered into the hands of sinful men, and be crucified, and the third day rise again" (Luke 24:6-7).

STATISTICS
Spouse: Chuza
First mention: Luke 8:3
Final mention: Luke 24:10
Frequency of her name: Referred to two times
Biblical books mentioning her: One book (Luke)
Important fact about her life: She helped Jesus financially in Galilee.

John the Apostle

CHRONOLOGICAL SUMMARY

I. The ministry of John

A. As recorded in the Gospel accounts

1. His call

a. John and his brother James were fishing partners with Andrew and Peter (Luke 5:10).

b. John was probably a well-to-do businessman, for his father had hired servants (Mark 1:20).

c. He may have been, along with Andrew, an early disciple of John the Baptist (John 1:35).

d. If so, he was first introduced to Christ by the Baptist—"And looking upon Jesus as he walked, he saith, Behold the Lamb of God! And the two disciples heard him speak, and they followed Jesus. Then Jesus turned, and saw them following, and saith unto them, What seek ye? They said unto him, Rabbi, (which is to say, being interpreted, Master,) where dwellest thou? He saith unto them, Come and see. They came and saw where he dwelt, and abode with him that day: for it was about the tenth hour" (John 1:36-39).

e. Later, while fishing on the Galilean Sea, upon being summoned by Christ, he forsook all and followed him (Mark 1:19-20).

2. His confidants—John performed most of his activities as a member of a trio or duet.

a. The trio (composed of Peter, James, and John)
   (1) They alone saw the raising from the dead of Jairus's daughter (Mark 5:37).
   (2) They alone saw the transfiguration of Christ (Matt. 17:1).
   (3) They alone saw the special sufferings of Christ in Gethsemane (Matt. 26:36-46).
      (a) He asked them on three specific occasions to pray for him.
      (b) On each occasion they fell asleep.

b. The duet (composed of Peter and John)
   (1) Christ sent these two men on a special mission just prior to his triumphal entry (Luke 19:28-35).
      (a) The place—"And it came to pass, when he was come nigh to Bethphage and Bethany, at the mount called the mount of Olives, he sent two of his disciples" (Luke 19:29).
      (b) The purpose—"Saying, Go ye into the village over against you; in the which at your entering ye shall find a colt tied, whereon yet never man sat: loose him, and bring him hither. And if any man ask you, Why do ye loose him? thus shall ye say unto him, Because the Lord hath need of him" (Luke 19:30-31).
      (c) The performance—"And they that were sent went their way, and found even as he had said unto them. . . . And they brought him to Jesus: and they cast their garments upon the colt, and they set Jesus thereon" (Luke 19:32, 35).
   (2) Christ later sent them to prepare for the final Passover (Luke 22:8-13).
      (a) The man —"And he said unto them, Behold, when ye are entered into the city, there shall a man meet you, bearing a pitcher of water; follow him into the house where he entereth in" (Luke 22:10).
      (b) The message—"And ye shall say unto the goodman of the house, The Master saith unto thee, Where is the guestchamber, where I shall eat the passover with my disciples?" (Luke 22:11).
      (c) The meeting place—"And he shall shew you a large upper room furnished: there make ready. And they went, and found as he had said unto them: and they made ready the passover" (Luke 22:12-13).
   (3) They both followed Christ afar off after his arrest in Gethsemane—"And Simon Peter followed Jesus, and so did another disciple: that disciple was known unto the high priest, and went in with Jesus into the palace of the high priest" (John 18:15).
   (4) They both examined the empty tomb of Christ (John 20:2-8).
      (a) The report—"The first day of the week cometh Mary Magdalene early, when it was yet dark, unto the sepulchre, and seeth the stone taken away from the sepulchre. Then she runneth, and cometh to Simon Peter, and to the other disciple, whom Jesus loved, and saith unto

them, They have taken away the Lord out of the sepulchre, and we know not where they have laid him" (John 20:1-2).

(b) The race—"Peter therefore went forth, and that other disciple, and came to the sepulchre. So they ran both together: and the other disciple did outrun Peter, and came first to the sepulchre. And he stooping down, and looking in, saw the linen clothes lying; yet went he not in" (John 20:3-5).

(c) The realization—"Then went in also that other disciple, which came first to the sepulchre, and he saw, and believed" (John 20:8).

3. His carnality—On at least three occasions, the fleshly nature of John was displayed.

a. As seen by a sectarian event—"And John answered him, saying, Master, we saw one casting out devils in thy name, and he followeth not us: and we forbad him, because he followeth not us. But Jesus said, Forbid him not: for there is no man which shall do a miracle in my name, that can lightly speak evil of me. For he that is not against us is on our part. For whosoever shall give you a cup of water to drink in my name, because ye belong to Christ, verily I say unto you, he shall not lose his reward" (Mark 9:38-41).

b. As seen by a selfish event

(1) The request of the two—"And James and John, the sons of Zebedee, come unto him, saying, Master, we would that thou shouldest do for us whatsoever we shall desire. And he said unto them, What would ye that I should do for you? They said unto him, Grant unto us that we may sit, one on thy right hand, and the other on thy left hand, in thy glory" (Mark 10:35-37).

(2) The resentment of the ten—"And when the ten heard it, they began to be much displeased with James and John" (Mark 10:41).

(3) The response of the Lord

(a) Toward the two—"And he saith unto them, Ye shall drink indeed of my cup, and be baptized with the baptism that I am baptized with: but to sit on my right hand, and on my left, is not mine to give, but it shall be given to them for whom it is prepared of my Father" (Matt. 20:23).

(b) Toward the ten—"But Jesus called them unto him, and said, Ye know that the princes of the Gentiles exercise dominion over them, and they that are great exercise authority upon them. But it shall not be so among you: but whosoever will be great among you, let him be your minister; and whosoever will be chief among you, let him be your servant: Even as the Son of man came not to be ministered unto, but to minister, and to give his life a ransom for many" (Matt. 20:25-28).

c. As seen by a spiteful event

(1) The refusal demonstrated by the Samaritans—"And it came to pass, when the time was come that he should be received up, he stedfastly set his face to go to Jerusalem, and sent messengers before

his face: and they went, and entered into a village of the Samaritans, to make ready for him. And they did not receive him, because his face was as though he would go to Jerusalem" (Luke 9:51-53).

(2) The retaliation demanded by the brothers—"And when his disciples James and John saw this, they said, Lord, wilt thou that we command fire to come down from heaven, and consume them, even as Elias did?" (Luke 9:54).

(3) The rebuke delivered by the Lord—"But he turned, and rebuked them, and said, Ye know not what manner of spirit ye are of. For the Son of man is not come to destroy men's lives, but to save them. And they went to another village" (Luke 9:55-56).

4. His concern—John questioned the when and who of two prophecies uttered by Christ.
   a. The when of the prophecy concerning the destruction of Jerusalem—"And as he went out of the temple, one of his disciples saith unto him, Master, see what manner of stones and what buildings are here! And Jesus answering said unto him, Seest thou these great buildings? there shall not be left one stone upon another, that shall not be thrown down. And as he sat upon the mount of Olives over against the temple, Peter and James and John and Andrew asked him privately, Tell us, when shall these things be? and what shall be the sign when all these things shall be fulfilled?" (Mark 13:1-4).
   b. The who of the prophecy concerning the betrayal of Jesus—"When Jesus had thus said, he was troubled in spirit, and testified, and said, Verily, verily, I say unto you, that one of you shall betray me. Then the disciples looked one on another, doubting of whom he spake. Now there was leaning on Jesus' bosom one of his disciples, whom Jesus loved. Simon Peter therefore beckoned to him, that he should ask who it should be of whom he spake. He then lying on Jesus' breast saith unto him, Lord, who is it? Jesus answered, He it is, to whom I shall give a sop, when I have dipped it. And when he had dipped the sop, he gave it to Judas Iscariot, the son of Simon" (John 13:21-26).
5. His courage—John alone of the 12 apostles was present at the crucifixion of Christ (John 19:26-27).
   a. Jesus' words to his mother—"When Jesus therefore saw his mother, and the disciple standing by, whom he loved, he saith unto his mother, Woman, behold thy son!" (John 19:26).
   b. Jesus' words to his disciple—"Then saith he to the disciple, Behold thy mother! And from that hour that disciple took her unto his own home" (John 19:27).

B. As recorded in the book of Acts
1. John and the cripple in Jerusalem (Acts 3:1-11; 4:13-22)
   a. The deliverance in Jesus' name—The lame man was healed by the power of Jesus (Acts 3:1-11).
   b. The defense of Jesus' name (Acts 4:13-22)—"Now when they saw the boldness of Peter and John, and perceived that they were unlearned and ignorant men, they marvelled; and they took knowledge of them, that they had been with Jesus. And beholding the man which was healed standing with them, they could say nothing against it. But when they had commanded

them to go aside out of the council, they conferred among themselves, Saying, What shall we do to these men? for that indeed a notable miracle hath been done by them is manifest to all them that dwell in Jerusalem; and we cannot deny it. But that it spread no further among the people, let us straitly threaten them, that they speak henceforth to no man in this name. And they called them, and commanded them not to speak at all nor teach in the name of Jesus. But Peter and John answered and said unto them, Whether it be right in the sight of God to hearken unto you more than unto God, judge ye. For we cannot but speak the things which we have seen and heard" (Acts 4:13-20).

2. John and the converts in Samaria—"Now when the apostles which were at Jerusalem heard that Samaria had received the word of God, they sent unto them Peter and John: Who, when they were come down, prayed for them, that they might receive the Holy Ghost" (Acts 8:14-15).

C. As recorded in the book of Galatians (Gal. 2:9)—John, along with Peter, James, and Barnabas, extended to Paul the right hand of fellowship during the apostle's second visit to Jerusalem as a believer.

D. As recorded in the book of Revelation

1. John was exiled to the Isle of Patmos in the Mediterranean Sea because of his testimony for Christ (Rev. 1:9).
2. He received in vision form the book of Revelation at that time (Rev. 1:10-20).
3. He was not permitted, however, to write down everything he heard (Rev. 10:4).
4. He was commanded to eat from a scroll held by an angel. It tasted as honey in his mouth but made his stomach sour (Rev. 10:8-10).
5. He was instructed to measure the temple of God in heaven (Rev. 11:1).
6. He fell down on two occasions and attempted to worship the angel who showed him the future. On each occasion he was rebuked.
   a. First occasion—"And I fell at his feet to worship him. And he said unto me, See thou do it not: I am thy fellowservant, and of thy brethren that have the testimony of Jesus: worship God: for the testimony of Jesus is the spirit of prophecy" (Rev. 19:10).
   b. Second occasion—"And I John saw these things, and heard them. And when I had heard and seen, I fell down to worship before the feet of the angel which shewed me these things. Then saith he unto me, See thou do it not: for I am thy fellowservant, and of thy brethren the prophets, and of them which keep the sayings of this book: worship God" (Rev. 22:8-9).
7. John was the last to see the Son of God in his glory—"And in the midst of the seven candlesticks one like unto the Son of man, clothed with a garment down to the foot, and girt about the paps with a golden girdle. His head and his hairs were white like wool, as white as snow; and his eyes were as a flame of fire; and his feet like unto fine brass, as if they burned in a furnace; and his voice as the sound of many waters. And he had in his right hand seven stars: and out of his mouth went a sharp twoedged sword: and his countenance was as the sun shineth in his strength" (Rev. 1:13-16).
8. John was the first to see the city of God in its glory—"And I saw a new heaven and a new earth: for the first heaven and the first earth were passed away; and there was no more sea. And I John saw the holy city, new Jerusalem, coming down

from God out of heaven, prepared as a bride adorned for her husband. And I heard a great voice out of heaven saying, Behold, the tabernacle of God is with men, and he will dwell with them, and they shall be his people, and God himself shall be with them, and be their God. And God shall wipe away all tears from their eyes; and there shall be no more death, neither sorrow, nor crying, neither shall there be any more pain: for the former things are passed away. . . . And he carried me away in the spirit to a great and high mountain, and shewed me that great city, the holy Jerusalem, descending out of heaven from God" (Rev. 21:1-4, 10).

II. The Manuscripts of John—He was the author of 5 of the 27 New Testament books.

THE GOSPEL OF JOHN

John emphasizes the deity of Christ.

I. The eternal Son of God (John 1:1-5)—"In the beginning was the Word, and the Word was with God, and the Word was God. The same was in the beginning with God. All things were made by him; and without him was not any thing made that was made. In him was life; and the life was the light of men. And the light shineth in darkness; and the darkness comprehended it not" (John 1:1-5).

II. The earthly Son of God (John 1:6–18:12)

A. The forerunner to his ministry (John 1:6-37)—"There was a man sent from God, whose name was John. The same came for a witness, to bear witness of the Light, that all men through him might believe. He was not that Light, but was sent to bear witness of that Light. . . . John bare witness of him, and cried, saying, This was he of whom I spake, He that cometh after me is preferred before me: for he was before me" (John 1:6-8, 15).

B. The fruits of his ministry

1. The zeal he displayed (John 2:13-25)—"And when he had made a scourge of small cords, he drove them all out of the temple, and the sheep, and the oxen; and poured out the changers' money, and overthrew the tables; and said unto them that sold doves, Take these things hence; make not my Father's house an house of merchandise. And his disciples remembered that it was written, The zeal of thine house hath eaten me up" (John 2:15-17).

2. The miracles he performed
   a. First miracle: Turning water into wine (John 2:1-12)
   b. Second miracle: Healing the nobleman's son (John 4:46-54)
   c. Third miracle: Healing of the impotent man (John 5:1-16)
   d. Fourth miracle: Feeding of the 5,000 (John 6:1-14)
   e. Fifth miracle: Walking on the water (John 6:15-21)
   f. Sixth miracle: Healing of the blind man (John 9:1-41)
   g. Seventh miracle: Raising of Lazarus (John 11:1-57)

3. The dialogues he had
   a. With Nicodemus (John 3:1-36)
   b. With the Samaritan woman (John 4:1-45)
   c. With the woman taken in adultery (John 8:1-11)

4. The sermons he preached
   a. On his relationship with the Father (John 5:17-47)
   b. On the bread of life (John 6:22-71)
   c. On the water of life (John 7:1-53)
   d. On his relationship with Abraham (John 8:12-59)
   e. On the Good Shepherd (John 10:1-42)
   f. On his death (John 12:23-50)
   g. On the Holy Spirit (John 14:1-31)
   h. On fruit bearing (John 15:1-16:33)

C. The final days of his ministry
1. His anointing by Mary (John 12:1-11)
2. The triumphal entry (John 12:12-22)
3. Events in the upper room (John 13:1-38)

a. Washing the apostles' feet (John 13:1-17)
b. Announcing his betrayal (John 13:18-35)
c. Predicting Peter's denials (John 13:36-38)
4. His great high priestly prayer (John 17:1-26)
5. His ordeal in Gethsemane (John 18:1-12)

III. The executed Son of God (John 18:12–19:42)
A. The denials by Peter (John 18:15-18, 24-27)
B. The unfair trials
1. Before Annas and Caiaphas (John 18:13-14, 19-24)
2. Before Pilate (John 18:28-40)
C. The scourging (John 19:1-15)
D. The crucifixion (John 19:16-42)

IV. The exalted Son of God (John 20:1–21:25)
A. His absence from the tomb (John 20:1-10)
B. His appearance from the tomb (John 20:11–21:25)
1. Before Mary Magdalene (John 20:1-18)
2. Before the apostles (John 20:24-31)
3. Before Thomas (John 20:24-31)
4. Before seven apostles (John 21:1-25)

THE FIRST EPISTLE OF JOHN

This epistle is outlined with the word "fellowship" in mind.

I. The source of this fellowship
A. The incarnation of Jesus Christ (1 John 1:1-2; 3:5, 8)
B. The atonement of Jesus Christ (1 John 2:2; 3:16; 4:9-10, 14)

II. The purpose of this fellowship
A. That we might know more about the Father
1. He is light (1 John 1:5)
2. He is righteous (1 John 3:7)
3. He is omniscient (1 John 3:20)
4. He is love (1 John 4:8, 16)
5. He is invisible (1 John 4:12)
6. He is life (1 John 5:11-12)
B. That we might love the Father and understand his love (1 John 3:16; 4:19)
C. That we might allow the Father's love to be perfected in us (1 John 2:5; 4:12)
D. That we might love the family of God (1 John 3:11, 23; 4:7, 11)
E. That we might experience the fullness of joy (1 John 1:4)
F. That we might receive assurance
1. Concerning our salvation (1 John 5:13)
2. Concerning our prayers (1 John 3:22; 5:14-15)

III. The requirements for this fellowship
A. Walk in the light (1 John 1:7).
B. Recognize our sin (1 John 1:8).
C. Confess our sin (1 John 1:9).
D. Keep his commandments (1 John 2:3-8; 5:2-3).
1. The old commandment (1 John 2:7)—Love others as you love yourself (Lev. 19:34; Deut. 10:19).
2. The new commandment—Love others as Christ loves you (1 John 2:8).
E. Abide in Christ (1 John 2:28).
F. Keep unspotted from the world (1 John 2:3; 5:21).
G. Help our brother in need (1 John 3:17).

IV. The tests of this fellowship
A. Do I conduct my life down here in view of the rapture? "And every man that hath this hope in him purifieth himself, even as he is pure" (1 John 3:3).
B. Do I continually dwell in sin (1 John 2:29)?
C. Do I hate my spiritual brother? "If a man say, I love God, and hateth his brother, he is a liar: for he that loveth not his brother whom he hath seen, how can he love God whom he hath not seen?" (1 John 4:20).
D. Do I desire to help my brother? "But whoso hath this world's good, and seeth his brother have need, and shutteth up his bowels of compassion from him, how dwelleth the love of God in him?" (1 John 3:17).
E. Do I really love my brother? "He that loveth his brother abideth in the light, and there is none occasion of stumbling in him" (1 John 2:10).
F. Do I really love God? "By this we know that we love the children of God, when

we love God, and keep his commandments" (1 John 5:2).

G. Do I enjoy a rapport with other servants of God? "We are of God: he that knoweth God heareth us; he that is not of God heareth not us. Hereby know we the spirit of truth, and the spirit of error" (1 John 4:6).

H. Am I plagued with constant fear? "There is no fear in love; but perfect love casteth out fear: because fear hath torment. He that feareth is not made perfect in love" (1 John 4:18).

I. Can I recognize false doctrine when it comes my way? "Hereby know ye the Spirit of God: Every spirit that confesseth that Jesus Christ is come in the flesh is of God: And every spirit that confesseth not that Jesus Christ is come in the flesh is not of God" (1 John 4:2-3a).

J. Am I straight on the deity of Christ? "Whosoever denieth the Son, the same hath not the Father: [but] he that acknowledgeth the Son hath the Father also" (1 John 2:23).

K. Am I straight on the work of Christ? "And ye know that he was manifested to take away our sins; and in him is no sin. He that committeth sin is of the devil; for the devil sinneth from the beginning. For this purpose the Son of God was manifested, that he might destroy the works of the devil" (1 John 3:5, 8).

L. Do I have the witness of the Spirit? "And he that keepeth his commandments dwelleth in him, and he in him. And hereby we know that he abideth in us, by the Spirit which he hath given us" (1 John 3:24).

V. The maintenance of this fellowship
   A. Accomplished through the occupation of the Son of God
      1. He serves as our advocate (1 John 2:1).
      2. He serves as our propitiation (1 John 2:2).
   B. Accomplished through the habitation of the Spirit of God (1 John 2:20, 27)
   C. Accomplished through the cooperation of the saints of God (1 John 1:8-9)

VI. The family members in this fellowship (1 John 3:1)
   A. Little children (new converts) (1 John 2:12-13)
   B. Young men (those saved for awhile) (1 John 2:13-14)
   C. Fathers (those mature in the faith) (1 John 2:13-14)

VII. The enemies of this fellowship (1 John 2:15; 5:19)
   A. The evil systems in this world
      1. The divisions (1 John 2:16)
         a. The lust of the flesh
         b. The lust of the eyes
         c. The pride of life
      2. The destruction
   B. The evil seducers in this world (1 John 2:26)
      1. Their appearance (1 John 2:18)
      2. Their apostasy (1 John 2:19)
   C. The evil spirits
      1. The fruit of these spirits (1 John 2:22)
      2. The root of these spirits (1 John 4:1-3)

VIII. The witnesses to this fellowship (1 John 5:6-8)
   A. The witnesses in heaven (1 John 5:7)
   B. The witnesses on earth (1 John 5:8)

IX. The separation from this fellowship (1 John 5:16-17)

X. The encouragements of this fellowship
   A. The promise of eternal life (1 John 2:25)
   B. Confidence at the rapture (1 John 2:28)
   C. The promise of a new body (1 John 3:2)
   D. Boldness at the judgment (1 John 4:17)
   E. A life without fear (1 John 3:19, 21; 4:18)

THE SECOND EPISTLE OF JOHN

I. An elect lady is commended by the Apostle John (2 John 1-4).

II. This lady is commanded by the Apostle John.
   A. That she walk in love (2 John 5)
   B. That she walk in truth (2 John 6)

III. This lady is cautioned by the Apostle John.
   A. Look out for Satan (2 John 7, 9-11).
   B. Look out for self (2 John 8).

IV. This lady is comforted by the Apostle John (2 John 12-13).

THE THIRD EPISTLE OF JOHN

I. The prosperity of Gaius the exhorter (3 John 1-8)
- A. John's prayer for him (3 John 1-2)
- B. John's praise of him
  1. His faithfulness to the message of God (3 John 3-4)
  2. His helpfulness to the messengers of God (3 John 5-8)

II. The pride of Diotrephes the egotist (3 John 9-10)
- A. He attempted to occupy the leading place (3 John 9).
- B. He refused to receive the Apostle John (3 John 9).
- C. He had slandered the apostles (3 John 10).
- D. He had refused to entertain missionaries (3 John 10).
- E. He attempted to excommunicate believers (3 John 10).
- F. He was not of God (3 John 10).

III. The praise of Demetrius the example (3 John 12)

THE BOOK OF REVELATION

I. Part 1: The witnesses of the Lamb instructed (Rev. 1–3)
- A. The servant of God (Rev. 1:1-10)—A heavenly message was revealed to a man on a lonely island some 20 centuries ago.
  1. The source of the message—"The Revelation of Jesus Christ, which God gave unto him" (Rev. 1:1).
  2. The recorder of the message—"His servant John" (Rev. 1:1).
  3. The nature of the message—"To shew unto his servants things which must shortly come to pass" (Rev. 1:1).
  4. The promise of the message—"Blessed is he that readeth, and they that hear the words of this prophecy, and keep those things which are written therein: for the time is at hand" (Rev. 1:3).
  5. The recipients of the message—The seven churches in Asia (Rev. 1:4)
  6. The greetings in the message
     - a. From the Father (Rev. 1:4)
     - b. From the seven spirits (or, sevenfold spirit, a possible reference to the Holy Spirit and his perfection) (Rev. 1:4)
     - c. From the Son (Rev. 1:5)
  7. The theme of the message—Jesus Christ
     - a. Who he is (Rev. 1:5)
     - b. What he has done (Rev. 1:5b-6)
     - c. What he shall do (Rev. 1:7)
  8. The authority behind the message—The Lord (Rev. 1:8)
  9. The location of the message—The Isle of Patmos (Rev. 1:9)
  10. The day of the message—The Lord's day (Rev. 1:10)
- B. The Son of God (Rev. 1:11-20)
  1. The designation (Rev. 1:11)
  2. The description (Rev. 1:12-16)
  3. The devastation (Rev. 1:17)
  4. The declaration (Rev. 1:18)
  5. The dictation (Rev. 1:19)
  6. The delineation (Rev. 1:20)
- C. The churches of God (Rev. 2–3)
  1. The church at Ephesus (Rev. 2:1-7)
  2. The church at Smyrna (Rev. 2:8-11)
  3. The church at Pergamos (Rev. 2:12-17)
  4. The church at Thyatira (Rev. 2:18-29)
  5. The church at Sardis (Rev. 3:1-6)
  6. The church at Philadelphia (Rev. 3:7-13)
  7. The church at Laodicea (Rev. 3:14-22)

II. Part 2: The worship of the Lamb invited (Rev. 4–5)—This section is the story of two songs of praise.
- A. The creation hymn of worship (Rev. 4)
  1. The place—heaven (Rev. 4:1)
  2. The persons
     - a. The Father (Rev. 4:2-3)
     - b. The 24 elders (Rev. 4:4)
     - c. The seven spirits of God (Rev. 4:5)
     - d. The four living creatures (Rev. 4:6-8)
  3. The praise (Rev. 4:9-11)
- B. The redemption hymn of worship (Rev. 5)
  1. The proclamation (Rev. 5:1-2)
  2. The investigation (Rev. 5:3)
  3. The lamentation (Rev. 5:4)

4. The manifestation (Rev. 5:5-7)
5. The adoration (Rev. 5:9-14)

III. Part 3: The wrath of the Lamb invoked (Rev. 6–19)

A. He pours out the seven seal judgments (Rev. 6–11).

1. First seal (Rev. 6:1-2)
2. Second seal (Rev. 6:3-4)
3. Third seal (Rev. 6:5-6)
4. Fourth seal (Rev. 6:7-8)
5. Fifth seal (Rev. 6:9-11)
   a. The altar for the saints (Rev. 6:9)
   b. The anger of the saints (Rev. 6:10)
   c. The answer to the saints (Rev. 6:11)
6. Sixth seal (Rev. 6:12-17)
   a. The destruction of earth's surface (Rev. 6:12, 14)
   b. The darkening of earth's skies (Rev. 6:12-14)
   c. The despair of earth's sinners (Rev. 6:15-17)
7. Interlude (Rev. 7:1-17)
   a. On earth: The sealing of the servants of God (Rev. 7:1-8)
      (1) The sealer—An angel (Rev. 7:2-3)
      (2) The sealed—The 144,000 from the 12 tribes of Israel (Rev. 7:4)
   b. In heaven: The singing of the servants of God (Rev. 7:9-17)
      (1) Their song (Rev. 7:10)
      (2) Their support (Rev. 7:11-12)
      (3) Their service (Rev. 7:15)
      (4) Their Savior (Rev. 7:17)
8. Seventh seal (Rev. 8–11)—The seventh seal actually consists of seven trumpets. The silence before the trumpets (Rev. 8:1-5): "And when he had opened the seventh seal, there was silence in heaven about the space of half an hour" (Rev. 8:1). The sounding of the trumpets (Rev. 8:6): "And the seven angels which had the seven trumpets prepared themselves to sound" (Rev. 8:6).
   a. First trumpet (Rev. 8:7)
   b. Second trumpet (Rev. 8:8-9)
   c. Third trumpet (Rev. 8:10-11)
   d. Fourth trumpet (Rev. 8:12-13)
      (1) The fearful darkening (Rev. 8:12)
      (2) The future destruction (Rev. 8:13)
   e. Fifth trumpet (Rev. 9:1-12)—This trumpet unleashes the first hellish invasion of demons upon the earth.
      (1) Their location (Rev. 9:1-2)
      (2) Their leader (Rev. 9:11)
      (3) Their torment (Rev. 9:3-5)—"And their torment was as the torment of a scorpion, when he striketh a man" (Rev. 9:5).
      (4) Their duration (Rev. 9:5-6)
      (5) Their description (Rev. 9:7-10)
   f. Sixth trumpet (Rev. 9:13-21)—This trumpet unleashes the second hellish invasion of demons upon the earth.
      (1) Their four leaders (Rev. 9:13-14)
      (2) Their mission (Rev. 9:15)
      (3) Their number (Rev. 9:16)
      (4) Their description (Rev. 9:17)
      (5) Their torment (Rev. 9:19)
      (6) Their effect (Rev. 9:20-21)
   g. Interlude (Rev. 10:1–11:14)—Seven events occur between the sixth and seventh trumpets.
      (1) The message of the angel of God (Rev. 10:1-2)
         (a) How he looked (Rev. 10:1-7)
         (b) How he sounded (Rev. 10:3-4)
         (c) What he said (Rev. 10:4-7)
      (2) The mission of the apostle of God (Rev. 10:8-11)
      (3) The measuring of the temple of God (Rev. 11:1-2)
      (4) The ministry of the witnesses of God (Rev. 11:3-6)
      (5) The martyrdom of the witnesses of God (Rev. 11:7-10)
      (6) The metamorphosis of the witnesses of God (Rev. 11:11-12)
      (7) The manifestation of the judgment of God (Rev. 11:13)

h. Seventh trumpet (Rev. 11:15-19)
(1) The proclamation (Rev. 11:15)
(2) The adoration (Rev. 11:16-17)
(3) The vindication (Rev. 11:18-19)

B. He allows Satan to reign on earth (Rev. 12–13).
1. Satan and Israel (Rev. 12)
a. His former hatred for the Jews (Rev. 12:1-5)
(1) Satan
(a) His sin in the beginning when he attempted to steal God's throne (Rev. 12:3-4)
(b) His sin at Bethlehem when he attempted to slaughter God's Son (Rev. 12:4)
(2) Israel
(a) Her rise—Israel began with Jacob's 12 sons (Rev. 12:1).
(b) Her prize—Israel gave birth to her Messiah (Rev. 12:2).
b. His future hatred for the Jews (Rev. 12:6-17)
(1) His defeat in heaven—Satan is cast out of the very heavenlies during the tribulation (Rev. 12:7-12).
(a) Heaven's reaction to his defeat (Rev. 12:10-11)
(b) Satan's reaction to his defeat (Rev. 12:12)
(2) His depravity on earth—Satan now instigates an all-out attempt to destroy Israel.
(a) The devil's persecution (Rev. 12:13, 15, 17)
(b) The Lord's protection (Rev. 12:6, 14, 16)
2. The devil and the world (Rev. 13)
a. His cohort, the Antichrist (Rev. 13:1-10)
(1) The description of the Antichrist (Rev. 13:1-2)
(2) The authority of the Antichrist—"And the dragon gave him his power, and his seat, and great authority" (Rev. 13:2).
(3) The healing of the Antichrist (Rev. 13:3)
(4) The worship of the Antichrist (Rev. 13:4, 8)
(5) The power of the Antichrist
(a) Its scope—Power is given him over all kindred, tongues, and nations (Rev. 13:7).
(b) Its duration—For 42 months (Rev. 13:5)
(6) The blasphemy of the Antichrist (Rev. 13:5-6)
b. His cohort, the false prophet (Rev. 13:11-18)
(1) His militancy—"And he exerciseth all the power of the first beast" (Rev. 13:12).
(2) His mission (Rev. 13:12)
(3) His miracles (Rev. 13:13-14)
(4) His mark—"And he causeth all, both small and great, rich and poor, free and bond, to receive a mark in their right hand, or in their foreheads: And that no man might buy or sell, save he that had the mark, or the name of the beast, or the number of his name. Here is wisdom. Let him that hath understanding count the number of the beast: for it is the number of a man; and his number is six hundred threescore and six" (Rev. 13:16-18).

C. He pours out the seven vial judgments (Rev. 14–16).
1. Those events preceding the vial judgments (Rev. 14–15)
a. The song of the witnesses of God (Rev. 14:1-5)
b. The messages of the angels of God (Rev. 14:6-12)
c. The assurance from the Spirit of God (Rev. 14:13)
d. The reaping of the harvest of God (Rev. 14:14-20)
e. The praise of the victors of God (Rev. 15:1-4)

f. The events in the temple of God (Rev. 15:5-8)
2. Those events accompanying the vial judgments (Rev. 16)
a. First vial judgment (Rev. 16:2)
b. Second vial judgment (Rev. 16:3)
c. Third vial judgment (Rev. 16:4-7)
(1) The action (Rev. 16:4)
(2) The reaction (Rev. 16:5-7)
d. Fourth vial judgment (Rev. 16:8-9)
(1) The action (Rev. 16:8)
(2) The reaction (Rev. 16:9)
e. Fifth vial judgment (Rev. 16:10-11)
(1) The action (Rev. 16:10)
(2) The reaction (Rev. 16:11)
f. Sixth vial judgment (Rev. 16:12-16)
g. Seventh vial judgment (Rev. 16:17-21)
(1) The world's greatest earthquake (Rev. 16:18-20)
(2) The world's greatest hailstorm (Rev. 16:21)
D. He destroys the world's religious systems (Rev. 17).
1. The history of this harlot (Rev. 17:1-6)
a. Depraved with the filth of hell (Rev. 17:2, 5)
b. Decked with the wealth of the world (Rev. 17:4)
c. Drunk with the blood of saints (Rev. 17:6)
2. The future of this harlot (Rev. 17:7-18)
a. To be teamed up (at first) with the Antichrist (Rev. 17:7-9)
b. To be destroyed (at last) by the Antichrist (Rev. 17:15-17)
E. He destroys the world's political and economic systems (Rev. 18). It is believed a literal city will become the headquarters of both these systems.
1. The designation of the city—"That great city Babylon, that mighty city!" (Rev. 18:10). A literal interpretation of this chapter would say that during the tribulation ancient Babylon will be rebuilt by the Antichrist as his headquarters.
2. The denunciation of the city (Rev. 18:1-2, 5, 21)
3. The degeneration of the city
a. Godless materialism (Rev. 18:3, 11-17)
b. Arrogance and pride (Rev. 18:7)
c. Immorality (Rev. 18:3)
d. Demonism and false religions (Rev. 18:2)
e. Drug peddling (Rev. 18:23)—The word *sorceries* is a probable reference to drugs.
f. Slavery (Rev. 18:13)
g. Bloodshedding (Rev. 18:24)
4. The destruction of the city
a. The source of its destruction—God himself (Rev. 18:8, 20)
b. The means of its destruction—Possibly by nuclear energy (Rev. 18:8-10)—This is suggested because of the speed and nature of the destruction.
c. The reaction to its destruction
(1) Despair on earth (Rev. 18:11, 19)
(2) Delight in heaven (Rev. 18:20)
F. He defeats his enemies at Armageddon (Rev. 19)
1. The celebration in heaven (Rev. 19:1-10)
a. Praising God for his wrath upon a cruel whore (Rev. 19:1-5)
b. Praising God for his wedding to a chaste wife (Rev. 19:6-10)
2. The confrontation on earth (Rev. 19:11-21)
a. Armageddon—The victory over Satan's horsemen (Rev. 19:15, 17-19)
b. Gehenna—The victory over Satan's henchmen (Rev. 19:19-20)
IV. Part 4: The reign of the Lamb instituted (Rev. 20)
A. The great chain (Rev. 20:1-3)—"And I saw an angel come down from heaven, having the key of the bottomless pit and a great chain in his hand. And he laid hold on the dragon, that old serpent, which is the Devil, and Satan, and bound him a thousand years" (Rev. 20:1-2).

B. The great reign (Rev. 20:4-6)
1. The resurrection of the just (Rev. 20:5-6)
2. The rule of the just (Rev. 20:4, 6)

C. The great revolt (Rev. 20:7-10)
1. The adversary (Rev. 20:7)
2. The arrogance (Rev. 20:8)
3. The attack (Rev. 20:9)
4. The abyss (Rev. 20:10)

D. The great throne (Rev. 20:11-15)
1. The judge (Rev. 20:11)
2. The judged (Rev. 20:12-13)
3. The judgment (Rev. 20:14-15)

V. Part 5: The wife of the Lamb introduced (Rev. 21:1–22:21)

A. Her habitation—The fabulous city (Rev. 21:1–22:5)—"And I saw a new heaven and a new earth: for the first heaven and the first earth were passed away; and there was no more sea. And I John saw the holy city, new Jerusalem, coming down from God out of heaven, prepared as a bride adorned for her husband" (Rev. 21:1-2).
1. Its occupants (Rev. 21:27)—"And there shall in no wise enter into it any thing that defileth, neither whatsoever worketh abomination, or maketh a lie: but they which are written in the Lamb's book of life" (Rev. 21:27).
2. Its wall (Rev. 21:12, 14, 17-18)—"And the wall of the city had twelve foundations, and in them the names of the twelve apostles of the Lamb" (Rev. 21:14).
3. Its gates (Rev. 21:12-13, 21, 25) —"And the twelve gates were twelve pearls; every several gate was of one pearl" (Rev. 21:21).
4. Its size and shape (Rev. 21:15-16)—"And he measured the city with the reed, twelve thousand furlongs. The length and the breadth and the height of it are equal" (Rev. 21:16).
5. Its 12 foundations—"And the foundations of the wall of the city were garnished with all manner of precious stones" (Rev. 21:19).
6. Its street—"And the street of the city was pure gold, as it were transparent glass" (Rev. 21:21).
7. Its light source (Rev. 21:23; 22:5)—"And the city had no need of the sun, neither of the moon, to shine in it: for the glory of God did lighten it, and the Lamb is the light thereof" (Rev. 21:23).
8. Its river—"And he shewed me a pure river of water of life, clear as crystal, proceeding out of the throne of God and of the Lamb" (Rev. 22:1).
9. Its tree of life—"In the midst of the street of it, and on either side of the river, was there the tree of life, which bare twelve manner of fruits, and yielded her fruit every month" (Rev. 22:2).
10. Its relationship to the earth (Rev. 21:24, 26)—"And they shall bring the glory and honour of the nations into it" (Rev. 21:26).
11. Its worship center—"And I saw no temple therein: for the Lord God Almighty and the Lamb are the temple of it" (Rev. 21:22).
12. Its throne (Rev. 22:1)
13. Its activities—What will we do in heaven?
    a. Learn about Christ (Rev. 22:4)
    b. Work for Christ (Rev. 22:3)
    c. Reign with Christ (Rev. 22:5)

B. Her husband—The faithful spouse (Rev. 22:6-21)
1. The comfort from Christ (Rev. 22:12, 14)
2. The character of Christ (Rev. 22:13, 16)
3. The counsel of Christ (Rev. 22:10)
4. The concern of Christ
    a. His concern about the water of life—"And the Spirit and the bride say, Come. And let him that heareth say, Come. And let him that is athirst come. And whosoever will, let him take the water of life freely" (Rev. 22:17).

b. His concern about the Word of life (Rev. 22:18-19)
    (1) That we not add to it (Rev. 22:18)
    (2) That we not take away from it (Rev. 22:19)

STATISTICS

Father: Zebedee (Matt. 4:21)
Mother: Salome (Mark 15:40)
Brother: James (Matt. 4:21)
First mention: Matthew 4:21
Final mention: Revelation 22:8
Meaning of his name: "The grace of Jehovah." Note: Both he and his brother James were nicknamed "Boanerges" by Christ, meaning "Sons of Thunder" (Mark 3:17)
Frequency of his name: Referred to 42 times: As John, 33 times; as "that disciple that Jesus loved" (John 13:23; 19:26; 20:2; 21:7, 20, 24), six times; as Boanerges, meaning "Son of rage, thunder" (Mark 3:17), once
Biblical books mentioning him: Six books (Matthew, Mark, Luke, Acts, Galatians, Revelation)
Occupation: Fisherman before becoming one of Christ's three key apostles
Place of birth: Probably Bethsaida in Galilee
Place of death: Tradition suggests it was in Ephesus.
Important fact about his life: He was Christ's beloved apostle who authored five New Testament books.

John the Baptist

(See also Part Two, Observations from the Life of John the Baptist)

CHRONOLOGICAL SUMMARY

I. The mission of John
  A. As foretold by the angel of God
    1. The declaration (Luke 1:5-17)—Zacharias the priest was visited by the angel Gabriel while offering incense. He heard a sixfold prophecy by this heavenly messenger.
      a. He and his wife, Elisabeth, would have a son (Luke 1:13).
      b. His name would be John (Luke 1:13).
      c. He would become a Spirit-filled Nazirite (Luke 1:15).
      d. He would have a successful ministry (Luke 1:16).
      e. He would prepare the way for the Messiah (Luke 1:17).
      f. His style would be similar to that of Elijah (Luke 1:17).
    2. The doubts—"And Zacharias said unto the angel, Whereby shall I know this? for I am an old man, and my wife well stricken in years" (Luke 1:18).
    3. The dumbness (Luke 1:19-20)—"And, behold, thou shalt be dumb, and not able to speak, until the day that these things shall be performed, because thou believest not my words, which shall be fulfilled in their season" (Luke 1:20).
    4. The delay (Luke 1:21-22)—"And the people waited for Zacharias, and marvelled that he tarried so long in the temple" (Luke 1:21).
    5. The devotion (Luke 1:23-25)— "And after those days his wife Elisabeth conceived, and hid herself five months, saying, Thus hath the Lord dealt with me in the days wherein he looked on me, to take away my reproach among men" (Luke 1:24-25).
  B. As foretold by the Spirit of God
    1. The witness of the Holy Spirit prior to John's birth—"And it came to pass, that, when Elisabeth heard the salutation of Mary, the babe leaped in her womb; and Elisabeth was filled with the Holy Ghost" (Luke 1:41).
    2. The will of the Holy Spirit at John's birth—"Now Elisabeth's full time came that she should be delivered; and she brought forth a son. And her neighbours and her cousins heard how the Lord had shewed great mercy upon her; and they rejoiced with her. And it came to pass, that on the eighth day they

came to circumcise the child; and they called him Zacharias, after the name of his father. And his mother answered and said, Not so; but he shall be called John. And they said unto her, There is none of thy kindred that is called by this name. And they made signs to his father, how he would have him called. And he asked for a writing table, and wrote, saying, His name is John. And they marvelled all. And his mouth was opened immediately, and his tongue loosed, and he spake, and praised God" (Luke 1:57-64).

3. The words of the Holy Spirit following John's birth—"And his father Zacharias was filled with the Holy Ghost . . . saying" (Luke 1:67).
   a. The praise of Zacharias
      (1) He thanked God for the Davidic covenant—"Blessed be the Lord God of Israel; for he hath visited and redeemed his people, and hath raised up an horn of salvation for us in the house of his servant David. . . . That we should be saved from our enemies, and from the hand of all that hate us" (Luke 1:68-69, 71).
      (2) He thanked God for the Abrahamic covenant—"The oath which he sware to our father Abraham" (Luke 1:73).
   b. The prediction of Zacharias—"And thou, child, shalt be called the prophet of the Highest: for thou shalt go before the face of the Lord to prepare his ways; to give knowledge of salvation unto his people by the remission of their sins, through the tender mercy of our God; whereby the dayspring from on high hath visited us, to give light to them that sit in darkness and in the shadow of death, to guide our feet into the way of peace" (Luke 1:76-79).

II. The message of John
   A. As predicted by Isaiah and Malachi
      1. Isaiah's prophecy (Isa. 40:3-5)—"In those days came John the Baptist, preaching in the wilderness of Judaea" (Matt. 3:1). "And he came into all the country about Jordan, preaching the baptism of repentance for the remission of sins; as it is written in the book of the words of Esaias the prophet, saying, The voice of one crying in the wilderness, Prepare ye the way of the Lord, make his paths straight. Every valley shall be filled, and every mountain and hill shall be brought low; and the crooked shall be made straight, and the rough ways shall be made smooth; and all flesh shall see the salvation of God" (Luke 3:3-6).
      2. Malachi's prophecy (Mal. 3:1)—"For this is he, of whom it is written, Behold, I send my messenger before thy face, which shall prepare thy way before thee" (Matt. 11:10).
   B. As proclaimed by John
      1. To the crowds
         a. His message to their hearts—"Repent ye; for the kingdom of heaven is at hand. . . . Prepare ye the way of the Lord, make his paths straight" (Matt. 3:2, 3b).
         b. His message to their hands—"And the people asked him, saying, What shall we do then? He answereth and saith unto them, He that hath two coats, let him impart to him that hath none; and he that hath meat, let him do likewise" (Luke 3:10-11).
      2. To the Pharisees and Sadducees—"But when he saw many of the Pharisees and Sadducees come to his baptism, he said unto them, O generation of vipers, who hath warned you to flee from the wrath to come? Bring forth therefore fruits meet for repentance: And think not to say within yourselves, We have Abra-

ham to our Father: for I say unto you, that God is able of these stones to raise up children unto Abraham. And now also the axe is laid unto the root of the trees: therefore every tree which bringeth not forth good fruit is hewn down, and cast into the fire" (Matt. 3:7-10).

3. To the tax collectors—"Then came also publicans to be baptized, and said unto him, Master, what shall we do? And he said unto them, Exact no more than that which is appointed you" (Luke 3:12-13).
4. To the soldiers—"And the soldiers likewise demanded of him, saying, And what shall we do? And he said unto them, Do violence to no man, neither accuse any falsely; and be content with your wages" (Luke 3:14).
5. To the world—"The next day John seeth Jesus coming unto him, and saith, Behold the Lamb of God, which taketh away the sin of the world" (John 1:29).

III. The ministry of John
- A. He baptized the converts of Israel—"Then went out to him Jerusalem, and all Judaea, and all the region round about Jordan, and were baptized of him in Jordan, confessing their sins" (Matt. 3:5-6).
- B. He baptized the Christ of Israel.
  1. The acquiescence—A reluctant John agreed to baptize Christ. "Then cometh Jesus from Galilee to Jordan unto John, to be baptized of him. But John forbad him, saying, I have need to be baptized of thee, and comest thou to me? And Jesus answering said unto him, Suffer it to be so now: for thus it becometh us to fulfil all righteousness. Then he suffered him" (Matt. 3:13-15).
  2. The anointing—"And Jesus, when he was baptized, went up straightway out of the water: and, lo, the heavens were opened unto him, and he saw the Spirit of God descending like a dove, and lighting upon him" (Matt. 3:16).
  3. The approval—"And lo a voice from heaven, saying, This is my beloved Son, in whom I am well pleased" (Matt. 3:17).
  4. The assurance—"And I knew him not: but he that sent me to baptize with water, the same said unto me, Upon whom thou shalt see the Spirit descending, and remaining on him, the same is he which baptizeth with the Holy Ghost. And I saw, and bare record that this is the Son of God" (John 1:33-34).

IV. The measure of John—Just what kind of man was John the Baptist?
- A. His private life
  1. He was a rugged and simple man—"And the same John had his raiment of camel's hair, and a leathern girdle about his loins; and his meat was locusts and wild honey" (Matt. 3:4).
  2. He was a man of prayer (Luke 11:1).
  3. He was a Spirit-controlled man—"There was a man sent from God, whose name was John" (John 1:6). "And the child grew, and waxed strong in spirit, and was in the deserts till the day of his shewing unto Israel" (Luke 1:80). "And the hand of the Lord was with him" (Luke 1:66).
- B. His public life
  1. He was a controversial man.
     - a. Most looked upon him as a prophet (Matt. 21:26).
     - b. Some, however, felt he was demon possessed (Matt. 11:18).
     - c. Jesus compared him to Elijah (Matt. 17:12-13).
     - d. A few thought he had come back from the dead in the person of Christ—"At that time Herod the tetrarch heard of the fame of Jesus, And said unto his servants, This is John the Baptist; he is risen from the dead; and therefore mighty works do shew forth themselves in him"

(Matt. 14:1-2). "When Jesus came into the coasts of Caesarea Philippi, he asked his disciples, saying, Whom do men say that I the Son of man am? and they said, Some say that thou art John the Baptist: some, Elias; and others, Jeremias, or one of the prophets" (Matt. 16:13-14).

2. He was a fearless man—John preached his message of repentance or judgment equally, to potentates, publicans, Pharisees, and the public in general.
3. He was an effective man—Although he worked no miracles, his ministry moved the masses (John 10:41).
4. He was a faithful man—"Ye sent unto John, and he bare witness unto the truth. . . . He was a burning and a shining light: and ye were willing for a season to rejoice in his light" (John 5:33, 35).

V. The magnificence of John—Christ himself delivered the greatest eulogy concerning John ever bestowed upon a mortal man. "And as they departed, Jesus began to say unto the multitudes concerning John, What went ye out into the wilderness to see? A reed shaken with the wind? But what went ye out for to see? A man clothed in soft raiment? behold, they that wear soft clothing are in kings' houses. But what went ye out for to see? A prophet? yea, I say unto you, and more than a prophet. For this is he, of whom it is written, Behold, I send my messenger before thy face, which shall prepare thy way before thee. Verily I say unto you, Among them that are born of women there hath not risen a greater than John the Baptist: notwithstanding he that is least in the kingdom of heaven is greater than he" (Matt. 11:7-11). "Ye sent unto John, and he bare witness unto the truth. . . . He was a burning and a shining light: and ye were willing for a season to rejoice in his light" (John 5:33, 35).

VI. The Messiah of John

A. John's loyalty to Christ
1. He correctly described his Savior to the public—"John bare witness of him, and cried, saying, This was he of whom I spake, He that cometh after me is preferred before me: for he was before me. And of his fulness have all we received, and grace for grace. For the law was given by Moses, but grace and truth came by Jesus Christ. No man hath seen God at any time; the only begotten Son, which is in the bosom of the Father, he hath declared him" (John 1:15-18).
2. He correctly described himself to the Pharisees—"And this is the record of John, when the Jews sent priests and Levites from Jerusalem to ask him, Who art thou? And he confessed, and denied not; but confessed, I am not the Christ. And they asked him, What then? Art thou Elias? And he saith, I am not. Art thou that prophet? And he answered, No. Then said they unto him, Who art thou? that we may give an answer to them that sent us. What sayest thou of thyself? He said, I am the voice of one crying in the wilderness, Make straight the way of the Lord, as said the prophet Esaias. And they which were sent were of the Pharisees. And they asked him, and said unto him, Why baptizest thou then, if thou be not that Christ, nor Elias, neither that prophet? John answered them, saying, I baptize with water: but there standeth one among you, whom ye know not; he it is, who coming after me is preferred before me, whose shoe's latchet I am not worthy to unloose" (John 1:19-27).

B. John's love for Christ—"Then there arose a question between some of John's disciples and the Jews about purifying. And they came unto John, and said unto him, Rabbi, he that was with thee beyond Jordan, to whom thou barest witness, behold, the same baptizeth, and all men come to him. John answered and said, A man can receive nothing, except it be given him from heaven. Ye yourselves bear me witness, that I said, I am not the Christ, but that I am sent before him. He that hath the bride is the bridegroom: but the friend of the bridegroom, which standeth and heareth him, rejoiceth greatly because of the bridegroom's voice: this my joy therefore is fulfilled. He must increase, but I must decrease" (John 3:25-30).

VII. The martyrdom of John
  A. The detainment of John—John was cast into prison.
    1. The who of the matter—"For Herod himself had sent forth and laid hold upon John, and bound him in prison for Herodias' sake, his brother Philip's wife: for he had married her" (Mark 6:17).
    2. The why of the matter—"For John had said unto Herod, It is not lawful for thee to have thy brother's wife. Therefore Herodias had a quarrel against him, and would have killed him; but she could not: For Herod feared John, knowing that he was a just man and an holy, and observed him; and when he heard him, he did many things, and heard him gladly" (Mark 6:18-20).
  B. The doubts of John
    1. His request to the Savior—"Now when John had heard in the prison the works of Christ, he sent two of his disciples, And said unto him, Art thou he that should come, or do we look for another?" (Matt. 11:2-3).
    2. His reassurance from the Savior—"And in that same hour he cured many of their infirmities and plagues, and of evil spirits; and unto many that were blind he gave sight. Then Jesus answering said unto them, Go your way, and tell John what things ye have seen and heard; how that the blind see, the lame walk, the lepers are cleansed, the deaf hear, the dead are raised, to the poor the gospel is preached" (Luke 7:21-22).
  C. The death of John
    1. The party—"And when a convenient day was come, that Herod on his birthday made a supper to his lords, high captains, and chief estates of Galilee" (Mark 6:21).
    2. The performance—"And when the daughter of the said Herodias came in, and danced, and pleased Herod and them that sat with him, the king said unto the damsel, Ask of me whatsoever thou wilt, and I will give it thee. And he sware unto her, Whatsoever thou shalt ask of me, I will give it thee, unto the half of my kingdom" (Mark 6:22-23)
    3. The plot—"And she went forth, and said unto her mother, What shall I ask? And she said, The head of John the Baptist. And she came in straightway with haste unto the king, and asked, saying, I will that thou give me by and by in a charger the head of John the Baptist. And the king was exceeding sorry; yet for his oath's sake, and for their sakes which sat with him, he would not reject her. And immediately the king sent an executioner, and commanded his head to be brought: and he went and beheaded him in the prison. And brought his head in a charger, and gave it to the damsel: and the damsel gave it to her mother" (Mark 6:24-28).

THEOLOGICAL SUMMARY

I. Christ referred to John just prior to His ascension—"For John truly baptized with water; but ye shall be baptized with the Holy Ghost not many days hence" (Acts 1:5).

II. Peter referred to John on two occasions:
  A. During his address to the 120 in the upper room (Acts 1:22)
  B. During his dealings with Cornelius in Caesarea (Acts 10:37)

III. Paul referred to John on two occasions:

A. During his address in the synagogue at Antioch of Pisidia (Acts 13:24-25)
B. During his conversation with John's disciples in Ephesus (Acts 19:3-4)

IV. Apollos referred to John in Ephesus—"He spake and taught diligently the things of the Lord, knowing only the baptism of John" (Acts 18:25).

STATISTICS

Father: Zacharias
Mother: Elisabeth
First mention: Matthew 3:1
Final mention: Acts 19:4
Meaning of his name: "Grace of God"
Frequency of his name: Referred to 90 times
Biblical books mentioning him: Five books (Matthew, Mark, Luke, John, Acts)
Occupation: Prophet and Nazirite evangelist
Place of birth: Hill country of Judaea
Place of death: In a dungeon near the Dead Sea
Circumstances of death: He was beheaded by the sword.
Age at death: Approximately 35
Important fact about his life: He was the forerunner of Christ; he both introduced and baptized the Messiah.

Joseph (1)

CHRONOLOGICAL SUMMARY

I. The distress of Joseph—"Now the birth of Jesus Christ was on this wise: When as his mother Mary was espoused to Joseph, before they came together, she was found with child of the Holy Ghost" (Matt. 1:18).

II. The decision of Joseph—"Then Joseph her husband, being a just man, and not willing to make her a publick example, was minded to put her away privily" (Matt. 1:19).

III. The dreams of Joseph
- A. First dream
  - 1. The contents of the dream
    - a. Concerning the purity of Mary—"But while he thought on these things, behold, the angel of the Lord appeared unto him in a dream, saying, Joseph, thou son of David, fear not to take unto thee Mary thy wife: for that which is conceived in her is of the Holy Ghost" (Matt. 1:20).
    - b. Concerning the person within Mary—"And she shall bring forth a son, and thou shalt call his name JESUS: for he shall save his people from their sins" (Matt. 1:21).
    - c. Concerning the prophecy about Mary—"Now all this was done, that it might be fulfilled which was spoken of the Lord by the prophet, saying, Behold, a virgin shall be with child, and shall bring forth a son, and they shall call his name Emmanuel, which being interpreted is, God with us" (Matt. 1:22-23).
  - 2. The consequences of the dream
    - a. The marriage in Nazareth—"Then Joseph being raised from sleep did as the angel of the Lord had bidden him, and took unto him his wife" (Matt. 1:24).
    - b. The manger in Bethlehem—"And Joseph also went up from Galilee, out of the city of Nazareth, into Judaea, unto the city of David, which is called Bethlehem; (because he was of the house and lineage of David:). . . . And she brought forth her firstborn son, and wrapped him in swaddling clothes, and laid him in a manger; because there was no room for them in the inn" (Luke 2:4, 7).
    - c. The message in Jerusalem (Luke 2:21-35)—An old man named Simeon delivered a message for Joseph and Mary as they dedicated the infant Jesus in the temple.
- B. Second dream—Upon the departure of the wise man, Joseph received his second dream. "And when they were departed, behold, the angel of the Lord

appeareth to Joseph in a dream, saying, Arise, and take the young child and his mother, and flee into Egypt, and be thou there until I bring thee word: for Herod will seek the young child to destroy him. When he arose, he took the young child and his mother by night, and departed into Egypt" (Matt. 2:13-14).

C. Third dream—"But when Herod was dead, behold, an angel of the Lord appeareth in a dream to Joseph in Egypt, Saying, Arise, and take the young child and his mother, and go into the land of Israel: for they are dead which sought the young child's life. And he arose, and took the young child and his mother, and came into the land of Israel" (Matt. 2:19-21).

D. Fourth dream—"But when he heard that Archelaus did reign in Judaea in the room of his father Herod, he was afraid to go thither: notwithstanding, being warned of God in a dream, he turned aside into the parts of Galilee: And he came and dwelt in a city called Nazareth: that it might be fulfilled which was spoken by the prophets, He shall be called a Nazarene" (Matt. 2:22-23).

STATISTICS

Father: Jacob (Matt. 1:16)
Spouse: Mary
Sons: James, Joseph, Simon, Judas (Matt. 13:55)
Daughters: Several unnamed (Matt. 13:56)
Famous ancestors: Abraham, David, Solomon
First mention: Matthew 1:16
Final mention: John 6:42
Meaning of his name: "Increaser, may God add"
Frequency of his name: Referred to 16 times
Biblical books mentioning him: Three books (Matthew, Luke, John)
Occupation: Carpenter
Place of birth: Bethlehem
Important fact about his life: He was the godly legal (but not physical) father of Jesus.

Joseph (2)

CHRONOLOGICAL SUMMARY

I. Requested the body of Jesus
  A. The character of Joseph
    1. He was a rich man (Matt. 27:57).
    2. He was a bold man (Mark 15:43).
    3. He was an honored member of the Sanhedrin (Mark 15:43).
    4. He was a good and upright man (Luke 23:50).
    5. He was a disciple of Jesus (Matt. 27:57).
    6. He was waiting for the kingdom of God (Mark 15:43).
  B. The companion of Joseph—Both Joseph and Nicodemus went to Pilate and asked that they might take down from the cross the lifeless body of Jesus and prepare it for proper burial (John 19:38-39).

II. Received the body of Jesus—"And Pilate marvelled if he were already dead: and calling unto him the centurion, he asked him whether he had been any while dead. And when he knew it of the centurion, he gave the body to Joseph" (Mark 15:44-45).
  A. Preparing it for the tomb—He wrapped Jesus' body in a clean linen cloth with spices (Matt. 27:59).
  B. Placing it in the tomb—He laid Jesus' body in his own new tomb (Matt. 27:60).
  C. Protecting it from outside the tomb—Joseph rolled a great stone in front of the entrance (Matt. 27:60).

STATISTICS

First mention: Matthew 27:57
Final mention: John 19:38
Meaning of his name: "Increaser, may God add"
Frequency of his name: Referred to five times
Biblical books mentioning him: Four books (Matthew, Mark, Luke, John)
Occupation: Wealthy businessman
Important fact about his life: He obtained the lifeless body of Jesus from the cross and placed it in his personal tomb.

Judas of Galilee

CHRONOLOGICAL SUMMARY

I. The uprising of Judas—"After this . . . rose up Judas of Galilee in the days of the taxing, and drew away much people after him" (Acts 5:37a).

II. The uprooting of Judas—"He also perished; and all, even as many as obeyed him, were dispersed" (Acts 5:37b).

STATISTICS

First mention: Acts 5:37
Final mention: Acts 5:37
Meaning of his name: "Praised"
Frequency of his name: Referred to one time
Biblical books mentioning him: One book (Acts)
Occupation: Rebel
Place of death: Somewhere in Galilee
Important fact about his life: The lawyer Gamaliel referred to Judas in his counsel to the Pharisees, warning them not to persecute the apostles.

Judas Iscariot

CHRONOLOGICAL SUMMARY

I. Judas, the apostle
  A. His call (Matt. 10:4; Mark 3:19; Luke 6:16)
  B. His city—The word *Iscariot* literally means "the man from Kerioth." Kerioth was a town in southern Judea. Thus Judas was the only non-Galilean among the 12 apostles.

II. Judas, the apostate
  A. The defection of Judas
    1. He was a thief (John 12:1-8).
      a. The circumstances involved—"Then took Mary a pound of ointment of spikenard, very costly, and anointed the feet of Jesus, and wiped his feet with her hair: and the house was filled with the odour of the ointment" (John 12:3).
      b. The criticism involved—"Then saith one of his disciples, Judas Iscariot, Simon's son, which should betray him, Why was not this ointment sold for three hundred pence, and given to the poor?" (John 12:4-5).
      c. The callousness involved—"This he said, not that he cared for the poor; but because he was a thief, and had the bag, and bare what was put therein" (John 12:6).
    2. He was a traitor—No less than 16 times does the New Testament speak of Judas's sin in betraying Christ (Matt. 10:4; 26:16, 25; Mark 3:19; 14:10-11; Luke 6:16; 22:4, 6; John 6:71; 12:4; 18:2, 5; Acts 1:16, 18, 25).
      a. The person behind Judas's crime
        (1) Satan had controlled him from the very beginning—"Jesus answered them, Have not I chosen you twelve, and one of you is a devil? He spake of Judas Iscariot the son of Simon: for he it was that should betray him, being one of the twelve" (John 6:70-71).
        (2) Satan was his spiritual father—Jesus referred to Judas as "the son of perdition" (John 17:12).
        (3) Satan put the desire in Judas' heart to betray Christ (John 13:2).
        (4) Satan actually entered into Judas on two occasions:
          (a) First occasion: Just prior to the upper room events—"Then entered Satan into Judas surnamed Iscariot, being of the number of the twelve" (Luke 22:3).
          (b) Second occasion: In the upper room—"And after the sop Satan entered into him. Then said Jesus unto him, That thou doest, do quickly" (John 13:27).
      b. The price received for Judas's crime—"Then one of the twelve, called Judas Iscariot, went unto the chief priests, and said unto

them, What will ye give me, and I will deliver him unto you? And they covenanted with him for thirty pieces of silver. And from that time he sought opportunity to betray him" (Matt. 26:14-16).

c. The prophecies concerning Judas's crime

(1) Foretold by the Psalms—Just prior to Pentecost, in the upper room, Peter reminded the 120 of these predictions, referring to three Old Testament psalms. "Men and brethren, this scripture must needs have been fulfilled, which the Holy Ghost by the mouth of David spake before concerning Judas, which was guide to them that took Jesus. For he was numbered with us, and had obtained part of this ministry" (Acts 1:16-17). See Psalm 41:9. "For it is written in the book of Psalms, Let his habitation be desolate, and let no man dwell therein: and his bishoprick let another take" (Acts 1:20). See Psalms 69:25 and 109:8.

(2) Foretold by the Savior—"When Jesus had thus said, he was troubled in spirit, and testified, and said, Verily, verily, I say unto you, that one of you shall betray me. . . . He then lying on Jesus' breast saith unto him, Lord, who is it? Jesus answered, He it is, to whom I shall give a sop, when I have dipped it. And when he had dipped the sop, he gave it to Judas Iscariot, the son of Simon. And after the sop Satan entered into him. Then said Jesus unto him, That thou doest, do quickly. Now no man at the table knew for what intent he spake this unto him. For some of them thought, because Judas had the bag, that Jesus had said unto him, Buy those things that we have need of against the feast; or, that he should give something to the poor. He then having received the sop went immediately out: and it was night" (John 13:21, 25-30).

d. The place of Judas's crime—"When Jesus had spoken these words, he went forth with his disciples over the brook Cedron, where was a garden, into the which he entered, and his disciples. And Judas also, which betrayed him, knew the place: for Jesus ofttimes resorted thither with his disciples. Judas then, having received a band of men and officers from the chief priests and Pharisees, cometh thither with lanterns and torches and weapons" (John 18:1-3). "Now he that betrayed him gave them a sign, saying, Whomsoever I shall kiss, that same is he: hold him fast. And forthwith he came to Jesus, and said, Hail, master; and kissed him. And Jesus said unto him, Friend, wherefore art thou come? Then came they, and laid hands on Jesus, and took him" (Matt. 26:48-50).

B. The death of Judas

1. The penitence of the traitor

a. The misery before his death—"Then Judas, which had betrayed him, when he saw that he was condemned, repented himself, and brought again the thirty pieces of silver to the chief priests and elders, saying, I have sinned in that I have betrayed the innocent blood. And they said, What is that to us? see thou to that" (Matt. 27:3-4).

b. The method of his death—"And he cast down the pieces of silver in the temple, and departed, and went and hanged himself" (Matt. 27:5). "Now this man purchased a field with the reward of iniquity; and falling headlong, he burst asunder in the midst, and all his bowels gushed out" (Acts 1:18).

2. The problem of the chief priests—"And they took counsel, and bought with them the potter's field, to bury strangers in. Wherefore that field was called, The field of blood, unto this day" (Matt. 27:7-8).
3. The prediction of the prophet—"Then was fulfilled that which was spoken by Jeremy the prophet, saying, And they took the thirty pieces of silver, the price of him that was valued, whom they of the children of Israel did value; and gave them for the potter's field, as the Lord appointed me" (Matt. 27:9-10).

STATISTICS

First mention: Matthew 10:4
Final mention: Acts 1:25
Meaning of his name: "Praise"
Frequency of his name: Referred to 22 times
Biblical books mentioning him: Five books (Matthew, Mark, Luke, John, Acts)
Occupation: Apostle
Place of birth: Probably in the Judean city of Kerioth
Place of death: In or near Jerusalem
Circumstances of death: He hanged himself (Matt. 27:5; Acts 1:18).
Important fact about his life: He was the apostle who betrayed Christ.

Jude

CHRONOLOGICAL SUMMARY

I. Jude, the agnostic
   A. Prior to the resurrection of Jesus (his half brother), Jude was an unbeliever (John 7:3-5)
   B. He was probably a married man (1 Cor. 9:5)
II. Jude, the associate—Assuming he was the Jude in Acts 15:22-23, we learn the following:
   A. He was a respected elder in the Jerusalem church
   B. He was a co-worker with Paul and Barnabas
   C. He was chosen to inform various churches of the all-important decision made by the Jerusalem council concerning the matter of circumcision.
III. Jude, the author—He was the author of the New Testament epistle that bears his name:

THE EPISTLE OF JUDE

I. The Problem of Apostasy (Jude 1-4)
   A. Jude's commendation (Jude 1-2)
   B. Jude's compulsion (Jude 3)
   C. Jude's concern—"For there are certain men crept in unawares" (Jude 4)
II. The Description of Apostasy—Apostates are:
   A. Ungodly (Jude 4)
   B. Twisters of God's grace (Jude 4)
   C. Christ deniers (Jude 4)
   D. Sensuous (Jude 8)
   E. Flesh defilers (Jude 8)
   F. Despisers of authority (Jude 8)
   G. Ignorant critics (Jude 10)
   H. Unreasoning animals (Jude 10)
   I. Immoral fault-finders (Jude 16)
   J. Arrogant to the core (Jude 16)
   K. Lying flatterers for personal gain (Jude 16)
   L. Divisive (Jude 19)
   M. Worldly minded (Jude 19)
   N. Devoid of the Spirit (Jude 19)
III. Historical examples and causes of apostasy—See also Numbers 14:22–23; Psalm 106:6-33; Hebrews 3:8-19.
   A. The nation Israel, caused by unbelief (Jude 5)
   B. The fallen angels, caused by disloyalty (Jude 6)—See also Genesis 6:1-4; 1 Peter 3:18-20; 2 Peter 2:4; Revelation 12:3-4.

C. The citizens of Sodom and Gomorrah, caused by sexual perversion (Jude 7)—See Genesis 13:13; 18:20-21; 19:4-13; 2 Peter 2:6.
D. The devil, caused by pride and self-will (Jude 9)—See Isaiah 14:12-15; Ezekiel 28:11-19.
E. Cain, caused by perversion of religion—"Woe unto them! for they have gone in the way of Cain" (Jude 11). See Genesis 4:1-8; 1 John 3:12.
F. Balaam, caused by greed for money—"And ran greedily after the error of Balaam for reward" (Jude 11). See Numbers 22:15-17.
G. Korah, caused by rejection of divine authority—"And perished in the gainsaying of Korah" (Jude 11). See Numbers 16:1-3.

IV. The metaphors of apostasy (Jude 12-13)
A. Hidden reefs—"These men are those who are hidden reefs in your love feasts when they feast with you without fear, caring for themselves" (Jude 12, NASB). This describes the unseen dangers of apostasy.
B. Waterless clouds—"Clouds they are without water, carried about of winds" (Jude 12). This describes the false claims of apostasy.
C. Dead autumn trees—"Autumn trees without fruit, doubly dead, uprooted" (Jude 12, NASB). This describes the wasted efforts of apostasy.
D. Wandering stars—"Wandering stars, to whom is reserved the blackness of darkness forever" (Jude 13). This describes the aimless purpose of apostasy.

V. The Judgment upon Apostasy (Jude 14-15)
A. The messenger—"And Enoch also, the seventh from Adam, prophesied of these" (Jude 14).
B. The message—"Behold, the Lord cometh with ten thousands of his saints, to execute judgment upon all and to convince all that are ungodly among them of all their ungodly deeds which they have ungodly committed, and all of their hard speeches which ungodly sinners have spoken against him" (Jude 14-15).

VI. The safeguards to apostasy (Jude 20-25)
A. The believer and himself
1. He is to build on the Word of God—"But ye, beloved, building up yourselves on your most holy faith" (Jude 20).
2. He is to pray with the Spirit of God—"Praying in the Holy Ghost" (Jude 20).
3. He is to keep in the love of God—"Keeps yourselves in the love of God" (Jude 21)
4. He is to look for the return of God—"Looking for the mercy of our Lord Jesus Christ unto eternal life" (Jude 21).
5. He is to testify to the glory of God—"To the only wise God our Savior, be glory and majesty, dominion and power, both now and ever. Amen" (Jude 25).

B. The believer and the lost
1. Concerning those in great doubt—"And have mercy on some, who are doubting" (Jude 22).
2. Concerning those who are in great danger—"And save others, snatching them out of the fire" (Jude 23).
3. Concerning those who are in great depravity—"And on some have mercy with fear, hating even the garment polluted by the flesh" (Jude 23, NASB).

C. The believer and the Lord
1. What he does for us now—"Now unto him that is able to keep you from falling" (Jude 24).
2. What he will do for us later—"And to present you faultless before the presence of his glory with exceeding joy" (Jude 24).

STATISTICS

Father: Joseph (Matt. 13:55)
Mother: Mary (Matt. 13:55)
Brothers: James, Joseph, Simon (Matt. 13:55)
Sisters: Several unnamed (Matt. 13:55)
First mention: Matthew 13:55

Final mention: Jude 1
Meaning of his name: "Praise"
Frequency of his name: Referred to four times
Biblical books mentioning him: Four books (Matthew, Mark, Acts, Jude)
Place of birth: Probably Nazareth
Important fact about his life: He was the half brother of Christ and the author of the New Testament book of Jude.

Julius

CHRONOLOGICAL SUMMARY

I. The charge of Julius—"And when it was determined that we should sail into Italy, they delivered Paul and certain other prisoners unto one named Julius a centurion of Augustus' band" (Acts 27:1).

II. The consideration of Julius—Paul was treated with respect and kindness by this Roman commanding officer.

A. As demonstrated in the city of Sidon—"And the next day we touched at Sidon. And Julius courteously entreated Paul, and gave him liberty to go unto his friends to refresh himself" (Acts 27:3).

B. As demonstrated near the Isle of Melita

1. The plot against Paul—"And the soldiers' counsel was to kill the prisoners, lest any of them should swim out, and escape" (Acts 27:42).

2. The protection of Paul—"But the centurion, willing to save Paul, kept them from their purpose; and commanded that they which could swim should cast themselves first into the sea, and get to land" (Acts 27:43).

STATISTICS

First mention: Acts 27:3
Final mention: Acts 27:43
Frequency of his name: Referred to two times
Biblical books mentioning him: One book (Acts)
Occupation: Roman military officer
Important fact about his life: He commanded the ship that carried Paul to Rome.

Lazarus (1)

CHRONOLOGICAL SUMMARY

I. Lazarus and the rich man: An earthly contrast

A. The rich man—"There was a certain rich man, which was clothed in purple and fine linen, and fared sumptuously every day" (Luke 16:19).

B. Lazarus

1. His pain—"And there was a certain beggar named Lazarus, which was laid at his gate, full of sores" (Luke 16:20).

2. His poverty—"And desiring to be fed with the crumbs which fell from the rich man's table: moreover the dogs came and licked his sores" (Luke 16:21).

II. Lazarus and the rich man: An eternal contrast

A. The rich man—"And in hell he lift up his eyes, being in torments, and seeth Abraham afar off, and Lazarus in his bosom. And he cried and said, Father Abraham, have mercy on me, and send Lazarus, that he may dip the tip of his finger in water, and cool my tongue; for I am tormented in this flame" (Luke 16:23-24).

B. Lazarus—"And it came to pass, that the beggar died, and was carried by the angels into Abraham's bosom" (Luke 16:22). "But Abraham said, Son, remember that thou in thy lifetime receivedst thy good things, and likewise Lazarus evil things: but now he is comforted, and thou art tormented" (Luke 16:25).

STATISTICS

First mention: Luke 16:20
Final mention: Luke 16:25
Meaning of his name: "Without life, helped by God"
Frequency of his name: Referred to four times
Biblical books mentioning him: One book (Luke)
Important fact about his life: He was the saved beggar carried by the angels into Abraham's bosom.

Lazarus (2)

CHRONOLOGICAL SUMMARY

I. The sickness of Lazarus (John 11:1-4)
  A. The concern by his sisters—"Therefore his sisters sent unto him, saying, Lord, behold, he whom thou lovest is sick" (John 11:3).
  B. The comment by his Savior—"When Jesus heard that, he said, This sickness is not unto death, but for the glory of God, that the Son of God might be glorified thereby" (John 11:4).
II. The sorrow over Lazarus
  A. Martha's sorrow—"Then said Martha unto Jesus, Lord, if thou hadst been here, my brother had not died" (John 11:21).
  B. Mary's sorrow—"Then when Mary was come where Jesus was, and saw him, she fell down at his feet, saying unto him, Lord, if thou hadst been here, my brother had not died" (John 11:32).
  C. Jesus' sorrow—"When Jesus therefore saw her weeping, and the Jews also weeping which came with her, he groaned in the spirit, and was troubled. . . . Jesus wept. . . . Jesus therefore again groaning in himself cometh to the grave. It was a cave, and a stone lay upon it" (John 11:33, 35, 38).
III. The summons to Lazarus—"And when he thus had spoken, he cried with a loud voice, Lazarus, come forth. And he that was dead came forth, bound hand and foot with graveclothes: and his face was bound about with a napkin. Jesus saith unto them, Loose him, and let him go" (John 11:43-44).
IV. The supper for Lazarus—"Then Jesus six days before the passover came to Bethany, where Lazarus was which had been dead, whom he raised from the dead. There they made him a supper; and Martha served: but Lazarus was one of them that sat at the table with him" (John 12:1-2).
V. The subtlety against Lazarus—"But the chief priests consulted that they might put Lazarus also to death; Because that by reason of him many of the Jews went away, and believed on Jesus" (John 12:10-11).

STATISTICS

Sisters: Mary and Martha (John 11:1)
First mention: John 11:1
Final mention: John 12:17
Meaning of his name: "Without help"
Frequency of his name: Referred to 11 times
Biblical books mentioning him: One book (John)
Place of birth: Probably in Bethany
Place of death: First time, Bethany; second time, probably Bethany
Important fact about his life: He was the last of three persons raised from the dead by Jesus during his earthly ministry.

Luke

CHRONOLOGICAL SUMMARY

I. The ministry of Luke
  A. He was a coworker with the Apostle Paul.
    1. Traveling with Paul during the second missionary journey
      a. Luke joined Paul, Silas, and Timothy at the city of Troas (Acts 16:8, 10).
      b. He ministered to Lydia and a demoniac girl at Philippi (Acts 16:14-18).
      c. For some reason, neither he nor Timothy were beaten and thrown into prison as were Paul and Silas (Acts 16:19-34).
    2. Traveling with Paul during the third missionary journey
      a. Luke again joined Paul at Troas, as he had during the previous trip (Acts 20:6).
      b. He participated in a prayer meeting on the seashore at Tyre (Acts 21:4-6).
      c. He visited with Philip the evangelist and his four daughters at Caesarea (Acts 21:8-9).

d. He urged Paul not to return to Jerusalem after hearing the prediction of Agabas the prophet—"And as we tarried there many days, there came down from Judaea a certain prophet, named Agabus. And when he was come unto us, he took Paul's girdle, and bound his own hands and feet, and said, Thus saith the Holy Ghost, So shall the Jews at Jerusalem bind the man that owneth this girdle, and shall deliver him into the hands of the Gentiles. And when we heard these things, both we, and they of that place, besought him not to go up to Jerusalem" (Acts 21:10-12).

e. Upon realizing Paul's determination, however, he resigned himself to this visit—"Then Paul answered, What mean ye to weep and to break mine heart? for I am ready not to be bound only, but also to die at Jerusalem for the name of the Lord Jesus. And when he would not be persuaded, we ceased, saying, The will of the Lord be done"(Acts 21:13-14).

3. Arriving in Jerusalem with Paul
   a. Upon returning, Luke stayed in the home of Mnason, a man originally from Cyprus, and one of the early Christian converts (Acts 21:16).
   b. He then visited briefly with James, half brother of the Lord (Acts 21:17-18).

B. He was a chaplain to the Apostle Paul. Luke faithfully ministered to Paul during his various imprisonments.
   1. Joining Paul in Caesarea during the apostle's two-year imprisonment (Acts 24:27; 27:1)
   2. Sailing with Paul for Rome (Acts 27:1)
      a. He endured the terrible storm at sea (Acts 27:18-20).
      b. He escaped safely (along with 275 other passengers) to the Isle of Melita (Acts 28:1).
      c. He stayed three days with Publius, governor of the island (Acts 28:7).
      d. He was treated kindly by the natives, especially after Paul had healed the governor's father of a fever and dysentery (Acts 28:8-10).
      e. Luke spent a total of three months on the island (Acts 28:11).
   3. Arriving in Rome with Paul (Acts 28:11-16)
   4. Joining Paul during the apostle's first Roman imprisonment (Acts 28:30-31; Col. 4:14; Philem. 24)
   5. Joining Paul during the apostle's second (and final) Roman imprisonment (2 Tim. 4:11)

II. The manuscripts of Luke—Luke authored two New Testament books, the Gospel of Luke and the book of Acts.

THE GOSPEL OF LUKE

I. Luke compiled his material from numerous sources (Luke 1:1-4).
   A. He was a highly educated man.
   B. He wrote from a Greek background and perspective.

II. Luke presents Christ as the Son of man, i.e., the perfect man.
   A. The explanation: Luke explained to his friend Theophilus his reason for writing an account of the Son of man (Luke 1:1-4).
   B. The annunciations: There were a number of heavenly announcements concerning both the Son of man and his forerunner, occurring before and after the Bethlehem event. Various parties were involved.
      1. Those involved preceding his birth
         a. Zacharias and Gabriel (Luke 1:5-25)
         b. Mary and Gabriel (Luke 1:26-38)
         c. Mary and Elisabeth (Luke 1:39-56)
         d. Zacharias and the infant John (Luke 1:57-80)

e. Mary and Joseph (Luke 2:1-7)
2. Those involved following his birth
a. The shepherds and the angels (Luke 2:8-15)
b. The shepherds and the Savior (Luke 2:16-20)
c. Simeon and the Savior (Luke 2:21-35)
d. Anna and the Savior (Luke 2:36-38)

C. The preparation: The quiet boyhood of Jesus prepared him for his role as the perfect Son of man.
1. He was seen in the home of his mother—"And when they had performed all things according to the law of the Lord, they returned into Galilee, to their own city Nazareth. And the child grew, and waxed strong in spirit, filled with wisdom: and the grace of God was upon him. . . . And Jesus increased in wisdom and stature, and in favour with God and man" (Luke 2:39-40, 52).
2. He was seen in the house of his Father (Luke 2:41-51)—"And it came to pass, that after three days they found him in the temple, sitting in the midst of the doctors, both hearing them, and asking them questions. And all that heard him were astonished at his understanding and answers. And when they saw him, they were amazed: and his mother said unto him, Son, why hast thou thus dealt with us? behold, thy father and I have sought thee sorrowing. And he said unto them, How is it that ye sought me? wist ye not that I must be about my Father's business?" (Luke 2:46-49).

D. The anticipation: The preaching of John the Baptist caused great interest in the promised appearance of the Son of man (Luke 3:1-20). "And he came into all the country about Jordan, preaching the baptism of repentance for the remission of sins; As it is written in the book of the words of Esaias the prophet, saying, The voice of one crying in the wilderness, Prepare ye the way of the Lord, make his paths straight. Every valley shall be filled, and every mountain and hill shall be brought low; and the crooked shall be made straight, and the rough ways shall be made smooth; And all flesh shall see the salvation of God" (Luke 3:3-6).

E. The validation: At his baptism the Father gave official approval of the Son of man (Luke 3:21-22). "And the Holy Ghost descended in a bodily shape like a dove upon him, and a voice came from heaven, which said, Thou art my beloved Son; in thee I am well pleased" (Luke 3:22).

F. The documentation: Luke followed the genealogy of the Son of man backward in time to Adam, tracing his line through Nathan, the second son of King David (Luke 3:23-38).

G. The temptation: The Son of man was unsuccessfully tempted in three areas by Satan (Luke 4:1-13).

H. The proclamation: The Son of man proclaimed his message throughout the land (Luke 4:14-15, 42-44). "And he said unto them, I must preach the kingdom of God to other cities also: for therefore am I sent" (Luke 4:43).
1. The sermons he delivered
a. The message at Nazareth on Isaiah 61 (Luke 4:16-30)
b. The Sermon on the Mount (Luke 6:17-49)
c. The Mount Olivet discourse (Luke 21:5-38)
2. The subjects he discussed
a. True spiritual relationships (Luke 8:19-21)
b. His future sufferings, death, and resurrection (Luke 9:22, 44-45; 17:25; 18:31-34)
c. Discipleship (Luke 9:23-26, 57-62; 14:25-33)
d. Greatness (Luke 9:46-48; 22:24-27)
e. Sectarianism (Luke 9:49-50)
f. The unbelief of and coming judgment upon his generation (Luke 11:29-32)
g. The Holy Spirit (Luke 12:10-12)

h. Covetousness (Luke 12:13-15; 16:14-15)
i. God's care for his own (Luke 12:6-7, 22-34)
j. Watchfulness (Luke 12:35-40)
k. His mission (Luke 12:49-53)
l. Repentance and confession (Luke 13:1-5; 12:8-9)
m. Signs of the times (Luke 12:54-57)
n. False religious profession (Luke 13:22-30)
o. The great white judgment throne (Luke 12:2-5)
p. Divorce (Luke 16:18)
q. Forgiveness (Luke 17:3-4)
r. Faith (Luke 17:22-37)
s. Final events (Luke 17:22-37)
t. Rewards (Luke 18:28-30; 22:28-30)

I. The eulogization: The Son of man paid great homage to the imprisoned John the Baptist (Luke 7:19-29).

J. The deputation: The Son of man chose and commissioned his apostles.
1. The 12 disciples
a. The call of Andrew, Peter, James, and John (Luke 5:1-11)
b. The call of Levi (Luke 5:27-29)
c. The selection of the Twelve (Luke 6:13-16)
d. The sending forth of the Twelve (Luke 9:1-11)
2. The Seventy (Luke 10:1-24)

K. The demonstrations: The Son of man exhibited his mighty power by performing 18 miracles, as recorded by Luke.
1. Casting of demons
a. The man at Capernaum (Luke 4:31-37)
b. The man at Gadara (Luke 8:26-40)
c. The boy at the base of Mount Hermon (Luke 9:37-43)
d. A man somewhere in Galilee (Luke 11:14)
2. Raising the dead
a. The widow's son at Nain (Luke 7:11-18)
b. Jairus's daughter in Galilee (Luke 8:41-42, 49-56)
3. Feeding the hungry (Luke 9:12-17)
4. Healing the sick
a. Peter's mother-in-law (Luke 4:38-39)
b. A leper (Luke 5:12-14)
c. Ten lepers (Luke 17:11-19)
d. A paralytic (Luke 5:17-26)
e. A man with a paralyzed hand (Luke 6:6-11)
f. A centurion's servant (Luke 7:1-10)
g. A woman with an issue of blood (Luke 8:43-48)
h. A woman with an 18-year infirmity (Luke 13:10-17)
i. A man with dropsy (Luke 14:1-6)
j. A blind man named Bartimaeus (Luke 18:35-43)
5. Calming the sea (Luke 8:22-25)

L. The illustrations: The Son of man illustrated his message and mission through the employment of parables. Here are the 25 parables as recorded by Luke:
1. The two debtors (Luke 7:40-43)
2. The sower and the soil (Luke 8:4-15)
3. The mustard seed (Luke 13:18-19)
4. The leaven (Luke 13:20-21)
5. The lighted lamp (Luke 8:16-18; 11:33-36)
6. The good Samaritan (Luke 10:25-37)
7. The generous father (Luke 11:11-13)
8. The persistent friend (Luke 11:5-8)
9. Reformation without regeneration (Luke 11:24-26)
10. The rich fool (Luke 12:16-21)
11. The faithful and faithless servants (Luke 12:41-48)
12. The fruitless fig tree (Luke 13:6-9)
13. The ambitious guest (Luke 14:7-14)
14. The great supper (Luke 14:15-24)
15. The lost sheep (Luke 15:1-7)
16. The lost coin (Luke 15:8-10)
17. The lost son (Luke 15:11-32)
18. The unjust steward (Luke 16:1-13)
19. The rich man and Lazarus (Luke 16:19-31)
20. When our best is but the least (Luke 17:7-10)
21. The persistent widow (Luke 18:1-8)
22. The publican and the Pharisee (Luke 18:9-14)
23. The ten pounds (Luke 19:11-27)

24. The angry vineyard owner (Luke 20:9-18)
25. The budding fig tree (Luke 21:29-32)

M. The supplications: The Son of man considered the subject of prayer to be an all-important one.
   1. His personal prayers—Jesus prayed:
      a. At his baptism (Luke 3:21)
      b. In the wilderness (Luke 5:16)
      c. Before choosing the Twelve (Luke 6:12)
      d. Prior to hearing Peter's great confession (Luke 9:18)
      e. During his transfiguration (Luke 9:29)
      f. After hearing the report of the returning Seventy—"In that hour Jesus rejoiced in spirit, and said, I thank thee, O Father, Lord of heaven and earth, that thou hast hid these things from the wise and prudent, and hast revealed them unto babes: even so, Father; for so it seemed good in thy sight. All things are delivered to me of my Father: and no man knoweth who the Son is, but the Father; and who the Father is, but the Son, and he to whom the Son will reveal him" (Luke 10:21-22).
      g. Before giving the model prayer (Luke 11:1)
      h. In the upper room for Peter—"And the Lord said, Simon, Simon, behold, Satan hath desired to have you, that he may sift you as wheat: But I have prayed for thee, that thy faith fail not: and when thou art converted, strengthen thy brethren" (Luke 22:31-32).
      i. In the garden—"And he was withdrawn from them about a stone's cast, and kneeled down, and prayed, Saying, Father, if thou be willing, remove this cup from me: nevertheless not my will, but thine, be done. And there appeared an angel unto him from heaven, strengthening him. And being in an agony he prayed more earnestly: and his sweat was as it were great drops of blood falling down to the ground" (Luke 22:41-44).
      j. On the cross—"Then said Jesus, Father, forgive them; for they know not what they do. And they parted his raiment, and cast lots. And when Jesus had cried with a loud voice, he said, Father, into thy hands I commend my spirit: and having said thus, he gave up the ghost" (Luke 23:34, 36).
   2. His pattern prayer—"And he said unto them, When ye pray, say, Our Father which art in heaven, Hallowed be thy name. Thy kingdom come. Thy will be done, as in heaven, so in earth. Give us day by day our daily bread. And forgive us our sins; for we also forgive every one that is indebted to us. And lead us not into temptation; but deliver us from evil" (Luke 11:2-4).
   3. His points on prayer (Luke 6:27-28; 11:9-10; 18:1; 21:36; 22:40)

N. The invitations: On two special occasions the Son of man issued a personal invitation.
   1. To the rich young ruler (Luke 18:18-24)—"Now when Jesus heard these things, he said unto him, Yet lackest thou one thing: sell all that thou hast, and distribute unto the poor, and thou shalt have treasure in heaven: and come, follow me" (Luke 18:22).
   2. To a short but rich tax collector (Luke 19:1-10)—"And when Jesus came to the place, he looked up, and saw him, and said unto him, Zacchaeus, make haste, and come down; for to day I must abide at thy house" (Luke 19:5).

O. The intolerance: The Son of man was rejected by the Samaritans (Luke 9:51-56)—"And they did not receive him, because his face was as though he would go to Jerusalem" (Luke 9:53).

P. The clarification: During his visit with Mary and Martha the Son of man gently corrected Martha for having her priorities in the wrong order (Luke 10:38-42).

Q. The consecration: Some children were brought to the Son of man to be blessed by him (Luke 18:15-17).

R. The lamentation: The Son of man wept over the city of Jerusalem (Luke 19:41-42).

S. The presentation: The Son of man presented himself to the Jerusalem crowds during the triumphal entry on Palm Sunday (Luke 19:28-40).

T. The purification: The Son of man cleansed the temple (Luke 19:45-48).

U. The observation: The Son of man commented concerning a poor widow and her offering in the temple (Luke 21:1-4).

V. The confrontations: The Son of man was often confronted by the wicked Jewish leaders.
   1. They said he was a blasphemer (Luke 5:21).
   2. They accused him of having a demon (Luke 11:15).
   3. They criticized him in various areas:
      a. For associating with sinners (Luke 5:30-32; 7:36-39)
      b. For not observing their ceremonial fastings (Luke 5:33-35)
      c. For not observing their ceremonial washings (Luke 11:37-38)
      d. For allowing his disciples to pick grain for food on the Sabbath (Luke 6:1-5)
      e. For healing on the Sabbath (Luke 6:6-11)
   4. They challenged his authority (Luke 20:1-8).
   5. They attempted to trap him concerning:
      a. The paying of tribute (Luke 20:19-26)
      b. The resurrection of the dead (Luke 20:27-33)

W. The condemnation: The Son of man utterly condemned the wicked Jewish leaders (Luke 7:30-35; 11:39-54; 20:45-47).

X. The symbolization: The Son of man used bread and wine to symbolize his sufferings in the upper room (Luke 22:7-20). "And he took bread, and gave thanks, and brake it, and gave unto them, saying, This is my body which is given for you: this do in remembrance of me. Likewise also the cup after supper, saying, This cup is the new testament in my blood, which is shed for you" (Luke 22:19-20).

Y. The repudiation: The Son of man was betrayed and denied by two followers.
   1. The betrayal by Judas (Luke 22:1-6, 47-48)
   2. The denials by Peter (Luke 22:34, 53-62)

Z. The interrogation: The Son of man was arrested in Gethsemane and subjected to several unfair trials.
   1. Before the high priest (Luke 22:54, 63-65)
   2. Before the Sanhedrin (Luke 22:66-71)
   3. Before Pilate for the first time (Luke 23:1-5)
   4. Before Herod (Luke 23:6-12)
   5. Before Pilate for the second time (Luke 23:13-25)

AA. The brutalization: The Son of man was cruelly placed on the cross of Calvary and crucified (Luke 23:33-49).

BB. The authorization: Joseph of Arimathea received permission from Pilate to remove the lifeless body of the Son of man and place it in a new tomb (Luke 23:50-53).

CC. The finalization: The women prepared spices and ointments for anointing the body of the Son of man for final burial (Luke 23:54-56).

DD. The vindication: The Son of man was vindicated through his glorious resurrection from the dead.
   1. The announcement to some women in the tomb (Luke 24:1-12)

2. The appearances to his disciples
a. Christ appeared to two of them en route to Emmaus (Luke 24:13-32).
b. Christ appeared to 10 of them in the upper room (Luke 24:33-44).
EE. The exaltation: The Son of man ascended into heaven (Luke 24:49-53).

THE BOOK OF ACTS Part 1: Operation Holy Land—The Greater Jerusalem Crusade (Acts 1–12). It was headed up by Peter, the fisherman, and assisted by Stephen and Philip.

I. Activities of Peter
A. Peter and the 120 (Acts 1:1-26)
1. On the Mount of Olives (Acts 1:1-12)
a. Receiving the assurance from Christ (Acts 1:6-8)
b. Witnessing the ascension of Christ (Acts 1:9-11)
2. In the upper room (Acts 1:13-26)
a. The prayer meeting (Acts 1:13-14)
b. The business meeting (Acts 1:15-26)
B. Peter and the crowd at Pentecost (Acts 2:1-47)
1. The cloven tongues (Acts 2:1-4)
2. The congregation (Acts 2:5-11)
3. The confusion (Acts 2:12-13)
4. The clarification (Acts 2:14-15)
5. The comparison (Acts 2:16-21)
a. The Old Testament prophet Joel (Acts 2:16)
b. The Old Testament prophecy of Joel (Acts 2:17-21)
6. The condemnation (Acts 2:22-28)
a. The Messiah had been crucified by his foes (Acts 2:22-24).
b. The Messiah had been resurrected by his Father (Acts 2:24).
7. The conclusion (Acts 2:29-36)
8. The conviction (Acts 2:37)
9. The command (Acts 2:38-39)
10. The conversions (Acts 2:41)
11. The communion (Acts 2:42-47)
C. Peter and the lame man (Acts 3:1-26)
1. The miracle (Acts 3:1-11)
a. The need for the healing (Acts 3:2)
b. The name in the healing (Acts 3:4-6)
c. The nature of the healing (Acts 3:8)
2. The message (Acts 3:12-26)—At this point, Peter delivered a powerful sermon about the cross.
a. The promoters of the cross—The Jewish leaders (Acts 3:13-15)
b. The prophecies about the cross—The Old Testament Scriptures (Acts 3:18)
c. The power of the cross (Acts 3:16, 26)
(1) It had sealed the body of one man (Acts 3:16).
(2) It could heal the souls of all men (Acts 3:26).
d. The program of the cross (Acts 3:15, 18-21)
e. The plea of the cross (Acts 3:19, 26)
D. Peter and the high priest (Acts 4:1-37)—Annas, the Jewish high priest, had Peter and John arrested.
1. The reason for the arrest (Acts 4:2)
2. The evidence supporting the arrest (Acts 4:4)
3. The dialogue in the arrest (Acts 4:8-12)
4. The conference during the arrest (Acts 4:13-17)
5. The warning accompanying the arrest (Acts 4:18-22)
6. The praise service following the arrest (Acts 4:23-30)
7. The blessings resulting from the arrest (Acts 4:31-37)
E. Peter and Ananias and Sapphira (Acts 5:1-11)
1. Their deception (Acts 5:1-2)
2. Their discovery (Acts 5:3-4)
3. Their deaths (Acts 5:5, 10)
F. Peter and the sick (Acts 5:12-16)
G. Peter and the lawyer Gamaliel (Acts 5:17-42)—For the second time Peter was arrested for preaching Christ.
1. The anger of the Sadducees (Acts 5:17-18)

2. The appearance of the Lord (Acts 5:19-20)
3. The astonishment of the jailors (Acts 5:21-26)
4. The address of Peter (Acts 5:27-32)
5. The advice of Gamaliel (Acts 5:34-39)
6. The attitude of the apostles (Acts 5:40-42)
   a. Their pain (Acts 5:40)
   b. Their praise (Acts 5:41)
   c. Their persistence (Acts 5:42)

H. Peter and Simon the Sorcerer (Acts 8:9-25)
1. The pride of Simon (Acts 8:9-11)
2. The perversion of Simon (Acts 8:18-19)
3. The punishment of Simon (Acts 8:20-21)
4. The plea of Simon (Acts 8:24)

I. Peter and Aeneas (Acts 9:32-35)
1. The misery (Acts 9:32-33)
2. The miracle (Acts 9:34)

J. Peter and Dorcas (Acts 9:36-42)
1. The deeds of Dorcas (Acts 9:36)
2. The death of Dorcas (Acts 9:37)
3. The deliverance of Dorcas (Acts 9:38-41)

K. Peter and Cornelius (Acts 9:43–10:48)
1. Cornelius, a religious sinner in Caesarea (Acts 10:1-8)
2. Peter, a reluctant soul winner in Joppa (Acts 10:9-23)
3. Peter and Cornelius, redeemed saints in Christ (Acts 10:24-48)

L. Peter and the Jewish believers at Jerusalem (Acts 11:1-18)
1. The accusation (Acts 11:1-3)
2. The argument (Acts 11:14-17)
3. The acceptance (Acts 11:18)

M. Peter and the angel of the Lord (Acts 12:1-17)
1. Peter's success in escaping a prison house (Acts 12:5-11)
2. Peter's struggle in entering a prayer house (Acts 12:12-16)

N. Peter and the Jerusalem council (Acts 15)
1. His comments (Acts 15:7-9)
2. His caution (Acts 15:10)
3. His conclusion (Acts 15:11)

II. Activities of Stephen (Acts 6:1–7:60):

A. The complaint of the laity (Acts 6:1)

B. The conference of the leaders (Acts 6:2-4)

C. The choice of the laborers (Acts 6:5-7)—The first seven deacons were chosen; Stephen was one of them.
1. The spiritual maturity of Stephen (Acts 6:5-10)
2. The miracles of Stephen (Acts 6:8)
3. The maligning of Stephen (Acts 6:9-14)
4. The meekness of Stephen (Acts 6:15)
5. The message of Stephen (Acts 7:1-53)
6. The martyrdom of Stephen (Acts 7:54-60)
   a. His persecutors (Acts 7:54, 57-58)
   b. His preview of glory (Acts 7:55-56)
   c. His prayer (Acts 7:59-60)
      (1) For himself (Acts 7:59)
      (2) For his enemies (Acts 7:60)

III. Activities of Philip (Acts 6:5; 8:5-8, 26-40)

A. The evangelist in Samaria
1. The message he preached (Acts 8:5)
2. The miracles he performed (Acts 8:6-8)

B. The soul winner in Gaza (Acts 8:26-40)
1. His mission from an angel (Acts 8:26)
2. His mission to a eunuch (Acts 8:27-40)
   a. The confusion of the eunuch (Acts 8:31-34)
   b. The conversion of the eunuch (Acts 8:36-37)
   c. The confession of the eunuch (Acts 8:38-40)

C. The family man in Caesarea (Acts 21:8-9)

THE BOOK OF ACTS: Part 2: Operation Whole Earth—The Global Crusade (Acts 13–28). It was headed up by Paul, the tentmaker, and assisted by Barnabas, Silas, Timothy, Mark, and Luke.

I. The conversion of Paul (Acts 9:1-19; 22:5-16; 26:12)

A. Paul's vendetta against the saints of God (Acts 9:1-2; 22:4; 26:9-12)

B. Paul's vision of the Son of God (Acts 9:3-9; 22:6-11; 26:12-18)
C. Paul's visitation by a servant of God (Acts 9:10-18; 22:13-16)

II. The early ministry of Paul (Acts 9:19-30; 11:24-30; 12:25–13:3; 22:21)—His first missionary journey (Acts 13:2–14:2)
A. First stop, Cyprus (Acts 13:4-12)
B. Second stop, Perga (Acts 13:13)—John Mark left the team at this point.
C. Third stop, Antioch in Pisidia (Acts 13:14-50)—Paul spent several weeks there and preached two sermons in the synagogue in Antioch.
D. Fourth stop, Iconium (Acts 13:51—14:5)
E. Fifth stop, Lystra (Acts 14:6-23)
F. Sixth stop, back to Antioch in Syria (Acts 14:24-28)

III. The Jerusalem council—Attended by Paul (Acts 15:1-35)
A. The reason for the council (Acts 15:1-2, 5-6)
B. The reports given in the council
1. Peter's report (Acts 15:7-11)
2. Paul's report (Acts 15:12)
3. James's report (Acts 15:13-21)
a. The summary: James summarized the position of no circumcision for Gentiles through two arguments.
(1) A practical argument—God had already saved Gentiles without the rite of circumcision (Acts 15:14).
(2) A prophetical argument—Amos the prophet had already predicted this would happen (Acts 15:15-18).
b. The suggestion (Acts 15:19-21)
C. The recommendation of the council (Acts 15:22-35)
1. The messengers who carried their recommendation (Acts 15:22-27)
2. The message contained in their recommendation (Acts 15:28-35)

IV. The disagreement between Paul and Barnabas (Acts 15:36-40)
A. The background of the disagreement (Acts 15:36-38)
B. The blessing from the disagreement (Acts 15:39-40)—As a result, there were twice as many missionaries on the field.

V. The second missionary journey of Paul (Acts 15:41–18:22)
A. First stop, Lystra (Acts 16:1-5)
1. The choosing of Timothy (Acts 16:1-2)
2. The circumcising of Timothy (Acts 16:3)
B. Second stop, Troas (Acts 16:6-10)
1. Forbidden by the Holy Spirit to go north or south (Acts 16:6-7)
2. Bidden by the Holy Spirit to go west (Acts 16:9-10)
C. Third stop, Philippi (Acts 16:11-40)—At Philippi three tremendous conversions took place.
1. The salvation of a business woman (Acts 16:13-15)
2. The salvation of a demoniac girl (Acts 16:16-18)
3. The salvation of a prison keeper (Acts 16:19-40)
D. Fourth stop, Thessalonica (Acts 17:1-9)
E. Fifth stop, Berea (Acts 17:10-14)—Timothy and Silas remained in Berea.
F. Sixth stop, Athens (Acts 17:15-34)—Paul preached his famous sermon on Mars Hill.
G. Seventh stop, Corinth (Acts 18:1-18)
1. Paul's friends in this city (Acts 18:1-5)
2. Paul's foes in this city (Acts 18:1-5)
3. Paul's fruits in this city (Acts 18:8, 11)
4. Paul's Heavenly Father in this city (Acts 18:9-10)
H. Eighth stop, Ephesus (Acts 18:19-21)

VI. The third missionary journey of Paul (Acts 18:23–21:14)
A. First stop, Asia Minor (Acts 18:23)—Paul revisited these churches to exhort and strengthen them.
B. Second stop, Ephesus (Acts 18:24–19:41)
1. The forerunner of Paul in Ephesus—Apollos (Acts 18:24-28)
a. The teaching of Apollos (Acts 18:24-28)
b. The teachers of Apollos (Acts 18:26)
2. The fruits of Paul in Ephesus (Acts 19:1-41)

C. Third stop, Greece (Acts 20:1-5)—After a stay of three months he left to escape a plot of the Jews to kill him.
D. Fourth stop, Troas (Acts 20:6-12)
1. The midnight address (Acts 20:7)
2. The midmorning accident (Acts 20:8-9)
3. The miraculous awakening (Acts 20:10-12)
E. Fifth stop, Miletus (Acts 20:15-38)
F. Sixth stop, Tyre (Acts 21:1-6)
G. Seventh stop, Ptolemais (Acts 21:7)
H. Eighth stop, Caesarea (Acts 21:8-14)

VII. Paul's final visit to Jerusalem (Acts 21:15-20)
A. The rumors against Paul (Acts 21:18-22, 27-30)
B. The reaction by Paul (Acts 21:23-26)—To counteract these false rumors, Paul agreed to put himself back under the Law, shave his head, and take a seven-day vow.
C. The rescue of Paul (Acts 21:30-32)—In spite of Paul's efforts, the rumors persisted and he was set upon by a murderous Jewish mob.
D. The replies by Paul (Acts 21:33–23:10)
E. The revelation to Paul (Acts 23:11)
F. The revenge against Paul (Acts 23:12-15)
G. The relative of Paul (Acts 23:16-22)
H. The removal of Paul (Acts 23:23-32)

VIII. Paul's imprisonment in Caesarea (Acts 23:33–26:32)
A. Paul before Felix (Acts 23:33–24:27)
B. Paul before Festus (Acts 25:1-12)
C. Paul before Agrippa (Acts 25:13–26:32)

IX. Paul's voyage to Rome (Acts 27:1–28:31)
A. Phase 1: From Caesarea to Fair Havens (Acts 27:1-12)
B. Phase 2: From Fair Havens to Melita (Acts 26:13–27:44)
C. Phase 3: At Melita (Acts 28:1-10)
D. Phase 4: From Melita to Rome (Acts 28:11-15)
E. Phase 5: At Rome (Acts 28:16-31)

STATISTICS

Brother: Some feel Titus may have been his brother (2 Cor. 8:18; 12:18).
First mention: Luke 1:3
Final mention: Philemon 24
Meaning of his name: "Light giving"
Frequency of his name: Referred to 41 times
Biblical books mentioning him: five books (Luke, Acts, Colossians, 2 Peter, Philemon)
Occupation: Medical doctor (Col. 4:14)
Place of birth: Probably born in Antioch in Syria
Place of death: Tradition says he died in Greece.
Circumstances of death: Tradition says he was crucified for his faith in Christ, along with the Apostle Andrew.
Important fact about his life: He was the author of the books of Luke and Acts and served as Paul's personal physician.

Lydia

CHRONOLOGICAL SUMMARY

I. Her business—"And a certain woman named Lydia, a seller of purple, of the city of Thyatira" (Acts 16:14a).
II. Her new birth—"Whose heart the Lord opened, that she attended unto the things which were spoken of Paul" (Acts 16:14b).
III. Her baptism—"And when she was baptized, and her household, she besought us, saying, If ye have judged me to be faithful to the Lord, come into my house, and abide there. And she constrained us" (Acts 16:15).

STATISTICS

First mention: Acts 16:14
Final mention: Acts 16:15
Frequency of her name: Referred to one time
Biblical books mentioning her: One book (Acts)
Occupation: Saleswoman in the purple dye trade
Important fact about her life: She was Paul's first female convert in Greece.

Malchus

CHRONOLOGICAL SUMMARY

I. The removing of his ear by Simon—"Then Simon Peter having a sword drew it, and smote the high priest's servant, and cut off his right ear. The servant's name was Malchus" (John 18:10).

II. The restoring of his ear by Jesus—"And Jesus answered and said, Suffer ye thus far. And he touched his ear, and healed him" (Luke 22:51).

STATISTICS

First mention: Luke 22:51
Final mention: John 18:10
Meaning of his name: "Counselor"
Frequency of his name: Referred to two times
Biblical books mentioning him: Two books (Luke, John)
Important fact about his life: Jesus restored to him his ear which Peter had cut off.

Mark

CHRONOLOGICAL SUMMARY

I. Mark, the failure
  A. He was brought to Antioch by Paul and his uncle, Barnabas (Acts 12:25).
  B. He accompanied Paul and Barnabas on their first missionary journey (Acts 13:5).
  C. When things became difficult, he abandoned the team at Perga and returned home (Acts 13:13).
  D. Paul later refused to allow John Mark to accompany him on his second missionary trip (Acts 15:36-38).
II. Mark, the fruitful
  A. John Mark and Barnabas—Barnabas left Paul and took John Mark with him to Cyprus for missionary purposes. Apparently this time, the young man rose to the occasion (Acts 15:39).
  B. John Mark and Paul
    1. He ministered to Paul in Rome during the apostle's first imprisonment (Philem. 24; Col. 4:10).
    2. He was summoned by Paul in Rome during the apostle's final imprisonment—"Only Luke is with me. Take Mark, and bring him with thee: for he is profitable to me for the ministry" (2 Tim. 4:11).
  C. John Mark and Peter—"The church that is at Babylon, elected together with you, saluteth you; and so doth Marcus my son" (1 Pet. 5:13).
III. Mark, the author—He was the author of the Gospel that bears his name.

THE GOSPEL OF MARK

Mark emphasizes the servanthood of Christ.

I. The setting apart of the servant
  A. His forerunner (Mark 1:1-8)
  B. His baptism (Mark 1:9-11)
  C. His temptation (Mark 1:12-13)
II. The spokesman of the servant
  A. The personal meeting with his apostles
    1. James, John, Peter, and Andrew (Mark 1:14-20)
    2. Matthew (Mark 2:13-14)
  B. The public ministry of his apostles
    1. The official call of the Twelve (Mark 3:13-21)
    2. The official commission to the Twelve (Mark 6:7-13)
III. The sermons and subjects of the Savior—"And he said unto them, Let us go into the next towns, that I may preach there also: for therefore came I forth" (Mark 1:38).
  A. The sermons he delivered
    1. The sower and the soils (Mark 4:1-34)
    2. A description of defilement (Mark 7:1-23)
    3. The Mount Olivet discourse (Mark 13:1-37)
  B. The subjects he discussed
    1. The unpardonable sin (Mark 3:22-30)
    2. True relationships (Mark 3:31-35)
    3. Discipleship (Mark 8:34-38)
    4. Greatness (Mark 9:33-37; 10:42-45)
    5. Sectarianism (Mark 9:38-41)
    6. Hell (Mark 9:42-50)
    7. Divorce (Mark 10:1-12)
    8. Rewards (Mark 10:28-31)
    9. Prayer and faith (Mark 11:20-26)
    10. The Messiah (Mark 12:35-37)
IV. The supernaturalness of the servant—"And whithersoever he entered, into villages, or cities, or country, they laid the sick in the streets, and besought him that they might touch if it were but the border of his garment: and as many as touched him were made whole"

(Mark 6:56). Mark records no less than 18 miracles performed by Jesus.

A. Casting out of demons
   1. From a man in Capernaum (Mark 1:21-28)
   2. From a man in Gadara (Mark 5:1-20)
   3. From a girl in Tyre (Mark 7:24-30)
   4. From a boy near Mount Hermon (Mark 9:14-29)

B. Healing of diseases
   1. Peter's mother-in-law (Mark 1:29-34)
   2. A leper (Mark 1:40-45)
   3. A palsied man (Mark 2:1-12)
   4. A withered hand (Mark 3:1-6)
   5. A woman with a bloody issue (Mark 5:25-34)
   6. A deaf and mute man (Mark 7:31-37)
   7. A blind man (Mark 8:22-26)
   8. A blind man named Bartimaeus (Mark 10:46-52)

C. Feeding the hungry
   1. The five thousand (Mark 6:30-44)
   2. The four thousand (Mark 8:1-9)

D. Controlling the elements (Mark 4:35-41)
   1. Stilling the storm (Mark 4:35-41)
   2. Walking on water (Mark 6:45-52)

E. Judging a fruitless fig tree (Mark 11:12-14)

F. Raising a girl from the dead (Mark 5:21-24, 35-43)

V. The skeptics of the servant—"And the scribes which came down from Jerusalem said, He hath Beelzebub, and by the prince of the devils casteth he out devils" (Mark 3:22). "And the Pharisees came forth, and began to question with him, seeking of him a sign from heaven, tempting him" (Mark 8:11). "And they send unto him certain of the Pharisees and of the Herodians, to catch him in his words" (Mark 12:13).

A. His confrontation with the skeptics
   1. They said he associated with sinners and did not observe all their legalism (Mark 2:16-22).
   2. They questioned his authority (Mark 11:27-33).
   3. They attempted to trap him:
      a. Concerning the subject of paying tribute (Mark 12:13-17)
      b. Concerning the subject of the resurrection (Mark 12:18-27)

B. His condemnation of the skeptics
   1. He suggested they might have committed the unpardonable sin (Mark 3:22-30).
   2. He refused to give them a sign (Mark 8:11-13).
   3. He warned against their hypocrisy (Mark 8:14-21).
   4. He compared them to some wicked and murderous laborers in a vineyard (Mark 12:1-12).
   5. He denounced their self-centeredness and pride (Mark 12:38-40).

VI. The seekers of the servant—In contrast to the wicked Jewish leaders who rejected him, there were those who sought him out for various reasons.

A. Some parents with their children (Mark 10:13-16)—"And he took them up in his arms, put his hands upon them, and blessed them" (Mark 10:16).

B. The rich young ruler (Mark 10:17-27)

C. James and John (Mark 10:35-41)—"They said unto him, Grant unto us that we may sit, one on thy right hand, and the other on thy left hand, in thy glory" (Mark 10:37).

D. A sincere scribe (Mark 12:28-34)—"And when Jesus saw that he answered discreetly, he said unto him, Thou art not far from the kingdom of God. And no man after that durst ask him any question" (Mark 12:34).

E. A woman in Bethany (Mark 14:3-9)—"And being in Bethany in the house of Simon the leper, as he sat at meat, there came a woman having an alabaster box of ointment of spikenard very precious; and she brake the box, and poured it on his head" (Mark 14:3).

VII. The splendor of the servant

A. A declaration of his deity (Mark 8:27-30)—"And Jesus went out, and his disciples, into the towns of Caesarea Philippi: and by the way he asked his disciples, saying unto them, Whom do men say that I am? And they answered, John the Baptist: but some say, Elias; and others, One of the prophets. And he saith unto them, But whom say ye that I am? And Peter answereth and saith unto him, Thou art the Christ" (Mark 8:27-29).

B. A demonstration of his deity (Mark 9:1-13)—"And after six days Jesus taketh with him Peter, and James, and John, and leadeth them up into an high mountain apart by themselves: and he was transfigured before them. And his raiment became shining, exceeding white as snow; so as no fuller on earth can white them" (Mark 9:2-3).

VIII. The sorrow of the servant

A. Over the disbelief in Nazareth (Mark 6:1-6)

B. Over the death of John (Mark 6:14-29)

IX. The showing of the servant (Mark 11:1-11)—"And they brought the colt to Jesus, and cast their garments on him; and he sat upon him. And many spread their garments in the way: and others cut down branches off the trees, and strawed them in the way. And they that went before, and they that followed, cried, saying, Hosanna; Blessed is he that cometh in the name of the Lord: Blessed be the kingdom of our father David, that cometh in the name of the Lord: Hosanna in the highest" (Mark 11:7-10).

X. The surveillance of the servant (Mark 11:15-19)—"And they come to Jerusalem: and Jesus went into the temple, and began to cast out them that sold and bought in the temple, and overthrew the tables of the moneychangers, and the seats of them that sold doves" (Mark 11:15).

XI. The supper of the servant (Mark 14:12-25)—"And as they did eat, Jesus took bread, and blessed, and brake it, and gave to them, and said, Take, eat: this is my body. And he took the cup, and when he had given thanks, he gave it to them: and they all drank of it. And he said unto them, This is my blood of the new testament, which is shed for many. Verily I say unto you, I will drink no more of the fruit of the vine, until that day that I drink it new in the kingdom of God" (Mark 14:22-25).

XII. The submission of the servant (Mark 14:32-42)—"And he went forward a little, and fell on the ground, and prayed that, if it were possible, the hour might pass from him. And he said, Abba, Father, all things are possible unto thee; take away this cup from me: nevertheless not what I will, but what thou wilt" (Mark 14:35-36).

XIII. The sufferings of the servant

A. He was plotted against—"After two days was the feast of the passover, and of unleavened bread: and the chief priests and the scribes sought how they might take him by craft, and put him to death. But they said, Not on the feast day, lest there be an uproar of the people" (Mark 14:1-2). "And Judas Iscariot, one of the twelve, went unto the chief priests, to betray him unto them. And when they heard it, they were glad, and promised to give him money. And he sought how he might conveniently betray him" (Mark 14:10-11).

B. He was filled with horror and distress in the garden.

1. The agony (Mark 14:32-42)
2. The arrest (Mark 14:43-49)
3. The abandonment (Mark 14:50)

C. He was denied by a friend.

1. The revelation of these denials (Mark 14:26-31)—"But Peter said unto him, Although all shall be offended, yet will not I. And Jesus saith unto him, Verily I say unto thee, That this day, even in this night, before the cock crow twice, thou shalt deny me thrice" (Mark 14:29-30).
2. The record of these denials (Mark 14:66-72)—"But he began to curse and to swear, saying, I know not this man of whom ye speak" (Mark 14:71).

D. He was betrayed by a follower (Mark 14:43-46)—"And he that betrayed him had given them a token, saying, Whomsoever I shall kiss, that same is he; take him, and lead him away safely. And as soon as he was come, he goeth straightway to him, and saith, Master, master; and kissed him" (Mark 14:44-45).

E. He was illegally tried.

1. Before the high priest (Mark 14:53-65)

a. Falsely accused (Mark 14:55-59)

b. Condemned to die (Mark 14:60-64)

c. Spit upon, blindfolded, struck, and ridiculed (Mark 14:65)

2. Before Pilate (Mark 15:1-15)

a. Slandered by the priests (Mark 15:1-5)

b. Scourged by Pilate (Mark 15:15)

3. Before the Roman soldiers (Mark 15:16-20)

a. He was mistreated.

b. He was mocked.

XIV. The sacrifice of the servant (Mark 15:20-47)

A. On the cross (Mark 15:20-41)

B. In the tomb (Mark 15:42-47)

XV. The sovereignty of the servant (Mark 16:1-20)

A. He arose from the grave (Mark 16:1-18).

1. The announcement (Mark 16:1-8)—"And when the sabbath was past, Mary Magdalene, and Mary the mother of James, and Salome, had bought sweet spices, that they might come and anoint him. . . . And entering into the sepulchre, they saw a young man sitting on the right side, clothed in a long white garment; and they were affrighted. And he saith unto them, Be not affrighted: Ye seek Jesus of Nazareth, which was crucified: he is risen; he is not here: behold the place where they laid him" (Mark 16:1, 5-6).

2. The appearances (Mark 16:9-11)

a. To Mary Magdalene (Mark 16:9-11)

b. To two disciples (Mark 16:12-13)

c. To the 11 (Mark 16:14-18)

B. He ascended into glory (Mark 16:19-20)—"So then after the Lord had spoken unto them, he was received up into heaven, and sat on the right hand of God" (Mark 16:19).

STATISTICS

Mother: Mary (Acts 12:12)

Uncle: Barnabas (Acts 12:25; Col 4:10)

First mention: Acts 12:25

Final mention: 1 Peter 5:13

Meaning of his name: John means "Grace of Jehovah"; Mark means "Large hammer."

Frequency of his name: Referred to 10 times

Biblical books mentioning him: Five books (Acts, Colossians, 2 Timothy, Philemon, 1 Peter)

Occupation: Author and missionary evangelist

Place of birth: Probably Jerusalem

Place of death: Tradition says he died in Alexandria, Egypt.

Circumstances of death: Tradition says he died a martyr's death, being dragged through the streets with a rope around his neck.

Important fact about his life: He authored the Gospel of Mark.

Martha

CHRONOLOGICAL SUMMARY

I. Martha's agitation concerning her sister Mary

A. Her complaint to Jesus—"Now it came to pass, as they went, that he entered into a certain village: and a certain woman named Martha received him into her house. And she had a sister called Mary, which also sat at Jesus' feet, and heard his word. But Martha was cumbered about much serving, and came to him, and said, Lord, dost thou not care that my sister hath left me to serve alone? bid her therefore that she help me" (Luke 10:38-40).

B. Her correction by Jesus

1. What she had been doing—"And Jesus answered and said unto her, Martha, Martha, thou art careful and troubled about many things" (Luke 10:41).

2. What she should be doing—"But one thing is needful: and Mary hath chosen that good part, which shall not be taken away from her" (Luke 10:42).

II. Martha's anguish concerning her brother Lazarus
  A. The dying brother
    1. Her message to Jesus—"Now a certain man was sick, named Lazarus, of Bethany, the town of Mary and her sister Martha. (It was that Mary which anointed the Lord with ointment, and wiped his feet with her hair, whose brother Lazarus was sick.) Therefore his sisters sent unto him, saying, Lord, behold, he whom thou lovest is sick" (John 11:1-3).
    2. Her meeting with Jesus—"Then Martha, as soon as she heard that Jesus was coming, went and met him: but Mary sat still in the house" (John 11:20).
      a. Martha's frustration—"Then said Martha unto Jesus, Lord, if thou hadst been here, my brother had not died" (John 11:21).
      b. Martha's faith
        (1) In the promise of Christ—"But I know, that even now, whatsoever thou wilt ask of God, God will give it thee. Jesus saith unto her, Thy brother shall rise again. Martha saith unto him, I know that he shall rise again in the resurrection at the last day. Jesus said unto her, I am the resurrection, and the life: he that believeth in me, though he were dead, yet shall he live" (John 11:22-25).
        (2) In the person of Christ—"And whosoever liveth and believeth in me shall never die. Believest thou this? She saith unto him, Yea, Lord: I believe that thou art the Christ, the Son of God, which should come into the world" (John 11:26-27).
    3. Her mission for Jesus—"And when she had so said, she went her way, and called Mary her sister secretly, saying, The Master is come, and calleth for thee" (John 11:28).
  B. The dead brother
    1. The request—"Jesus said, Take ye away the stone" (John 11:39a).
    2. The reluctance—"Martha, the sister of him that was dead, saith unto him, Lord, by this time he stinketh, for he hath been dead four days" (John 11:39b).
    3. The reminder—"Jesus saith unto her, Said I not unto thee, that, if thou wouldest believe, thou shouldest see the glory of God?" (John 11:40).
  C. The delivered brother—"Then Jesus six days before the passover came to Bethany, where Lazarus was which had been dead, whom he raised from the dead. There they made him a supper; and Martha served: but Lazarus was one of them that sat at the table with him" (John 12:1-2).

STATISTICS

Brother: Lazarus
Sister: Mary
First mention: Luke 10:38
Final mention: John 12:2
Meaning of her name: "Lady, mistress"
Frequency of her name: Referred to 12 times
Biblical books mentioning her: Two books (Luke, John)
Important fact about her life: She saw Christ raise her dead brother Lazarus.

Mary

CHRONOLOGICAL SUMMARY

I. Mary and Gabriel (the angel of the Lord)
  A. His announcement about Mary
    1. Concerning the father of her unborn Son—"Now the birth of Jesus Christ was on this wise: When as his mother Mary was espoused to Joseph, before they came together, she was found with child of the Holy Ghost. Then Joseph her husband, being a just man, and not willing to make her a publick example, was minded to put her away

privily. But while he thought on these things, behold, the angel of the Lord appeared unto him in a dream, saying, Joseph, thou son of David, fear not to take unto thee Mary thy wife: for that which is conceived in her is of the Holy Ghost" (Matt. 1:18-20).

2. Concerning the fruits of her unborn Son—"And she shall bring forth a son, and thou shalt call his name JESUS: for he shall save his people from their sins" (Matt. 1:21).

B. His announcement to Mary

1. The salutation—"And in the sixth month the angel Gabriel was sent from God unto a city of Galilee, named Nazareth, to a virgin espoused to a man whose name was Joseph, of the house of David; and the virgin's name was Mary. And the angel came in unto her, and said, Hail, thou that art highly favoured, the Lord is with thee: blessed art thou among women. And when she saw him, she w as troubled at his saying, and cast in her mind what manner of salutation this should be" (Luke 1:26-29).

a. Concerning the birth of Jesus

(1) The choice of Mary—"And the angel said unto her, Fear not, Mary: for thou hast found favour with God" (Luke 1:30).

(2) The child in Mary—"And, behold, thou shalt conceive in thy womb, and bring forth a son, and shalt call his name JESUS. He shall be great, and shall be called the Son of the Highest: and the Lord God shall give unto him the throne of his father David: And he shall reign over the house of Jacob for ever; and of his kingdom there shall be no end" (Luke 1:31-33).

(3) The concern of Mary—"Then said Mary unto the angel, How shall this be, seeing I know not a man?" (Luke 1:34).

(4) The clarification to Mary—"And the angel answered and said unto her, The Holy Ghost shall come upon thee, and the power of the Highest shall overshadow thee: therefore also that holy thing which shall be born of thee shall be called the Son of God" (Luke 1:35).

b. Concerning the birth of John—"And, behold, thy cousin Elisabeth, she hath also conceived a son in her old age: and this is the sixth month with her, who was called barren. For with God nothing shall be impossible" (Luke 1:36-37).

2. The submission—"And Mary said, Behold the handmaid of the Lord; be it unto me according to thy word. And the angel departed from her" (Luke 1:38).

II. Mary and Elisabeth (the affirmation of the Lord)—God reassured both Mary and Elisabeth, each of which had experienced a supernatural conception.

A. The meeting—"And Mary arose in those days, and went into the hill country with haste, into a city of Juda; and entered into the house of Zacharias, and saluted Elisabeth" (Luke 1:39-40).

B. The miracle

1. Elisabeth's babe—"And it came to pass, that, when Elisabeth heard the salutation of Mary, the babe leaped in her womb; and Elisabeth was filled with the Holy Ghost" (Luke 1:41).

2. Elisabeth's blessing—"And she spake out with a loud voice, and said, Blessed art thou among women, and blessed is the fruit of thy womb. And whence is this to me, that the mother of my Lord should come to me? For, lo, as soon as the voice of thy salutation sounded in mine ears, the babe

leaped in my womb for joy. And blessed is she that believed: for there shall be a performance of those things which were told her from the Lord" (Luke 1:42-45).

C. The Magnificat (Luke 1:46-56)—In these verses Mary quoted from at least 15 Old Testament sources and praised God for his various attributes:

1. His grace (Luke 1:46-48)
2. His power (Luke 1:49)
3. His mercy (Luke 1:50)
4. His holiness (Luke 1:49)
5. His goodness (Luke 1:53)
6. His faithfulness (Luke 1:54-56)

III. Mary and Jesus (the Anointed of the Lord)

A. Jesus, the infant—"But Mary kept all these things, and pondered them in her heart. . . . And Joseph and his mother marvelled at those things which were spoken of him" (Luke 2:19, 33).

1. Events in Bethlehem

a. The birth of Jesus—"And so it was, that, while they were there, the days were accomplished that she should be delivered. And she brought forth her firstborn son, and wrapped him in swaddling clothes, and laid him in a manger; because there was no room for them in the inn" (Luke 2:6-7).

b. The worship of Jesus—"And it came to pass, as the angels were gone away from them into heaven, the shepherds said one to another, Let us now go even unto Bethlehem, and see this thing which is come to pass, which the Lord hath made known unto us. And they came with haste, and found Mary, and Joseph, and the babe lying in a manger" (Luke 2:15-16).

c. The circumcision of Jesus "And when eight days were accomplished for the circumcising of the child, his name was called JESUS, which was so named of the angel before he was conceived in the womb" (Luke 2:21).

2. Events in Jerusalem

a. The dedication of the Babe—"And when the days of her purification according to the law of Moses were accomplished, they brought him to Jerusalem, to present him to the Lord . . . . And to offer a sacrifice according to that which is said in the law of the Lord, A pair of turtledoves, or two young pigeons" (Luke 2:22, 24).

b. The declaration concerning the Babe—"And, behold, there was a man in Jerusalem, whose name was Simeon; and the same man was just and devout, waiting for the consolation of Israel: and the Holy Ghost was upon him" (Luke 2:25).

(1) His words concerning the Messiah—"For mine eyes have seen thy salvation, which thou hast prepared before the face of all people; a light to lighten the Gentiles, and the glory of thy people Israel. . . . And Simeon blessed them, and said unto Mary his mother, Behold, this child is set for the fall and rising again of many in Israel; and for a sign which shall be spoken against" (Luke 2:30-32, 34).

(2) His words concerning the mother—"(Yea, a sword shall pierce through thy own soul also,) that the thoughts of many hearts may be revealed" (Luke 2:35).

B. Jesus, the young child

1. The testimony of the wise men (Matt. 2:1-12)—"And when they were come into the house, they saw the young child with Mary his mother, and fell down, and worshipped him: and when they had opened their treasures, they presented unto him gifts; gold, and frankincense, and myrrh" (Matt. 2:11).

2. The trip to Egypt—"And when they were departed, behold, the angel of the Lord appeareth to Joseph in a dream, saying, Arise, and take the young child and his mother, and flee into Egypt, and be thou there until I bring thee word: for Herod will seek the young child to destroy him. When he arose, he took the young child and his mother by night, and departed into Egypt: and was there until the death of Herod: that it might be fulfilled which was spoken of the Lord by the prophet, saying, Out of Egypt have I called my son" (Matt. 2:13-15).

C. Jesus, the boy—"Now his parents went to Jerusalem every year at the feast of the passover. And when he was twelve years old, they went up to Jerusalem after the custom of the feast. And when they had fulfilled the days, as they returned, the child Jesus tarried behind in Jerusalem; and Joseph and his mother knew not of it" (Luke 2:41-43).

1. The concern of Mary—"And when they saw him, they were amazed: and his mother said unto him, Son, why hast thou thus dealt with us? behold, thy father and I have sought thee sorrowing" (Luke 2:48).
2. The correction by Jesus—"And he said unto them, How is it that ye sought me? wist ye not that I must be about my Father's business?" (Luke 2:49).

D. Jesus, the man

1. His words to Mary in the city of Cana
   a. Mary and the Savior
      (1) Her request—"And the third day there was a marriage in Cana of Galilee; and the mother of Jesus was there: and both Jesus was called, and his disciples, to the marriage. And when they wanted wine, the mother of Jesus saith unto him, They have no wine" (John 2:1-3).
      (2) His reply—"Jesus saith unto her, Woman, what have I to do with thee? mine hour is not yet come" (John 2:4).
   b. Mary and the servants—"His mother saith unto the servants, Whatsoever he saith unto you, do it" (John 2:5).
2. His words to Mary on the cross of Calvary—"When Jesus therefore saw his mother, and the disciple standing by, whom he loved, he saith unto his mother, Woman, behold thy son! Then saith he to the disciple, Behold thy mother! And from that hour that disciple took her unto his own home" (John 19:26-27).

IV. Mary and the 120 (the ambassadors of the Lord)—She was numbered with the 120 in the upper room on the day of Pentecost (Acts 1:12-15). "These all continued with one accord in prayer and supplication, with the women, and Mary the mother of Jesus, and with his brethren" (Acts 1:14).

STATISTICS

Spouse: Joseph
Sons: Jesus, James, Joseph, Simon, Judas (Luke 2:7; Matt. 13:55)
Daughters: Several unnamed (Matt. 13:56)
First mention: Matthew 1:16
Final mention: Acts 1:14
Meaning of her name: "Bitter"
Frequency of her name: Referred to 19 times
Biblical books mentioning her: Four books (Matthew, Mark, Luke, Acts)
Place of birth: Probably Bethlehem
Important fact about her life: She was God's chosen vessel to give birth to the Savior of the world.

Mary Magdalene

CHRONOLOGICAL SUMMARY

I. Events before the cross

A. Mary's salvation—She had seven demons cast from her by the Savior (Mark 16:9; Luke 8:2).

B. Mary's service—After her conversion, she contributed to the support of Jesus and his disciples (Luke 8:2-3).

II. Events at the cross

A. The presence of Mary—She was present during the crucifixion of Jesus (Mark 15:40; John 19:25).

B. The preparation by Mary—She helped prepare the body of Jesus for burial (Matt. 27:56, 61; Mark 15:46-47).

III. Events after the cross

A. Her trip to the tomb—"And when the sabbath was past, Mary Magdalene, and Mary the mother of James, and Salome, had bought sweet spices, that they might come and anoint him" (Mark 16:1).

B. Her testimony about the tomb— "The first day of the week cometh Mary Magdalene early, when it was yet dark, unto the sepulchre, and seeth the stone taken away from the sepulchre. Then she runneth, and cometh to Simon Peter, and to the other disciple, whom Jesus loved, and saith unto them, They have taken away the Lord out of the sepulchre, and we know not where they have laid him" (John 20:1-2).

C. Her tears at the tomb—"But Mary stood without at the sepulchre weeping: and as she wept, she stooped down, and looked into the sepulchre, and seeth two angels in white sitting, the one at the head, and the other at the feet, where the body of Jesus had lain. And they say unto her, Woman, why weepest thou? She saith unto them, Because they have taken away my Lord, and I know not where they have laid him" (John 20:11-13).

1. Mary's error—"And when she had thus said, she turned herself back, and saw Jesus standing, and knew not that it was Jesus. Jesus saith unto her, Woman, why weepest thou? whom seekest thou? She, supposing him to be the gardener, saith unto him, Sir, if thou have borne him hence, tell me where thou hast laid him, and I will take him away" (John 20:14-15).

2. Mary's ecstasy—She became the first person to see the resurrected Christ (Mark 16:9). "Jesus saith unto her, Mary. She turned herself, and saith unto him, Rabboni; which is to say, Master. Jesus saith unto her, Touch me not; for I am not yet ascended to my Father: but go to my brethren, and say unto them, I ascend unto my Father, and your Father; and to my God, and your God. Mary Magdalene came and told the disciples that she had seen the Lord, and that he had spoken these things unto her" (John 20:16-18).

STATISTICS

First mention: Matthew 27:56
Final mention: John 20:18
Meaning of her name: "Bitter"
Frequency of her name: Referred to 15 times
Biblical books mentioning her: Four books (Matthew, Mark, Luke, John)
Important fact about her life: She was a woman who had been demon-possessed but became a believer and the first person to see the resurrected Christ.

Mary, the Mother of James and Joses

CHRONOLOGICAL SUMMARY

I. Mary, the worker for Christ—Her role during his earthly life: "(Who also, when he was in Galilee, followed him, and ministered unto him;) and many other women which came up with him unto Jerusalem" (Mark 15:41).

II. Mary, the watcher for Christ—Her role during his death

A. She was at the cross—"There were also women looking on afar off: among whom was Mary Magdalene, and Mary the mother of James the less and of Joses, and Salome" (Mark 15:40).

B. She was at the cemetery—"And Mary Magdalene and Mary the mother of Joses beheld where he was laid" (Mark 15:47).

III. Mary, the witness concerning Christ—Her role during his resurrection

A. She saw the glory of the risen Christ—"And when the sabbath was past, Mary Magdalene, and Mary the mother of James, and Salome, had bought sweet spices, that they might come and anoint him. And very early in the morning the first day of the week, they came unto the sepulchre at the rising of the sun. And they said among themselves, Who shall roll us away the stone from the door of the sepulchre? And when they looked, they saw that the stone was rolled away: for it was very great" (Mark 16:1-4).

1. As announced by an angel

a. His revelation—"And the angel answered and said unto the women, Fear not ye: for I know that ye seek Jesus, which was crucified. He is not here: for he is risen, as he said. Come, see the place where the Lord lay" (Matt. 28:5-6). "But go your way, tell his disciples and Peter that he goeth before you into Galilee: there shall ye see him, as he said unto you" (Mark 16:7).

b. His reminder—"Remember how he spake unto you . . . Saying, the Son of man must be delivered into the hands of sinful men, and be crucified, and the third day rise again. And they remembered his words" (Luke 24:6-8).

2. As announced by the Savior—"And they departed quickly from the sepulchre with fear and great joy; and did run to bring his disciples word. And as they went to tell his disciples, behold, Jesus met them, saying, All hail. And they came and held him by the feet, and worshipped him. Then said Jesus unto them, Be not afraid: go tell my brethren that they go into Galilee, and there shall they see me" (Matt. 28:8-10).

B. She shared the glory of the risen Christ—"And returned from the sepulchre, and told all these things unto the eleven, and to all the rest. It was Mary Magdalene, and Joanna, and Mary the mother of James, and other women that were with them, which told these things unto the apostles. And their words seemed to them as idle tales, and they believed them not" (Luke 24:9-11).

STATISTICS

Sons: James and Joses (Matt. 27:56)
First mention: Matthew 27:56
Final mention: Luke 24:10
Meaning of her name: "Bitter"
Frequency of her name: Referred to seven times
Biblical books mentioning her: Three books (Matthew, Mark, Luke)
Important fact about her life: She helped Christ financially and was present at his crucifixion and resurrection.

Mary, the Sister of Martha

CHRONOLOGICAL SUMMARY

I. Mary, the Bible student—"Which also sat at Jesus' feet, and heard his word" (Luke 10:39b). "Mary hath chosen that good part, which shall not be taken away from her" (Luke 10:42b).

II. Mary, the bereaved sister

A. Her message to Jesus—"Now a certain man was sick, named Lazarus, of Bethany, the town of Mary and her sister Martha. (It was that Mary which anointed the Lord with ointment, and wiped his feet with her hair, whose brother Lazarus was sick.) Therefore his sisters sent unto him, saying, Lord, behold, he whom thou lovest is sick" (John 11:1-3).

B. Her meeting with Jesus—"Martha saith unto him, I know that he shall rise again in the resurrection at the last day. . . . And when she had so said, she went her way, and called Mary her sister secretly, saying, The Master is come, and calleth for thee. As soon as she heard that, she arose quickly, and came unto him" (John 11:24, 28-29).
   1. The sorrow of the sister—"Then when Mary was come where Jesus was, and saw him, she fell down at his feet, saying unto him, Lord, if thou hadst been here, my brother had not died" (John 11:32).
   2. The sorrow of the Savior—"When Jesus therefore saw her weeping, and the Jews also weeping which came with her, he groaned in the spirit, and was troubled" (John 11:33).

III. Mary, the bountiful servant—"Then Jesus six days before the passover came to Bethany, where Lazarus was which had been dead, whom he raised from the dead. There they made him a supper; and Martha served: but Lazarus was one of them that sat at the table with him" (John 12:1-2).

A. Her gift was precious.
   1. The cost—"Then took Mary a pound of ointment of spikenard, very costly, and anointed the feet of Jesus, and wiped his feet with her hair: and the house was filled with the odour of the ointment" (John 12:3).
   2. The criticism—"Then saith one of his disciples, Judas Iscariot, Simon's son, which should betray him, Why was not this ointment sold for three hundred pence, and given to the poor? This he said, not that he cared for the poor; but because he was a thief, and had the bag, and bare what was put therein" (John 11:4-6).

B. Her gift was prophetical.
   1. In regard to the burial of Christ—"And Jesus said, Let her alone; why trouble ye her? she hath wrought a good work on me. For ye have the poor with you always, and whensoever ye will ye may do them good: but me ye have not always. She hath done what she could: she is come aforehand to anoint my body to the burying" (Mark 14:6-8).
   2. In regard to the body of Christ (the church)—"Verily I say unto you, Wheresoever this gospel shall be preached in the whole world, there shall also this, that this woman hath done, be told for a memorial of her" (Matt. 26:13).

STATISTICS

Brother: Lazarus
Sister: Martha
First mention: Luke 10:39
Final mention: John 12:3
Meaning of her name: "Bitter"
Frequency of her name: Referred to 11 times
Biblical books mentioning her: Two books (Luke, John)
Important fact about her life: She prepared the body of Christ for burial while he was still living by anointing it with precious oil.

Matthew

CHRONOLOGICAL SUMMARY

I. Matthew, the apostle

A. His call by Christ—"And after these things he went forth, and saw a publican, named Levi, sitting at the receipt of custom: and he said unto him, Follow me" (Luke 5:27).

B. His consecration to Christ—"And he left all, rose up, and followed him. And Levi made him a great feast in his own house: and there was a great company of publicans and of others that sat down with them" (Luke 5:28-29).

II. Matthew, the author—He was the author of the Gospel that bears his name.

THE GOSPEL OF MATTHEW

Matthew emphasizes the kingship of Christ.

I. The preparation of the King (Matt. 1–4)
  A. His genealogy (Matt. 1:1-17)
  B. His birth announcement (Matt. 1:18-25)
  C. His worship by the wise men (Matt. 2:1-12)
  D. His trip to Egypt (Matt. 2:13-20)
  E. His early years in Nazareth (Matt. 2:21-23)
  F. His forerunner (Matt. 3:13-17)
  G. His baptism (Matt. 3:13-17)
  H. His temptation (Matt. 4:1-11)
  I. His first disciples (Matt. 4:18-22)
  J. His early Galilean ministry (Matt. 4:23-25)

II. The principles of the King (Matt. 5–7)—Jesus laid out his moral and spiritual standards during the Sermon on the Mount.

III. The power of the King—His mighty power was shown through his miracles.
  A. General healing accounts (Matt. 4:23-25; 8:16-17; 9:35; 12:15; 14:14, 34-36; 15:29-31)
  B. Healing of a leper (Matt. 8:1-4)
  C. Healing of the centurion's servant (Matt. 8:5-13)
  D. Healing of Peter's mother-in-law (Matt. 8:14-15)
  E. Stilling of the winds and waves (Matt. 8:23-27)
  F. Casting demons from two Gadarene men (Matt. 8:28-34)
  G. Healing a paralytic (Matt. 9:1-8)
  H. Healing a woman with an issue of blood (Matt. 9:20-22)
  I. Raising Jairus's daughter (Matt. 9:18-19, 23-26)
  J. Healing two blind men (Matt. 9:27-31)
  K. Healing a Galilean demoniac (Matt. 9:32-33)
  L. Healing a man with a paralyzed hand (Matt. 12:10-13)
  M. Feeding five thousand (Matt. 14:15-21)
  N. Walking on water (Matt. 14:22-33)
  O. Healing a Syro-phoenician girl of a demon (Matt. 15:21-28)
  P. Feeding four thousand (Matt. 15:32-39)
  Q. Providing tax money from a fish (Matt. 17:24-27)
  R. Healing two blind men (Matt. 20:29-34)

IV. The program of the King (Matt. 13)—The kingdom of heaven's plan and program are described and overviewed by Jesus in Matthew 13.

V. The preachers of the King
  A. John the Baptist
    1. His ministry (Matt. 3:1-12; 11:1-15)
    2. His martyrdom (Matt. 14:1-12)
  B. The 12 apostles (Matt. 10:1-42)-- "And when he had called unto him his twelve disciples, he gave them power against unclean spirits, to cast them out, and to heal all manner of sickness and all manner of disease" (Matt. 10:1).

VI. The proclamations of the King—In addition to those topics mentioned during his Sermon on the Mount, Jesus touched upon various subjects.
  A. True greatness (Matt. 18:1-5; 20:20-28)
  B. God's love for children (Matt. 18:6-11; 19:13-15)
  C. God's love for the lost (Matt. 18:11-14)
  D. Church discipline (Matt. 18:15-20)
  E. Forgiveness (Matt. 18:21-35)
  F. Divorce (Matt. 19:1-12)
  G. Danger of riches (Matt. 19:16-26)
  H. Rewards (Matt. 19:27-30)
  I. Discipleship (Matt. 8:18-22; 16:24-26)
  J. Vain traditions (Matt. 15:1-20)
  K. The unpardonable sin (Matt. 12:24-37)
  L. His family (Matt. 12:46-50; 13:53-56)
  M. Hypocrisy (Matt. 16:5-12)
  N. His authority (Matt. 12:1-8; 21:23-27)
  O. The giving of tribute (Matt. 22:15-22)
  P. The resurrection (Matt. 22:23-33)
  Q. The greatest commandment (Matt. 22:34-40)
  R. The Messiah (Matt. 22:41-46)

VII. The parables of the King
  A. The two builders (Matt. 7:24-27)
  B. The sower and the soils (Matt. 13:1-9, 18-23)
  C. The wheat and the tares (Matt. 13:24-30, 36-43)
  D. The mustard seed (Matt. 13:31-32)
  E. The leaven (Matt. 13:33)
  F. The hidden treasure (Matt. 13:44)
  G. The pearl of great price (Matt. 13:45-46)
  H. The dragnet (Matt. 13:47-51)
  I. The householder (Matt. 13:52)
  J. The morning, noon, and evening laborers (Matt. 20:1-16)

K. The two sons (Matt. 21:28-32)
L. The angry vineyard owner (Matt. 21:33-41)
M. The marriage feast (Matt. 22:1-14)
N. The fig tree (Matt. 24:32-35)
O. The faithful and faithless servants (Matt. 24:42-51)
P. The ten virgins (Matt. 25:1-13)
Q. The three servants and their talents (Matt. 25:14-30)
R. The sheep and the goats (Matt. 25:31-46)

VIII. The person of the King (Matt. 16:13-23)—"When Jesus came into the coasts of Caesarea Philippi, he asked his disciples, saying, Whom do men say that I the Son of man am? And they said, Some say that thou art John the Baptist: some, Elias; and others, Jeremias, or one of the prophets. He saith unto them, But whom say ye that I am? And Simon Peter answered and said, Thou art the Christ, the Son of the living God" (Matt. 16:13-16).

IX. The preeminence of the King (Matt. 17:1-13)—"And after six days Jesus taketh Peter, James, and John his brother, and bringeth them up into an high mountain apart, and was transfigured before them: and his face did shine as the sun, and his raiment was white as the light" (Matt. 17:1-2).

X. The plea of the King—"Come unto me, all ye that labour and are heavy laden, and I will give you rest. Take my yoke upon you, and learn of me; for I am meek and lowly in heart: and ye shall find rest unto your souls. For my yoke is easy, and my burden is light" (Matt. 11:28-30).

XI. The performance of the King—"Behold my servant, whom I have chosen; my beloved, in whom my soul is well pleased: I will put my spirit upon him, and he shall shew judgment to the Gentiles. He shall not strive, nor cry; neither shall any man hear his voice in the streets. A bruised reed shall he not break, and smoking flax shall he not quench, till he send forth judgment unto victory. And in his name shall the Gentiles trust" (Matt. 12:18-21).

XII. The pity of the King—"But when he saw the multitudes, he was moved with compassion on them, because they fainted, and were scattered abroad, as sheep having no shepherd. Then saith he unto his disciples, The harvest truly is plenteous, but the labourers are few; pray ye therefore the Lord of the harvest, that he will send forth labourers into his harvest" (Matt. 9:36-38).

XIII. The provoking of the King—The righteous indignation of Christ was aroused on several occasions.
A. He rebuked his generation (Matt. 11:16-19; 12:38-45; 16:1-4; 17:17).
B. He rebuked the unbelieving Galilean cities (Matt. 11:20-24).
C. He rebuked the Pharisees (Matt. 15:1-9; 21:42-45; 23:1-36).

XIV. The predictions of the King (Matt. 23–24)—"And Jesus went out, and departed from the temple: and his disciples came to him for to shew him the buildings of the temple. And Jesus said unto them, See ye not all these things? verily I say unto you, There shall not be left here one stone upon another, that shall not be thrown down. And as he sat upon the mount of Olives, the disciples came unto him privately, saying, Tell us, when shall these things be? and what shall be the sign of thy coming, and of the end of the world? And Jesus answered and said unto them, Take heed that no man deceive you" (Matt. 24:1-4).

XV. The presentation of the King (Matt. 21:1-11)—"And when they drew nigh unto Jerusalem, and were come to Bethphage, unto the mount of Olives, then sent Jesus two disciples, saying unto them, Go into the village over against you, and straightway ye shall find an ass tied, and a colt with her: loose them, and bring them unto me. . . . And the disciples went, and did as Jesus commanded them, and brought the ass, and the colt, and put on them their clothes, a nd they set him thereon. And a very great multitude spread their garments in the way; others cut down branches from the trees, and strawed them in the way. And the multitudes that went before, and that followed, cried, saying, Hosanna to the Son of David: Blessed is he that cometh in the name of the Lord; Hosanna in the highest" (Matt. 21:1-2, 6-9).

XVI. The purging by the King (Matt. 21:12-16)—"And Jesus went into the temple of God, and cast out all them that sold and bought in the temple, and overthrew the tables of the moneychangers, and the seats of them that sold doves" (Matt. 21:12).

XVII. The pain of the King—"O Jerusalem, Jerusalem, thou that killest the prophets, and stonest them which are sent unto thee, how often would I have gathered thy children together, even as a hen gathereth her chickens under her wings, and ye would not! Behold, your house is left unto you desolate. For I say unto you, Ye shall not see me henceforth, till ye shall say, Blessed is he that cometh in the name of the Lord" (Matt. 23:37-39).

XVIII. The Passover of the King (Matt. 26:17-30)

XIX. The prayers of the King (Matt. 26:30-46)—"Then cometh Jesus with them unto a place called Gethsemane, and saith unto the disciples, Sit ye here, while I go and pray yonder. And he went a little farther, and fell on his face, and prayed, saying, O my Father, if it be possible, let this cup pass from me: nevertheless not as I will, but as thou wilt" (Matt. 26:36, 39).

XX. The persecution of the King—Throughout his earthly ministry, Christ experienced persecution and hostility from sinful men.

A. He was accused of being a demon-possessed blasphemer (Matt. 9:3, 34; 12:24; 26:65).

B. He was plotted against (Matt. 12:14).

C. He was denied by a friend (Matt. 26:69-75).

D. He was betrayed by a follower (Matt. 26:47-50).

E. He was illegally tried.

1. Before Caiaphas and the Jewish leaders (Matt. 26:57, 59-68)
2. Before Pilate (Matt. 27:11-26)
3. Before the Roman soldiers (Matt. 27:27-31)

F. He was spit upon (Matt. 26:67).

G. He was slapped (Matt. 26:67).

H. He was ridiculed (Matt. 26:68; 27:28-30).

I. He was severely beaten (Matt. 27:26).

XXI. The passion of the King

A. The foretelling of his passion—Christ often predicted his death on the cross.

1. First occasion (Matt. 16:21-23)—"From that time forth began Jesus to shew unto his disciples, how that he must go unto Jerusalem, and suffer many things of the elders and chief priests and scribes, and be killed, and be raised again the third day" (Matt. 16:21).
2. Second occasion (Matt. 17:22-23)
3. Third occasion (Matt. 20:17-19)
4. Fourth occasion (Matt. 26:6-13)—After being anointed by a woman in Bethany, Jesus said: "For in that she hath poured this ointment on my body, she did it for my burial" (Matt. 26:12).
5. Fifth occasion (Matt. 26:28)—"For this is my blood of the new testament, which is shed for many for the remission of sins" (Matt. 26:28).

B. The facts of his passion (Matt. 27:31-50)—"And when they were come unto a place called Golgotha, that is to say, a place of a skull, they gave him vinegar to drink mingled with gall: and when he had tasted thereof, he would not drink. And they crucified him, and parted his garments, casting lots: that it might be fulfilled which was spoken by the prophet, They parted my garments among them, and upon my vesture did they cast lots" (Matt. 27:33-35).

XXII. The proof of the King (Matt. 28:1-20)—"In the end of the sabbath, as it began to dawn toward the first day of the week, came Mary Magdalene and the other Mary to see the sepulchre. And, behold, there was a great earthquake: for the angel of the Lord descended from heaven, and came and rolled back the stone from the door, and sat upon it. His countenance was like lightning, and his raiment white as snow" (Matt. 28:1-3).

A. As confirmed by his foes (Matt. 28:4, 11-15)
B. As confirmed by his friends
1. The women (Matt. 28:5-10)
2. The 11 (Matt. 28:16-20)

STATISTICS
Father: Alphaeus (Mark 2:14)
Brother: James the less (one of the 12 apostles) may have been his brother.
First mention: Matthew 9:9
Final mention: Acts 1:13
Meaning of his name: Matthew means "gift of God"; Levi means "joiner."
Frequency of his name: Referred to eight times
Biblical books mentioning him: Four books (Matthew, Mark, Luke, Acts)
Occupation: Tax collector before becoming an apostle (Matt. 9:9; 10:3)
Place of birth: Possibly Capernaum, a Galilean city (Matt. 9:1, 9)
Place of death: Tradition says he died in Ethiopia.
Circumstances of death: Tradition says he died as a martyr.
Important fact about his life: He authored the Gospel of Matthew.

Matthias

CHRONOLOGICAL SUMMARY
I. The character of Matthias—"Wherefore of these men which have companied with us all the time that the Lord Jesus went in and out among us, beginning from the baptism of John, unto that same day that he was taken up from us, must one be ordained to be a witness with us of his resurrection" (Acts 1:21-22).
II. The choice of Matthias
A. The men involved—"And they appointed two, Joseph called Barsabas, who was surnamed Justus, and Matthias" (Acts 1:23).
B. The ministry involved—"And they prayed, and said, Thou, Lord, which knowest the hearts of all men, shew whether of these two thou hast chosen, that he may take part of this ministry and apostleship, from which Judas by transgression fell, that he might go to his own place" (Acts 1:24-25).
C. The method involved—"And they gave forth their lots; and the lot fell upon Matthias; and he was numbered with the eleven apostles" (Acts 1:26).

STATISTICS
First mention: Acts 1:23
Final mention: Acts 1:26
Meaning of his name: "Gift of Jehovah"
Frequency of his name: Referred to two times
Biblical books mentioning him: One book (Acts)
Important fact about his life: He was selected to take the place of Judas Iscariot.

Nathanael/ Bartholomew

CHRONOLOGICAL SUMMARY
I. The skepticism of Nathanael
A. The identification—"Philip findeth Nathanael, and saith unto him, We have found him, of whom Moses in the law, and the prophets, did write, Jesus of Nazareth, the son of Joseph" (John 1:45).
B. The intolerance—"And Nathanael said unto him, Can there any good thing come out of Nazareth?" (John 1:46a).
C. The invitation—"Philip saith unto him, Come and see" (John 1:46b).
II. The surprise of Nathanael—"Jesus saw Nathanael coming to him, and saith of him, Behold an Israelite indeed, in whom is no guile! Nathanael saith unto him, Whence knowest thou me? Jesus answered and said unto him, Before that Philip called thee, when thou wast under the fig tree, I saw thee" (John 1:47-48).
III. The salvation of Nathanael
A. His faith in Christ—"Nathanael answered and saith unto him, Rabbi, thou art the Son of God; thou art the King of Israel" (John 1:49).

B. His future in Christ—"Jesus answered and said unto him, Because I said unto thee, I saw thee under the fig tree, believest thou? thou shalt see greater things than these. And he saith unto him, Verily, verily, I say unto you, Hereafter ye shall see heaven open, and the angels of God ascending and descending upon the Son of man" (John 1:50-51).

STATISTICS

First mention: Matthew 10:3
Final mention: Acts 1:13
Meaning of his name: "Gift of God"
Frequency of his name: Referred to 10 times
Biblical books mentioning him: Five books (Matthew, Mark, Luke, John, Acts)
Occupation: Apostle
Place of birth: Probably Bethsaida
Important fact about his life: Philip witnessed to him under a fig tree and brought him to Christ.

Nicodemus

CHRONOLOGICAL SUMMARY

I. The character of Nicodemus
- A. He was a Jewish religious leader (John 3:1).
- B. He was a member of the Pharisees (John 3:1).
- C. He was a well-known teacher (John 3:10).

II. The confession of Nicodemus—"The same came to Jesus by night, and said unto him, Rabbi, we know that thou art a teacher come from God: for no man can do these miracles that thou doest, except God be with him" (John 3:2).

III. The concern of Nicodemus—He probably scheduled the meeting with Jesus to learn more about the new birth. This is indicated by Jesus' opening statement: "Jesus answered and said unto him, Verily, verily, I say unto thee, Except a man be born again, he cannot see the kingdom of God" (John 3:3).

IV. The confusion of Nicodemus
- A. The ruler's ignorance—"Nicodemus saith unto him, How can a man be born when he is old? can he enter the second time into his mother's womb, and be born?" (John 3:4)
  1. His rank may have confused him (John 3:1).
  2. His religion may have confused him (John 3:1, 10).
- B. The Redeemer's illustrations—Jesus offered three illustrations to help Nicodemus understand the new birth.
  1. A physical illustration—"That which is born of the flesh is flesh; and that which is born of the Spirit is spirit" (John 3:6).
  2. A natural illustration—"The wind bloweth where it listeth, and thou hearest the sound thereof, but canst not tell whence it cometh, and whither it goeth: so is every one that is born of the Spirit" (John 3:8).
  3. A scriptural illustration—"And as Moses lifted up the serpent in the wilderness, even so must the Son of man be lifted up" (John 3:14).

V. The chastisement of Nicodemus—"Jesus answered and said unto him, Art thou a master of Israel, and knowest not these things? . . . If I have told you earthly things, and ye believe not, how shall ye believe, if I tell you of heavenly things?" (John 3:10, 12).

VI. The conversion of Nicodemus—The evidence strongly suggests that Nicodemus accepted Christ at this time, perhaps after hearing the most important verse in the Bible (John 3:16).

VII. The courage of Nicodemus
- A. He defended Jesus before the Sanhedrin— "Nicodemus saith unto them, (he that came to Jesus by night, being one of them,) Doth our law judge any man, before it hear him, and know what he doeth? They answered and said unto him, Art thou also of Galilee? Search, and look: for out of Galilee ariseth no prophet" (John 7:50-52).

B. He helped prepare the body of Christ for burial—"And there came also Nicodemus, which at the first came to Jesus by night, and brought a mixture of myrrh and aloes, about an hundred pound weight" (John 19:39).

STATISTICS
First mention: John 3:1
Final mention: John 19:39
Meaning of his name: "Victor over the people"
Frequency of his name: Referred to five times
Biblical books mentioning him: One book (John)
Occupation: Jewish religious ruler
Important fact about his life: He came to Christ by night, asking about the new birth.

Onesimus

CHRONOLOGICAL SUMMARY

I. Paul's appeal and plea for Onesimus—"I beseech thee for my son Onesimus, whom I have begotten in my bonds" (Philem. 10).
  A. The background of this appeal—Onesimus, a slave who stole from his master Philemon and escaped to Rome, had been led to Christ by Paul. He was being sent back with a request that he be received as a Christian brother.
  B. The basis for this appeal—Paul listed three reasons why Philemon should forgive Onesimus.
    1. Forgive him for your sake—"Which in time past was to thee unprofitable, but now profitable to thee and to me. For perhaps he therefore departed for a season, that thou shouldest receive him for ever" (Philem. 11, 15).
    2. Forgive him for his sake—"Not now as a servant, but above a servant, a brother beloved, specially to me, but how much more unto thee, both in the flesh, and in the Lord?" (Philem. 16).
    3. Forgive him for my sake—"Yet for love's sake I rather beseech thee, being such an one as Paul the aged, and now also a prisoner of Jesus Christ. If thou count me therefore a partner, receive him as myself" (Philem. 9, 17).

II. Paul's assurance and pledge for Onesimus—"If he hath wronged thee, or oweth thee ought, put that on mine account; I Paul have written it with mine own hand, I will repay it: albeit I do not say to thee how thou owest unto me even thine own self besides" (Philem. 18-19).

STATISTICS
First mention: Colossians 4:9
Final mention: Philemon 10
Meaning of his name: "Useful, profitable"
Frequency of his name: Referred to two times
Biblical books mentioning him: Two books (Colossians, Philemon)
Occupation: Slave
Important fact about his life: He was a runaway slave whom Paul led to Christ and sent back to his master.

Onesiphorus

CHRONOLOGICAL SUMMARY

I. His ministry to Paul in Ephesus—"How many things he ministered unto me at Ephesus" (2 Tim. 1:18b).

II. His ministry to Paul in Rome
  A. The persistence of Onesiphorus
    1. He diligently sought out Paul in Rome—"But, when he was in Rome, he sought me out very diligently, and found me" (2 Tim. 1:17).
    2. He encouraged and refreshed the imprisoned apostle (2 Tim. 1:16a).
    3. He was not ashamed to be associated with Paul and his chains (2 Tim. 1:16b).
  B. The prayer for Onesiphorus—Paul prayed that Onesiphorus would be especially rewarded at the coming of Christ (2 Tim. 1:18a).

STATISTICS
First mention: 2 Timothy 1:16
Final mention: 2 Timothy 4:19
Meaning of his name: "Bringing a gift"
Frequency of his name: Referred to two times
Biblical books mentioning him: One book (2 Timothy)
Important fact about his life: He was a faithful associate of Paul who ministered to the apostle.

Paul (Saul)

(See also Part Two, Observations from the Life of Paul)

THE PRE-CONVERSION ACTIVITIES OF PAUL

I. His background
   A. Ancestry and youth (Acts 21:39; 22:3; 23:34; Rom. 11:1; 2 Cor. 11:22; Phil. 3:4-5).
      1. He was born and raised in Tarsus in Cilicia (Acts 21:39).
      2. He was of the tribe of Benjamin (Rom. 11:1).
      3. He was a "Hebrew of the Hebrews" (Phil. 3:5).
   B. Education (Acts 22:3; 23:6; 26:4-5; Gal. 1:13-14; Phil. 3:5)
      1. He was taught by Gamaliel (Acts 22:3).
      2. He was a Pharisee and the son of a Pharisee (Acts 23:6).
   C. Political status—He was a Roman citizen (Acts 16:37; 22:25-29).
   D. Character (Phil. 3:6; 1 Tim. 1:12-13; 2 Tim. 1:3)
      1. To the best of his ability he had attempted to keep the Law (Phil. 3:6).
      2. He performed everything he did with great zeal (Phil 3:6).
      3. In ignorance, he persecuted the church (1 Tim. 1:13).
   E. Personal appearance
      1. He probably was of slight build, as indicated by his given name, Paul, which means "small."
      2. He may have had a severe eye infirmity, as suggested by his words in the book of Galatians—"Where is then the blessedness ye spake of? for I bear you record, that, if it had been possible, ye would have plucked out your own eyes, and have given them to me. . . . Ye see how large a letter I have written unto you with mine own hand" (Gal. 4:15; 6:11). (Many Bible students feel this was the "thorn in the flesh" given him by Satan as described in 2 Cor. 12:7-10.)
      3. According to his own evaluation, Paul was not an especially handsome or impressive man (2 Cor. 10:7-10).
      4. He apparently was not an eloquent speaker (2 Cor. 10:10; 11:6).

II. His war against the church (Acts 7:57-58; 8:1-4; 22:4-5, 19-20; 26:9-11; 1 Cor. 15:9; Gal. 1:13, 22-24; Phil. 3:6; 1 Tim. 1:3)
   A. He "kept the raiment" of those who murdered Stephen, and consented to his death (Acts 7:57-58; 8:1-2; 22:20).
   B. He made havoc of the church (Acts 8:3). This word describes the act of a wild hog viciously uprooting a vineyard.
   C. He entered the homes of Christians and dragged them out to prison (Acts 8:3).
   D. In various cities he hounded Christians to their death (Acts 22:5).
   E. He beat believers (Acts 22:19).
   F. He voted to have them put to death (Acts 26:10).
   G. He attempted through torture to force them into cursing Christ (Acts 26:11).
   H. He persecuted the church beyond measure and "wasted it" (Gal. 1:13).

THE CONVERSION OF PAUL

I. His vision of the Son of God (Acts 9:3-9; 22:6-11; 26:1-18)
   A. What he saw—A blinding light brighter than the noonday sun (Acts 9:3; 22:6; 26:13).

B. What he heard

1. The Savior saying, "I am the One you have been persecuting" (Acts 9:4-5; 22:7-8; 26:15).
2. The Savior saying, "I am the One you shall be proclaiming" (Acts 9:6; 22:10; 26:16-18). "But rise, and stand upon thy feet: for I have appeared unto thee for this purpose, to make thee a minister and a witness both of these things which thou hast seen, and of those things in the which I will appear unto thee; delivering thee from the people, and from the Gentiles, unto whom now I send thee, to open their eyes, and to turn them from darkness to light, and from the power of Satan unto God, that they may receive forgiveness of sins, and inheritance among them which are sanctified by faith that is in me" (Acts 26:16-18).

II. His visitation by a servant of God (Acts 9:10-18; 22:13-16)

A. Ananias protesting—"And the Lord said unto him, Arise, and go into the street which is called Straight, and enquire in the house of Judas for one called Saul of Tarsus: for, behold, he prayeth. Then Ananias answered, Lord, I have heard by many of this man, how much evil he hath done to thy saints at Jerusalem: and here he hath authority from the chief priests to bind all that call on thy name. But the Lord said unto him, Go thy way: for he is a chosen vessel unto me, to bear my name before the Gentiles, and kings, and the children of Israel: for I will shew him how great things he must suffer for my name's sake" (Acts 9:11, 13-16).

B. Ananias pastoring—"And Ananias went his way, and entered into the house; and putting his hands on him said, Brother Saul, the Lord, even Jesus, that appeared unto thee in the way as thou camest, hath sent me, that thou mightest receive thy sight, and be filled with the Holy Ghost. And immediately there fell from his eyes as it had been scales: and he received sight forthwith, and arose, and was baptized" (Acts 9:17-18).

C. Ananias predicting—"And he said, The God of our fathers hath chosen thee, that thou shouldest know his will, and see that Just One, and shouldest hear the voice of his mouth. For thou shalt be his witness unto all men of what thou hast seen and heard" (Acts 22:14-15).

THE POST-CONVERSION ACTIVITIES OF PAUL

I. His early ministry (Acts 9:19-30; 11:22-30; 12:25–13:3; Gal. 2:1; 2:1-14)

A. Preaching Christ in the Damascus synagogues (Acts 9:19-21)—"And when he had received meat, he was strengthened. Then was Saul certain days with the disciples which were at Damascus. And straightway he preached Christ in the synagogues, that he is the Son of God. But all that heard him were amazed, and said; Is not this he that destroyed them which called on this name in Jerusalem, and came hither for that intent, that he might bring them bound unto the chief priests?" (Acts 9:19-21).

B. Retiring to the Arabian desert for a period of several years (Gal. 1:16-17)—"Neither went I up to Jerusalem to them which were apostles before me; but I went into Arabia, and returned again unto Damascus" (Gal. 1:17).

C. Returning to Damascus with greater knowledge and preaching power (Acts 9:22; Gal. 1:17)—"But Saul increased the more in strength, and confounded the Jews which dwelt at Damascus, proving that this is very Christ" (Acts 9:22).

D. Escaping from Damascus (Acts 9:23-25)—"And after that many days were fulfilled, the Jews took counsel to kill him: but their laying await was known of Saul. And they watched the gates day and night to kill him. Then the disciples took him by night, and let him down by the wall in a basket" (Acts 9:23-25).

E. Visiting Jerusalem for the first time since his conversion (Acts 9:26-29; Gal. 1:18-19).
   1. The duration of this visit (Gal. 1:18-19)—"But other of the apostles saw I none, save James the Lord's brother" (Gal. 1:19).
   2. The difficulties during this visit (Acts 9:26-29)
      a. The fears—"And when Saul was come to Jerusalem, he assayed to join himself to the disciples: but they were all afraid of him, and believed not that he was a disciple" (Acts 9:26).
      b. The fellowship—"But Barnabas took him, and brought him to the apostles, and declared unto them how he had seen the Lord in the way, and that he had spoken to him, and how he had preached boldly at Damascus in the name of Jesus" (Acts 9:27).

F. Escaping from Jerusalem and settling in Tarsus (Acts 9:29-30; 22:17-21; Gal. 1:21)
   1. The villains in the plot to kill Paul—"And he spake boldly in the name of the Lord Jesus, and disputed against the Grecians: but they went about to slay him" (Acts 9:29).
   2. The vision about the plot to kill Paul—"And it came to pass, that, when I was come again to Jerusalem, even while I prayed in the temple, I was in a trance; and saw him saying unto me, Make haste, and get thee quickly out of Jerusalem: for they will not receive thy testimony concerning me. And I said, Lord, they know that I imprisoned and beat in every synagogue them that believed on thee: and when the blood of thy martyr Stephen was shed, I also was standing by, and consenting unto his death, and kept the raiment of them that slew him. And he said unto me, Depart: for I will send thee far hence unto the Gentiles" (Acts 22:17-21).

G. Struggling over his old sin nature (Rom. 7:15-25)—"For I know that in me (that is, in my flesh,) dwelleth no good thing: for to will is present with me; but how to perform that which is good I find not. For the good that I would I do not: but the evil which I would not, that I do. I find then a law, that, when I would do good, evil is present with me. For I delight in the law of God after the inward man: but I see another law in my members, warring against the law of my mind, and bringing me into captivity to the law of sin which is in my members. O wretched man that I am! who shall deliver me from the body of this death? I thank God through Jesus Christ our Lord. So then with the mind I myself serve the law of God; but with the flesh the law of sin" (Rom. 7:18-19, 21-25). Paul may have experienced what he described here during this time.

H. Joining Barnabas in the work at Antioch (Acts 11:19-26)
   1. The background of the Antioch church (Acts 11:19-21)—It was started by Christians who were driven from Jerusalem following the persecution at the time of Stephen's death.
   2. The missionary pastor of the Antioch church (Acts 11:22-24)—"Then tidings of these things came unto the ears of the church which was in Jerusalem: and they sent forth Barnabas, that he should go as far as Antioch. Who, when he came, and had seen the grace of God, was glad, and exhorted them all, that with purpose of heart they would cleave unto the Lord. For he was a good man, and full of the Holy Ghost and of faith: and much people was added unto the Lord" (Acts 11:22-24).
   3. The associate pastor of the Antioch church (Acts 11:25-26)—"Then departed Barnabas to Tarsus, for to seek Saul: and when he had found him, he brought him unto Antioch. And it came to pass, that a whole

year they assembled themselves with the church, and taught much people. And the disciples were called Christians first in Antioch" (Acts 11:25-26).

I. Visiting Jerusalem for the second time carrying a love offering for the needy there (Acts 11:27-30; Gal. 2:1)
   1. The messages from the Spirit of God directing the visit (Acts 11:28; Gal. 2:2)
      a. The revelation to Agabus (Acts 11:28)—"And there stood up one of them named Agabus, and signified by the Spirit that there should be great dearth throughout all the world: which came to pass in the days of Claudius Caesar" (Acts 11:28).
      b. The revelation to Paul (Gal. 2:2)
   2. The meeting with the saints of God during the visit (Gal. 2:9)—"And when James, Cephas, and John, who seemed to be pillars, perceived the grace that was given unto me, they gave to me and Barnabas the right hands of fellowship; that we should go unto the heathen, and they unto the circumcision" (Gal. 2:9).

J. Returning to Antioch to preach and teach the Word (Acts 12:25–13:1)—"And Barnabas and Saul returned from Jerusalem, when they had fulfilled their ministry, and took with them John, whose surname was Mark. Now there were in the church that was at Antioch certain prophets and teachers; as Barnabas, and Simeon that was called Niger, and Lucius of Cyrene, and Manaen, which had been brought up with Herod the tetrarch, and Saul" (Acts 12:25; 13:1).

II. His first missionary journey (Acts 13:2–14:28)—"As they ministered to the Lord, and fasted, the Holy Ghost said, Separate me Barnabas and Saul for the work whereunto I have called them. And when they had fasted and prayed, and laid their hands on them, they sent them away" (Acts 13:2-3).

A. First stop, Cyprus (Acts 13:4-12)
   1. Preaching at Salamis, the island's eastern city (Acts 13:5)—"And when they were at Salamis, they preached the word of God in the synagogues of the Jews: and they had also John to their minister" (Acts 13:5).
   2. Preaching at Paphos, the island's western city (Acts 13:6-12)
      a. The opportunity (13:6)—Paul and his companions had the opportunity to preach to Sergius Paulus, the governor of the island. In fact, he was anxious to hear God's Word.
      b. The opposition (13:6, 8-11)
         (1) The brazenness of Elymas (13:6, 8)—"And when they had gone through the isle unto Paphos, they found a certain sorcerer, a false prophet, a Jew, whose name was Barjesus. But Elymas the sorcerer (for so is his name by interpretation) withstood them, seeking to turn away the deputy from the faith" (Acts 13:6, 8).
         (2) The blindness of Elymas (13:9-11)—"Then Saul, (who also is called Paul,) filled with the Holy Ghost, set his eyes on him, and said, O full of all subtilty and all mischief, thou child of the devil, thou enemy of all righteousness, wilt thou not cease to pervert the right ways of the Lord? And now, behold, the hand of the Lord is upon thee, and thou shalt be blind, not seeing the sun for a season. And immediately there fell on him a mist and a darkness; and he went about seeking some to lead him by the hand" (Acts 13:9-11).
      c. The open heart (13:12)—"Then the deputy, when he saw what was done, believed, being astonished at the doctrine of the Lord" (Acts 13:12).

B. Second stop, Perga (Acts 13:13)—John Mark left the team at that point.

C. Third stop, Antioch in Pisidia (13:14-50)—Paul spent several weeks there and preached two sermons in the synagogue in Antioch. These sermons described a Savior.

1. His first sermon (Acts 13:14-43)
   a. The preparation for this Savior
      (1) Historical preparations
         (a) God chose a nation—Israel (13:17).
         (b) He led that nation out of Egypt into Canaan (13:18-19).
         (c) He sent judges to deliver them (13:20).
         (d) He chose kings to rule over them (13:21).
      (2) Prophetical preparations—The Psalms had predicted his death and resurrection (13:33-37).
      (3) Homiletical preparation (13:24-25)—John the Baptist had preached sermons on him.
   b. The identity of this Savior
      (1) He came from the seed of David (13:23).
      (2) His name is Jesus (13:23).
   c. The rejection of this Savior (13:27-29)—"And though they found no cause of death in him, yet desired they Pilate that he should be slain. And when they had fulfilled all that was written of him, they took him down from the tree, and laid him in a sepulchre" (Acts 13:28-29).
   d. The resurrection of this Savior (13:30-32)—"But God raised him from the dead: and he was seen many days of them which came up with him from Galilee to Jerusalem, who are his witnesses unto the people. And we declare unto you glad tidings, how that the promise which was made unto the fathers" (Acts 13:30-32).
   e. The salvation offered by this Savior (13:38-39)—"Be it known unto you therefore, men and brethren, that through this man is preached unto you the forgiveness of sins: and by him all that believe are justified from all things, from which ye could not be justified by the law of Moses" (Acts 13:38-39).
2. His second sermon (13:44-50)—"And the next sabbath day came almost the whole city together to hear the word of God" (Acts 13:44).
   a. Rejected by the Jewish listeners (13:45-46, 50)—"But when the Jews saw the multitudes, they were filled with envy, and spake against those things which were spoken by Paul, contradicting and blaspheming. Then Paul and Barnabas waxed bold, and said, It was necessary that the word of God should first have been spoken to you: but seeing ye put it from you, and judge yourselves unworthy of everlasting life, lo, we turn to the Gentiles" (Acts 13:45-46).
   b. Received by the Gentile listeners (13:47-49)—"For so hath the Lord commanded us, saying, I have set thee to be a light of the Gentiles, that thou shouldest be for salvation unto the ends of the earth" (Acts 13:47).
      (1) They accepted the message of God—"And when the Gentiles heard this, they were glad, and glorified the word of the Lord: and as many as were ordained to eternal life believed" (Acts 13:48).
      (2) They assisted the messenger of God—"Ye know how through infirmity of the flesh I preached the gospel unto you at the first. And my temptation which was in my flesh ye despised not, nor rejected;

but received me as an angel of God, even as Christ Jesus. Where is then the blessedness ye spake of? for I bear you record, that, if it had been possible, ye would have plucked out your own eyes, and have given them to me" (Gal. 4:13-15).

D. Fourth stop, Iconium (Acts 13:51–14:5)—"Long time therefore abode they speaking boldly in the Lord, which gave testimony unto the word of his grace, and granted signs and wonders to be done by their hands. But the multitude of the city was divided: and part held with the Jews, and part with the apostles" (Acts 14:3-4).

E. Fifth stop, Lystra (14:6-23)

1. The cripple (14:8)—"And there sat a certain man at Lystra, impotent in his feet, being a cripple from his mother's womb, who never had walked" (Acts 14:8).
2. The cure (14:9-10)—"The same heard Paul speak: who stedfastly beholding him, and perceiving that he had faith to be healed, said with a loud voice, Stand upright on thy feet. And he leaped and walked" (Acts 14:9-10).
3. The commotion (14:11)—"And when the people saw what Paul had done, they lifted up their voices, saying in the speech of Lycaonia, The gods are come down to us in the likeness of men" (Acts 14:11).
4. The confusion (14:12)—"And they called Barnabas, Jupiter; and Paul, Mercurius, because he was the chief speaker" (Acts 14:12).
5. The corruption (14:13)—"Then the priest of Jupiter, which was before their city, brought oxen and garlands unto the gates, and would have done sacrifice with the people" (Acts 14:13).
6. The consternation (14:14)—"Which when the apostles, Barnabas and Paul, heard of, they rent their clothes, and ran in among the people, crying out" (Acts 14:14).
7. The correction (14:15-18)—"And saying, Sirs, why do ye these things? We also are men of like passions with you, and preach unto you that ye should turn from these vanities unto the living God, which made heaven, and earth, and the sea, and all things that are therein" (Acts 14:15).
8. The condemnation (14:19-20)—"And there came thither certain Jews from Antioch and Iconium, who persuaded the people, and, having stoned Paul, drew him out of the city, supposing he had been dead. Howbeit, as the disciples stood round about him, he rose up, and came into the city: and the next day he departed with Barnabas to Derbe" (Acts 14:19-20).
9. The confirmation (14:21-23)—"Confirming the souls of the disciples, and exhorting them to continue in the faith, and that we must through much tribulation enter into the kingdom of God. And when they had ordained them elders in every church, and had prayed with fasting, they commended them to the Lord, on whom they believed" (Acts 14:22-23).

F. Sixth stop, back to Antioch in Syria (14:24-28)—"And when they were come, and had gathered the church together, they rehearsed all that God had done with them, and how he had opened the door of faith unto the Gentiles" (Acts 14:27).

III. His role in the Jerusalem church council (Acts 14:1–15:35; Gal. 2:1-10)

A. The revelation to attend the council—"Then fourteen years after I went up again to Jerusalem with Barnabas, and took Titus with me also. And I went up by revelation, and communicated unto them that gospel which I preach among the Gentiles, but privately to them which were of reputation, lest by any means I should run, or had run, in vain" (Gal. 2:1-2).

B. The reason for the council (Acts 15:1-2, 5-6)—"And certain men which came down from Judaea taught the brethren, and said, Except ye be circumcised after the manner of Moses, ye cannot be saved. . . . And the apostles and elders came together for to consider of this matter" (Acts 15:1, 6).

C. The reports given in the council
   1. Peter's report (15:7-11)—"And when there had been much disputing, Peter rose up, and said unto them, Men and brethren, ye know how that a good while ago God made choice among us, that the Gentiles by my mouth should hear the word of the gospel, and believe. . . . Now therefore why tempt ye God, to put a yoke upon the neck of the disciples, which neither our fathers nor we were able to bear? But we believe that through the grace of the Lord Jesus Christ we shall be saved, even as they" (Acts 15:7, 10-11).
   2. Paul's report (15:12)—"Then all the multitude kept silence, and gave audience to Barnabas and Paul, declaring what miracles and wonders God had wrought among the Gentiles by them" (Acts 15:12).
   3. James's report (15:13-21)
      a. The summary: James summarized the position of no circumcision for the Gentiles, using two arguments.
         (1) A practical argument—God had already saved Gentiles without the rite of circumcision (15:14). "Simeon hath declared how God at the first did visit the Gentiles, to take out of them a people for his name" (Acts 15:14).
         (2) A prophetical argument—Amos the prophet had already predicted this would happen (15:15-18). "And to this agree the words of the prophets; as it is written, After this I will return, and will build again the tabernacle of David, which is fallen down; and I will build again the ruins thereof, and I will set it up: that the residue of men might seek after the Lord, and all the Gentiles, upon whom my name is called, saith the Lord, who doeth all these things" (Acts 15:15-17).
      b. The suggestion (15:19-21)—"Wherefore my sentence is, that we trouble not them, which from among the Gentiles are turned to God" (Acts 15:19).

D. The recommendation of the council (15:22-35)
   1. The messengers who carried this recommendation (15:22-27)—"Then pleased it the apostles and elders, with the whole church, to send chosen men of their own company to Antioch with Paul and Barnabas; namely, Judas surnamed Barsabas, and Silas, chief men among the brethren. . . . Men that have hazarded their lives for the name of our Lord Jesus Christ" (Acts 15:22, 26).
   2. The message contained in this recommendation (15:28-35)—"For it seemed good to the Holy Ghost, and to us, to lay upon you no greater burden than these necessary things; that ye abstain from meats offered to idols, and from blood, and from things strangled, and from fornication: from which if ye keep yourselves, ye shall do well. Fare ye well" (Acts 15:28-29).

E. The results of the council
   1. Paul refused the demands of the Jewish legalizers that he circumcise Titus, his young Gentile coworker in the faith (Gal. 2:3-5).

2. Paul's divinely ordered preaching mission to the Gentiles was recognized by the Jewish Christian leaders (Gal. 2:6-7).
3. Paul and Barnabas were given the official right hand of fellowship by James, Peter, and John (Gal. 2:9).

F. The return from the council—"So when they were dismissed, they came to Antioch: and when they had gathered the multitude together, they delivered the epistle. Paul also and Barnabas continued in Antioch, teaching and preaching the word of the Lord, with many others also" (Acts 15:30, 35).

G. The rebuke following the council—"But when Peter was come to Antioch, I withstood him to the face, because he was to be blamed. For before that certain came from James, he did eat with the Gentiles: but when they were come, he withdrew and separated himself, fearing them which were of the circumcision. And the other Jews dissembled likewise with him; insomuch that Barnabas also was carried away with their dissimulation. But when I saw that they walked not uprightly according to the truth of the gospel, I said unto Peter before them all, If thou, being a Jew, livest after the manner of Gentiles, and not as do the Jews, why compellest thou the Gentiles to live as do the Jews?" (Gal. 2:11-14).

IV. His disagreement with Barnabas (Acts 15:36-40)

A. The background of the disagreement (15:36-38)—"And Barnabas determined to take with them John, whose surname was Mark. But Paul thought not good to take him with them, who departed from them from Pamphylia, and went not with them to the work" (Acts 15: 37-38).

B. The blessing from the disagreement (15:39-40)—"And the contention was so sharp between them, that they departed asunder one from the other: and so Barnabas took Mark, and sailed unto Cyprus; and Paul chose Silas, and departed, being recommended by the brethren unto the grace of God" (Acts 15:39-40).

V. His second missionary journey (Acts 15:41–18:22)

A. First stop, Lystra (16:1-5)
1. The choosing of Timothy (16:1-2)
2. The circumcising of Timothy (16:3)

B. Second stop, Troas (16:6-10)
1. Forbidden by the Holy Spirit to go north or south (16:6-7)
2. Bid by the Holy Spirit to go west (16:9-10)—"And a vision appeared to Paul in the night; there stood a man of Macedonia, and prayed him, saying, Come over into Macedonia, and help us. And after he had seen the vision, immediately we endeavoured to go into Macedonia, assuredly gathering that the Lord had called us for to preach the gospel unto them" (Acts 16:9-10). Note: Observe the "we" in 16:10, indicating that Luke, the author of Acts, had joined the team.

C. Third stop, Philippi (16:11-40)—At Philippi three tremendous conversions took place.
1. The salvation of a business woman (16:13-15)—"And on the sabbath we went out of the city by a river side, where prayer was wont to be made; and we sat down, and spake unto the women which resorted thither. And a certain woman named Lydia, a seller of purple, of the city of Thyatira, which worshipped God, heard us: whose heart the Lord opened, that she attended unto the things which were spoken of Paul. And when she was baptized, and her household, she besought us, saying, If ye have judged me to be faithful to the Lord, come into my house, and abide there. And she constrained us" (Acts 16:13-15).
2. The salvation of a demoniac girl (16:16-18)—"And it came to pass, as we went to prayer, a certain damsel possessed with a spirit of divination

met us, which brought her masters much gain by soothsaying: the same followed Paul and us, and cried, saying, These men are the servants of the most high God, which shew unto us the way of salvation. And this did she many days. But Paul, being grieved, turned and said to the spirit, I command thee in the name of Jesus Christ to come out of her. And he came out the same hour" (Acts 16:16-18).

3. The salvation of a prison keeper (16:19-40)
   a. Paul the slandered (16:19-21)—"And when her masters saw that the hope of their gains was gone, they caught Paul and Silas, and drew them into the marketplace unto the rulers, and brought them to the magistrates, saying, these men, being Jews, do exceedingly trouble our city, and teach customs, which are not lawful for us to receive, neither to observe, being Romans" (Acts 16:19-21).
   b. Paul the sufferer (16:22-24)—"And the multitude rose up together against them: and the magistrates rent off their clothes, and commanded to beat them. And when they had laid many stripes upon them, they cast them into prison, charging the jailor to keep them safely: who, having received such a charge, thrust them into the inner prison, and made their feet fast in the stocks" (Acts 16:22-24).
   c. Paul the singer (16:25)—"And at midnight Paul and Silas prayed, and sang praises unto God: and the prisoners heard them" (Acts 16:25).
   d. Paul the spokesman (16:26-28)—"And suddenly there was a great earthquake, so that the foundations of the prison were shaken: and immediately all the doors were opened, and every one's bands were loosed. And the keeper of the prison awaking out of his sleep, and seeing the prison doors open, he drew out his sword, and would have killed himself, supposing that the prisoners had been fled. But Paul cried with a loud voice, saying, Do thyself no harm: for we are all here" (Acts 16:26-28).
   e. Paul the soul winner (16:29-34)—"Then he called for a light, and sprang in, and came trembling, and fell down before Paul and Silas, and brought them out, and said, Sirs, what must I do to be saved? And they said, Believe on the Lord Jesus Christ, and thou shalt be saved, and thy house. And they spake unto him the word of the Lord, and to all that were in his house. And he took them the same hour of the night, and washed their stripes; and was baptized, he and all his, straightway. And when he had brought them into his house, he set meat before them, and rejoiced, believing in God with all his house" (Acts 16:29-34).
   f. Paul the citizen (16:35-40)—"And when it was day, the magistrates sent the serjeants, saying, Let those men go. And the keeper of the prison told this saying to Paul, The magistrates have sent to let you go: now therefore depart, and go in peace. But Paul said unto them, They have beaten us openly uncondemned, being Romans, and have cast us into prison; and now do they thrust us out privily? nay verily; but let them come themselves and fetch us out. And the serjeants told these words unto the magistrates: and they feared, when they heard that they were Romans" (Acts 16:35-38).

D. Fourth stop, Thessalonica (Acts 17:1-9)
   1. Paul, the tireless worker—"For ye remember, brethren, our labour and travail: for labouring night and day, because we would not be chargeable unto any of you, we preached unto you the gospel of God" (1 Thess. 2:9). "For yourselves know how ye ought to follow us: for we behaved not ourselves disorderly among you; neither did we eat any man's bread for nought; but wrought with labour and travail night and day, that we might not be chargeable to any of you: not because we have not power, but to make ourselves an ensample unto you to follow us. For even when we were with you, this we commanded you, that if any would not work, neither should he eat" (2 Thess. 3:7-10).
   2. Paul, the tireless witness—"And Paul, as his manner was, went in unto them, and three sabbath days reasoned with them out of the scriptures, opening and alleging, that Christ must needs have suffered, and risen again from the dead; and that this Jesus, whom I preach unto you, is Christ. And some of them believed, and consorted with Paul and Silas; and of the devout Greeks a great multitude, and of the chief women not a few. But the Jews which believed not, moved with envy, took unto them certain lewd fellows of the baser sort, and gathered a company, and set all the city on an uproar, and assaulted the house of Jason, and sought to bring them out to the people" (Acts 17:2-5).

E. Fifth stop, Berea (17:10-14)—"These were more noble than those in Thessalonica, in that they received the word with all readiness of mind, and searched the scriptures daily, whether those things were so. Therefore many of them believed; also of honourable women which were Greeks, and of men, not a few" (Acts 17:11-12).

F. Sixth stop, Athens (17:15-34)—There Paul preached his famous sermon on Mars Hill.
   1. The need for this sermon (17:16-17)—"Now while Paul waited for them at Athens, his spirit was stirred in him, when he saw the city wholly given to idolatry" (Acts 17: 16).
   2. The audience of this sermon (17:18-21)—"Then certain philosophers of the Epicureans, and of the Stoicks, encountered him. And some said, What will this babbler say? other some, He seemeth to be a setter forth of strange gods: because he preached unto them Jesus, and the resurrection. (For all the Athenians and strangers which were there spent their time in nothing else, but either to tell, or to hear some new thing)" (Acts 17:18, 21).
   3. The introduction to this sermon (17:22)—"Then Paul stood in the midst of Mars' hill, and said, Ye men of Athens, I perceive that in all things ye are too superstitious" (Acts 17:22).
   4. The text of this sermon (17:24-31) — "For as I passed by, and beheld your devotions, I found an altar with this inscription, TO THE UNKNOWN GOD. Whom therefore ye ignorantly worship, him declare I unto you" (Acts 17:23).
   5. The points in this sermon (17:24-31)
      a. Regarding the past: God was the Creator of all people (17:24-26, 28-29).
      b. Regarding the present: God desires to be the Savior of all people (17:27, 30).
         (1) Providing they reach out (17:27)—"That they should seek the Lord, if haply they might feel after him, and find him, though he be not far from every one of us" (Acts 17:27).

(2) Providing they repent (17:30)—"And the times of this ignorance God winked at; but now commandeth all men every where to repent" (Acts 17:30).

c. Regarding the future: God will judge all people (17:31)—"Because he hath appointed a day, in the which he will judge the world in righteousness by that man whom he hath ordained; whereof he hath given assurance unto all men, in that he hath raised him from the dead" (Acts 17:31).

6. The reaction to this sermon (17:32-34)
   a. Some mocked (17:32).
   b. Some delayed (17:32).
   c. Some believed (17:34).

G. Seventh stop, Corinth (Acts 18:1-18)—"And I, brethren, when I came to you, came not with excellency of speech or of wisdom, declaring unto you the testimony of God. For I determined not to know any thing among you, save Jesus Christ, and him crucified. And I was with you in weakness, and in fear, and in much trembling. And my speech and my preaching was not with enticing words of man's wisdom, but in demonstration of the Spirit and of power" (1 Cor. 2:1-4).

1. Paul's friends in this city (Acts 18:1-5)
   a. The tentmakers (18:1-3)—He met a godly couple, Aquila and Priscilla, who, like Paul, were tentmakers by trade.
   b. The team members (18:5)—Silas and Timothy caught up with him from Macedonia.

2. Paul's foes in this city (18:5-6, 12-17)
   a. Their identity (18:5)—"And when Silas and Timotheus were come from Macedonia, Paul was pressed in the spirit, and testified to the Jews that Jesus was Christ" (Acts 18:5).
   b. Their insolence (18:6)—"And when they opposed themselves, and blasphemed, he shook his raiment, and said unto them, Your blood be upon your own heads; I am clean: from henceforth I will go unto the Gentiles" (Acts 18:6).
   c. Their insurrection (18:12-17)
      (1) The futility of their efforts (18:12-16)—They unsuccessfully attempted to indict Paul before Gallio, the Roman deputy.
      (2) The irony of their efforts (18:17)—"Then all the Greeks took Sosthenes, the chief ruler of the synagogue, and beat him before the judgment seat. And Gallio cared for none of those things" (Acts 18:17).

3. Paul's fruits in this city (18:8, 11)—"And Crispus, the chief ruler of the synagogue, believed on the Lord with all his house; and many of the Corinthians hearing believed, and were baptized. And he continued there a year and six months, teaching the word of God among them" (Acts 18:8, 11).

4. Paul's heavenly Father in this city (18:9-10)—"Then spake the Lord to Paul in the night by a vision, Be not afraid, but speak, and hold not thy peace: for I am with thee, and no man shall set on thee to hurt thee: for I have much people in this city" (Acts 18:9-10). Paul wrote 1 and 2 Thessalonians from Corinth.

H. Eighth stop, Ephesus (18:19-21)

1. He was accompanied by his friends Aquila and Priscilla (18:18).
2. He was asked by his converts to dwell in Ephesus (18:20-21)—"But bade them farewell, saying, I must by all means keep this feast that cometh in Jerusalem: but I will return again unto you, if God will. And he sailed from Ephesus" (Acts 18:21).

I. Final stop, back to Antioch (18:22)

VI. His third missionary journey (Acts 18:23–21:14)
   A. First stop, Asia Minor (18:24–19:41)—Paul revisited these churches to exhort and instruct them.
   B. Second stop, Ephesus (18:24)
      1. The forerunner of Paul in Ephesus (18:24-28)—"And a certain Jew named Apollos, born at Alexandria, an eloquent man, and mighty in the scriptures, came to Ephesus" (Acts 18:24).
         a. The teaching of Apollos (18:25)—"This man was instructed in the way of the Lord; and being fervent in the spirit, he spake and taught diligently the things of the Lord, knowing only the baptism of John" (Acts 18:25).
         b. The teachers of Apollos (18:26)—"And he began to speak boldly in the synagogue: whom when Aquila and Priscilla had heard, they took him unto them, and expounded unto him the way of God more perfectly" (Acts 18:26).
      2. The fruits of Paul in Ephesus (19:1-41)
         a. The disciples of John (19:1-7)—Paul found 12 disciples of John the Baptist who knew only of the ministry of Christ and nothing of Pentecost. He brought them up to date. "When they heard this, they were baptized in the name of the Lord Jesus. And when Paul had laid his hands upon them, the Holy Ghost came on them; and they spake with tongues, and prophesied" (Acts 19:5-6).
         b. The duration with Tyrannus (19:8-10)—"And he went into the synagogue, and spake boldly for the space of three months, disputing and persuading the things concerning the kingdom of God. But when divers were hardened, and believed not, but spake evil of that way before the multitude, he departed from them, and separated the disciples, disputing daily in the school of one Tyrannus. And this continued by the space of two years; so that all they which dwelt in Asia heard the word of the Lord Jesus, both Jews and Greeks" (Acts 19:8-10).
         c. The distribution of prayer cloths (19:11-12)—"And God wrought special miracles by the hands of Paul: so that from his body were brought unto the sick handkerchiefs or aprons, and the diseases departed from them, and the evil spirits went out of them" (Acts 19:11-12).
         d. The divinations of Sceva (19:13-17)—"Then certain of the vagabond Jews, exorcists, took upon them to call over them which had evil spirits the name of the Lord Jesus, saying, We adjure you by Jesus whom Paul preacheth. And there were seven sons of one Sceva, a Jew, and chief of the priests, which did so. And the evil spirit answered and said, Jesus I know, and Paul I know; but who are ye? And the man in whom the evil spirit was leaped on them, and overcame them, and prevailed against them, so that they fled out of that house naked and wounded" (Acts 19:13-16).
         e. The dedication of the converts (19:18-20)—"And many that believed came, and confessed, and shewed their deeds. Many of them also which used curious arts brought their books together, and burned them before all men: and they counted the price of them, and found it fifty thousand pieces of silver. So mightily grew the word of God and prevailed" (Acts 19:18-20).
         f. The decision of Paul (19:21-22)—Paul determined to someday visit Rome.

g. The defenders of Diana (19:23-41)
  (1) The libel of Demetrius (19:23-28)—A meeting to oppose Paul was conducted by Demetrius, a silversmith who had profited by making silver shrines for the goddess statue Diana. At the meeting he said: "Moreover ye see and hear, that not alone at Ephesus, but almost throughout all Asia, this Paul hath persuaded and turned away much people, saying that they be no gods, which are made with hands: so that not only this our craft is in danger to be set at nought; but also that the temple of the great goddess Diana should be despised, and her magnificence should be destroyed, whom all Asia and the world worshippeth" (Acts 19:26-27).
  (2) The lunacy of the crowd (19:29-34)—"And certain of the chief of Asia, which were his friends, sent unto him, desiring him that he would not adventure himself into the theatre. Some therefore cried one thing, and some another: for the assembly was confused; and the more part knew not wherefore they were come together" (Acts 19:31-32). For the next two hours this mob screamed out: "Great is Diana of the Ephesians" (Acts 19:34).
  (3) The logic of the town clerk (19:35-41)—This intelligent Greek official calmed down the mob through four logical arguments.
    (a) One: The divinity of the statue (19:35-36)—"And when the townclerk had appeased the people, he said, Ye men of Ephesus, what man is there that knoweth not how that the city of the Ephesians is a worshipper of the great goddess Diana, and of the image which fell down from Jupiter? Seeing then that these things cannot be spoken against, ye ought to be quiet, and to do nothing rashly" (Acts 19:35-36).
    (b) Two: The honesty of the opponents (19:37)—"For ye have brought hither these men, which are neither robbers of churches, nor yet blasphemers of your goddess" (Acts 19:37).
    (c) Three: The legality of the matter (19:38-39)—"Wherefore if Demetrius, and the craftsmen which are with him, have a matter against any man, the law is open, and there are deputies: let them implead one another" (Acts 19:38).
    (d) Four: The (possible) hostility of the Romans (19:40)—"For we are in danger to be called in question for this day's uproar, there being no cause whereby we may give an account of this concourse" (Acts 19:40).

3. The follow-up of Paul in Ephesus
  a. While in Ephesus, Paul received some disturbing news from the house of Chloe concerning the sad state of the church in Corinth (1 Cor. 1:11).
  b. He then wrote 1 Corinthians from Ephesus.
  c. He had previously written a letter (now lost) to this church (see 1 Cor. 5:9).
  d. Paul made a quick follow-up trip to Corinth (implied by 2 Cor. 2:1; 12:14; 13:1-2).
  e. Upon returning he wrote 2 Corinthians from Ephesus.

C. Third stop, Greece (Acts 20:1-5)
   1. After a stay of three months he left to escape a plot of the Jews to kill him.
   2. Paul wrote Romans from Greece.

D. Fourth stop, Troas (20:6-12)
   1. The midnight address (20:7)—"And upon the first day of the week, when the disciples came together to break bread, Paul preached unto them, ready to depart on the morrow; and continued his speech until midnight" (Acts 20:7).
   2. The midmorning accident (20:8-9)—"And there sat in a window a certain young man named Eutychus, being fallen into a deep sleep: and as Paul was long preaching, he sunk down with sleep, and fell down from the third loft, and was taken up dead" (Acts 20:9).
   3. The miraculous awakening (20:10-12)—"And Paul went down, and fell on him, and embracing him said, Trouble not yourselves; for his life is in him. And they brought the young man alive, and were not a little comforted" (Acts 20:10, 12).

E. Fifth stop, Miletus (20:13-38)—"And from Miletus he sent to Ephesus, and called the elders of the church" (Acts 20:17).
   1. He reviewed the past—"Therefore watch, and remember, that by the space of three years I ceased not to warn every one night and day with tears" (Acts 20:31).
      a. His role as a servant of Christ (20:19)—"Serving the Lord with all humility of mind, and with many tears, and temptations, which befell me by the lying in wait of the Jews" (Acts 20:19).
      b. His role as a teacher of saints (20:20, 27)—"And how I kept back nothing that was profitable unto you, but have shewed you, and have taught you publickly, and from house to house. For I have not shunned to declare unto you all the counsel of God" (Acts 20:20, 27).
      c. His role as a witness to sinners (20:21, 26)—"Testifying both to the Jews, and also to the Greeks, repentance toward God, and faith toward our Lord Jesus Christ. Wherefore I take you to record this day, that I am pure from the blood of all men" (Acts 20:21, 26).
      d. His role as an example to all (20:33-35)—"I have coveted no man's silver, or gold, or apparel. Yea, ye yourselves know, that these hands have ministered unto my necessities, and to them that were with me. I have shewed you all things, how that so labouring ye ought to support the weak, and to remember the words of the Lord Jesus, how he said, It is more blessed to give than to receive" (Acts 20:33-35).
   2. He viewed the present.
      a. Summarizing his situation (20:22-23, 25)—"And now, behold, I go bound in the spirit unto Jerusalem, not knowing the things that shall befall me there: save that the Holy Ghost witnesseth in every city, saying that bonds and afflictions abide me. And now, behold, I know that ye all, among whom I have gone preaching the kingdom of God, shall see my face no more" (Acts 20:22-23, 25).
      b. Summarizing their situation (20:28, 32)
         (1) What they were to do (20:28)—"Take heed therefore unto yourselves, and to all the flock, over the which the Holy Ghost hath made you overseers, to feed the church of God, which he hath purchased with his own blood" (Acts 20:28).

(2) How they were to do it (20:32)—"And now, brethren, I commend you to God, and to the word of his grace, which is able to build you up, and to give you an inheritance among all them which are sanctified" (Acts 20:32).

3. He previewed the future.
   a. What his desire was (20:24)—"But none of these things move me, neither count I my life dear unto myself, so that I might finish my course with joy, and the ministry, which I have received of the Lord Jesus, to testify the gospel of the grace of God" (Acts 20:24).
   b. What their dangers would be (20:29-30)—"For I know this, that after my departing shall grievous wolves enter in among you, not sparing the flock. Also of your own selves shall men arise, speaking perverse things, to draw away disciples after them" (Acts 20:29-30).

F. Sixth stop, Tyre (21:1-6)
   1. A message from the Spirit (21:4)—"And finding disciples, we tarried there seven days: who said to Paul through the Spirit, that he should not go up to Jerusalem" (Acts 21:4).
   2. A meeting on the sand (21:5-6)—"And when we had accomplished those days, we departed and went our way; and they all brought us on our way, with wives and children, till we were out of the city: and we kneeled down on the shore, and prayed" (Acts 21:5).

G. Seventh stop, Ptolemais (21:7)—"And when we had finished our course from Tyre, we came to Ptolemais, and saluted the brethren, and abode with them one day" (Acts 21:7).

H. Eighth stop, Caesarea (21:8-14)
   1. The warrior of God (21:8)—"And the next day we that were of Paul's company departed, and came unto Caesarea: and we entered into the house of Philip the evangelist, which was one of the seven; and abode with him" (Acts 21:8).
   2. The women of God (21:9)—"And the same man had four daughters, virgins, which did prophesy" (Acts 21:9).
   3. The warning from God (21:10-11)—"And as we tarried there many days, there came down from Judaea a certain prophet, named Agabus. And when he was come unto us, he took Paul's girdle, and bound his own hands and feet, and said, Thus saith the Holy Ghost, So shall the Jews at Jerusalem bind the man that owneth this girdle, and shall deliver him into the hands of the Gentiles" (Acts 21:10-11).
   4. The will of God (21:12-14)—"And when we heard these things, both we, and they of that place, besought him not to go up to Jerusalem. Then Paul answered, What mean ye to weep and to break mine heart? for I am ready not to be bound only, but also to die at Jerusalem for the name of the Lord Jesus. And when he would not be persuaded, we ceased, saying, The will of the Lord be done" (Acts 21:12-14).

VII. His arrest in Jerusalem (Acts 21:15–23:32)—"And after those days we took up our carriages, and went up to Jerusalem. And when we were come to Jerusalem, the brethren received us gladly. And the day following Paul went in with us unto James; and all the elders were present" (Acts 21:15, 17-18).

A. The rumors against Paul (21:18-22, 27-30)
   1. That he had denounced the Law of Moses (21:18-21)—James informed Paul that many Jews were saying this about him. "And they are informed of thee, that thou teachest all the Jews which are among the Gentiles to forsake Moses, saying that they ought not to circumcise

their children, neither to walk after the customs" (Acts 21:21).
2. That he had desecrated the temple of God (21:27-30)—He was incorrectly accused of bringing a Gentile named Trophimus into the temple.

B. The reaction by Paul (21:23-26)—To counteract these false rumors, Paul agreed to put himself back under the Law, shaved his head, and took a seven-day vow.

C. The rescue of Paul (21:30-32)—In spite of Paul's efforts, the rumors persisted, and he was set upon by a murderous Jewish mob. "And all the city was moved, and the people ran together: and they took Paul, and drew him out of the temple: and forthwith the doors were shut. And as they went about to kill him, tidings came unto the chief captain of the band, that all Jerusalem was in an uproar. Who immediately took soldiers and centurions, and ran down unto them: and when they saw the chief captain and the soldiers, they left beating of Paul" (Acts 21:30-32).

D. The replies by Paul (21:33–23:10)
1. His reply to the chief captain
a. First dialogue (21:33-39)
(1) The captain's confusion—"Art not thou that Egyptian, which before these days madest an uproar, and leddest out into the wilderness four thousand men that were murderers?" (Acts 21:38).
(2) The apostle's correction—"But Paul said, I am a man which am a Jew of Tarsus, a city in Cilicia, a citizen of no mean city: and, I beseech thee, suffer me to speak unto the people" (Acts 21:39).
b. Second dialogue (22:24-30)
(1) The command of the captain (22:24)—In an attempt to secure more information, the captain ordered Paul to be scourged. The apostle then said: "And as they bound him with thongs, Paul said unto the centurion that stood by, Is it lawful for you to scourge a man that is a Roman, and uncondemned?" (Acts 22:25).
(2) The concern of the captain (22:28-29)—"And the chief captain answered, With a great sum obtained I this freedom. And Paul said, But I was free born. Then straightway they departed from him which should have examined him: and the chief captain also was afraid, after he knew that he was a Roman, and because he had bound him" (Acts 22:28-29).
2. His reply to the Jewish mob (21:40—22:23)—"And when he had given him licence, Paul stood on the stairs, and beckoned with the hand unto the people. And when there was made a great silence, he spake unto them in the Hebrew tongue" (Acts 21:40).
a. The speech (22:1-21)
(1) His conversion (22:1-16)—"And it came to pass, that, as I made my journey, and was come nigh unto Damascus about noon, suddenly there shone from heaven a great light round about me. And I fell unto the ground, and heard a voice saying unto me, Saul, Saul, why persecutest thou me? And I answered, Who art thou, Lord? And he said unto me, I am Jesus of Nazareth, whom thou persecutest. . . . And I said, What shall I do, Lord? And the Lord said unto me, Arise, and go into Damascus; and there it shall be told thee of all things which are appointed for thee to do" (Acts 22:6-8, 10).
(2) His call—"And it came to pass, that, when I was come

again to Jerusalem, even while I prayed in the temple, I was in a trance; and saw him saying unto me, Make haste, and get thee quickly out of Jerusalem: for they will not receive thy testimony concerning me. . . . And he said unto me, Depart: for I will send thee far hence unto the Gentiles" (Acts 22:17-18, 21).

b. The screams (22:22-23)—"And they gave him audience unto this word, and then lifted up their voices, and said, Away with such a fellow from the earth: for it is not fit that he should live. And as they cried out, and cast off their clothes, and threw dust into the air" (Acts 22:22-23).

3. His reply to the Sanhedrin (23:1-10)

a. The reprisal (23:1-2)—"And Paul, earnestly beholding the council, said, Men and brethren, I have lived in all good conscience before God unto this day. And the high priest Ananias commanded them that stood by him to smite him on the mouth" (Acts 23:1-2).

b. The retaliation (23:3)—"Then said Paul unto him, God shall smite thee, thou whited wall: for sittest thou to judge me after the law, and commandest me to be smitten contrary to the law?" (Acts 23:3).

c. The regret (23:4-5)—"And they that stood by said, Revilest thou God's high priest? Then said Paul, I wist not, brethren, that he was the high priest: for it is written, Thou shalt not speak evil of the ruler of thy people" (Acts 23:4-5).

d. The ruse (23:6-10)—"But when Paul perceived that the one part were Sadducees, and the other Pharisees, he cried out in the council, Men and brethren, I am a Pharisee, the son of a Pharisee: of the hope and resurrection of the dead I am called in question. And when he had so said, there arose a dissension between the Pharisees and the Sadducees: and the multitude was divided. For the Sadducees say that there is no resurrection, neither angel, nor spirit: but the Pharisees confess both. And there arose a great cry: and the scribes that were of the Pharisees' part arose, and strove, saying, We find no evil in this man: but if a spirit or an angel hath spoken to him, let us not fight against God. And when there arose a great dissension, the chief captain, fearing lest Paul should have been pulled in pieces of them, commanded the soldiers to go down, and to take him by force from among them, and to bring him into the castle" (Acts 23:6-10).

E. The revelation to Paul (23:11)—"And the night following the Lord stood by him, and said, Be of good cheer, Paul: for as thou hast testified of me in Jerusalem, so must thou bear witness also at Rome" (Acts 23:11).

F. The revenge against Paul (23:12-15)—"And when it was day, certain of the Jews banded together, and bound themselves under a curse, saying that they would neither eat nor drink till they had killed Paul. And they were more than forty which had made this conspiracy. And they came to the chief priests and elders, and said, We have bound ourselves under a great curse, that we will eat nothing until we have slain Paul. Now therefore ye with the council signify to the chief captain that he bring him down unto you to morrow, as though ye would enquire something more perfectly concerning him: and we, or ever he come near, are ready to kill him" (Acts 23:12-15).

G. The relative of Paul (23:16-22)—"And when Paul's sister's son heard of their lying in wait, he went and entered into the castle, and told Paul. Then Paul called one of the centurions unto him, and said, Bring this young man unto the chief captain: for he hath a certain thing to tell him. . . . So the chief captain then let the young man depart, and charged him, See thou tell no man that thou hast shewed these things to me" (Acts 23:16-17, 22).

H. The removal of Paul (23:23-32)

1. The soldiers (23:23-24)—"And he called unto him two centurions, saying, Make ready two hundred soldiers to go to Caesarea, and horsemen threescore and ten, and spearmen two hundred, at the third hour of the night; and provide them beasts, that they may set Paul on, and bring him safe unto Felix the governor" (Acts 23:23-24).
2. The salutation (23:25-32)—The chief captain wrote a letter to Felix explaining the circumstances surrounding Paul's arrest.

VIII. His imprisonment in Caesarea (Acts 23:33–26:32)

A. Paul before Felix (23:33–24:27)

1. The accusations of Tertullus (24:1-9)—He was an articulate Jewish lawyer who accused Paul of being three things:
   a. A political rebel (24:5)—"For we have found this man a pestilent fellow, and a mover of sedition . . . throughout the world" (Acts 24:5).
   b. A religious heretic (24:5)—"And a ringleader of the sect of the Nazarenes" (Acts 24:5).
   c. A temple desecrator (24:6)—"Who also hath gone about to profane the temple" (Acts 24:6).
2. The answer of Paul (24:10-21)
   a. Concerning the first and third charges—Innocent. "Because that thou mayest understand, that there are yet but twelve days since I went up to Jerusalem for to worship. And they neither found me in the temple disputing with any man, neither raising up the people, neither in the synagogues, nor in the city: neither can they prove the things whereof they now accuse me" (Acts 24:11-13).
   b. Concerning the second charge—Guilty. "But this I confess unto thee, that after the way which they call heresy, so worship I the God of my fathers, believing all things which are written in the law and in the prophets: and have hope toward God, which they themselves also allow, that there shall be a resurrection of the dead, both of the just and unjust. And herein do I exercise myself, to have always a conscience void of offence toward God, and toward men. . . . Or else let these same here say, if they have found any evil doing in me, while I stood before the council, except it be for this one voice, that I cried standing among them, Touching the resurrection of the dead I am called in question by you this day" (Acts 24:14-16, 20-21).
3. The apprehension of Felix (24:22-27)—"And after certain days, when Felix came with his wife Drusilla, which was a Jewess, he sent for Paul, and heard him concerning the faith in Christ. And as he reasoned of righteousness, temperance, and judgment to come, Felix trembled, and answered, Go thy way for this time; when I have a convenient season, I will call for thee" (Acts 24:24-25).

B. Paul before Festus (25:1-12)

1. The trip (25:1-6)—Upon succeeding Felix, Festus visited Jerusalem and invited the Jews to once again

present their case against Paul in Caesarea.

2. The tormentors (25:7)—"And when he was come, the Jews which came down from Jerusalem stood round about, and laid many and grievous complaints against Paul, which they could not prove" (Acts 25:7).
3. The tormented (25:8)—"While he answered for himself, Neither against the law of the Jews, neither against the temple, nor yet against Caesar, have I offended any thing at all" (Acts 25:8).
4. The treachery (25:9)—"But Festus, willing to do the Jews a pleasure, answered Paul, and said, Wilt thou go up to Jerusalem, and there be judged of these things before me?" (Acts 25:9).
5. The transfer (25:10-12)—"Then said Paul, I stand at Caesar's judgment seat, where I ought to be judged: to the Jews have I done no wrong, as thou very well knowest. For if I be an offender, or have committed any thing worthy of death, I refuse not to die: but if there be none of these things whereof these accuse me, no man may deliver me unto them. I appeal unto Caesar. Then Festus, when he had conferred with the council, answered, Hast thou appealed unto Caesar? unto Caesar shalt thou go" (Acts 25:10-12).

C. Paul before Agrippa (25:13–26:32)
1. The summarizer
   a. His activities as a religious man (26:2-5, 9-11)—"My manner of life from my youth, which was at the first among mine own nation at Jerusalem, know all the Jews; which knew me from the beginning, if they would testify, that after the most straitest sect of our religion I lived a Pharisee" (Acts 26:4-5).
   b. His activities as a redeemed man
      (1) His conversion (26:12-15)
      (2) His call (26:16-18)—"But rise, and stand upon thy feet: for I have appeared unto thee for this purpose, to make thee a minister and a witness both of these things which thou hast seen, and of those things in the which I will appear unto thee; delivering thee from the people, and from the Gentiles, unto whom now I send thee" (Acts 26:16-17).
      (3) His consecration (26:19)—"Whereupon, O king Agrippa, I was not disobedient unto the heavenly vision" (Acts 26:19).
      (4) His conflicts (26:21)—"For these causes the Jews caught me in the temple, and went about to kill me" (Acts 26:21).
      (5) His consistency (26:22-23)—"Having therefore obtained help of God, I continue unto this day, witnessing both to small and great, saying none other things than those which the prophets and Moses did say should come: that Christ should suffer, and that he should be the first that should rise from the dead, and should shew light unto the people, and to the Gentiles" (Acts 26:22-23).
2. The soul winner (26:24-32)
   a. Paul and Festus (26:24-25)—"And as he thus spake for himself, Festus said with a loud voice, Paul, thou art beside thyself; much learning doth make thee mad. But he said, I am not mad, most noble Festus; but I speak forth the words of truth and soberness" (Acts 26:24-25).
   b. Paul and Agrippa (26:26-32)—"King Agrippa, believest thou the prophets? I know that thou believest. Then Agrippa said unto Paul, Almost thou

persuadest me to be a Christian. And Paul said, I would to God, that not only thou, but also all that hear me this day, were both almost, and altogether such as I am, except these bonds" (Acts 26:27-29).

Paul may have written Hebrews from Caesarea. Note: If the apostle was indeed the author of Hebrews, he probably wrote it at this time.

IX. His voyage to Rome (27:1–28:15)
   A. Phase 1: From Caesarea to Fair Havens (27:1-12)
      1. Julius's kindness to Paul (27:1, 3)—"And when it was determined that we should sail into Italy, they delivered Paul and certain other prisoners unto one named Julius a centurion of Augustus' band. . . . And entering into a ship of Adramyttium, we launched, meaning to sail by the coasts of Asia; one Aristarchus, a Macedonian of Thessalonica, being with us. And the next day we touched at Sidon. And Julius courteously entreated Paul, and gave him liberty to go unto his friends to refresh himself" (Acts 27:1, 3).
      2. Paul's caution to Julius (27:9-11)—"Now when much time was spent, and when sailing was now dangerous, because the fast was now already past, Paul admonished them, and said unto them, Sirs, I perceive that this voyage will be with hurt and much damage, not only of the lading and ship, but also of our lives. Nevertheless the centurion believed the master and the owner of the ship, more than those things which were spoken by Paul" (Acts 27:9-11).
   B. Phase 2: From Fair Havens to Melita (27:13-44)
      1. The fearful storm (27:14-20)—"But not long after there arose against it a tempestuous wind, called Euroclydon. And when the ship was caught, and could not bear up into the wind, we let her drive. And we being exceedingly tossed with a tempest, the next day they lightened the ship; and the third day we cast out with our own hands the tackling of the ship. And when neither sun nor stars in many days appeared, and no small tempest lay on us, all hope that we should be saved was then taken away" (Acts 27: 14-15, 18-20).
      2. The cheerful saint (27:21-26, 33-37)—"But after long abstinence Paul stood forth in the midst of them, and said, Sirs, ye should have hearkened unto me, and not have loosed from Crete, and to have gained this harm and loss. And now I exhort you to be of good cheer" (Acts 27:21-22).
         a. The prophetical aspect—"For there stood by me this night the angel of God, whose I am, and whom I serve, saying, Fear not, Paul; thou must be brought before Caesar: and, lo, God hath given thee all them that sail with thee. Wherefore, sirs, be of good cheer: for I believe God, that it shall be even as it was told me" (Acts 27:23-25).
            (1) There would be no loss of life (27:22).
            (2) Only the ship would be lost (27:22).
            (3) They would be cast on an island (27:26).
         b. The practical aspect (27:33-37)—"And while the day was coming on, Paul besought them all to take meat, saying, This day is the fourteenth day that ye have tarried and continued fasting, having taken nothing. Wherefore I pray you to take some meat: for this is for your health: for there shall not an hair fall from the head of any of you. And when he had thus spoken, he took bread, and gave thanks to God in presence of them all: and when he had broken it, he began to eat.

Then were they all of good cheer, and they also took some meat. And we were in all in the ship two hundred threescore and sixteen souls" (Acts 27:33-37).

c. The political aspect (27:39-44)—"And falling into a place where two seas met, they ran the ship aground; and the forepart stuck fast, and remained unmoveable, but the hinder part was broken with the violence of the waves. And the soldiers' counsel was to kill the prisoners, lest any of them should swim out, and escape. But the centurion, willing to save Paul, kept them from their purpose; and commanded that they which could swim should cast themselves first into the sea, and get to land: and the rest, some on boards, and some on broken pieces of the ship. And so it came to pass, that they escaped all safe to land" (Acts 27:41-44).

C. Phase 3: At Melita (28:1-10)

1. Paul and the people (28:1-6)

a. First viewed as a murderer (28:2-4)—"And the barbarous people shewed us no little kindness: for they kindled a fire, and received us every one, because of the present rain, and because of the cold. And when Paul had gathered a bundle of sticks, and laid them on the fire, there came a viper out of the heat, and fastened on his hand. And when the barbarians saw the venomous beast hang on his hand, they said among themselves, No doubt this man is a murderer, whom, though he hath escaped the sea, yet vengeance suffereth not to live" (Acts 28:2-4).

b. Finally viewed as a messiah (28:5, 7)—"And he shook off the beast into the fire, and felt no harm. Howbeit they looked when he should have swollen, or fallen down dead suddenly: but after they had looked a great while, and saw no harm come to him, they changed their minds, and said that he was a god" (Acts 28:5-6).

2. Paul and Publius (28:7-10)

a. Healing his father (28:8)— "And it came to pass, that the father of Publius lay sick of a fever and of a bloody flux: to whom Paul entered in, and prayed, and laid his hands on him, and healed him" (Acts 28:8).

b. Healing his friends (28:9)

D. Phase 4: From Melita to Rome (28:11-15)

X. His first Roman imprisonment (Acts 28:16-31)

A. The two meetings, during which the gospel was explained to the Roman Jews (28:17-29)

1. First meeting (28:17-22)

a. The review of the apostle: He gave them the background for his appearing there in chains (28:17-20).

b. The reaction of the audience (28:21-22)—"And they said unto him, We neither received letters out of Judaea concerning thee, neither any of the brethren that came shewed or spake any harm of thee. But we desire to hear of thee what thou thinkest: for as concerning this sect, we know that every where it is spoken against" (Acts 28:21-22).

2. Second meeting (28:23-29)

a. The sermon of God expounded—"And when they had appointed him a day, there came many to him into his lodging; to whom he expounded and testified the kingdom of God, persuading them concerning Jesus, both out of the law of Moses, and out of the prophets, from morning till evening. And some believed the things which were spoken, and some believed not" (Acts 28:23-24).

b. The Scriptures of God employed—"And when they agreed not among themselves, they departed, after that Paul had spoken one word, Well spake the Holy Ghost by Esaias the prophet unto our fathers, saying, Go unto this people, and say, Hearing ye shall hear, and shall not understand; and seeing ye shall see, and not perceive" (Acts 28:25-26).

c. The salvation of God expanded—"Be it known therefore unto you, that the salvation of God is sent unto the Gentiles, and that they will hear it" (Acts 28:28).

B. The two years, during which the gospel was explained to all (28:30-31)—"And Paul dwelt two whole years in his own hired house, and received all that came in unto him, preaching the kingdom of God, and teaching those things which concern the Lord Jesus Christ, with all confidence, no man forbidding him" (Acts 28:30-31). Paul wrote Ephesians, Colossians, Philemon, and Philippians from Rome.

XI. His release—It is believed by most Bible students that Paul was released after the two-year period he spent in his Roman imprisonment. The apostle himself anticipated this release in the following verses: "That your rejoicing may be more abundant in Jesus Christ for me by my coming to you again" (Phil. 1:26). "But I trust in the Lord that I also myself shall come shortly" (Phil. 2:24). "But withal prepare me also a lodging: for I trust that through your prayers I shall be given unto you" (Philem. 22).

XII. His final missionary journey

A. At Ephesus (1 Tim. 1:3; 3:14-15)—Paul left Timothy to pastor the church in Ephesus.

B. In Macedonia (1 Tim. 1:3)—Paul wrote 1 Timothy from Macedonia.

C. Possibly in Spain, as indicated by his words in Romans 15:24, 28

D. At Crete (Titus 1:5)—Paul left Titus to oversee the church at Crete.

E. At Corinth (2 Tim. 4:20)—He left Erastus at Corinth. Paul wrote Titus from Corinth.

F. At Miletus (2 Tim. 4:20)—He left a friend named Trophimus sick at Miletus.

G. At Troas (2 Tim. 4:13)—"The cloak that I left at Troas with Carpus, when thou comest, bring with thee, and the books, but especially the parchments" (2 Tim. 4:13).

H. At Nicopolis (Titus 3:12)—Paul planned to spend the winter there. It was probably at Nicopolis where he was rearrested by the Roman officials and brought back to Rome.

XIII. His final Roman imprisonment

A. He wrote 2 Timothy.

B. He was abandoned by most of his friends, including Phygellus, Hermogenes, and Demas (2 Tim. 1:15; 4:10).

C. This occurred during his first trial (2 Tim. 4:16).

D. Only Onesiphorus, his family, and Luke remained true (2 Tim. 1:16; 4:11).

E. Paul requested that Timothy come to him soon, before winter if possible (2 Tim. 4:9, 21).

F. When he came, he was to bring John Mark with him, as well as his cloak and books (2 Tim. 4:13).

XIV. His death as a martyr for Christ—"For I am now ready to be offered, and the time of my departure is at hand. I have fought a good fight, I have finished my course, I have kept the faith: Henceforth there is laid up for me a crown of righteousness, which the Lord, the righteous judge, shall give me at that day: and not to me only, but unto all them also that love his appearing" (2 Tim. 4:6-8).

STATISTICS

Father: A Pharisee (Acts 23:6)
Sister: See Acts 23:16.
First mention: Saul (Acts 7:58); Paul (Acts 13:9)

Final mention: Saul (Acts 26:14); Paul (2 Pet. 3:15)
Meaning of his name: Saul means "one who asks"; Paul means "little, small."
Frequency of his name: Referred to 180 times: As Saul, 22 times; as Paul, 158 times
Biblical books mentioning him: 15 books (Acts, Romans, 1 Corinthians, 2 Corinthians, Galatians, Ephesians, Philippians, Colossians, 1 Thessalonians, 2 Thessalonians, 1 Timothy, 2 Timothy, Titus, Philemon, 2 Peter)
Occupation: Tentmaker and apostle to the Gentiles (Acts 18:1-3; Eph. 3:6-8)
Place of birth: The city of Tarsus, in Asia Minor (Acts 9:11; 22:3)
Place of death: Rome (2 Tim. 4:6-8)
Circumstances of death: He was killed by the sword.
Important fact about his life: He was the greatest missionary, church planter, soul winner, and theologian in church history; he wrote 13 (perhaps 14) of the 27 New Testament books.

Peter

(See also Part Two, Observations from the Life of Peter)

CHRONOLOGICAL SUMMARY

I. Peter, the unstable apostle
  A. The fisherman
    1. He was from the city of Bethsaida in Galilee (John 1:44).
    2. He was the brother of Andrew (John 1:40).
    3. He and Andrew were fishing partners with James and John (Matt. 4:21-22; Mark 1:19-20; Luke 5:10). "And so were also James and John, the sons of Zebedee, who were partners with Simon" (Luke 5:10).
    4. He was a married man (Matt. 8:14).
    5. He was brought to Christ by Andrew—"He first findeth his own brother Simon, and saith unto him, We have found the Messias, which is, being interpreted, the Christ" (John 1:41).
    6. His name was changed by Christ—"And he brought him to Jesus. And when Jesus beheld him, he said, Thou art Simon the son of Jona: thou shalt be called Cephas, which is by interpretation, A stone" (John 1:42). "And when it was day, he called unto him his disciples: and of them he chose twelve, whom also he named apostles; Simon, (whom he also named Peter,) and Andrew his brother, James and John, Philip and Bartholomew" (Luke 6:13-14).
    7. He was officially called into full-time service while fishing on the Sea of Galilee (Matt. 4:18-20; Mark 1:16-18; Luke 5:1-11).
      a. The request—"And he entered into one of the ships, which was Simon's, and prayed him that he would thrust out a little from the land. And he sat down, and taught the people out of the ship. Now when he had left speaking, he said unto Simon, Launch out into the deep, and let down your nets for a draught" (Luke 5:3-4).
      b. The reluctance—"And Simon answering said unto him, Master, we have toiled all the night, and have taken nothing: nevertheless at thy word I will let down the net" (Luke 5:5).
      c. The results—"And when they had this done, they inclosed a great multitude of fishes: and their net brake" (Luke 5:6).
      d. The remorse—"When Simon Peter saw it, he fell down at Jesus' knees, saying, Depart from me; for I am a sinful man, O Lord" (Luke 5:8).
      e. The reassurance—"And Jesus said unto Simon, Fear not; from henceforth thou shalt catch men" (Luke 5:10).
  B. The follower
    1. The event at Caesarea Philippi—Christ heard Peter's confession and

promised to build his (Christ's) church (Matt. 16:13-21; Mark 8:27-31; Luke 9:18-22).

a. The recognition by Peter—"When Jesus came into the coasts of Caesarea Philippi, he asked his disciples, saying, Whom do men say that I the Son of man am? And they said, Some say that thou art John the Baptist: some, Elias; and others, Jeremias, or one of the prophets. He saith unto them, But whom say ye that I am? And Simon Peter answered and said, Thou art the Christ, the Son of the living God" (Matt. 16:13-16).

b. The revelation to Peter—"And Jesus answered and said unto him, Blessed art thou, Simon Bar-jona: for flesh and blood hath not revealed it unto thee, but my Father which is in heaven. And I say also unto thee, That thou art Peter, and upon this rock I will build my church; and the gates of hell shall not prevail against it. And I will give unto thee the keys of the kingdom of heaven: and whatsoever thou shalt bind on earth shall be bound in heaven: and whatsoever thou shalt loose on earth shall be loosed in heaven" (Matt. 16:17-19).

c. The rebuke of Peter—"From that time forth began Jesus to shew unto his disciples, how that he must go unto Jerusalem, and suffer many things of the elders and chief priests and scribes, and be killed, and be raised again the third day. Then Peter took him, and began to rebuke him, saying, Be it far from thee, Lord: this shall not be unto thee. But he turned, and said unto Peter, Get thee behind me, Satan: thou art an offence unto me: for thou savourest not the things that be of God, but those that be of men" (Matt. 16:21-23).

2. The event on Mount Hermon—Peter was present when Christ was transfigured (Matt. 17:1-8; Mark 9:2-8; Luke 9:28-36).

a. The prophecy—"Verily I say unto you, There be some standing here, which shall not taste of death, till they see the Son of man coming in his kingdom" (Matt. 16:28).

b. The personalities

(1) The Savior—"And was transfigured before them: and his face did shine as the sun, and his raiment was white as the light" (Matt. 17:2).

(2) The Father

(3) Moses and Elijah

(4) Peter, James, and John

c. The particulars

(1) The heavenly conversation—"And, behold, there talked with him two men, which were Moses and Elias: who appeared in glory, and spake of his decease which he should accomplish at Jerusalem" (Luke 9:30-31).

(2) The earthly conversation

(a) Peter's foolish talk—"And it came to pass, as they departed from him, Peter said unto Jesus, Master, it is good for us to be here: and let us make three tabernacles; one for thee, and one for Moses, and one for Elias: not knowing what he said" (Luke 9:33).

(b) Peter's fearful talk—"For he wist not what to say; for they were sore afraid" (Mark 9:6).

d. The pronouncement—"While he yet spake, behold, a bright cloud overshadowed them: and behold a voice out of the cloud, which said, This is my beloved Son, in whom I am well pleased; hear ye him" (Matt. 17:5).

3. The event on the Sea of Galilee—Peter was allowed to walk on the water (Matt. 14:28-33).
   a. His request
      (1) Bid me!—"And Peter answered him and said, Lord, if it be thou, bid me come unto thee on the water. And he said, Come. And when Peter was come down out of the ship, he walked on the water, to go to Jesus" (Matt. 14:28-29).
      (2) Save me!—"But when he saw the wind boisterous, he was afraid; and beginning to sink, he cried, saying, Lord, save me" (Matt. 14:30).
   b. His rescue—"And immediately Jesus stretched forth his hand, and caught him, and said unto him, O thou of little faith, wherefore didst thou doubt?" (Matt. 14:31).
4. The events in Capernaum
   a. At Christ's command, he caught a fish with a coin in its mouth (Matt. 17:24-27).
      (1) The tax—"And when they were come to Capernaum, they that received tribute money came to Peter, and said, Doth not your master pay tribute?" (Matt. 17:24).
      (2) The truth—"He saith, Yes. And when he was come into the house, Jesus prevented him, saying, What thinkest thou, Simon? of whom do the kings of the earth take custom or tribute? of their own children, or of strangers? Peter saith unto him, Of strangers. Jesus saith unto him, Then are the children free" (Matt. 17:25-26).
      (3) The testimony—"Notwithstanding, lest we should offend them, go thou to the sea, and cast an hook, and take up the fish that first cometh up; and when thou hast opened his mouth, thou shalt find a piece of money: that take, and give unto them for me and thee" (Matt. 17:27).
   b. Peter learned about forgiveness (Matt. 18:21-22).
      (1) The confusion—"Then came Peter to him, and said, Lord, how oft shall my brother sin against me, and I forgive him? till seven times?" (Matt. 18:21).
      (2) The clarification—"Jesus saith unto him, I say not unto thee, Until seven times: but, Until seventy times seven" (Matt. 18:22).
   c. Peter was present at the raising of Jairus's daughter by the Lord. Only he, along with James and John, were allowed in the house (Mark 5:37; Luke 8:51).
   d. Peter responded to Christ's question asked during the healing of a sick woman (Luke 8:43-46).
      (1) The cause for the question—"And a woman having an issue of blood twelve years, which had spent all her living upon physicians, neither could be healed of any, came behind him, and touched the border of his garment: and immediately her issue of blood stanched" (Luke 8:43-44).
      (2) The comment on the question—"And Jesus said, Who touched me? When all denied, Peter and they that were with him said, Master, the multitude throng thee and press thee, and sayest thou, Who touched me? And Jesus

said, Somebody hath touched me: for I perceive that virtue is gone out of me" (Luke 8:45-46).

e. Peter asked Christ to explain the parable of the faithful servant (Luke 12:35-41).

f. Peter responded to Christ's question concerning discipleship (John 6:66-69).

(1) The faithless ones—"From that time many of his disciples went back, and walked no more with him. Then said Jesus unto the twelve, Will ye also go away?" (John 6:66-67).

(2) The faithful ones—"Then Simon Peter answered him, Lord, to whom shall we go? thou hast the words of eternal life. And we believe and are sure that thou art that Christ, the Son of the living God" (John 6:68-69).

5. The events in Jerusalem

a. Peter asked about future rewards (Matt. 19:27-30; Mark 10:28-31; Luke 18:28-30).

(1) What he had renounced for Christ—"Then answered Peter and said unto him, Behold, we have forsaken all, and followed thee; what shall we have therefore?" (Matt. 19:27).

(2) What he would receive from Christ—"And Jesus said unto them, Verily I say unto you, That ye which have followed me, in the regeneration when the Son of man shall sit in the throne of his glory, ye also shall sit upon twelve thrones, judging the twelve tribes of Israel. And every one that hath forsaken houses, or brethren, or sisters, or father, or mother, or wife, or children, or lands, for my name's sake, shall receive an hundredfold, and shall inherit everlasting life" (Matt. 19:28-29).

b. Peter commented on the miracle of the withered fig tree and learned about faith (Mark 11:20-24).

c. Peter, James, and John asked Christ concerning the prophecy of the destruction of Jerusalem (Mark 13:3-4).

C. The foolish

1. At Bethany (Matt. 26:17-19; Mark 14:12-16; Luke 22:8-13)

a. The mission—"And he sent Peter and John, saying, Go and prepare us the passover, that we may eat. And they said unto him, Where wilt thou that we prepare?" (Luke 22:8-9).

b. The man—"And he said unto them, Behold, when ye are entered into the city, there shall a man meet you, bearing a pitcher of water; follow him into the house where he entereth in. And ye shall say unto the goodman of the house, The Master saith unto thee, Where is the guestchamber, where I shall eat the passover with my disciples? And he shall shew you a large upper room furnished: there make ready. And they went, and found as he had said unto them: and they made ready the passover" (Luke 22:10-13).

2. In the upper room (John 13)

a. He had his feet washed by Christ (John 13:5-10).

(1) Lagging behind in the will of God—"Then cometh he to Simon Peter: and Peter saith unto him, Lord, dost thou wash my feet? Jesus answered and said unto him, What I do thou knowest not now; but thou shalt know hereafter. Peter saith unto him, Thou shalt never wash my feet. Jesus answered him,

If I wash thee not, thou hast no part with me" (John 13:6-8).

(2) Lunging ahead in the will of God—"Simon Peter saith unto him, Lord, not my feet only, but also my hands and my head. Jesus saith to him, He that is washed needeth not save to wash his feet, but is clean every whit: and ye are clean, but not all" (John 13:9-10).

b. He signaled for John to ask Christ concerning the identity of the betrayer (John 13:21-26)—"Now there was leaning on Jesus' bosom one of his disciples, whom Jesus loved. Simon Peter therefore beckoned to him, that he should ask who it should be of whom he spake. He then lying on Jesus' breast saith unto him, Lord, who is it? Jesus answered, he it is, to whom I shall give a sop, when I have dipped it. And when he had dipped the sop, he gave it to Judas Iscariot, the son of Simon" (John 13:23-26).

c. He was warned by Christ for the first time concerning his future denials (John 13:36-38)—"Simon Peter said unto him, Lord, whither goest thou? Jesus answered him, Whither I go, thou canst not follow me now; but thou shalt follow me afterwards. Peter said unto him, Lord, why cannot I follow thee now? I will lay down my life for thy sake. Jesus answered him, Wilt thou lay down thy life for my sake? Verily, verily, I say unto thee, The cock shall not crow, till thou hast denied me thrice" (John 13:36-38).

3. At the Mount of Olives (Matt. 26:30-35; Mark 14:26-31)—He was warned by Christ for the second time concerning his future denials.

4. In Gethsemane

a. He was asked by Christ on three occasions to watch and pray (Matt. 26:36-38; Mark 14:32-33; Luke 22:40). "Then cometh Jesus with them unto a place called Gethsemane, and saith unto the disciples, Sit ye here, while I go and pray yonder. And he took with him Peter and the two sons of Zebedee, and began to be sorrowful and very heavy. Then saith he unto them, My soul is exceeding sorrowful, even unto death: tarry ye here, and watch with me" (Matt. 26:36-38).

b. He fell asleep on all three occasions (Matt. 26:40-46; Mark 14:34-42; Luke 22:45-46)—"And he cometh unto the disciples, and findeth them asleep, and saith unto Peter, What, could ye not watch with me one hour? Watch and pray, that ye enter not into temptation: the spirit indeed is willing, but the flesh is weak. And he came and found them asleep again: for their eyes were heavy. . . . Then cometh he to his disciples, and saith unto them, Sleep on now, and take your rest: behold, the hour is at hand, and the Son of man is betrayed into the hands of sinners" (Matt. 26:40-41, 43, 45).

c. He cut off the ear of Malchus, servant to the Jewish high priest (Matt. 26:51; Mark 14:47; Luke 22:50; John 18:10-11).

(1) The reason for Peter's rash act—"Rise up, let us go; lo, he that betrayeth me is at hand. And immediately, while he yet spake, cometh Judas, one of the twelve, and with him a great multitude with swords

and staves, from the chief priests and the scribes and the elders" (Mark 14:42-43).

(2) The rebuke of Peter's rash act—"Then said Jesus unto him, Put up again thy sword into his place: for all they that take the sword shall perish with the sword. Thinkest thou that I cannot now pray to my Father, and he shall presently give me more than twelve legions of angels?" (Matt. 26:52-53).

D. The frightened

1. He fled and followed Christ afar off (Matt. 26:56-58; Mark 14:50, 53-54; Luke 22:54; John 18:15).
2. He warmed himself outside the Sanhedrin court (Mark 14:54; Luke 22:55).
3. He denied Christ three times (Matt. 26:69-74; Mark 14:66-72; Luke 22:56-60; John 18:16-18, 25-27)—"Now Peter sat without in the palace: and a damsel came unto him, saying, Thou also wast with Jesus of Galilee. But he denied before them all, saying, I know not what thou sayest. And when he was gone out into the porch, another maid saw him, and said unto them that were there, This fellow was also with Jesus of Nazareth. And again he denied with an oath, I do not know the man. And after a while came unto him they that stood by, and said to Peter, Surely thou also art one of them; for thy speech bewrayeth thee. Then began he to curse and to swear, saying, I know not the man. And immediately the cock crew" (Matt. 26:69-74).
4. He was looked upon by Christ—"And the Lord turned, and looked upon Peter. And Peter remembered the word of the Lord, how he had said unto him, Before the cock crow, thou shalt deny me thrice" (Luke 22:61).
5. He went out and wept (Matt. 26:75; Mark 14:72; Luke 22:62). "And Peter went out, and wept bitterly" (Luke 22:62).

E. The favored—Of all the apostles, Peter alone experienced a personal post-resurrection appearance of Christ himself (Luke 24:34; 1 Cor. 15:5).

1. The report of Mary—"The first day of the week cometh Mary Magdalene early, when it was yet dark, unto the sepulchre, and seeth the stone taken away from the sepulchre. Then she runneth, and cometh to Simon Peter, and to the other disciple, whom Jesus loved, and saith unto them, They have taken away the Lord out of the sepulchre, and we know not where they have laid him" (John 20:1-2).
2. The reaction of Peter—"Peter therefore went forth, and that other disciple, and came to the sepulchre. So they ran both together: and the other disciple did outrun Peter, and came first to the sepulchre. And he stooping down, and looking in, saw the linen clothes lying; yet went he not in. Then cometh Simon Peter following him, and went into the sepulchre, and seeth the linen clothes lie, and the napkin, that was about his head, not lying with the linen clothes, but wrapped together in a place by itself" (John 20:3-7).
3. The revelation of Christ—"Saying, The Lord is risen indeed, and hath appeared to Simon" (Luke 24:34). "And that he was seen of Cephas, then of the twelve" (1 Cor. 15:5).

F. The forgiven (John 21)

1. Peter and the fishermen—"There were together Simon Peter, and Thomas called Didymus, and Nathanael of Cana in Galilee, and the sons of Zebedee, and two other of his disciples. Simon Peter saith unto them, I go a fishing. They say unto him, We also go with thee.

They went forth, and entered into a ship immediately; and that night they caught nothing" (John 21:2-3).

2. Peter and the fisher of men—"But when the morning was now come, Jesus stood on the shore: but the disciples knew not that it was Jesus" (John 21:4).
   a. The call—"Then Jesus saith unto them, Children, have ye any meat? They answered him, No" (John 21:5).
   b. The command—"And he said unto them, Cast the net on the right side of the ship, and ye shall find. They cast therefore, and now they were not able to draw it for the multitude of fishes" (John 21:6).
   c. The commitment—"Therefore that disciple whom Jesus loved saith unto Peter, It is the Lord. Now when Simon Peter heard that it was the Lord, he girt his fisher's coat unto him, (for he was naked,) and did cast himself into the sea" (John 21:7).
   d. The communion—"Simon Peter went up, and drew the net to land full of great fishes, an hundred and fifty and three: and for all there were so many, yet was not the net broken. Jesus saith unto them, Come and dine. And none of the disciples durst ask him, Who art thou? knowing that it was the Lord. Jesus then cometh, and taketh bread, and giveth them, and fish likewise" (John 21:11-13).
   e. The confession—"So when they had dined, Jesus saith to Simon Peter, Simon, son of Jonas, lovest thou me more than these? He saith unto him, Yea, Lord; thou knowest that I love thee. He saith unto him, Feed my lambs. He saith to him again the second time, Simon, son of Jonas, lovest thou me? He saith unto him, Yea, Lord; thou knowest that I love thee. He saith unto him, Feed my sheep. He saith unto him the third time, Simon, son of Jonas, lovest thou me? Peter was grieved because he said unto him the third time, Lovest thou me? And he said unto him, Lord, thou knowest all things; thou knowest that I love thee. Jesus saith unto him, Feed my sheep" (John 21:15-17).
   f. The cross—"Verily, verily, I say unto thee, When thou wast young, thou girdedst thyself, and walkedst whither thou wouldest: but when thou shalt be old, thou shalt stretch forth thy hands, and another shall gird thee, and carry thee whither thou wouldest not. This spake he, signifying by what death he should glorify God. And when he had spoken this, he saith unto him, Follow me" (John 21:18-19).
   g. The confusion—"Then Peter, turning about, seeth the disciple whom Jesus loved following; which also leaned on his breast at supper, and said, Lord, which is he that betrayeth thee? Peter seeing him saith to Jesus, Lord, and what shall this man do? Jesus saith unto him, If I will that he tarry till I come, what is that to thee? follow thou me. Then went this saying abroad among the brethren, that that disciple should not die: yet Jesus said not unto him, He shall not die; but, If I will that he tarry till I come, what is that to thee?" (John 21:20-23).

II. Peter, the unshakable apostle—His witnessing for Christ (as seen in the book of Acts)
  A. Peter and the 120 (Acts 1:1-26)
    1. On the Mount of Olives (Acts 1:1-12)
      a. Receiving the assurance from Christ
        (1) The confusion—"When they therefore were come together,

they asked of him, saying, Lord, wilt thou at this time restore again the kingdom to Israel?" (Acts 1:6).

(2) The commission—"And he said unto them, It is not for you to know the times or the seasons, which the Father hath put in his own power. But ye shall receive power, after that the Holy Ghost is come upon you: and ye shall be witnesses unto me both in Jerusalem, and in all Judaea, and in Samaria, and unto the uttermost part of the earth" (Acts 1:7-8).

b. Witnessing the ascension of Christ

(1) The action—"And when he had spoken these things, while they beheld, he was taken up; and a cloud received him out of their sight" (Acts 1:9).

(2) The attendants—"And while they looked stedfastly toward heaven as he went up, behold, two men stood by them in white apparel" (Acts 1:10).

(3) The announcement—"Which also said, Ye men of Galilee, why stand ye gazing up into heaven? this same Jesus, which is taken up from you into heaven, shall so come in like manner as ye have seen him go into heaven" (Acts 1:11).

2. In the upper room (Acts 1:13-26)

a. The prayer meeting (Acts 1:13-14)—"These all continued with one accord in prayer and supplication, with the women, and Mary the mother of Jesus, and with his brethren" (Acts 1:14).

b. The business meeting (Acts 1:15-26)

(1) Concerning the defection of Judas (Acts 1:15-20)—"For he was numbered with us, and had obtained part of this ministry. . . . For it is written in the book of Psalms, Let his habitation be desolate, and let no man dwell therein: and his bishoprick let another take" (Acts 1:17, 20).

(2) Concerning the election of Matthias (Acts 1:21-26)—"And they prayed, and said, Thou, Lord, which knowest the hearts of all men, shew whether of these two thou hast chosen. . . . And they gave forth their lots; and the lot fell upon Matthias; and he was numbered with the eleven apostles" (Acts 1:24, 26).

B. Peter and the crowd at Pentecost (Acts 2:1-47)

1. The cloven tongues (Acts 2:1-4)—"And there appeared unto them cloven tongues like as of fire, and it sat upon each of them. And they were all filled with the Holy Ghost, and began to speak with other tongues, as the Spirit gave them utterance" (Acts 2:3-4).

2. The congregation (Acts 2:5-11)—"And they were all amazed and marvelled, saying one to another, Behold, are not all these which speak Galilaeans? And how hear we every man in our own tongue, wherein we were born?" (Acts 2:7-8).

3. The confusion (Acts 2:12-13)—"And they were all amazed, and were in doubt, saying one to another, What meaneth this? Others mocking said, These men are full of new wine" (Acts 2:12-13).

4. The clarification (Acts 2:14-15)—"For these are not drunken, as ye suppose, seeing it is but the third hour of the day" (Acts 2:15).

5. The comparison (Acts 2:16-21)

a. The Old Testament prophet—"But this is that which was spoken by the prophet Joel" (Acts 2:16).
b. The Old Testament prophecy—"And it shall come to pass in the last days, saith God, I will pour out of my Spirit upon all flesh: and your sons and your daughters shall prophesy, and your young men shall see visions, and your old men shall dream dreams: and on my servants and on my handmaidens I will pour out in those days of my Spirit; and they shall prophesy: and I will shew wonders in heaven above, and signs in the earth beneath; blood, and fire, and vapour of smoke: The sun shall be turned into darkness, and the moon into blood, before that great and notable day of the Lord come: And it shall come to pass, that whosoever shall call on the name of the Lord shall be saved" (Acts 2:17-21).

6. The condemnation (Acts 2:22-28)
   a. The Messiah had been crucified by his foes (Acts 2:22-24)—"Him, being delivered by the determinate counsel and foreknowledge of God, ye have taken, and by wicked hands have crucified and slain" (Acts 2:23).
   b. The Messiah had been resurrected by his Father (Acts 2:24)—"Whom God hath raised up, having loosed the pains of death: because it was not possible that he should be holden of it" (Acts 2:24).
7. The conclusion (Acts 2:29-36)—"This Jesus hath God raised up, whereof we all are witnesses. Therefore being by the right hand of God exalted, and having received of the Father the promise of the Holy Ghost, he hath shed forth this, which ye now see and hear. For David is not ascended into the heavens: but he saith himself, The LORD said unto my Lord, Sit thou on my right hand, until I make thy foes thy footstool. Therefore let all the house of Israel know assuredly, that God hath made that same Jesus, whom ye have crucified, both Lord and Christ" (Acts 2:32-36).
8. The conviction (Acts 2:37)—"Now when they heard this, they were pricked in their heart, and said unto Peter and to the rest of the apostles, Men and brethren, what shall we do?" (Acts 2:37).
9. The command—"Then Peter said unto them, Repent, and be baptized every one of you in the name of Jesus Christ for the remission of sins, and ye shall receive the gift of the Holy Ghost. For the promise is unto you, and to your children, and to all that are afar off, even as many as the Lord our God shall call" (Acts 2:38-39).
10. The conversions (Acts 2:41)—"Then they that gladly received his word were baptized: and the same day there were added unto them about three thousand souls" (Acts 2:41).
11. The communion (Acts 2:42-47)—"And they continued stedfastly in the apostles' doctrine and fellowship, and in breaking of bread, and in prayers. . . . And all that believed were together, and had all things common" (Acts 2:42, 44).

C. Peter and the lame man (Acts 3:1-26)
   1. The miracle (Acts 3:1-11)
      a. The need for the healing—"And a certain man lame from his mother's womb was carried, whom they laid daily at the gate of the temple which is called Beautiful, to ask alms of them that entered into the temple" (Acts 3:2).
      b. The name in the healing—"And Peter, fastening his eyes upon him with John, said, Look on us.

And he gave heed unto them, expecting to receive something of them. Then Peter said, Silver and gold have I none; but such as I have give I thee: In the name of Jesus Christ of Nazareth rise up and walk" (Acts 3:4-6).

c. The nature of the healing—"And he leaping up stood, and walked, and entered with them into the temple, walking, and leaping, and praising God" (Acts 3:8).

2. The message (Acts 3:12-26)—Peter delivered a powerful sermon on the cross.

a. The promoters of the cross—The Jewish leaders. "The God of Abraham, and of Isaac, and of Jacob, the God of our fathers, hath glorified his Son Jesus; whom ye delivered up, and denied him in the presence of Pilate, when he was determined to let him go. But ye denied the Holy One and the Just, and desired a murderer to be granted unto you; and killed the Prince of life, whom God hath raised from the dead; whereof we are witnesses" (Acts 3:13-15).

b. The prophecies about the cross—The Old Testament Scriptures. "But those things, which God before had shewed by the mouth of all his prophets, that Christ should suffer, he hath so fulfilled" (Acts 3:18).

c. The power of the cross (Acts 3:16, 26)

(1) It had healed the body of one man—"And his name through faith in his name hath made this man strong, whom ye see and know: yea, the faith which is by him hath given him this perfect soundness in the presence of you all" (Acts 3:16).

(2) It could heal the souls of all men—"Unto you first God, having raised up his Son Jesus, sent him to bless you, in turning away every one of you from his iniquities" (Acts 3:26).

d. The program of the cross (Acts 3:15, 18, 21)

(1) Christ would suffer and die (Acts 3:18).

(2) God would raise him from the dead (Acts 3:15).

(3) He would be taken up for awhile (Acts 3:21)—"Whom the heaven must receive until the times of restitution of all things, which God hath spoken by the mouth of all his holy prophets since the world began" (Acts 3:21).

(4) He will come again (Acts 3:19-20)—"Repent ye therefore, and be converted, that your sins may be blotted out, when the times of refreshing shall come from the presence of the Lord" (Acts 3:19).

e. The plea of the cross (Acts 3:19, 26)—"Unto you first God, having raised up his Son Jesus, sent him to bless you, in turning away every one of you from his iniquities" (Acts 3:26).

D. Peter and the high priest (Acts 4:1-37)—Annas, the Jewish high priest, had Peter and John arrested.

1. The reason for the arrest—"Being grieved that they taught the people, and preached through Jesus the resurrection from the dead" (Acts 4:2).

2. The evidence supporting the arrest—"Howbeit many of them which heard the word believed; and the number of the men was about five thousand" (Acts 4:4).

3. The dialogue in the arrest

a. Their question—"And when they had set them in the midst, they asked, By what power, or by what name, have ye done this?" (Acts 4:7).

b. Peter's answer (Acts 4:8-12)—"Be it known unto you all, and to all the people of Israel, that by the name of Jesus Christ of Nazareth, whom ye crucified, whom God raised from the dead, even by him doth this man stand here before you whole. . . . Neither is there salvation in any other: for there is none other name under heaven given among men, whereby we must be saved" (Acts 4:10, 12).

4. The conference during the arrest (Acts 4:13-17)—"Now when they saw the boldness of Peter and John, and perceived that they were unlearned and ignorant men, they marvelled; and they took knowledge of them, that they had been with Jesus. And beholding the man which was healed standing with them, they could say nothing against it. But when they had commanded them to go aside out of the council, they conferred among themselves, saying, What shall we do to these men? for that indeed a notable miracle hath been done by them is manifest to all them that dwell in Jerusalem; and we cannot deny it" (Acts 4:13-16).

5. The warning accompanying the arrest (Acts 4:18-22)
   a. You can't continue—"And they called them, and commanded them not to speak at all nor teach in the name of Jesus" (Acts 4:18).
   b. We must continue—"But Peter and John answered and said unto them, Whether it be right in the sight of God to hearken unto you more than unto God, judge ye. For we cannot but speak the things which we have seen and heard" (Acts 4:19-20).

6. The praise service following the arrest (Acts 4:23-30)—"And being let go, they went to their own company, and reported all that the chief priests and elders had said unto them. And when they heard that, they lifted up their voice to God with one accord, and said, Lord, thou art God, which hast made heaven, and earth, and the sea, and all that in them is. . . . And now, Lord, behold their threatenings: and grant unto thy servants, that with all boldness they may speak thy word" (Acts 4:23-24, 29).

7. The blessings resulting from the arrest (Acts 4:31-37)
   a. The believers were filled with the Spirit of God—"And when they had prayed, the place was shaken where they were assembled together; and they were all filled with the Holy Ghost, and they spake the word of God with boldness" (Acts 4:31).
   b. The brotherhood was supplied by the grace of God—"And the multitude of them that believed were of one heart and of one soul: neither said any of them that ought of the things which he possessed was his own; but they had all things common. . . . Neither was there any among them that lacked: for as many as were possessors of lands or houses sold them, and brought the prices of the things that were sold, and laid them down at the apostles' feet: and distribution was made unto every man according as he had need" (Acts 4:32, 34-35).
   c. Among those who sacrificed this way was Barnabas (Acts 4:36).

E. Peter and Ananias and Sapphira (Acts 5:1-11)

1. Their deception—"But a certain man named Ananias, with Sapphira his wife, sold a possession, and kept back part of the price, his wife also being privy to it, and brought a certain part, and laid it at the apostles' feet" (Acts 5:1-2).

2. Their discovery—"But Peter said, Ananias, why hath Satan filled thine

heart to lie to the Holy Ghost, and to keep back part of the price of the land? Whiles it remained, was it not thine own? and after it was sold, was it not in thine own power? why hast thou conceived this thing in thine heart? thou hast not lied unto men, but unto God" (Acts 5:3-4).

3. Their deaths—"And Ananias hearing these words fell down, and gave up the ghost: and great fear came on all them that heard these things. . . . Then fell she down straightway at his feet, and yielded up the ghost: and the young men came in, and found her dead, and, carrying her forth, buried her by her husband" (Acts 5:5, 10).

F. Peter and the sick (Acts 5:12-16)—"Insomuch that they brought forth the sick into the streets, and laid them on beds and couches, that at the least the shadow of Peter passing by might overshadow some of them. There came also a multitude out of the cities round about unto Jerusalem, bringing sick folks, and them which were vexed with unclean spirits: and they were healed every one" (Acts 5:15-16).

G. Peter and the lawyer Gamaliel (Acts 5:17-42)—For the second time Peter was arrested for preaching Christ.

1. The anger of the Sadducees (Acts 5:17-18)
2. The appearance of the Lord—"But the angel of the Lord by night opened the prison doors, and brought them forth, and said, Go, stand and speak in the temple to the people all the words of this life" (Acts 5:19-20).
3. The astonishment of the jailers (Acts 5:21-26)—"But when the officers came, and found them not in the prison, they returned, and told, saying, The prison truly found we shut with all safety, and the keepers standing without before the doors: but when we had opened, we found no man within. . . . Then came one and told them, saying, Behold, the men whom ye put in prison are standing in the temple, and teaching the people" (Acts 5:22-23, 25).
4. The address of Peter (Acts 5:27-32)—"The God of our fathers raised up Jesus, whom ye slew and hanged on a tree. Him hath God exalted with his right hand to be a Prince and a Saviour, for to give repentance to Israel, and forgiveness of sins. And we are his witnesses of these things; and so is also the Holy Ghost, whom God hath given to them that obey him" (Acts 5:30-32).
5. The advice of Gamaliel (Acts 5:33-39)—"And now I say unto you, Refrain from these men, and let them alone: for if this counsel or this work be of men, it will come to nought: but if it be of God, ye cannot overthrow it; lest haply ye be found even to fight against God" (Acts 5:38-39).
6. The attitude of the apostles (Acts 5:40-42)
   a. Their pain—"And to him they agreed: and when they had called the apostles, and beaten them, they commanded that they should not speak in the name of Jesus, and let them go" (Acts 5:40).
   b. Their praise—"And they departed from the presence of the council, rejoicing that they were counted worthy to suffer shame for his name" (Acts 5:41).
   c. Their persistence—"And daily in the temple, and in every house, they ceased not to teach and preach Jesus Christ" (Acts 5:42).

H. Peter and Simon the sorcerer (Acts 8:9-25)

1. His pride (Acts 8:9-11)—"But there was a certain man, called Simon, which beforetime in the same city used sorcery, and bewitched the people of Samaria, giving out that himself was some great one" (Acts 8:9).

2. His perversion—"And when Simon saw that through laying on of the apostles' hands the Holy Ghost was given, he offered them money, saying, Give me also this power, that on whomsoever I lay hands, he may receive the Holy Ghost" (Acts 8:18-19).
3. His punishment—"But Peter said unto him, Thy money perish with thee, because thou hast thought that the gift of God may be purchased with money. Thou hast neither part nor lot in this matter: for thy heart is not right in the sight of God" (Acts 8:20-21).
4. His plea—"Then answered Simon, and said, Pray ye to the Lord for me, that none of these things which ye have spoken come upon me" (Acts 8:24).

I. Peter and Aeneas (Acts 9:32-35)
1. The misery—"And it came to pass, as Peter passed throughout all quarters, he came down also to the saints which dwelt at Lydda. And there he found a certain man named Aeneas, which had kept his bed eight years, and was sick of the palsy" (Acts 9:32-33).
2. The miracle—"And Peter said unto him, Aeneas, Jesus Christ maketh thee whole: arise, and make thy bed. And he arose immediately" (Acts 9:34).

J. Peter and Dorcas (Acts 9:36-42)
1. The deeds of Dorcas—"Now there was at Joppa a certain disciple named Tabitha, which by interpretation is called Dorcas: this woman was full of good works and almsdeeds which she did" (Acts 9:36).
2. The death of Dorcas—"And it came to pass in those days, that she was sick, and died: whom when they had washed, they laid her in an upper chamber" (Acts 9:37).
3. The deliverance of Dorcas
   a. The call for Peter—"And forasmuch as Lydda was nigh to Joppa, and the disciples had heard that Peter was there, they sent unto him two men, desiring him that he would not delay to come to them. Then Peter arose and went with them. When he was come, they brought him into the upper chamber: and all the widows stood by him weeping, and shewing the coats and garments which Dorcas made, while she was with them" (Acts 9:38-39).
   b. The command of Peter—"But Peter put them all forth, and kneeled down, and prayed; and turning him to the body said, Tabitha, arise. And she opened her eyes: and when she saw Peter, she sat up. And he gave her his hand, and lifted her up, and when he had called the saints and widows, presented her alive" (Acts 9:40-41).

K. Peter and Cornelius (Acts 9:43–10:48)
1. Cornelius—A religious sinner in Caesarea (Acts 10:1-8)
   a. His veneration for God (Acts 10:1-2)—"There was a certain man in Caesarea called Cornelius, a centurion of the band called the Italian band, a devout man, and one that feared God with all his house, which gave much alms to the people, and prayed to God alway" (Acts 10:1-2).
   b. His visitation from God (Acts 10:3-8)
      (1) The messenger—"He saw in a vision evidently about the ninth hour of the day an angel of God coming in to him, and saying unto him, Cornelius. And when he looked on him, he was afraid, and said, What is it, Lord? And he said unto him, Thy prayers and thine alms are

come up for a memorial before God" (Acts 10:3-4).

(2) The message—"And now send men to Joppa, and call for one Simon, whose surname is Peter: He lodgeth with one Simon a tanner, whose house is by the sea side: he shall tell thee what thou oughtest to do" (Acts 10:5-6).

2. Peter—A reluctant soul winner in Joppa (Acts 10:9-23). "On the morrow, as they went on their journey, and drew nigh unto the city, Peter went up upon the housetop to pray about the sixth hour: And he became very hungry, and would have eaten: but while they made ready, he fell into a trance" (Acts 10:9-10).

a. The message of the trance (Acts 10:11-14)—"And saw heaven opened, and a certain vessel descending unto him, as it had been a great sheet knit at the four corners, and let down to the earth: wherein were all manner of fourfooted beasts of the earth, and wild beasts, and creeping things, and fowls of the air. And there came a voice to him, Rise, Peter; kill, and eat. But Peter said, Not so, Lord; for I have never eaten any thing that is common or unclean" (Acts 10:11-14).

b. The meaning of the trance (Acts 10:15-23)—"And the voice spake unto him again the second time, What God hath cleansed, that call not thou common. This was done thrice: and the vessel was received up again into heaven. Now while Peter doubted in himself what this vision which he had seen should mean, behold, the men which were sent from Cornelius had made enquiry for Simon's house, and stood before the gate. . . . While Peter thought on the vision, the Spirit said unto him, Behold, three men seek thee. Arise therefore, and get thee down, and go with them, doubting nothing: for I have sent them" (Acts 10:15-17, 19-20).

3. Peter and Cornelius—Redeemed saints in Christ (Acts 10:24-48)

a. The conversation with Cornelius (Acts 10:24-35)

(1) The reception—"And as Peter was coming in, Cornelius met him, and fell down at his feet, and worshipped him. But Peter took him up, saying, Stand up; I myself also am a man" (Acts 10:25-26).

(2) The perception—"And he said unto them, Ye know how that it is an unlawful thing for a man that is a Jew to keep company, or come unto one of another nation; but God hath shewed me that I should not call any man common or unclean. . . . Then Peter opened his mouth, and said, Of a truth I perceive that God is no respecter of persons: But in every nation he that feareth him, and worketh righteousness, is accepted with him" (Acts 10:28, 34-35).

b. The clarification to Cornelius (Acts 10:36-43)—Peter's sermon

(1) He talked about the Word of God—"The word which God sent unto the children of Israel, preaching peace by Jesus Christ: (he is Lord of all:) That word, I say, ye know, which was published throughout all Judaea, and began from Galilee, after the baptism which John preached" (Acts 10:36-37).

(2) He talked about the work of God—"How God anointed Jesus of Nazareth with the Holy Ghost and with power:

who went about doing good, and healing all that were oppressed of the devil; for God was with him" (Acts 10:38).

(3) He talked about the witness of God—"And we are witnesses of all things which he did both in the land of the Jews, and in Jerusalem; whom they slew and hanged on a tree: him God raised up the third day, and shewed him openly; not to all the people, but unto witnesses chosen before of God, even to us, who did eat and drink with him after he rose from the dead" (Acts 10:39-41).

(4) He talked about the will of God—"And he commanded us to preach unto the people, and to testify that it is he which was ordained of God to be the Judge of quick and dead. To him give all the prophets witness, that through his name whosoever believeth in him shall receive remission of sins" (Acts 10:42-43).

c. The conversion of Cornelius (Acts 10:44-48)

(1) The divine baptizer—"While Peter yet spake these words, the Holy Ghost fell on all them which heard the word. And they of the circumcision which believed were astonished, as many as came with Peter, because that on the Gentiles also was poured out the gift of the Holy Ghost" (Acts 10:44-45).

(2) The human baptizer—"For they heard them speak with tongues, and magnify God. They answered Peter, Can any man forbid water, that these should not be baptized, which have received the Holy Ghost as well as we? And he commanded them to be baptized in the name of the Lord. Then prayed they him to tarry certain days" (Acts 10:46-48).

L. Peter and the Jewish believers at Jerusalem (Acts 11:1-18)

1. The accusation (Acts 11:1-3)—"And when Peter was come up to Jerusalem, they that were of the circumcision contended with him, saying, Thou wentest in to men uncircumcised, and didst eat with them" (Acts 11:2-3).

2. The argument (Acts 11:4-17)

a. Peter presented his case—"But Peter rehearsed the matter from the beginning, and expounded it by order unto them, saying. . . . And as I began to speak, the Holy Ghost fell on them, as on us at the beginning. Then remembered I the word of the Lord, how that he said, John indeed baptized with water; but ye shall be baptized with the Holy Ghost" (Acts 11:4, 15-16).

b. Peter presented his conclusion—"Forasmuch then as God gave them the like gift as he did unto us, who believed on the Lord Jesus Christ; what was I, that I could withstand God?" (Acts 11:17).

3. The acceptance—"When they heard these things, they held their peace, and glorified God, saying, Then hath God also to the Gentiles granted repentance unto life" (Acts 11:18).

M. Peter and the angel of the Lord (Acts 12:1-17)

1. The success of Peter in escaping a prison house—"Peter therefore was kept in prison: but prayer was made without ceasing of the church unto God for him. And when Herod would have brought him forth, the same night Peter was sleeping

between two soldiers, bound with two chains: and the keepers before the door kept the prison. And, behold, the angel of the Lord came upon him, and a light shined in the prison: and he smote Peter on the side, and raised him up, saying, Arise up quickly. And his chains fell off from his hands. . . . When they were past the first and the second ward, they came unto the iron gate that leadeth unto the city; which opened to them of his own accord: and they went out, and passed on through one street; and forthwith the angel departed from him" (Acts 12:5-7, 10).

2. The struggle of Peter in entering a prayer house—"And when he had considered the thing, he came to the house of Mary the mother of John, whose surname was Mark; where many were gathered together praying. And as Peter knocked at the door of the gate, a damsel came to hearken, named Rhoda. And when she knew Peter's voice, she opened not the gate for gladness, but ran in, and told how Peter stood before the gate. And they said unto her, Thou art mad. But she constantly affirmed that it was even so. Then said they, It is his angel. But Peter continued knocking: and when they had opened the door, and saw him, they were astonished" (Acts 12:12-16).

N. Peter and the Jerusalem council (Acts 15)—"And certain men which came down from Judaea taught the brethren, and said, Except ye be circumcised after the manner of Moses, ye cannot be saved. . . . And the apostles and elders came together for to consider of this matter" (Acts 15:1, 6).

1. His comments—"And when there had been much disputing, Peter rose up, and said unto them, Men and brethren, ye know how that a good while ago God made choice among us, that the Gentiles by my mouth should hear the word of the gospel, and believe. And God, which knoweth the hearts, bare them witness, giving them the Holy Ghost, even as he did unto us; and put no difference between us and them, purifying their hearts by faith" (Acts 15:7-9).
2. His caution—"Now therefore why tempt ye God, to put a yoke upon the neck of the disciples, which neither our fathers nor we were able to bear?" (Acts 15:10).
3. His conclusion—"But we believe that through the grace of the Lord Jesus Christ we shall be saved, even as they" (Acts 15:11).

O. Peter and Paul

1. The contacts between these two men— Peter and Paul met on three recorded occasions.
   a. First meeting: In Jerusalem—"Then after three years I went up to Jerusalem to see Peter, and abode with him fifteen days" (Gal. 1:18).
   b. Second meeting: In Jerusalem—"Then fourteen years after I went up again to Jerusalem with Barnabas, and took Titus with me also. . . . And when James, Cephas, and John, who seemed to be pillars, perceived the grace that was given unto me, they gave to me and Barnabas the right hands of fellowship; that we should go unto the heathen, and they unto the circumcision" (Gal. 2:1, 9).
   c. Third meeting: In Antioch
      (1) The rebuke—"But when Peter was come to Antioch, I withstood him to the face, because he was to be blamed" (Gal. 2:11).
      (2) The reason—"For before that certain came from James, he did eat with the Gentiles: but when they were come, he withdrew and separated himself, fearing them which were

of the circumcision. And the other Jews dissembled likewise with him; insomuch that Barnabas also was carried away with their dissimulation" (Gal. 2:12-13).

(3) The rationale—"But when I saw that they walked not uprightly according to the truth of the gospel, I said unto Peter before them all, If thou, being a Jew, livest after the manner of Gentiles, and not as do the Jews, why compellest thou the Gentiles to live as do the Jews?" (Gal. 2:14).

2. The comparison of these two men
   a. One (Paul) was the official messenger to the Gentiles, while the other (Peter) was God's spokesman to the Jews (Gal. 2:7-8).
   b. Both played important roles in the Jerusalem Council (Acts 15).
   c. Both healed a lame man (Acts 3:1-8; 14:8-12).
   d. Both dealt with satanic pretenders.
      (1) Peter confronted Simon the sorcerer at Samaria (Acts 8:9-24).
      (2) Paul confronted Bar-jesus the sorcerer at Salamis on the Isle of Cyprus (Acts 13:5-11).
   e. Both were released from prison miraculously.
      (1) God sent an angel to free Peter (Acts 12:5-10).
      (2) God sent an earthquake to free Paul (Acts 16:25-39).
   f. Both raised the dead.
      (1) Peter raised Dorcas from the dead (Acts 9:40).
      (2) Paul raised Eutychus from the dead (Acts 20:12).
   g. Both received heavenly visions to minister to the lost.
      (1) Peter saw his vision at Joppa (Acts 10:9-23).
      (2) Paul saw his vision at Troas (Acts 16:8-10).
   h. Both authored New Testament books.
      (1) Peter wrote two epistles.
      (2) Paul wrote 13 (possibly 14) epistles.
   i. Both wrote key passages on the subject of biblical inspiration (2 Pet. 1:19-21; 2 Tim. 3:16-17).
   j. Both knew they would die as martyrs for Christ.
      (1) Peter's testimony—"Yea, I think it meet, as long as I am in this tabernacle, to stir you up by putting you in remembrance; knowing that shortly I must put off this my tabernacle, even as our Lord Jesus Christ hath shewed me" (2 Pet. 1:13-14).
      (2) Paul's testimony—"For I am now ready to be offered, and the time of my departure is at hand. I have fought a good fight, I have finished my course, I have kept the faith" (2 Tim. 4:6-7).

III. Peter, the author—He was the author of the two New Testament epistles that bear his name.

THE FIRST EPISTLE OF PETER

I. Peter wrote concerning the salvation of the believer (1 Pet. 1:1–2:12).
   A. The source of our salvation—According to Peter, the entire Trinity is included in our salvation (1 Pet. 1:2).
      1. The Father elected us—"Elect according to the foreknowledge of God the Father" (1 Pet. 1:2a).
      2. The Son redeemed us—"And sprinkling of the blood of Jesus Christ" (1 Pet. 1:2c).
      3. The Spirit sanctified us—"Through sanctification of the Spirit, unto obedience" (1 Pet. 1:2b).
   B. The blessing of our salvation—This blessing has to do with the word *hope.*
      1. A living hope—"Blessed be the God and Father of our Lord Jesus Christ, which according to his abundant

mercy hath begotten us again unto a lively hope by the resurrection of Jesus Christ from the dead" (1 Pet. 1:3).

2. A lasting hope—"To an inheritance incorruptible, and undefiled, and that fadeth not away, reserved in heaven for you" (1 Pet. 1:4). According to Peter:
   a. This hope is perfect (it is incorruptible).
   b. This hope is pure (it is undefiled).
   c. This hope is permanent (it does not fade away).

C. The guarantee of our salvation—"Who are kept by the power of God through faith unto salvation ready to be revealed in the last time" (1 Pet. 1:5).

D. The trials in our salvation (1 Pet. 1:6-9)
1. The necessity of these trials—"Wherein ye greatly rejoice, though now for a season, if need be, ye are in heaviness through manifold temptations" (1 Pet. 1:6).
2. The reasons for these trials—Peter listed two reasons for our trials:
   a. They strengthen our faith in Christ—"That the trial of your faith, being much more precious than of gold that perisheth, though it be tried with fire, might be found unto praise and honour and glory at the appearing of Jesus Christ" (1 Pet. 1:7).
   b. They strengthen our love for Christ—"Whom having not seen, ye love; in whom, though now ye see him not, yet believing, ye rejoice with joy unspeakable and full of glory" (1 Pet. 1:8).

E. The Old Testament prophets and our salvation—"Of which salvation the prophets have enquired and searched diligently, who prophesied of the grace that should come unto you: searching what, or what manner of time the Spirit of Christ which was in them did signify, when it testified beforehand the sufferings of Christ, and the glory that should follow" (1 Pet. 1:10-11). These verses bring out two facts:
1. The Old Testament prophets (such as Isaiah) did not always understand their inspired prophecies about the future Messiah.
2. When they sought to know, they were told the predictions would be understood only at a later date (New Testament times).

F. The holy angels and our salvation—"Unto whom it was revealed, that not unto themselves, but unto us they did minister the things, which are now reported unto you by them that have preached the gospel unto you with the Holy Ghost sent down from heaven; which things the angels desire to look into" (1 Pet. 1:12). One of the accomplishments of our salvation is to serve as an object lesson to heaven's elect angels. They do not experience our redemption, but they are intensely interested in observing it.

G. The awesome cost of our salvation
1. The price—"Forasmuch as ye know that ye were not redeemed with corruptible things, as silver and gold, from your vain conversation received by tradition from your fathers; but with the precious blood of Christ, as of a lamb without blemish and without spot" (1 Pet. 1:18-19).
2. The planning—"Who verily was foreordained before the foundation of the world, but was manifest in these last times for you" (1 Pet. 1:20).

H. The vehicle of our salvation—"Being born again, not of corruptible seed, but of incorruptible, by the word of God, which liveth and abideth for ever. For all flesh is as grass, and all the glory of man as the flower of grass. The grass withereth, and the flower thereof falleth away: But the word of the Lord endureth for ever. And this is the word which by the gospel is preached unto you" (1 Pet. 1:23-25).

I. The relationships in our salvation
   1. We are members of the same family.
      a. We have experienced the same birth—"Being born again, not of corruptible seed, but of incorruptible, by the word of God, which liveth and abideth for ever" (1 Pet. 1:23).
      b. We partake of the same food—"Wherefore laying aside all malice, and all guile, and hypocrisies, and envies, and all evil speakings" (1 Pet. 2:1).
   2. We are stones in the same building—"Ye also, as lively stones, are built up a spiritual house, an holy priesthood" (1 Pet. 2:5a).
   3. We are priests in the same temple—We are to: "Offer up spiritual sacrifices, acceptable to God by Jesus Christ" (1 Pet. 2:5b).
   4. We are citizens of the same nation—"Which in time past were not a people, but are now the people of God: which had not obtained mercy, but now have obtained mercy" (1 Pet. 2:10).
   5. We are pilgrims on the same journey—"Dearly beloved, I beseech you as strangers and pilgrims, abstain from fleshly lusts, which war against the soul" (1 Pet. 2:11).

II. Peter wrote concerning the submission of the believer (1 Pet. 2:13–3:12).
   A. His exhortation to submission
      1. We are to submit to civil authorities—"Submit yourselves to every ordinance of man for the Lord's sake: whether it be to the king, as supreme; or unto governors, as unto them that are sent by him for the punishment of evildoers, and for the praise of them that do well" (1 Pet. 2:13-14).
      2. We are to submit to our employer—"Servants, be subject to your masters with all fear; not only to the good and gentle, but also to the froward. For this is thankworthy, if a man for conscience toward God endure grief, suffering wrongfully. For what glory is it, if, when ye be buffeted for your faults, ye shall take it patiently? but if, when ye do well, and suffer for it, ye take it patiently, this is acceptable with God" (1 Pet. 2:18-20).
      3. We are to submit in our homes.
         a. The believing wife (1 Pet. 3:1-6)—"Likewise, ye wives, be in subjection to your own husbands; that, if any obey not the word, they also may without the word be won by the conversation of the wives. . . . Whose adorning let it not be that outward adorning of plaiting the hair, and of wearing of gold, or of putting on of apparel; but let it be the hidden man of the heart, in that which is not corruptible, even the ornament of a meek and quiet spirit, which is in the sight of God of great price. For after this manner in the old time the holy women also, who trusted in God, adorned themselves, being in subjection unto their own husbands: even as Sara obeyed Abraham, calling him lord: whose daughters ye are, as long as ye do well, and are not afraid with any amazement" (1 Pet. 3:1, 3-6).
         b. The believing husband (1 Pet. 3:7)—"Likewise, ye husbands, dwell with them according to knowledge, giving honour unto the wife, as unto the weaker vessel, and as being heirs together of the grace of life; that your prayers be not hindered" (1 Pet. 3:7).
      4. We are to submit in the church—"Finally, be ye all of one mind, having compassion one of another, love as brethren, be pitiful, be courteous: not rendering evil for evil, or railing for railing: but contrariwise blessing; knowing that ye are thereunto called, that ye should inherit a blessing" (1 Pet. 3:8-9).

B. His example of submission
1. The sufferings of Christ—"For even hereunto were ye called: because Christ also suffered for us, leaving us an example, that ye should follow his steps" (1 Pet. 2:21).
2. The silence of Christ—"Who did no sin, neither was guile found in his mouth: who, when he was reviled, reviled not again; when he suffered, he threatened not; but committed himself to him that judgeth righteously" (1 Pet. 2:22-23).
3. The salvation of Christ—"Who his own self bare our sins in his own body on the tree, that we, being dead to sins, should live unto righteousness: by whose stripes ye were healed. For ye were as sheep going astray; but are now returned unto the Shepherd and Bishop of your souls" (1 Pet. 2:24-25).

III. Peter wrote concerning the suffering of the believer (1 Pet. 3:13–4:19).
A. Suffering provides the opportunity to witness—"But sanctify the Lord God in your hearts: and be ready always to give an answer to every man that asketh you a reason of the hope that is in you with meekness and fear" (1 Pet. 3:15).
B. Suffering helps purify a life—"Forasmuch then as Christ hath suffered for us in the flesh, arm yourselves likewise with the same mind: for he that hath suffered in the flesh hath ceased from sin" (1 Pet. 4:1).
C. Suffering should be expected—"Beloved, think it not strange concerning the fiery trial which is to try you, as though some strange thing happened unto you" (1 Pet. 4:12).
D. Suffering, if rightly understood, will bring rejoicing—"But rejoice, inasmuch as ye are partakers of Christ's sufferings; that, when his glory shall be revealed, ye may be glad also with exceeding joy. If ye be reproached for the name of Christ, happy are ye; for the spirit of glory and of God resteth upon you: on their part he is evil spoken of, but on your part he is glorified" (1 Pet. 4:13-14).
E. Suffering should not be self-induced—"But let none of you suffer as a murderer, or as a thief, or as an evildoer, or as a busybody in other men's matters. Yet if any man suffer as a Christian, let him not be ashamed; but let him glorify God on this behalf" (1 Pet. 4:15-16).
F. Suffering should be looked upon as a special calling from God—"For what glory is it, if, when ye be buffeted for your faults, ye shall take it patiently? but if, when ye do well, and suffer for it, ye take it patiently, this is acceptable with God. For even hereunto were ye called: because Christ also suffered for us, leaving us an example, that ye should follow his steps" (1 Pet. 2:20-21).
G. Suffering is the root of which glory is the fruit—"The sufferings of Christ, and the glory that should follow" (1 Pet. 1:11).

IV. Peter wrote concerning the service of the believer (1 Pet. 5:1-14).
A. Serving as a shepherd
1. The responsibilities—"The elders which are among you I exhort, who am also an elder, and a witness of the sufferings of Christ, and also a partaker of the glory that shall be revealed: Feed the flock of God which is among you, taking the oversight thereof, not by constraint, but willingly; not for filthy lucre, but of a ready mind; Neither as being lords over God's heritage, but being ensamples to the flock" (1 Pet. 5:1-3).
2. The rewards—"And when the chief Shepherd shall appear, ye shall receive a crown of glory that fadeth not away" (1 Pet. 5:4).
B. Serving as a servant
1. We are to serve the saints—"Likewise, ye younger, submit yourselves unto the elder. Yea, all of you be subject one to another, and be clothed

with humility: for God resisteth the proud, and giveth grace to the humble" (1 Pet. 5:5).
2. We are to serve the Savior (1 Pet. 5:6-7).

C. Serving as a soldier
1. The predator—"Be sober, be vigilant; because your adversary the devil, as a roaring lion, walketh about, seeking whom he may devour" (1 Pet. 5:8).
2. The plan—"Whom resist stedfast in the faith, knowing that the same afflictions are accomplished in your brethren that are in the world" (1 Pet. 5:9).
3. The purpose—What is the purpose of serving? Why does God sometimes allow us to suffer when we are faithfully serving him? Here is the answer to both questions: "But the God of all grace, who hath called us unto his eternal glory by Christ Jesus, after that ye have suffered a while, make you perfect, stablish, strengthen, settle you. To him be glory and dominion for ever and ever. Amen" (1 Pet. 5:10-11).

THE SECOND EPISTLE OF PETER

I. The proclamation of the power of God (2 Pet. 1:1-3)—"According as his divine power hath given unto us all things that pertain unto life and godliness, through the knowledge of him that hath called us to glory and virtue" (2 Pet. 1:3).

II. The application of the promise of God (2 Pet. 1:4-9)—"Whereby are given unto us exceeding great and precious promises: that by these ye might be partakers of the divine nature, having escaped the corruption that is in the world through lust" (2 Pet. 1:4).

A. The what of these promises (2 Pet. 1:5-7)—"And beside this, giving all diligence, add to your faith virtue; and to virtue knowledge; and to knowledge temperance; and to temperance patience; and to patience godliness; and to godliness brotherly kindness; and to brotherly kindness charity" (2 Pet. 1:5-7).

B. The why of these promises (2 Pet. 1:8-9)
1. To apply them leads to fruitfulness—"For if these things be in you, and abound, they make you that ye shall neither be barren nor unfruitful in the knowledge of our Lord Jesus Christ" (2 Pet. 1:8).
2. To avoid them leads to blindness (2 Pet. 1:9).

III. The examination of the calling of God (2 Pet. 1:10-12)—"Wherefore the rather, brethren, give diligence to make your calling and election sure: for if ye do these things, ye shall never fall" (2 Pet. 1:10).

IV. The revelation to the apostle of God (2 Pet. 1:13-15)—"Yea, I think it meet, as long as I am in this tabernacle, to stir you up by putting you in remembrance; Knowing that shortly I must put off this my tabernacle, even as our Lord Jesus Christ hath shewed me" (2 Pet. 1:13-14).

V. The transfiguration of the Son of God (2 Pet. 1:16-18)

A. The glorious sight—"For we have not followed cunningly devised fables, when we made known unto you the power and coming of our Lord Jesus Christ, but were eyewitnesses of his majesty" (2 Pet. 1:16).

B. The glorious sound—"For he received from God the Father honour and glory, when there came such a voice to him from the excellent glory, This is my beloved Son, in whom I am well pleased. And this voice which came from heaven we heard, when we were with him in the holy mount" (2 Pet. 1:17-18).

VI. The inspiration of the Word of God—(2 Pet. 1:19-21)

A. Its importance—"We have also a more sure word of prophecy; whereunto ye do well that ye take heed, as unto a light that shineth in a dark place, until the day dawn, and the day star arise in your hearts" (2 Pet. 1:19).

B. Its interpretation—"Knowing this first, that no prophecy of the scripture is of any private interpretation" (2 Pet. 1:20).

C. Its impartation—"For the prophecy came not in old time by the will of man: but holy men of God spake as they were moved by the Holy Ghost" (2 Pet. 1:21).

VII. The deviation of the enemies of God (2 Pet. 2:1–3:4)—"This second epistle, beloved, I now write unto you; in both which I stir up your pure minds by way of remembrance: that ye may be mindful of the words which were spoken before by the holy prophets, and of the commandment of us the apostles of the Lord and Saviour" (2 Pet. 3:1-2).

A. The identity of these enemies

1. In former days

a. Wicked angels (2 Pet. 2:4)—"For if God spared not the angels that sinned, but cast them down to hell, and delivered them into chains of darkness, to be reserved unto judgment" (2 Pet. 2:4).

b. Those living in Noah's day (2 Pet. 2:5)

(1) The godless—"And spared not the old world . . . bringing in the flood upon the world of the ungodly" (2 Pet. 2:5a, c).

(2) The godly—"but saved Noah the eighth person, a preacher of righteousness" (2 Pet. 2:5b).

c. Those living in Lot's day (2 Pet. 2:6-9)

(1) The godless—"And turning the cities of Sodom and Gomorrha into ashes condemned them with an overthrow, making them an ensample unto those that after should live ungodly" (2 Pet. 2:6).

(2) The godly—"And delivered just Lot, vexed with the filthy conversation of the wicked: (For that righteous man dwelling among them, in seeing and hearing, vexed his righteous soul from day to day with their unlawful deeds:); the Lord knoweth how to deliver the godly out of temptations, and to reserve the unjust unto the day of judgment to be punished" (2 Pet. 2:7-9).

d. False prophets such as Balaam—"But there were false prophets" (2 Pet. 2:1). "Which have forsaken the right way, and are gone astray, following the way of Balaam the son of Bosor, who loved the wages of unrighteousness; but was rebuked for his iniquity: the dumb ass speaking with man's voice forbad the madness of the prophet" (2 Pet. 2:15-16).

2. In the latter days

a. False teachers (2 Pet. 2:1)

b. Scoffers—"Knowing this first, that there shall come in the last days scoffers, walking after their own lusts" (2 Pet. 3:3).

B. The iniquity of these enemies

1. Inventors of heresies (2 Pet. 2:1)
2. Christ deniers (2 Pet. 2:1)
3. Sensuous flesh indulgers (2 Pet. 2:2, 10, 14)
4. Truth maligners (2 Pet. 2:2)
5. Greedy materialists (2 Pet. 2:3)
6. Exploiters (2 Pet. 2:3)
7. Despisers of all authority (2 Pet. 2:10)
8. Self-willed (2 Pet. 2:10)
9. Unreasoning brute animals (2 Pet. 2:12)
10. Ignorant revilers (2 Pet. 2:12)
11. Committed to the playboy philosophy (2 Pet. 2:13)
12. Cancers upon society (2 Pet. 2:13)
13. Eaten with lust (2 Pet. 2:14)
14. Totally forsaking the right way (2 Pet. 2:15)
15. Empty clouds (2 Pet. 2:17)
16. Waterless wells (2 Pet. 2:17)
17. Arrogant rabble rousers (2 Pet. 2:18)
18. Blind captives attempting to lead other blind captives (2 Pet. 2:19)

19. Cold-blooded apostates (2 Pet. 2:21)
20. Filthy hogs and dogs (2 Pet. 2:22)
21. Scoffers of the second coming (2 Pet. 3:3-4)
22. Closed-minded fools (2 Pet. 3:5)

VIII. The condemnation of the former world of God (2 Pet. 3:5-6)—"For this they willingly are ignorant of, that by the word of God the heavens were of old, and the earth standing out of the water and in the water: whereby the world that then was, being overflowed with water, perished" (2 Pet. 3:5-6).

IX. The annihilation of the present world of God (2 Pet. 3:7-12)

A. The certainty—"But the heavens and the earth, which are now, by the same word are kept in store, reserved unto fire against the day of judgment and perdition of ungodly men. But, beloved, be not ignorant of this one thing, that one day is with the Lord as a thousand years, and a thousand years as one day" (2 Pet. 3:7-8).

B. The compassion (2 Pet. 3:9)—"The Lord is not slack concerning his promise, as some men count slackness; but is longsuffering to us-ward, not willing that any should perish, but that all should come to repentance" (2 Pet. 3:9).

C. The chronology—"But the day of the Lord will come as a thief in the night; in the which the heavens shall pass away with a great noise, and the elements shall melt with fervent heat, the earth also and the works that are therein shall be burned up" (2 Pet. 3:10).

D. The challenge

1. Be righteous—"Seeing then that all these things shall be dissolved, what manner of persons ought ye to be in all holy conversation and godliness" (2 Pet. 3:11).
2. Be ready—"Looking for and hasting unto the coming of the day of God, wherein the heavens being on fire shall be dissolved, and the elements shall melt with fervent heat?" (2 Pet. 3:12).

X. The new creation of the future world of God (2 Pet. 3:13-18)

A. The anticipation of this new world—"Nevertheless we, according to his promise, look for new heavens and a new earth, wherein dwelleth righteousness. Wherefore, beloved, seeing that ye look for such things, be diligent that ye may be found of him in peace, without spot, and blameless" (2 Pet. 3:13-14).

B. The preparation for this new world

1. A proper relationship to the Scriptures

a. Heed them carefully—"And account that the longsuffering of our Lord is salvation; even as our beloved brother Paul also according to the wisdom given unto him hath written unto you; as also in all his epistles, speaking in them of these things; in which are some things hard to be understood, which they that are unlearned and unstable wrest, as they do also the other scriptures, unto their own destruction" (2 Pet. 3:15-16).

b. Read them carefully—"Ye therefore, beloved, seeing ye know these things before, beware lest ye also, being led away with the error of the wicked, fall from your own stedfastness" (2 Pet. 3:17).

2. A proper relationship to the Savior—"But grow in grace, and in the knowledge of our Lord and Saviour Jesus Christ. To him be glory both now and for ever. Amen" (2 Pet. 3:18).

STATISTICS

Father: Jonah (John 1:42)
Spouse: Unnamed (Matt. 8:14)
Brother: Andrew (John 1:40)
First mention: Matthew 4:18
Final mention: 2 Peter 1:1
Meaning of his name: Simon means "hearing"; Peter means "rock" (Greek); Cephas means "rock" (Aramaic).
Frequency of his name: Referred to 183 times

Biblical books mentioning him: Nine books (Matthew, Mark, Luke, John, Acts, 1 Corinthians, Galatians, 1 Peter, 2 Peter)
Occupation: Fisherman and apostle
Place of birth: Bethsaida in Galilee (John 1:44)
Place of death: Tradition says he died in Rome.
Circumstances of death: Tradition says he was crucified upside down.
Important fact about his life: He was one of the chief apostles and author of two New Testament books.

Philemon

CHRONOLOGICAL SUMMARY

I. The appreciation for and praise of Philemon (Philem. 1-7)
  A. Philemon was a friend.
    1. To Paul in Rome—"And to our beloved Apphia, and Archippus our fellow-soldier, and to the church in thy house" (Philem. 2).
    2. To Christians in Colosse (Philem. 5)—"Your love has given me great joy and encouragement, because you, brother, have refreshed the hearts of the saints"(Philem. 7, NIV).
  B. Philemon was a family man (Philem. 2)—Note: Apphia was probably Philemon's wife, and Archippus, his son.
II. The appeal and plea to Philemon (Philem. 8-17)—"I beseech thee for my son Onesimus, whom I have begotten in my bonds" (Philem. 10).
  A. The background of this appeal—Onesimus, Philemon's runaway slave, had been led to Christ in Rome by Paul, and was now being sent back to Philemon with a request that he be received as a Christian brother.
  B. The basis of this appeal
    1. Forgive him for your sake—"Which in time past was to thee unprofitable, but now profitable to thee and to me: For perhaps he therefore departed for a season, that thou shouldest receive him for ever" (Philem. 11, 15).
    2. Forgive him for his sake—"No longer as a slave, but better than a slave, as a dear brother" (Philem. 16, NIV).
    3. Forgive him for my sake—"Yet for love's sake I rather beseech thee, being such an one as Paul the aged, and now also a prisoner of Jesus Christ. . . . If thou count me therefore a partner, receive him as myself. If he hath wronged thee, or oweth thee ought, put that on mine account" (Philem. 9, 17-18).
III. The assurance and pledge to Philemon (Philem. 19-25)—"I Paul have written it with mine own hand, I will repay it: albeit I do not say to thee how thou owest unto me even thine own self besides" (Philem. 19).
  A. His confidence in Philemon—"Having confidence in thy obedience I wrote unto thee, knowing that thou wilt also do more than I say" (Philem. 21).
  B. His request to Philemon—"But withal prepare me also a lodging: for I trust that through your prayers I shall be given unto you" (Philem. 22).

STATISTICS

Spouse: Apphia (Philem. 2)
Son: Archippus (Philem. 2)
First mention: Philemon 1
Final mention: Philemon 1
Meaning of his name: "Loving"
Frequency of his name: Referred to one time
Biblical books mentioning him: One book (Philemon)
Occupation: Wealthy slave owner
Place of birth: Probably Colosse
Important fact about his life: Paul addressed one of his New Testament epistles to Philemon.

Philip

CHRONOLOGICAL SUMMARY

I. His first meeting with Christ
  A. Philip's willingness—"The day following Jesus would go forth into Galilee,

and findeth Philip, and saith unto him, Follow me" (John 1:43).

B. Philip's witness—"Philip findeth Nathanael, and saith unto him, We have found him, of whom Moses in the law, and the prophets, did write, Jesus of Nazareth, the son of Joseph" (John 1:45).

C. Philip's wisdom—"And Nathanael said unto him, Can there any good thing come out of Nazareth? Philip saith unto him, Come and see" (John 1:46).

II. His full-time ministry for Christ

A. Philip and the Savior

1. By the Galilean sea—The wrong reaction: "When Jesus then lifted up his eyes, and saw a great company come unto him, he saith unto Philip, Whence shall we buy bread, that these may eat? And this he said to prove him: for he himself knew what he would do. Philip answered him, Two hundred pennyworth of bread is not sufficient for them, that every one of them may take a little" (John 6:5-7).

2. In the upper room—The wrong request: "Philip saith unto him, Lord, shew us the Father, and it sufficeth us. Jesus saith unto him, Have I been so long time with you, and yet hast thou not known me, Philip? he that hath seen me hath seen the Father; and how sayest thou then, Shew us the Father?" (John 14:8-9).

B. Philip and the seekers—"And there were certain Greeks among them that came up to worship at the feast: The same came therefore to Philip, which was of Bethsaida of Galilee, and desired him, saying, Sir, we would see Jesus. Philip cometh and telleth Andrew: and again Andrew and Philip tell Jesus" (John 12:20-22).

STATISTICS

First mention: Matthew 10:3
Final mention: Acts 1:13
Meaning of his name: "Lover of horses"
Frequency of his name: Referred to 16 times
Biblical books mentioning him: Five books (Matthew, Mark, Luke, John, Acts)
Occupation: Apostle
Place of birth: Probably the Galilean city of Bethsaida (John 1:44)
Place of death: Tradition says he died at Hierapolis, a city near Colosse and Laodicia.
Important fact about his life: He led Nathanael to Christ (John 1:45-46).

Philip the Evangelist

CHRONOLOGICAL SUMMARY

I. The deacon in Jerusalem—Philip was one of seven men chosen by the early church to serve in the office of a deacon.

A. The reason for this election—"And in those days, when the number of the disciples were multiplied, there arose a murmuring of the Grecians against the Hebrews, because their widows were neglected in the daily ministration. Then the twelve called the multitude of the disciples unto them, and said, It is not reason that we should leave the word of God, and serve tables" (Acts 6:1-2).

B. The requirements for this election—"Wherefore, brethren, look ye out among you seven men of honest report, full of the Holy Ghost and wisdom, whom we may appoint over this business. But we will give ourselves continually to prayer, and to the ministry of the word" (Acts 6:3-4). "And the saying pleased the whole multitude: and they chose . . . Philip" (Acts 6:5a).

II. The evangelist in Samaria (Acts 8:5-8)

A. The message he preached—"Then Philip went down to the city of Samaria, and preached Christ unto them" (Acts 8:5).

B. The miracles he performed—"And the people with one accord gave heed unto those things which Philip spake, hearing and seeing the miracles which he did. For unclean spirits, crying with loud voice, came out of many that were possessed with them: and many taken with palsies, and that were lame, were healed. And there was great joy in that city" (Acts 8:6-8).

III. The soul winner in Gaza (Acts 8:26-40)
   A. His message from an angel—"And the angel of the Lord spake unto Philip, saying, Arise, and go toward the south unto the way that goeth down from Jerusalem unto Gaza, which is desert" (Acts 8:26).
   B. His ministry to a eunuch
      1. The charge of the eunuch—"And he arose and went: and, behold, a man of Ethiopia, an eunuch of great authority under Candace queen of the Ethiopians, who had the charge of all her treasure, and had come to Jerusalem for a worship" (Acts 8:27).
      2. The confusion of the eunuch
         a. The passage—"Was returning, and sitting in his chariot read Esaias the prophet. . . . The place of the scripture which he read was this, He was led as a sheep to the slaughter; and like a lamb dumb before his shearer, so opened he not his mouth: In his humiliation his judgment was taken away: and who shall declare his generation? for his life is taken from the earth" (Acts 8:28, 32-33).
         b. The problem—"Then the Spirit said unto Philip, Go near, and join thyself to this chariot. And Philip ran thither to him, and heard him read the prophet Esaias, and said, Understandest thou what thou readest? . . . And the eunuch answered Philip, and said, I pray thee, of whom speaketh the prophet this? of himself, or of some other man?" (Acts 8:29-30, 34).
      3. The clarification to the eunuch—"Then Philip opened his mouth, and began at the same scripture, and preached unto him Jesus" (Acts 8:35).
   C. The conversion of the eunuch—"And as they went on their way, they came unto a certain water: and the eunuch said, See, here is water; what doth hinder me to be baptized? And Philip said, If thou believest with all thine heart, thou mayest. And he answered and said, I believe that Jesus Christ is the Son of God" (Acts 8:36-37).
   D. The confession of the eunuch—"And he commanded the chariot to stand still: and they went down both into the water, both Philip and the eunuch; and he baptized him. And when they were come up out of the water, the Spirit of the Lord caught away Philip, that the eunuch saw him no more: and he went on his way rejoicing" (Acts 8:38-39).

IV. The family man in Caesarea—"But Philip was found at Azotus: and passing through he preached in all the cities, till he came to Caesarea" (Acts 8:40).
   A. The visitors to Philip's home—"And the next day we that were of Paul's company departed, and came unto Caesarea: and we entered into the house of Philip the evangelist, which was one of the seven; and abode with him" (Acts 21:8).
   B. The virgins in Philip's home—"And the same man had four daughters, virgins, which did prophesy" (Acts 21:9).

STATISTICS

First mention: Acts 6:5
Final mention: Acts 21:8
Meaning of his name: "Lover of horses"
Frequency of his name: Referred to 16 times
Biblical books mentioning him: One book (Acts)
Occupation: Evangelist
Place of death: Probably Caesarea
Important fact about his life: He led the Ethiopian eunuch to Christ in the desert of Gaza.

Phoebe (Phebe)

CHRONOLOGICAL SUMMARY

I. Her ministry to Paul—She had assisted Paul while he was in the city of Corinth (Rom. 16:1).

II. Her mission for Paul—"That ye receive her in the Lord, as becometh saints, and that ye assist her in whatsoever business she hath need of you: for she hath been a succourer of many, and of myself also" (Rom. 16:2).

A. Where she went—The apostle sent her to Rome.

B. Why she went—She carried with her Paul's epistle to the Roman church.

STATISTICS

First mention: Romans 16:1
Final mention: Romans 16:1
Meaning of her name: "Bright, radiant"
Frequency of her name: Referred to one time
Biblical books mentioning her: One book (Romans)
Important fact about her life: She carried Paul's epistle of Romans to the church at Rome.

Pilate

CHRONOLOGICAL SUMMARY

I. Pilate and the teaching of Jesus—"There were present at that season some that told him of the Galilaeans, whose blood Pilate had mingled with their sacrifices. And Jesus answering said unto them, Suppose ye that these Galilaeans were sinners above all the Galilaeans, because they suffered such things? I tell you, Nay: but, except ye repent, ye shall all likewise perish" (Luke 13:1-3).

II. Pilate and the trials of Jesus

A. The first trial (Matt. 27:2, 11-14; Mark 15:1-5; Luke 23:1-5; John 18:28-38)

1. The charges against Jesus

a. The hypocrisy of the Jews—"Then led they Jesus from Caiaphas unto the hall of judgment: and it was early; and they themselves went not into the judgment hall, lest they should be defiled; but that they might eat the passover" (John 18:28).

b. The hostility of the Jews—"Pilate then went out unto them, and said, What accusation bring ye against this man? They answered and said unto him, If he were not a malefactor, we would not have delivered him up unto thee. Then said Pilate unto them, Take ye him, and judge him according to your law. The Jews therefore said unto him, It is not lawful for us to put any man to death" (John 18:29-31).

(1) They accused Jesus of subverting the nation (Luke 23:2a).

(2) They accused Jesus of opposing payment of taxes to Caesar (Luke 23:2b).

(3) They accused Jesus of claiming to be the Messiah and King (Luke 23:2c).

2. The conversation with Jesus

a. Pilate learned about the King—"And Jesus stood before the governor: and the governor asked him, saying, Art thou the King of the Jews? And Jesus said unto him, Thou sayest. And when he was accused of the chief priests and elders, he answered nothing. Then said Pilate unto him, Hearest thou not how many things they witness against thee? And he answered him to never a word; insomuch that the governor marvelled greatly" (Matt. 27:11-14).

b. Pilate learned about the kingdom—"Jesus answered, My kingdom is not of this world: if my kingdom were of this world, then would my servants fight, that I should not be delivered to the Jews: but now is my kingdom not from hence. Pilate therefore said unto him, Art thou a king then? Jesus answered, Thou sayest that I am a king. To this end was I born, and for this cause came I into the world, that I should bear witness unto the truth. Every one that is of the truth heareth my voice" (John 18:36-37).

3. The conclusion concerning Christ—"Pilate saith unto him, What is truth? And when he had said this, he went out again unto the Jews, and saith unto them, I find in him no fault at all" (John 18:38).
4. The consignment of Christ—"When Pilate heard of Galilee, he asked whether the man were a Galilaean" (Luke 23:6).
5. The coalition through Christ—"And Herod with his men of war set him at nought, and mocked him, and arrayed him in a gorgeous robe, and sent him again to Pilate. And the same day Pilate and Herod were made friends together: for before they were at enmity between themselves" (Luke 23:11-12).

B. The final trial (Matt. 27:15-26; Mark 15:6-15; Luke 23:13-25; John 18:39–19:1, 4-16)
   1. The selection of the murderer
      a. The observation—"And Pilate, when he had called together the chief priests and the rulers and the people, said unto them, Ye have brought this man unto me, as one that perverteth the people: and, behold, I, having examined him before you, have found no fault in this man touching those things whereof ye accuse him: No, nor yet Herod: for I sent you to him; and, lo, nothing worthy of death is done unto him. . . . Pilate therefore, willing to release Jesus, spake again to them" (Luke 23:13-15, 20).
      b. The outrage—In spite of this, Pilate agreed to have Jesus flogged. "I will therefore chastise him, and release him" (Luke 23:16).
      c. The offer—"Now at that feast the governor was wont to release unto the people a prisoner, whom they would. And they had then a notable prisoner, called Barabbas. Therefore when they were gathered together, Pilate said unto them, Whom will ye that I release unto you? Barabbas, or Jesus which is called Christ?" (Matt. 27:15-17).
      d. The objection—"When he was set down on the judgment seat, his wife sent unto him, saying, Have thou nothing to do with that just man: for I have suffered many things this day in a dream because of him" (Matt. 27:19).
      e. The orchestration—"But the chief priests and elders persuaded the multitude that they should ask Barabbas, and destroy Jesus. The governor answered and said unto them, Whether of the twain will ye that I release unto you? They said, Barabbas. Pilate saith unto them, What shall I do then with Jesus which is called Christ? They all say unto him, Let him be crucified. And the governor said, Why, what evil hath he done? But they cried out the more, saying, Let him be crucified" (Matt. 27:20-23).
      f. The outcome—"When Pilate saw that he could prevail nothing, but that rather a tumult was made, he took water, and washed his hands before the multitude, saying, I am innocent of the blood of this just person: see ye to it. Then answered all

the people, and said, His blood be on us, and on our children" (Matt. 27:24-25).

2. The scourging of the Messiah
   a. Pilate's travesty against Jesus—"And they were instant with loud voices, requiring that he might be crucified. And the voices of them and of the chief priests prevailed. And Pilate gave sentence that it should be as they required. And he released unto them him that for sedition and murder was cast into prison, whom they had desired; but he delivered Jesus to their will" (Luke 23:23-25). "Then Pilate therefore took Jesus, and scourged him" (John 19:1).
   b. Pilate's talk with Jesus
      (1) The confusion of the governor—"And went again into the judgment hall, and saith unto Jesus, Whence art thou? But Jesus gave him no answer. Then saith Pilate unto him, Speakest thou not unto me? knowest thou not that I have power to crucify thee, and have power to release thee?" (John 19:9-10).
      (2) The correction by the Savior—"Jesus answered, Thou couldest have no power at all against me, except it were given thee from above: therefore he that delivered me unto thee hath the greater sin" (John 19:11).
   c. Pilate's transferring of Jesus—"Then delivered he him therefore unto them to be crucified. And they took Jesus, and led him away" (John 19:16).

III. Pilate and the title of Jesus
   A. The placing of the sign—"And Pilate wrote a title, and put it on the cross. And the writing was, JESUS OF NAZARETH THE KING OF THE JEWS. This title then read many of the Jews: for the place where Jesus was crucified was nigh to the city: and it was written in Hebrew, and Greek, and Latin" (John 19:19-20).
   B. The protest against the sign
      1. The demand by the priests—"Then said the chief priests of the Jews to Pilate, Write not, The King of the Jews; but that he said, I am King of the Jews" (John 19:21).
      2. The denial by the governor—"Pilate answered, What I have written I have written" (John 19:22).

IV. Pilate and the tomb of Jesus
   A. Jesus' foes wanted Pilate to kill the Savior on the cross—"The Jews therefore, because it was the preparation, that the bodies should not remain upon the cross on the sabbath day, (for that sabbath day was an high day,) besought Pilate that their legs might be broken, and that they might be taken away. Then came the soldiers, and brake the legs of the first, and of the other which was crucified with him. But when they came to Jesus, and saw that he was dead already, they brake not his legs" (John 19:31-33).
   B. Jesus' foes wanted Pilate to keep the Savior in the tomb.
      1. The reason for their request—"Now the next day, that followed the day of the preparation, the chief priests and Pharisees came together unto Pilate, saying, Sir, we remember that that deceiver said, while he was yet alive, After three days I will rise again. Command therefore that the sepulchre be made sure until the third day, lest his disciples come by night, and steal him away, and say unto the people, He is risen from the dead: so the last error shall be worse than the first" (Matt. 27:62-64).

2. The response to their request—"Pilate said unto them, Ye have a watch: go your way, make it as sure as ye can" (Matt. 27:65).
3. The results of their request—"So they went, and made the sepulchre sure, sealing the stone, and setting a watch" (Matt. 27:66).

STATISTICS

First mention: Matthew 27:2
Final mention: 1 Timothy 6:13
Meaning of his name: "Pikeman, one armed with a javelin"
Frequency of his name: Referred to 53 times
Biblical books mentioning him: Six books (Matthew, Mark, Luke, John, Acts, 1 Timothy)
Occupation: Governor over Palestine
Important fact about his life: He condemned Jesus to be crucified.

Priscilla (Prisca)

CHRONOLOGICAL SUMMARY

I. The tentmaker—"After these things Paul departed from Athens, and came to Corinth; and found a certain Jew named Aquila, born in Pontus, lately come from Italy, with his wife Priscilla; (because that Claudius had commanded all Jews to depart from Rome:) and came unto them. And because he was of the same craft, he abode with them, and wrought: for by their occupation they were tentmakers" (Acts 18:1-3).
II. The traveler—Both Aquila and Priscilla accompanied Paul on one occasion from Corinth to Ephesus (Acts 18:18-19).
III. The teacher—"And a certain Jew named Apollos, born at Alexandria, an eloquent man, and mighty in the scriptures, came to Ephesus. This man was instructed in the way of the Lord; and being fervent in the spirit, he spake and taught diligently the things of the Lord, knowing only the baptism of John. And he began to speak boldly in the synagogue: whom when Aquila and Priscilla had heard, they took him unto them, and expounded unto him the way of God more perfectly" (Acts 18:24-26).
IV. The trustee (Rom. 16:3-5; 1 Cor. 16:19)—"Greet Priscilla and Aquila my helpers in Christ Jesus: Who have for my life laid down their own necks: unto whom not only I give thanks, but also all the churches of the Gentiles" (Rom. 16:3-4).

STATISTICS

First mention: Acts 18:2
Final mention: 2 Timothy 4:19
Meaning of her name: "Ancient"
Frequency of her name: Referred to six times
Biblical books mentioning her: Four books (Acts, Romans, 1 Corinthians, 2 Timothy)
Occupation: Tentmaker
Important fact about her life: She and her husband greatly assisted and encouraged the Apostle Paul.

Publius

CHRONOLOGICAL SUMMARY

I. The hospitality he rendered to Paul—"In the same quarters were possessions of the chief man of the island, whose name was Publius; who received us, and lodged us three days courteously" (Acts 28:7).
II. The healing he received from Paul—"And it came to pass, that the father of Publius lay sick of a fever and of a bloody flux: to whom Paul entered in, and prayed, and laid his hands on him, and healed him" (Acts 28:8).

STATISTICS

First mention: Acts 28:7
Final mention: Acts 28:8
Meaning of his name: "Common"
Frequency of his name: Referred to two times
Biblical books mentioning him: One book (Acts)
Occupation: Governor of the Isle of Melita
Important fact about his life: He showed great kindness to Paul after the apostle's traumatic shipwreck.

Rhoda

CHRONOLOGICAL SUMMARY

I. Rhoda and the stranger without
  A. She recognized the voice of Peter—"And when he had considered the thing, he came to the house of Mary the mother of John, whose surname was Mark; where many were gathered together praying. And as Peter knocked at the door of the gate, a damsel came to hearken, named Rhoda" (Acts 12:12-13). "And when she knew Peter's voice, she opened not the gate for gladness" (Acts 12:14a).
  B. She reported the visit of Peter—"But ran in, and told how Peter stood before the gate" (Acts 12:14b).

II. Rhoda and the skeptics within
  A. They said it was her imagination—"And they said unto her, Thou art mad. But she constantly affirmed that it was even so" (Acts 12:15a).
  B. They said it was his apparition—"Then said they, It is his angel" (Acts 12:15b).

STATISTICS

First mention: Acts 12:13
Final mention: Acts 12:13
Meaning of her name: "A rose"
Frequency of her name: Referred to one time
Biblical books mentioning her: One book (Acts)
Important fact about her life: She reported the release of Simon Peter from prison.

Salome

CHRONOLOGICAL SUMMARY

I. Salome and Christ (before the cross)—She contributed financially to the needs of Christ and his disciples (Luke 8:2-3; Mark 15:40-41).

II. Salome and Christ (at the cross)—She, along with several faithful women, was present during the crucifixion of Christ (Mark 15:40).

III. Salome and Christ (after the cross)
  A. The anointing—Salome and some women came to the tomb Sunday morning to anoint the body of Christ (Mark 16:1).
  B. The announcement—Entering into the empty sepulchre, they saw an angel. "And he saith unto them, Be not affrighted: Ye seek Jesus of Nazareth, which was crucified: he is risen; he is not here: behold the place where they laid him" (Mark 16:6).

STATISTICS

First mention: Mark 15:40
Final mention: Mark 16:1
Meaning of her name: "Peaceful"
Frequency of her name: Referred to two times
Biblical books mentioning her: One book (Mark)
Important fact about her life: She was present during the crucifixion and resurrection of Christ.

Sapphira

CHRONOLOGICAL SUMMARY

I. Her deception—"But a certain man named Ananias, with Sapphira his wife, sold a possession, and kept back part of the price, his wife also being privy to it, and brought a certain part, and laid it at the apostles' feet" (Acts 5:1-2).

II. Her discovery—"And it was about the space of three hours after, when his wife, not knowing what was done, came in. And Peter answered unto her, Tell me whether ye sold the land for so much? And she said, Yea, for so much" (Acts 5:7-8).

III. Her denunciation—"Then Peter said unto her, How is it that ye have agreed together to tempt the Spirit of the Lord? behold, the feet of them which have buried thy husband are at the door, and shall carry thee out" (Acts 5:9).

IV. Her death—"Then fell she down straightway at his feet, and yielded up the ghost: and the young men came in, and found her dead, and, carrying her forth, buried her by her husband" (Acts 5:10).

STATISTICS
Spouse: Ananias
First mention: Acts 5:1
Final mention: Acts 5:1
Meaning of her name: "Beautiful"
Frequency of her name: Referred to one time
Biblical books mentioning her: One book (Acts)
Important fact about her life: She was struck dead for her sin of lying to the Holy Spirit.

Saul *(see Paul)*

Sceva

CHRONOLOGICAL SUMMARY
I. Sceva, the false Jewish priest—"Then certain of the vagabond Jews, exorcists, took upon them to call over them which had evil spirits the name of the Lord Jesus, saying, We adjure you by Jesus whom Paul preacheth. And there were seven sons of one Sceva, a Jew, and chief of the priests, which did so" (Acts 19:13-14).

II. Sceva, the foolish Jewish priest—He and his sons attempted to subdue an evil spirit without the power of the Holy Spirit.
   A. The hostile answer of the evil spirit—"And the evil spirit answered and said, Jesus I know, and Paul I know; but who are ye?" (Acts 19:15).
   B. The hostile action of the evil spirit—"And the man in whom the evil spirit was leaped on them, and overcame them, and prevailed against them, so that they fled out of that house naked and wounded" (Acts 19:16).

STATISTICS
First mention: Acts 19:14
Final mention: Acts 19:14
Frequency of his name: Referred to one time
Biblical books mentioning him: One book (Acts)
Occupation: False prophet
Important fact about his life: He was a false prophet who was punished for misusing the name of Jesus.

Sergius Paulus

CHRONOLOGICAL SUMMARY
I. The openness to the Word of God—"And when they had gone through the isle unto Paphos, they found a certain sorcerer, a false prophet, a Jew, whose name was Barjesus: which was with the deputy of the country, Sergius Paulus, a prudent man; who called for Barnabas and Saul, and desired to hear the word of God" (Acts 13:6-7).

II. The opposition to the Word of God
   A. The blasphemy of Elymas—"But Elymas the sorcerer (for so is his name by interpretation) withstood them, seeking to turn away the deputy from the faith" (Acts 13:8).
   B. The blindness of Elymas
      1. The judge—"Then Saul, (who also is called Paul,) filled with the Holy Ghost, set his eyes on him, and said, O full of all subtilty and all mischief, thou child of the devil, thou enemy of all righteousness, wilt thou not cease to pervert the right ways of the Lord?" (Acts 13:9-10).
      2. The judgment—"And now, behold, the hand of the Lord is upon thee, and thou shalt be blind, not seeing the sun for a season. And immediately there fell on him a mist and a darkness; and he went about seeking some to lead him by the hand" (Acts 13:11).

III. The obedience to the Word of God—"Then the deputy, when he saw what was done, believed, being astonished at the doctrine of the Lord" (Acts 13:12).

STATISTICS
First mention: Acts 13:7
Final mention: Acts 13:7
Frequency of his name: Referred to one time

Biblical books mentioning him: One book (Acts)
Occupation: Governor of the Isle of Cyprus
Important fact about his life: He was the Apostle Paul's first recorded convert.

Silas

CHRONOLOGICAL SUMMARY

I. Silas, the messenger
- A. His attendance at the Jerusalem council (Acts 15:22)
- B. His assignment by the Jerusalem council—"Then pleased it the apostles and elders, with the whole church, to send chosen men of their own com-pany to Antioch with Paul and Barnabas: namely, Judas surnamed Barsabas, and Silas, chief men among the brethren. . . . We have sent therefore Judas and Silas, who shall also tell you the same things by mouth. For it seemed good to the Holy Ghost, and to us, to lay upon you no greater burden than these necessary things; that ye abstain from meats offered to idols, and from blood, and from things strangled, and from fornication: from which if ye keep yourselves, ye shall do well. Fare ye well" (Acts 15:22, 27-29).
- C. His assistance to the Jerusalem council—"And Judas and Silas, being prophets also themselves, exhorted the brethren with many words, and confirmed them" (Acts 15:32).

II. Silas, the missionary
- A. His selection by Paul—"And Paul chose Silas, and departed, being recommended by the brethren unto the grace of God" (Acts 15:40).
- B. His service with Paul at Philippi
  1. Silas, the sufferer—"And when her masters saw that the hope of their gains was gone, they caught Paul and Silas, and drew them into the marketplace unto the rulers. . . . And when they had laid many stripes upon them, they cast them into prison, charging the jailer to keep them safely: who, having received such a charge, thrust them into the inner prison, and made their feet fast in the stocks" (Acts 16:19, 23-24).
  2. Silas, the singer—"And at midnight Paul and Silas prayed, and sang praises unto God: and the prisoners heard them" (Acts 16:25).
  3. Silas, the soul winner—"And suddenly there was a great earthquake, so that the foundations of the prison were shaken: and immediately all the doors were opened, and every one's bands were loosed. And the keeper of the prison awaking out of his sleep, and seeing the prison doors open, he drew out his sword, and would have killed himself, supposing that the prisoners had been fled. But Paul cried with a loud voice, saying, Do thyself no harm: for we are all here. Then he called for a light, and sprang in, and came trembling, and fell down before Paul and Silas, and brought them out, and said, Sirs, what must I do to be saved? And they said, Believe on the Lord Jesus Christ, and thou shalt be saved, and thy house" (Acts 16:26-31).

STATISTICS

First mention: Acts 15:22
Final mention: Acts 18:5
Meaning of his name: "Asked of God"
Frequency of his name: Referred to 13 times
Biblical books mentioning him: One book (Acts)
Occupation: Prophet and missionary (Acts 15:32, 40)
Important fact about his life: He was Paul's faithful associate during his second missionary journey.

Simeon

CHRONOLOGICAL SUMMARY

I. The righteousness of Simeon—"And, behold, there was a man in Jerusalem, whose name was Simeon; and the same man was just and devout, waiting for the consolation of Israel: and the Holy Ghost was upon him" (Luke 2:25).

II. The revelation to Simeon—"And it was revealed unto him by the Holy Ghost, that he should not see death, before he had seen the Lord's Christ" (Luke 2:26).

III. The recognition by Simeon

A. Simeon and the Messiah

1. Who he was—"And he came by the Spirit into the temple: and when the parents brought in the child Jesus, to do for him after the custom of the law, then took he him up in his arms, and blessed God, and said, Lord, now lettest thou thy servant depart in peace, according to thy word: For mine eyes have seen thy salvation" (Luke 2:27-30).

2. What he would do—"Which thou hast prepared before the face of all people; a light to lighten the Gentiles, and the glory of thy people Israel" (Luke 2:31-32).

B. Simeon and the mother—"And Joseph and his mother marvelled at those things which were spoken of him. And Simeon blessed them, and said unto Mary his mother, Behold, this child is set for the fall and rising again of many in Israel; and for a sign which shall be spoken against; (Yea, a sword shall pierce through thy own soul also,) that the thoughts of many hearts may be revealed" (Luke 2:33-35).

STATISTICS

First mention: Luke 2:25
Final mention: Luke 2:34
Meaning of his name: "Hearing"
Frequency of his name: Referred to two times
Biblical books mentioning him: One book (Luke)
Place of birth: Probably Jerusalem
Important fact about his life: He blessed the infant Jesus in the Jerusalem temple.

Simon the Cyrenian

CHRONOLOGICAL SUMMARY

I. Simon, the parent—He was the father of two sons, Alexander and Rufus (Mark 15:21)

II. Simon, the pilgrim—Both Mark (15:21) and Luke (23:26) describe him as "coming from the country" (NASB). Inasmuch as this was Passover time, he may have been en route to the temple to offer a sacrifice.

III. Simon, the participant—Simon is forced to carry Jesus' cross, thus involving him in the crucifixion event.

STATISTICS

Sons: Alexander and Rufus (Mark 15:21)
First Mention: Matthew 27:32
Final Mention: Luke 23:26
Meaning of his name: "Hearing"
Frequency of his name: Referred to three times
Biblical books mentioning him: Three books (Matthew, Mark, Luke)
*Important fact about his life:*He carried Jesus' cross to Calvary.

Simon the Leper

CHRONOLOGICAL SUMMARY

I. Simon the healed—Although the event is not recorded, there is strong evidence to indicate Christ had previously healed Simon of leprosy.

II. Simon the host—He prepared a supper in his home that was attended by Christ.

A. The occasion for the meal—"Now when Jesus was in Bethany, in the house of Simon the leper" (Matt. 26:6). "Then Jesus six days before the pass-over came to Bethany, where Lazarus was which had been dead, whom he raised from the dead. There they made him a supper; and Martha served: but Lazarus was one of them that sat at the table with him" (John 12:1-2).

B. The offering after the meal—"Then took Mary a pound of ointment of spikenard, very costly, and anointed the feet of Jesus, and wiped his feet with her hair: and the house was filled with the odour of the ointment" (John 12:3).

STATISTICS

First mention: Matthew 26:6
Final mention: Mark 14:3
Meaning of his name: "Hearing"
Frequency of his name: Referred to two times
Biblical books mentioning him: Two books (Matthew, Mark)
Important fact about his life: He hosted a supper to celebrate the raising of Lazarus.

Simon the Pharisee

CHRONOLOGICAL SUMMARY

I. Simon the host—"And one of the Pharisees desired him that he would eat with him. And he went into the Pharisee's house, and sat down to meat" (Luke 7:36).

II. Simon the hypocrite—"And, behold, a woman in the city, which was a sinner, when she knew that Jesus sat at meat in the Pharisee's house, brought an alabaster box of ointment, and stood at his feet behind him weeping, and began to wash his feet with tears, and did wipe them with the hairs of her head, and kissed his feet, and anointed them with the ointment. Now when the Pharisee which had bidden him saw it, he spake within himself, saying, This man, if he were a prophet, would have known who and what manner of woman this is that toucheth him: for she is a sinner" (Luke 7:37-39).

III. Simon the humbled

A. Jesus' illustration—"And Jesus answering said unto him, Simon, I have somewhat to say unto thee. And he saith, Master, say on. There was a certain creditor which had two debtors: the one owed five hundred pence, and the other fifty. And when they had nothing to pay, he frankly forgave them both. Tell me therefore, which of them will love him most? Simon answered and said, I suppose that he, to whom he forgave most. And he said unto him, Thou hast rightly judged" (Luke 7:40-43).

B. Jesus' application—"And he turned to the woman, and said unto Simon, Seest thou this woman? I entered into thine house, thou gavest me no water for my feet: but she hath washed my feet with tears, and wiped them with the hairs of her head. Thou gavest me no kiss: but this woman since the time I came in hath not ceased to kiss my feet. My head with oil thou didst not anoint: but this woman hath anointed my feet with ointment. Wherefore I say unto thee, Her sins, which are many, are forgiven; for she loved much: but to whom little is forgiven, the same loveth little" (Luke 7:44-47).

STATISTICS

First mention: Luke 7:40
Final mention: Luke 7:44
Meaning of his name: "Hearing"
Frequency of his name: Referred to three times
Biblical books mentioning him: One book (Luke)
Important fact about his life: Jesus ate supper in Simon's home but had to rebuke him for the sin of hypocrisy.

Simon the Sorcerer

CHRONOLOGICAL SUMMARY

I. The pride of Simon—"But there was a certain man, called Simon, which beforetime in the same city used sorcery, and bewitched the people of Samaria, giving out that himself was some great one" (Acts 8:9).

II. The popularity of Simon—"To whom they all gave heed, from the least to the greatest, saying, This man is the great power of God. And to him they had regard, because that of long time he had bewitched them with sorceries" (Acts 8:10-11).
III. The pretense of Simon—"But when they believed Philip preaching the things concerning the kingdom of God, and the name of Jesus Christ, they were baptized, both men and women. Then Simon himself believed also: and when he was baptized, he continued with Philip, and wondered, beholding the miracles and signs which were done" (Acts 8:12-13).
IV. The perversion of Simon
   A. The bribe—"And when Simon saw that through laying on of the apostles' hands the Holy Ghost was given, he offered them money" (Acts 8:18).
   B. The blasphemy—"Saying, Give me also this power, that on whomsoever I lay hands, he may receive the Holy Ghost" (Acts 8:19).
V. The problem of Simon
   A. Peter told Simon just what he was doing—"But Peter said unto him, Thy money perish with thee, because thou hast thought that the gift of God may be purchased with money. Thou hast neither part nor lot in this matter: for thy heart is not right in the sight of God. Repent therefore of this thy wickedness, and pray God, if perhaps the thought of thine heart may be forgiven thee" (Acts 8:20-22).
   B. Peter told Simon just why he was doing it—"For I perceive that thou art in the gall of bitterness, and in the bond of iniquity" (Acts 8:23).
VI. The plea of Simon—"Then answered Simon, and said, Pray ye to the Lord for me, that none of these things which ye have spoken come upon me" (Acts 8:24).

STATISTICS

First mention: Acts 8:9
Final mention: Acts 8:24
Meaning of his name: "Hearing"
Frequency of his name: Referred to four times
Biblical books mentioning him: One book (Acts)
Important fact about his life: Peter severely rebuked him for attempting to buy the power of the Holy Spirit.

Simon Peter *(see Peter)*

Simon the Zealot

CHRONOLOGICAL SUMMARY

I. The call of Simon (Matt. 10:4; Mark 3:18)
II. The convictions of Simon—This apostle belonged to a right-wing political party known as the Zealots (Luke 6:15; Acts 1:13).

STATISTICS

First mention: Matthew 10:4
Final mention: Acts 1:13
Meaning of his name: "Hearing"
Frequency of his name: Referred to four times
Biblical books mentioning him: Four books (Matthew, Mark, Luke, Acts)
Occupation: Apostle
Important fact about his life: He was the political conservative among Christ's 12 disciples.

Sosthenes

CHRONOLOGICAL SUMMARY

I. Sosthenes, the mistreated—"Then all the Greeks took Sosthenes, the chief ruler of the synagogue, and beat him before the judgment seat. And Gallio cared for none of those things" (Acts 18:17).
II. Sosthenes, the missionary—"Paul, called to be an apostle of Jesus Christ through the will of God, and Sosthenes our brother" (1 Cor. 1:1).

STATISTICS

First mention: Acts 18:17
Final mention: 1 Corinthians 1:1
Frequency of his name: Referred to two times

Biblical books mentioning him: Two books (Acts, 1 Corinthians)
Occupation: Ruler of the synagogue in Corinth
Important fact about his life: In a turn of events, he was beaten by a Gentile mob instead of Paul, the intended victim.

Stephanas

CHRONOLOGICAL SUMMARY

I. Stephanas: The first convert in Greece—"I beseech you, brethren, (ye know the house of Stephanas, that it is the firstfruits of Achaia, and that they have addicted themselves to the ministry of the saints). . . . And I baptized also the household of Stephanas: besides, I know not whether I baptized any other" (1 Cor. 16:15; 1:16).

II. Stephanas: The fruitful convert of Greece—He and two other believers had traveled from Corinth to Ephesus where they assisted the Apostle Paul. "I am glad of the coming of Stephanas and Fortunatus and Achaicus: for that which was lacking on your part they have supplied. For they have refreshed my spirit and yours: therefore acknowledge ye them that are such" (1 Cor. 16:17-18).

STATISTICS

First mention: 1 Corinthians 1:16
Final mention: 1 Corinthians 16:17
Meaning of his name: "Crown, wreath"
Frequency of his name: Referred to three times
Biblical books mentioning him: One book (1 Corinthians)
Important fact about his life: He was Paul's first male convert in Greece.

Stephen

CHRONOLOGICAL SUMMARY

I. The complaint of the laity—"And in those days, when the number of the disciples was multiplied, there arose a murmuring of the Grecians against the Hebrews, because their widows were neglected in the daily ministration" (Acts 6:1).

II. The conference of the leaders—"Then the twelve called the multitude of the disciples unto them, and said, It is not reason that we should leave the word of God, and serve tables" (Acts 6:2).

III. The choice of the laborers—"Wherefore, brethren, look ye out among you seven men of honest report, full of the Holy Ghost and wisdom, whom we may appoint over this business. But we will give ourselves continually to prayer, and to the ministry of the word" (Acts 6:3-4).

   A. The maturity of Stephen—"And the saying pleased the whole multitude: and they chose Stephen, a man full of faith and of the Holy Ghost" (Acts 6:5a).

   B. The miracles of Stephen—"And Stephen, full of faith and power, did great wonders and miracles among the people" (Acts 6:8).

   C. The maligning of Stephen—Stephen was viciously slandered by a group of religious men.

      1. Who they were—"Then there arose certain of the synagogue, which is called the synagogue of the Libertines, and Cyrenians, and Alexandrians, and of them of Cilicia and of Asia, disputing with Stephen" (Acts 6:9).

      2. What they did—"Then they suborned men, which said, We have heard him speak blasphemous words against Moses, and against God. And they stirred up the people, and the elders, and the scribes, and came upon him, and caught him, and brought him to the council, and set up false witnesses, which said, This man ceaseth not to speak blasphemous words against this holy place, and the law: For we have heard him say, that this Jesus of Nazareth shall destroy this place, and shall change the customs which Moses delivered us" (Acts 6:11-14).

3. Why they did it—"And they were not able to resist the wisdom and the spirit by which he spake" (Acts 6:10).

D. The meekness of Stephen—"And all that sat in the council, looking stedfastly on him, saw his face as it had been the face of an angel" (Acts 6:15).

E. The message of Stephen—As has been seen (Acts 6:13-14), the charge against Stephen was that he had been predicting the future destruction of both the Jewish temple (the Herodian, second temple) and the Jewish Law. In his defense, Stephen pointed out the following:

1. Israel had been blessed by God even before possession of the first temple, built by Solomon.
   a. God had led Abraham into Canaan (Acts 7:2-8).
   b. God had protected his seed while in Egypt (Acts 7:9-17).
   c. God had brought Israel out of Egypt (Acts 7:18-36).
   d. God had led them back to Canaan (Acts 7:37-45).
2. Israel had nevertheless turned from God.
   a. During the days of its first temple
   b. During the days of its second temple—"Ye stiffnecked and uncircumcised in heart and ears, ye do always resist the Holy Ghost: as your fathers did, so do ye. Which of the prophets have not your fathers persecuted? and they have slain them which shewed before of the coming of the Just One; of whom ye have been now the betrayers and murderers: Who have received the law by the disposition of angels, and have not kept it" (Acts 7:51-53).

F. The martyrdom of Stephen

1. His persecutors—"When they heard these things, they were cut to the heart, and they gnashed on him with their teeth. . . . Then they cried out with a loud voice, and stopped their ears, and ran upon him with one accord, and cast him out of the city, and stoned him: and the witnesses laid down their clothes at a young man's feet, whose name was Saul" (Acts 7:54, 57-58).
2. His preview of glory—"But he, being full of the Holy Ghost, looked up stedfastly into heaven, and s aw the glory of God, and Jesus standing on the right hand of God, and said, Behold, I see the heavens opened, and the Son of man standing on the right hand of God" (Acts 7:55-56).
3. His prayers
   a. For himself—"And they stoned Stephen, calling upon God, and saying, Lord Jesus, receive my spirit" (Acts 7:59).
   b. For his enemies—"And he kneeled down, and cried with a loud voice, Lord, lay not this sin to their charge" (Acts 7:60a).
4. His passing—"And when he had said this, he fell asleep" (Acts 7:60b).

STATISTICS

First mention: Acts 6:5
Final mention: Acts 22:20
Meaning of his name: "Crown, wreath"
Frequency of his name: Referred to seven times
Biblical books mentioning him: One book (Acts)
Occupation: Deacon and evangelist
Place of death: Jerusalem
Circumstances of death: He was stoned to death.
Important fact about his life: He was the first recorded martyr in the early church.

Syntyche

CHRONOLOGICAL SUMMARY

I. Her faithfulness—She had rendered great assistance to the Apostle Paul. "Which laboured with me in the gospel" (Phil. 4:3b).

II. Her feud—She was at odds with another woman in the Philippian church. "I beseech Euodias, and beseech Syntyche, that they be of the same mind in the Lord" (Phil. 4:2).

III. Her friend—Paul requested that a mutual friend of these two women attempt to reconcile them. "And I entreat thee also, true yokefellow, help those women" (Phil. 4:3a).

STATISTICS

First mention: Philippians 4:2
Final mention: Philippians 4:2
Meaning of her name: "Fortunate"
Frequency of her name: Referred to one time
Biblical books mentioning her: One book (Philippians)
Important fact about her life: This godly helper of Paul had experienced a falling out with another woman in the church at Philippi.

Tertullus

CHRONOLOGICAL SUMMARY

I. Tertullus, the Jewish spokesman against Paul—"And after five days Ananias the high priest descended with the elders, and with a certain orator named Tertullus, who in-formed the governor against Paul" (Acts 24:1).

II. Tertullus, the Jewish slanderer against Paul
  A. His flattery concerning the governor—"And when he was called forth, Tertullus began to accuse him, saying, Seeing that by thee we enjoy great quietness, and that very worthy deeds are done unto this nation by thy providence, we accept it always, and in all places, most noble Felix, with all thankfulness. Notwithstanding, that I be not further tedious unto thee, I pray thee that thou wouldest hear us of thy clemency a few words" (Acts 24:2-4).
  B. His fabrications concerning the apostle—Paul was accused of three things:
    1. That he was a troublemaker, stirring up riots among the Jews all over the world (Acts 24:5a)
    2. That he was a ringleader of the Nazarene sect (Acts 24:5b)
    3. That he was a defiler of the Jewish temple (Acts 24:6a)

STATISTICS

First mention: Acts 24:1
Final mention: Acts 24:2
Frequency of his name: Referred to two times
Biblical books mentioning him: One book (Acts)
Occupation: Jewish lawyer
Important fact about his life: He assumed the role of prosecuting attorney against Paul before the Roman governor, Felix.

Thaddaeus

CHRONOLOGICAL SUMMARY

I. The confusion of Thaddaeus (also called Judas)—"Judas saith unto him, not Iscariot, Lord, how is it that thou wilt manifest thyself unto us, and not unto the world?" (John 14:22).

II. The clarification to Thaddaeus—"Jesus answered and said unto him, If a man love me, he will keep my words: and my Father will love him, and we will come unto him, and make our abode with him" (John 14:23).

STATISTICS

Father: James (Acts 1:13)
First mention: Matthew 10:3
Final mention: Acts 1:13
Meaning of his name: Thaddaeus means "courageous"; Judas means "praise"; Labbaeus means "man of heart."
Frequency of his name: Referred to six times
Biblical books mentioning him: Five books (Matthew, Mark, Luke, John, Acts)
Occupation: Apostle
Important fact about his life: He was the last of three apostles who asked Jesus a question during the final Passover in the upper room.

Theophilus

CHRONOLOGICAL SUMMARY

I. Luke wrote a letter to him, describing the earthly ministry of the Son of God—the Gospel of Luke. "Forasmuch as many have taken in hand to set forth in order a declaration of those things which are most surely believed among us, even as they delivered them unto us, which from the beginning were eye-witnesses, and ministers of the word; it seemed good to me also, having had perfect understanding of all things from the very first, to write unto thee in order, most excellent Theophilus, that thou mightest know the certainty of those things, wherein thou hast been instructed" (Luke 1:1-4).

II. Luke wrote a letter to him, describing the earthly ministry of the Spirit of God—the book of Acts. "The former treatise have I made, O Theophilus, of all that Jesus began both to do and teach, until the day in which he was taken up, after that he through the Holy Ghost had given commandments unto the apostles whom he had chosen: To whom also he shewed himself alive after his passion by many infallible proofs, being seen of them forty days, and speaking of the things pertaining to the kingdom of God: And, being assembled together with them, commanded them that they should not depart from Jerusalem, but wait for the promise of the Father, which, saith he, ye have heard of me. For John truly baptized with water; but ye shall be baptized with the Holy Ghost not many days hence" (Acts 1:1-5).

STATISTICS

First mention: Luke 1:3
Final mention: Acts 1:1
Meaning of his name: "Loved by God"
Frequency of his name: Referred to two times
Biblical books mentioning him: Two books (Luke, Acts)
Important fact about his life: Luke addressed both of his New Testament books to this man.

Theudas

CHRONOLOGICAL SUMMARY

I. Theudas the anarchist—"To whom a number of men, about four hundred, joined themselves" (Acts 5:36b).

II. Theudas the arrogant—"Boasting himself to be somebody" (Acts 5:36a).

III. Theudas the assassinated—"Who was slain; and all, as many as obeyed him, were scattered, and brought to nought" (Acts 5:36c).

STATISTICS

First mention: Acts 5:36
Final mention: Acts 5:36
Meaning of his name: "Gift of God"
Frequency of his name: Referred to one time
Biblical books mentioning him: One book (Acts)
Occupation: Rebel
Important fact about his life: Gamaliel referred to Theudas as an example, warning the Pharisees against undue persecution of the apostles.

Thomas

CHRONOLOGICAL SUMMARY

I. The call of Thomas (Matt. 10:3; Mark 3:18; Luke 6:15)

II. The confusion of Thomas (John 14:1-7)—"In my Father's house are many mansions: if it were not so, I would have told you. I go to prepare a place for you. And if I go and prepare a place for you, I will come again, and receive you unto myself; that where I am, there ye may be also. And whither I go ye know, and the way ye know. Thomas saith unto him, Lord, we know not whither thou goest; and how can we know the way? Jesus saith unto him, I am the way, the truth, and the life: no man cometh unto the Father, but by me" (John 14:2-6).

III. The conflicts of Thomas

A. His despair preceding the resurrection of Lazarus (John 11:7-16)—"Then after that saith he to his disciples, Let us go into Judaea again. His disciples say unto him, Master, the Jews of late sought to stone thee; and goest thou thither again? . . . These things said he: and after that he saith unto them, Our friend Lazarus sleepeth; but I go, that I may awake him out of sleep. Then said his disciples, Lord, if he sleep, he shall do well. Howbeit Jesus spake of his death: but they thought that he had spoken of taking of rest in sleep. Then said Jesus unto them plainly, Lazarus is dead. And I am glad for your sakes that I was not there, to the intent ye may believe; nevertheless let us go unto him. Then said Thomas, which is called Didymus, unto his fellow disciples, Let us also go, that we may die with him" (John 11:7-8, 11-16).

B. His doubt following the resurrection of Christ (John 20:24-29)
   1. The report to Thomas (John 20:24-25)—"But Thomas, one of the twelve, called Didymus, was not with them when Jesus came. The other disciples therefore said unto him, We have seen the Lord" (John 20:24-25a).
   2. The reluctance of Thomas—"But he said unto them, Except I shall see in his hands the print of the nails, and put my finger into the print of the nails, and thrust my hand into his side, I will not believe" (John 20:25b).

IV. The convincing of Thomas (John 20:26-29)
   A. The manifestation—"And after eight days again his disciples were within, and Thomas with them: then came Jesus, the doors being shut, and stood in the midst, and said, Peace be unto you" (John 20:26).
   B. The invitation—"Then saith he to Thomas, Reach hither thy finger, and behold my hands; and reach hither thy hand, and thrust it into my side: and be not faithless, but believing" (John 20:27).
   C. The adoration—"And Thomas answered and said unto him, My Lord and my God" (John 20:28).
   D. The observation—"Jesus saith unto him, Thomas, because thou hast seen me, thou hast believed: blessed are they that have not seen, and yet have believed" (John 20:29).

STATISTICS

Brother: Thomas had an unnamed twin brother (John 11:16; 20:24; 21:2).
First mention: Matthew 10:3
Final mention: Acts 1:13
Meaning of his name: Thomas means "twin" (from the Greek); Didymus also means "twin" (from the Aramaic).
Frequency of his name: Referred to 15 times
Biblical books mentioning him: Five books (Matthew, Mark, Luke, John, Acts)
Occupation: Apostle
Place of birth: The area of Galilee
Place of death: Tradition says he died in India.
Circumstances of death: Tradition says he died a martyr, killed by arrows as he was praying.
Important fact about his life: He was known as the doubting apostle.

Timothy

CHRONOLOGICAL SUMMARY

I. Timothy, the person
   A. He was from Lystra and probably was saved during Paul's first missionary trip (Acts 14:19-20; 16:1-2).
   B. His mother (Eunice) and grandmother (Lois) were godly Jewish women, but his father was a pagan Greek (Acts 16:1-2; 2 Tim. 1:5).
   C. He had been brought up on God's Word (2 Tim. 3:14-15).
   D. He was a man of great faith (2 Tim. 1:5).
   E. Paul regarded him as his own son in the faith (1 Tim. 1:2; 2 Tim. 1:2).
   F. Timothy may have been a somewhat reserved individual who did not always enjoy robust health (1 Tim. 4:12, 14-16).
   G. He was, nevertheless, a man of God (see 1 Tim. 6:11).

II. Timothy, the partner—Timothy became a faithful coworker with the Apostle Paul.
  A. He was invited by Paul to "join the team" during the apostle's second trip (Acts 16:3)—This team would consist of Silas, Paul, and Luke. Timothy may have been chosen to take John Mark's place. (See Acts 13:5.)
  B. He was circumcised by Paul so that he might have freedom to preach the gospel in various Jewish synagogues (Acts 16:3; see also 1 Cor. 9:20).
  C. Timothy was formally ordained by Paul and the presbytery (1 Tim. 4:14; 2 Tim. 1:6).
  D. He also accompanied Paul during the third missionary trip (Acts 19:22; 20:4; 2 Cor. 1:1, 19).
  E. He became Paul's close companion during the apostle's first imprisonment (see Phil. 1:1; Col. 1:1; Philem. 1).
  F. Paul's final request before his martyrdom in Rome was for Timothy to be at his side (2 Tim. 4:9, 21).

III. Timothy, the pastor
  A. His witnessing for Paul—At the apostle's request, Timothy performed a ministry in at least five New Testament churches. These were:
    1. The church at Thessalonica—"Wherefore when we could no longer forbear, we thought it good to be left at Athens alone; and sent Timotheus, our brother, and minister of God, and our fellowlabourer in the gospel of Christ, to establish you, and to comfort you concerning your faith. . . . But now when Timotheus came from you unto us, and brought us good tidings of your faith and charity, and that ye have good remembrance of us always, desiring greatly to see us, as we also to see you" (1 Thess. 3:1-2, 6).
    2. The church at Corinth—"For this cause have I sent unto you Timotheus, who is my beloved son, and faithful in the Lord, who shall bring you into remembrance of my ways which be in Christ, as I teach every where in every church. . . . Now if Timotheus come, see that he may be with you without fear: for he worketh the work of the Lord, as I also do. Let no man therefore despise him: but conduct him forth in peace, that he may come unto me: for I look for him with the brethren" (1 Cor. 4:17; 16:10-11).
    3. The church at Philippi—"But I trust in the Lord Jesus to send Timotheus shortly unto you, that I also may be of good comfort, when I know your state. For I have no man likeminded, who will naturally care for your state. For all seek their own, not the things which are Jesus Christ's. But ye know the proof of him, that, as a son with the father, he hath served with me in the gospel" (Phil. 2:19-22).
    4. The church at Berea (Acts 17:14)
    5. The church at Ephesus—"As I besought thee to abide still at Ephesus, when I went into Macedonia, that thou mightest charge some that they teach no other doctrine" (1 Tim. 1:3).
  B. His writings from Paul—While at Ephesus, Timothy received two letters from Paul, 1 and 2 Timothy. In these epistles Paul exhorted and encouraged Timothy.
    1. Stir up your gift—"Neglect not the gift that is in thee, which was given thee by prophecy, with the laying on of the hands of the presbytery. Meditate upon these things; give thyself wholly to them; that thy profiting may appear to all" (1 Tim. 4:14-15).
    2. Be a good soldier—"This charge I commit unto thee, son Timothy, according to the prophecies which went before on thee, that thou by them mightest war a good warfare" (1 Tim. 1:18). "Fight the good fight of faith, lay hold on eternal life, whereunto thou art also called, and hast professed a good profession before many witnesses"

(1 Tim. 6:12). "Thou therefore endure hardness, as a good soldier of Jesus Christ" (2 Tim. 2:3).

3. Watch your own life—"Take heed unto thyself, and unto the doctrine; continue in them: for in doing this thou shalt both save thyself, and them that hear thee" (1 Tim. 4:16).
4. Be gentle—"And the servant of the Lord must not strive; but be gentle unto all men, apt to teach, patient, in meekness instructing those that oppose themselves; if God peradventure will give them repentance to the acknowledging of the truth" (2 Tim. 2:24-25).
5. Be impartial—"I charge thee before God, and the Lord Jesus Christ, and the elect angels, that thou observe these things without preferring one before another, doing nothing by partiality" (1 Tim. 5:21).
6. Flee from sin—"Flee also youthful lusts: but follow righteousness, faith, charity, peace, with them that call on the Lord out of a pure heart" (2 Tim. 2:22).
7. Denounce sin—"Them that sin rebuke before all, that others also may fear" (1 Tim. 5:20).
8. Follow after righteousness—"But thou, O man of God, flee these things; and follow after righteousness, godliness, faith, love, patience, meekness" (1 Tim. 6:11).
9. Bring others to Christ—"But watch thou in all things, endure afflictions, do the work of an evangelist, make full proof of thy ministry" (2 Tim. 4:5).
10. Give priority to the Word of God.
    a. Study it—"Study to shew thyself approved unto God, a workman that needeth not to be ashamed, rightly dividing the word of truth" (2 Tim. 2:15).
    b. Continue in it—"But continue thou in the things which thou hast learned and hast been assured of, knowing of whom thou hast learned them" (2 Tim. 3:14).
    c. Preach it—"Preach the word; be instant in season, out of season; reprove, rebuke, exhort with all longsuffering and doctrine" (2 Tim. 4:2).
    d. Commit it to others— "And the things that thou hast heard of me among many witnesses, the same commit thou to faithful men, who shall be able to teach others also" (2 Tim. 2:2).

STATISTICS

Mother: Eunice
First mention: Acts 16:1
Final mention: Hebrews 13:23
Meaning of his name: "Honored of God"
Frequency of his name: Referred to 24 times
Biblical books mentioning him: 12 books (Acts, Romans, 1 Corinthians, 2 Corinthians, Philippians, Colossians, 1 Thessalonians, 2 Thessalonians, 1 Timothy, 2 Timothy, Philemon, Hebrews)
Occupation: Missionary and pastor
Place of birth: Lystra
Important fact about his life: Paul addressed two New Testament epistles to him.

Titus

CHRONOLOGICAL SUMMARY

I. Titus, the man
   A. He was a Gentile Greek, probably from Syrian Antioch.
   B. Paul probably led him to Christ (Acts 11:26; Titus 1:4).
   C. Some believe he may have been the brother of Luke.
   D. He became one of Paul's most trusted associates. The apostle refers to him as:
      1. His true son in the faith (Titus 1:4)
      2. His spiritual brother (2 Cor. 2:13)
      3. His partner and helper (2 Cor. 8:23)
      4. A positive role model (2 Cor. 8:23)

II. Titus, the missionary
  A. He accompanied Paul to Jerusalem after the apostle's first missionary journey—"Then fourteen years after I went up again to Jerusalem with Barnabas, and took Titus with me also. But neither Titus, who was with me, being a Greek, was compelled to be circumcised" (Gal. 2:1, 3).
  B. He joined Paul during his third missionary journey.

III. Titus, the messenger—On at least two occasions during his third missionary journey, Paul sent Titus to straighten out certain problems that developed in the church at Corinth.
  A. Paul had learned while in Ephesus of the opposition that had developed against him in the Corinthian church.
  B. Attempting to correct this, he sent a letter (which he called his "sorrowful letter"; 2 Cor. 2:4; 7:8) by way of Titus to the church.
  C. This letter may have been 1 Corinthians, or a lost letter.
  D. Paul, anxious to learn the results of his letter, went to Troas and Macedonia, looking for Titus.
    1. His grief upon not finding Titus at Troas—"Furthermore, when I came to Troas to preach Christ's gospel, and a door was opened unto me of the Lord, I had no rest in my spirit, because I found not Titus my brother: but taking my leave of them, I went from thence into Macedonia" (2 Cor. 2:12-13). "For, when we were come into Macedonia, our flesh had no rest, but we were troubled on every side; without were fightings, within were fears" (2 Cor. 7:5).
    2. His gladness upon finding Titus in Macedonia—"Nevertheless God, that comforteth those that are cast down, comforted us by the coming of Titus; and not by his coming only, but by the consolation wherewith he was comforted in you, when he told us your earnest desire, your mourning, your fervent mind toward me; so that I rejoiced the more. . . . And his inward affection is more abundant toward you, whilst he remembereth the obedience of you all, how with fear and trembling ye received him" (2 Cor. 7:6-7, 15).
  E. Even though Paul's letter had caused the majority of the Corinthians to repent of their hostility against the apostle, there was still a minority opposition, led by a group of Judaizers (2 Cor. 10–13).
  F. Paul then wrote 2 Corinthians and sent it with Titus and another brother (2 Cor. 8:16-24).

IV. Titus, the minister—"For this cause left I thee in Crete, that thou shouldest set in order the things that are wanting, and ordain elders in every city, as I had appointed thee" (Titus 1:5). At Paul's direction, Titus settled on the Isle of Crete to pastor the church there. During the apostle's second and final Roman imprisonment, he wrote his epistle to Titus. In this letter Titus was instructed to do the following:
  A. Rebuke the slothful life-style of the Cretans (Titus 1:10-13).
  B. Reject all heresy and warn the heretics (Titus 3:10).
  C. Preach sound doctrine (Titus 2:1).
  D. Avoid foolish philosophical speculations (Titus 3:9).
  E. Exhort with all authority (Titus 2:15).
  F. Meet the apostle in Nicopolis (Titus 3:12).
  G. Help Zenas the lawyer and Apollos with their trip (Titus 3:13).

STATISTICS

First mention: 2 Corinthians 2:13
Final mention: Titus 1:4
Frequency of his name: Referred to 12 times
Biblical books mentioning him: Four (2 Corinthians, Galatians, 2 Timothy, Titus)
Occupation: Missionary and pastor
Important fact about his life: Paul addressed a New Testament epistle to him.

Trophimus

CHRONOLOGICAL SUMMARY

I. Trophimus and Paul: The anarchy in Jerusalem (Acts 21:27-32)
  A. The reason for this anarchy—A Jewish mob mistakenly concluded that Paul had brought Trophimus, a Gentile, into the sacred temple area (Acts 21:27-29).
  B. The results of this anarchy—"And all the city was moved, and the people ran together: and they took Paul, and drew him out of the temple: and forthwith the doors were shut. And as they went about to kill him, tidings came unto the chief captain of the band, that all Jerusalem was in an uproar. Who immediately took soldiers and centurions, and ran down unto them: and when they saw the chief captain and the soldiers, they left beating of Paul" (Acts 21:30-32).

II. Trophimus and Paul: The affliction in Miletus—"Erastus abode at Corinth: but Trophimus have I left at Miletum sick" (2 Tim. 4:20).

STATISTICS

First mention: Acts 20:4
Final mention: 2 Timothy 4:20
Meaning of his name: "Nourishing, lover of God"
Frequency of his name: Referred to three times
Biblical books mentioning him: Two books (Acts, 2 Timothy)
Important fact about his life: He was the faithful associate whom the Apostle Paul left sick at Miletus.

Tychicus

CHRONOLOGICAL SUMMARY

I. Tychicus, the man—He was described by Paul as:
  A. A beloved brother (Eph. 6:21)
  B. A faithful minister (Eph. 6:21)
  C. A fellow servant (Col. 4:7)

II. Tychicus, the missionary—He joined Paul during one leg of the apostle's third missionary journey (Acts 20:4).

III. Tychicus, the messenger
  A. He was sent to Ephesus by Paul during the apostle's first Roman imprisonment, carrying with him the New Testament Ephesian epistle (Eph. 6:21).
  B. He was sent to Colosse by Paul during the apostle's first Roman imprisonment, carrying with him the New Testament Colossian epistle (Col. 4:7).
  C. He was sent by Paul to help Titus in Crete between the apostle's first and second Roman imprisonments (Titus 3:12).
  D. He was sent back to Ephesus by Paul during the apostle's final Roman imprisonment (2 Tim. 4:12).

IV. Tychicus, the minister
  A. He ministered to Paul during the first Roman imprisonment (Eph. 6:21; Col. 4:7).
  B. He ministered to Paul during the second and final Roman imprisonments (2 Tim. 4:12).

STATISTICS

First mention: Acts 20:4
Final mention: Titus 3:12
Meaning of his name: "Fortunate"
Frequency of his name: Referred to five times
Biblical books mentioning him: Five books (Acts, Ephesians, Colossians, 2 Timothy, Titus)
Important fact about his life: He faithfully ministered to Paul during both of the apostle's Roman imprisonments.

Zacchaeus

CHRONOLOGICAL SUMMARY

I. Zacchaeus, the sinner—"And Jesus entered and passed through Jericho. And, behold, there was a man named Zacchaeus, which was the chief among the publicans, and he was rich" (Luke 19:1-2).

II. Zacchaeus, the seeker—He desired to meet the Savior, but first had to overcome a problem.
  A. The source of his problem—"And he sought to see Jesus who he was; and could not for the press, because he was little of stature" (Luke 19:3).
  B. The solution to his problem—"And he ran before, and climbed up into a sycomore tree to see him: for he was to pass that way" (Luke 19:4).
III. Zacchaeus, the saved
  A. Jesus' request—"And when Jesus came to the place, he looked up, and saw him, and said unto him, Zacchaeus, make haste, and come down; for to day I must abide at thy house" (Luke 19:5).
  B. Zacchaeus's response—"And he made haste, and came down, and received him joyfully" (Luke 19:6).
IV. Zacchaeus, the Spirit-controlled—Two spoken testimonies immediately made it clear that he had indeed passed from death to life, and was being controlled by the Holy Spirit of God.
  A. Zacchaeus's testimony—"And Zacchaeus stood, and said unto the Lord; Behold, Lord, the half of my goods I give to the poor; and if I have taken any thing from any man by false accusation, I restore him fourfold" (Luke 19:8).
  B. Jesus' testimony—"And Jesus said unto him, This day is salvation come to this house forsomuch as he also is a son of Abraham" (Luke 19:9).

STATISTICS

First mention: Luke 19:2
Final mention: Luke 19:8
Meaning of his name: "Pure"
Frequency of his name: Referred to three times
Occupation: Tax collector
Important fact about his life: This dishonest tax collector met Jesus while in a sycamore tree.

Zacharias

CHRONOLOGICAL SUMMARY

I. Zacharias, the priest
  A. His devotion to God—Both he and his wife Elisabeth loved the Lord. "And they were both righteous before God, walking in all the commandments and ordinances of the Lord blameless" (Luke 1:6).
  B. His duties for God
    1. Zacharias and the altar of the Lord—"And it came to pass, that while he executed the priest's office before God in the order of his course, according to the custom of the priest's office, his lot was to burn incense when he went into the temple of the Lord. And the whole multitude of the people were praying without at the time of incense" (Luke 1:8-10).
    2. Zacharias and the angel of the Lord
      a. The reassurance—"And there appeared unto him an angel of the Lord standing on the right side of the altar of incense. And when Zacharias saw him, he was troubled, and fear fell upon him. But the angel said unto him, Fear not Zacharias: for thy prayer is heard" (Luke 1:11-13).
      b. The revelation—Zacharias heard a sixfold prophecy from this heavenly angel whose name was Gabriel:
        (1) He and Elisabeth would have a son (Luke 1:13).
        (2) His name would be John (Luke 1:13).
        (3) He would become a Spirit-filled Nazirite (Luke 1:15).
        (4) He would have a successful ministry (Luke 1:16).
        (5) He would prepare the way for the Messiah (Luke 1:17).
        (6) His style would be similar to that of Elijah (Luke 1:17).

c. The response—"And Zacharias said unto the angel, Whereby shall I know this? for I am an old man and my wife well stricken in years" (Luke 1:18).

d. The rebuke—"And the angel answering said unto him, I am Gabriel, that stand in the presence of God; and am sent to speak unto thee, and to shew thee these glad tidings. And, behold, thou shalt be dumb, and not able to speak, until the day that these things shall be performed, because thou believest not my words, which shall be fulfilled in their season" (Luke 1:19-20).

e. The results—"And the people waited for Zacharias, and marvelled that he tarried so long in the temple. And when he came out, he could not speak unto them: and they perceived that he had seen a vision in the temple: for he beckoned unto them, and remained speechless" (Luke 1:21-22).

f. The rejoicing—"And it came to pass, that, as soon as the days of his ministration were accomplished, he departed to his own house. And after those days his wife Elisabeth conceived, and hid herself five months, saying, Thus hath the Lord dealt with me in the days wherein he looked on me, to take away my reproach among men" (Luke 1:23-25).

II. Zacharias, the parent

A. Writing—the silent words of Zacharias

1. The celebration—"Now Elisabeth's full time came that she should be delivered; and she brought forth a son. And her neighbours and her cousins heard how the Lord had shewed great mercy upon her; and they rejoiced with her" (Luke 1:57-58).

2. The circumcision—"And it came to pass, that on the eighth day they came to circumcise the child; and they called him Zacharias, after the name of his father" (Luke 1:59).

3. The confusion—"And his mother answered and said, Not so; but he shall be called John. And they said unto her, There is none of thy kindred that is called by this name" (Luke 1:60-61).

4. The confirmation—"And they made signs to his father, how he would have him called. And he asked for a writing table, and wrote, saying, His name is John. And they marvelled all" (Luke 1:62-63).

B. Worshiping—The spoken words of Zacharias. "And his mouth was opened immediately, and his tongue loosed, and he spake, and praised God" (Luke 1:64).

III. Zacharias, the prophet

A. His words to his Savior—"And his father Zacharias was filled with the Holy Ghost, and prophesied, saying, Blessed be the Lord God of Israel; for he hath visited and redeemed his people" (Luke 1:67-68).

1. He thanked God for the Davidic Covenant—"And hath raised up an horn of salvation for us in the house of his servant David" (Luke 1:69).

2. He thanked God for the Abrahamic Covenant—"The oath which he sware to our father Abraham" (Luke 1:73).

B. His words to his son—"And thou, child, shalt be called the prophet of the Highest: for thou shalt go before the face of the Lord to prepare his ways; to give knowledge of salvation unto his people by the remission of their sins, through the tender mercy of our God; whereby the dayspring from on high hath visited us, to give light to them that sit in darkness and in the shadow of death, to guide our feet into the way of peace" (Luke 1:76-79).

STATISTICS
Spouse: Elisabeth
Son: John the Baptist
First mention: Luke 1:5
Final mention: Luke 3:2
Meaning of his name: "God remembers"
Frequency of his name: Referred to eight times
Biblical books mentioning him: One book (Luke)
Occupation: Priest
Important fact about his life: He was the father of John the Baptist.

Unnamed People of the New Testament

The Capernaum Demoniac

I. The predicament of the man—"And there was in their synagogue a man with an unclean spirit; and he cried out" (Mark 1:23).

II. The acknowledgment of the demon—"Saying, Let us alone; what have we to do with thee, thou Jesus of Nazareth? art thou come to destroy us? I know thee who thou art, the Holy One of God" (Mark 1:24).

III. The commandment of the Lord—"And Jesus rebuked him, saying, Hold thy peace, and come out of him" (Mark 1:25).

IV. The amazement of the crowd—"And when the unclean spirit had torn him, and cried with a loud voice, he came out of him. And they were all amazed, insomuch that they questioned among themselves saying, What thing is this? what new doctrine is this? for with authority commandeth he even the unclean spirits, and they do obey him" (Mark 1:26-27).

Peter's Mother-in-Law

I. The suffering mother-in-law—"And when Jesus was come into Peter's house, he saw his wife's mother laid, and sick of a fever" (Matt. 8:14).

II. The serving mother-in-law—"And he touched her hand, and the fever left her: and she arose, and ministered unto them" (Matt. 8:15).

A Galilean Leper

I. The tears of the leper—"And there came a leper to him, beseeching him, and kneeling down to him, and saying unto him, If thou wilt, thou canst make me clean" (Mark 1:40).

II. The transformation of the leper—"And Jesus, moved with compassion, put forth his hand, and touched him, and saith unto him, I will; be thou clean. And as soon as he had spoken, immediately the leprosy departed from him, and he was cleansed" (Mark 1:41-42).

III. The testimony of the leper—"And he straitly charged him, and forthwith sent him away; and saith unto him, See thou say nothing to any man: but go thy way, shew thyself to the priest, and offer for thy cleansing those things which Moses commanded, for a testimony unto them. But he went out, and began to publish it much, and to blaze abroad the matter, insomuch that Jesus could no more openly enter into the city, but was without in desert places: and they came to him from every quarter" (Mark 1:43-45).

The Capernaum Paralytic

I. His helplessness
   A. The intervention of his friends—"And they come unto him, bringing one sick of the palsy, which was borne of four" (Mark 2:3).
   B. The ingenuity of his friends—"And when they could not come nigh unto him for the press, they uncovered the roof where he was: and when they had broken it up, they let down the bed wherein the sick of the palsy lay" (Mark 2:4).

II. His healing
   A. Spiritual healing—"When Jesus saw their faith, he said unto the sick of the palsy, Son, thy sins be forgiven thee" (Mark 2:5).

B. Physical healing—"I say unto thee, Arise, and take up thy bed, and go thy way into thine house. And immediately he arose, took up the bed, and went forth before them all; insomuch that they were all amazed, and glorified God, saying, We never saw it on this fashion" (Mark 2:11-12).

The Man with the Withered Right Hand

I. The victim—"And he [Jesus] entered again into the synagogue; and there was a man there which had a withered hand" (Mark 3:1).

II. The villains—"And they watched him, whether he would heal him on the sabbath day; that they might accuse him" (Mark 3:2).

III. The victor—"And he saith unto the man which had the withered hand, Stand forth" (Mark 3:3).

IV. The valuable—"And he said unto them, What man shall there be among you, that shall have one sheep, and if it fall into a pit on the sabbath day, will he not lay hold on it, and lift it out? How much then is a man better than a sheep? Wherefore it is lawful to do well on the sabbath days" (Matt. 12:11-12).

V. The victory—"Then saith he to the man, Stretch forth thine hand. And he stretched it forth; and it was restored whole, like as the other" (Matt. 12:13).

The Centurion

I. His concern for an individual

A. The problem—"And a certain centurion's servant, who was dear unto him, was sick, and ready to die" (Luke 7:2).

B. The plea—"And when he heard of Jesus, he sent unto him the elders of the Jews, beseeching him that he would come and heal his servant" (Luke 7:3).

II. His love for Israel—"And when they came to Jesus, they besought him instantly, saying, That he was worthy for whom he should do this: For he loveth our nation, and he hath built us a synagogue" (Luke 7:4-5).

III. His faith in Immanuel

A. The centurion's confidence in Christ—"Then Jesus went with them. And when he was now not far from the house, the centurion sent friends to him, saying unto him, Lord, trouble not thyself: for I am not worthy that thou shouldest enter under my roof: Wherefore neither thought I myself worthy to come unto thee: but say in a word, and my servant shall be healed. For I also am a man set under authority, having under me soldiers, and I say unto one, Go, and he goeth; and to another, Come, and he cometh; and to my servant, Do this, and he doeth it" (Luke 7:6-8).

B. The centurion's commendation by Christ—"When Jesus heard these things, he marvelled at him, and turned him about, and said unto the people that followed him, I say unto you, I have not found so great faith, no, not in Israel. And they that were sent, returning to the house, found the servant whole that had been sick" (Luke 7:9-10).

The Widow of Nain

I. The widow's sorrow—"Now when he came nigh to the gate of the city, behold, there was a dead man carried out, the only son of his mother, and she was a widow: and much people of the city was with her" (Luke 7:12).

II. The widow's Savior—"And when the Lord saw her, he had compassion on her, and said unto her, Weep not" (Luke 7:13).

III. The widow's son

A. Resurrected by the Messiah—"And he came and touched the bier: and they that bare him stood still. And he said, Young man, I say unto thee, Arise" (Luke 7:14).

B. Reunited to the mother—"And he that was dead sat up, and began to speak. And he delivered him to his mother" (Luke 7:15).

The Gerasene Maniac

I. The madman of Gadara
   A. The Gerasene maniac, controlled by demons
      1. His home—"Who had his dwelling among the tombs" (Mark 5:3).
      2. His helplessness
         a. He was naked (Luke 8:27).
         b. He was "exceeding fierce" (Matt. 8:28).
         c. He was totally unmanageable (Mark 5:3-4).
         d. He was constantly crying and cutting himself with stones (Mark 5:5).
         e. He was seized upon and driven about by a legion of demons (Luke 8:29; Mark 5:9).
   B. The Galilean Messiah, controller of demons
      1. They knew him—"And, behold, they cried out, saying, What have we to do with thee, Jesus, thou Son of God?" (Matt. 8:29a).
      2. They feared him—"Art thou come hither to torment us before the time?" (Matt. 8:29b). "I adjure thee by God, that thou torment me not" (Mark 5:7b).
      3. They obeyed him.
         a. The rebuke—"For he said unto him, Come out of the man, thou unclean spirit" (Mark 5:8).
         b. The renegades—"And he asked him, What is thy name? And he answered, saying, My name is Legion: for we are many" (Mark 5:9).
         c. The request—"And he besought him much that he would not send them away out of the country. Now there was there nigh unto the mountains a great herd of swine feeding. And all the devils besought him, saying, Send us into the swine, that we may enter into them" (Mark 5:10-12).
         d. The release—"And forthwith Jesus gave them leave. And the unclean spirits went out, and entered into the swine: and the herd ran violently down a steep place into the sea, (they were about two thousand;) and were choked in the sea" (Mark 5:13).

II. The missionary from Gadara
   A. His deliverance by Christ—"Then they went out to see what was done; and came to Jesus, and found the man, out of whom the devils were departed, sitting at the feet of Jesus, clothed, and in his right mind: and they were afraid" (Luke 8:35).
   B. His desire (as expressed) to Christ
      1. Let me go with you—"And when he was come into the ship, he that had been possessed with the devil prayed him that he might be with him" (Mark 5:18).
      2. I want you to go for me— "Howbeit Jesus suffered him not, but saith unto him, Go home to thy friends, and tell them how great things the Lord hath done for thee, and hath had compassion on thee" (Mark 5:19).
   C. His declaration for Christ—"And he departed, and began to publish in Decapolis how great things Jesus had done for him: and all men did marvel" (Mark 5:20).

The Woman with the Issue of Blood

I. The hurting patient
   A. Her years of frustration—"And a certain woman, which had an issue of blood twelve years, and had suffered many things of many physicians, and had spent all that she had, and was nothing bettered, but rather grew worse, when she had heard of Jesus, came in the press behind, and touched his garment" (Mark 5:25-27).
   B. Her hour of expectation—"For she said, If I may touch but his clothes, I shall be whole" (Mark 5:28).
   C. Her moment of realization—"And straightway the fountain of her blood

was dried up; and she felt in her body that she was healed of that plague" (Mark 5:29).

II. The healing physician
  A. The announcement—"And Jesus said, Who touched me? When all denied, Peter and they that were with him said, Master, the multitude throng thee and press thee, and sayest thou, Who touched me? And Jesus said, Somebody hath touched me: for I perceive that virtue is gone out of me" (Luke 8:45-46).
  B. The acknowledgment—"And when the woman saw that she was not hid, she came trembling, and falling down before him, she declared unto him before all the people for what cause she had touched him, and how she was healed immediately" (Luke 8:47).
  C. The assurance—"And he said unto her, Daughter, thy faith hath made thee whole; go in peace, and be whole of thy plague" (Mark 5:34).

Two Galilean Blind Men

I. The request of the sightless—"And when Jesus departed thence, two blind men followed him, crying, and saying, Thou Son of David, have mercy on us" (Matt. 9:27).

II. The response of the sinless
  A. The test of Jesus—"And when he was come into the house, the blind men came to him: and Jesus saith unto them, Believe ye that I am able to do this? They said unto him, Yea, Lord" (Matt. 9:28).
  B. The touch of Jesus—"Then touched he their eyes, saying, According to your faith be it unto you" (Matt. 9:29).
  C. The testimony for Jesus—"And their eyes were opened; and Jesus straitly charged them, saying, See that no man know it. But they, when they were departed, spread abroad his fame in all that country" (Matt. 9:30-31).

The Man Who Had Been a Cripple for 38 Years

I. The cripple and the Christ (first meeting)
  A. Wallowing on his bed of affliction
    1. The misery by the Bethesda waters—"Now there is at Jerusalem by the sheep market a pool, which is called in the Hebrew tongue Bethesda, having five porches" (John 5:2).
      a. A great multitude was there—"In these lay a great multitude of impotent folk, of blind, halt, withered" (John 5:3a).
      b. A certain man was there—"And a certain man was there, which had an infirmity thirty and eight years" (John 5:5).
    2. The moving of the Bethesda waters—"Waiting for the moving of the waters" (John 5:3b). "For an angel went down at a certain sea-son into the pool, and troubled the water: whosoever then first after the troubling of the water stepped in was made whole of whatsoever disease he had" (John 5:4).
    3. The miracle at the Bethesda waters
      a. The Savior's invitation—"When Jesus saw him lie, and knew t hat he had been now a long time in that case, he saith unto him, Wilt thou be made whole?" (John 5:6).
      b. The sick man's ignorance—He did not realize to whom he was speaking. "The impotent man answered him, Sir, I have no man, when the water is troubled, to put me into the pool: but while I am coming, another steppeth down before me" (John 5:7).
  B. Walking with his bed of affliction—"Jesus saith unto him, Rise, take up thy bed, and walk. And immediately the man was made whole, and took up his bed, and walked: and on the same day was the sabbath" (John 5:8-9).

II. The cripple and the critics
  A. First round—"The Jews therefore said unto him that was cured, It is the sabbath day: it is not lawful for thee

to carry thy bed. He answered them, He that made me whole, the same said unto me, Take up thy bed, and walk" (John 5:10-11).

B. Second round—"Then asked they him, What man is that which said unto thee, Take up thy bed, and walk? And he that was healed wist not who it was: for Jesus had conveyed himself away, a multitude being in that place" (John 5:12-13).

III. The cripple and the Christ (final meeting)

A. His warning from Jesus—"Afterward Jesus findeth him in the temple, and said unto him, Behold, thou art made whole: sin no more, lest a worse thing come unto thee" (John 5:14).

B. His witness for Jesus—"The man departed, and told the Jews that it was Jesus, which had made him whole" (John 5:15).

The Boy with a Lunch

I. The meager lunch of the boy—"One of his disciples, Andrew, Simon Peter's brother, saith unto him, There is a lad here, which hath five barley loaves, and two small fishes: but what are they among so many?" (John 6:8-9).

II. The miraculous lunch of the boy—It was used by Jesus to feed 5,000 men plus their families. "And when he had taken the five loaves and the two fishes, he looked up to heaven, and blessed, and brake the loaves, and gave them to his disciples to set before them; and the two fishes divided he among them all. And they did all eat, and were filled" (Mark 6:41-42).

The Mother of a Demoniac Girl

I. The brokenhearted mother

A. The place—"Then Jesus went thence, and departed into the coasts of Tyre and Sidon" (Matt. 15:21).

B. The problem—"For a certain woman, whose young daughter had an unclean spirit, heard of him, and came and fell at his feet" (Mark 7:25).

C. The plea—"And, behold, a woman of Canaan came out of the same coasts, and cried unto him, saying, Have mercy on me, O Lord, thou Son of David; my daughter is grievously vexed with a devil" (Matt. 15:22).

II. The hardhearted ministers—"But he answered her not a word. And his disciples came and besought him, saying, Send her away; for she crieth after us" (Matt. 15:23).

III. The kindhearted Messiah

A. His gentle reminder—"But he answered and said, I am not sent but unto the lost sheep of the house of Israel. . . . But he answered and said, It is not meet to take the children's bread, and to cast it to dogs" (Matt. 15:24, 26).

B. Her graceful reaction

1. Her worship of Jesus—"Then came she and worshipped him" (Matt. 15:25a).

2. Her words to Jesus

a. The reasoning—"And she answered and said unto him, Yes, Lord: yet the dogs under the table eat of the children's crumbs" (Mark 7:28).

b. The reward—"Then Jesus answered and said unto her, O woman, great is thy faith: be it unto thee even as thou wilt. And her daughter was made whole from that very hour" (Matt. 15:28).

The Deaf Man with a Speech Impediment

I. The request to Jesus—"And they bring unto him one that was deaf, and had an impediment in his speech; and they beseech him to put his hand upon him" (Mark 7:32).

II. The reaction by Jesus

A. He touched and held the man—"And he took him aside from the multitude, and put his fingers into his ears, and he spit, and touched his tongue" (Mark 7:33).

B. He transformed and healed the man—"And looking up to heaven, he sighed, and saith unto him, Ephphatha, that is, Be opened. And straightway his ears were opened, and the string of his tongue was loosed, and he spake plain" (Mark 7:34-35).

III. The report concerning Jesus—"And he charged them that they should tell no man: but the more he charged them, so much the more a great deal they published it; and were beyond measure astonished, saying, He hath done all things well: he maketh both the deaf to hear, and the dumb to speak" (Mark 7:36-37).

The Blind Man of Bethsaida

I. The first touch by the Savior
  A. The request—"And he cometh to Bethsaida; and they bring a blind man unto him, and besought him to touch him" (Mark 8:22).
  B. The reaction—"And he took the blind man by the hand, and led him out of the town; and when he had spit on his eyes, and put his hands upon him, he asked him if he saw ought" (Mark 8:23).
  C. The results—"And he looked up, and said, I see men as trees, walking" (Mark 8:24).

II. The final touch by the Savior
  A. Restoring—"After that he put his hands again upon his eyes, and made him look up: and he was restored, and saw every man clearly" (Mark 8:25).
  B. Requesting—"And he sent him away to his house, saying, Neither go into the town, nor tell it to any in the town" (Mark 8:26).

The Man Born Blind

I. Inconsideration—The disciples and the blind man: "And as Jesus passed by, he saw a man which was blind from his birth. And his disciples asked him, saying, Master, who did sin, this man, or his parents, that he was born blind?" (John 9:1-2).

II. Evangelization—The Savior and the blind man (first meeting)
  A. Jesus viewed the man as a subject of God's plan—"Jesus answered, Neither hath this man sinned, nor his parents: but that the works of God should be made manifest in him" (John 9:3).
  B. Jesus viewed himself as a servant in God's plan.
    1. The mission—"I must work the works of him that sent me, while it is day: the night cometh, when no man can work. As long as I am in the world, I am the light of the world" (John 9:4-5).
    2. The miracle—"When he had thus spoken, he spat on the ground, and made clay of the spittle, and he anointed the eyes of the blind man with the clay, and said unto him, Go, wash in the pool of Siloam, (which is by interpretation, Sent.) He went his way therefore, and washed, and came seeing" (John 9:6-7).

III. Speculation—The neighbors and the blind man
  A. Their confusion—"The neighbours therefore, and they which before had seen him that he was blind, said, Is not this he that sat and begged? Some said, This is he: others said, He is like him: but he said, I am he" (John 9:8-9).
  B. His clarification—"Therefore said they unto him, How were thine eyes opened? He answered and said, A man that is called Jesus made clay, and anointed mine eyes, and said unto me, Go to the pool of Siloam, and wash: and I went and washed, and I received sight" (John 9:10-11).

IV. Interrogation—The parents and the blind man
  A. The demands—"But the Jews did not believe concerning him, that he had been blind, and received his sight, until they called the parents of him that had received his sight. And they asked them, saying, Is this your son, who ye say was born blind? how then doth he now see?" (John 9:18-19).
  B. The denials—"His parents answered them and said, We know that this is our son, and that he was born blind: But by what means he now seeth, we know not; or who hath opened his eyes,

we know not: he is of age; ask him: he shall speak for himself. These words spake his parents, because they feared the Jews: for the Jews had agreed already, that if any man did confess that he was Christ, he should be put out of the synagogue. Therefore said his parents, He is of age; ask him" (John 9:20-23).

V. Castigation—The Pharisees and the blind man
  A. First round:
    1. The denunciation of Christ by the critics—"Therefore said some of the Pharisees, This man is not of God, because he keepeth not the sabbath day. Others said, How can a man that is a sinner do such miracles? And there was a division among them" (John 9:16).
    2. The defense of Christ by the convert—"They say unto the blind man again, What sayest thou of him, that he hath opened thine eyes? He said, He is a prophet" (John 9:17).
  B. Second round:
    1. The denunciation of Christ by the critics
      a. They said he was ungodly—"Then again called they the man that was blind, and said unto him, Give God the praise: we know that this man is a sinner" (John 9:24).
      b. They said he was unknown—"Then they reviled him, and said, Thou art his disciple; but we are Moses' disciples. We know that God spake unto Moses: as for this fellow, we know not from whence he is" (John 9:28-29).
    2. The defense of Christ by the convert
      a. He offered a personal argument—"He answered and said, Whether he be a sinner or no, I know not: one thing I know, that, whereas I was blind, now I see" (John 9:25).
      b. He offered a philosophical argument—"The man answered and said unto them, Why herein is a marvellous thing, that ye know not from whence he is, and yet he hath opened mine eyes. Now we know that God heareth not sinners: but if any man be a worshipper of God, and doeth his will, him he heareth. Since the world began was it not heard that any man opened the eyes of one that was born blind. If this man were not of God, he could do nothing" (John 9:30-33).
  C. Third round: Unable to destroy his testimony, the frustrated Pharisees excommunicated the cured man from the synagogue—"They answered and said unto him, Thou wast altogether born in sins, and dost thou teach us? And they cast him out" (John 9:34).

VI. Summarization—The Savior and the blind man (final meeting)—"And Jesus said, For judgment I am come into this world" (John 9:39a).
  A. "That they which see not might see" (John 9:39b). All converts to Christ belong to this group.
    1. Jesus' words to the former blind man—"Jesus heard that they had cast him out; and when he had found him, he said unto him, Dost thou believe on the Son of God? He answered and said, Who is he, Lord, that I might believe on him? And Jesus said unto him, Thou hast both seen him, and it is he that talketh with thee" (John 9:35-37).
    2. Jesus' worship by the former blind man—"And he said, Lord, I believe. And he worshipped him" (John 9:38).
  B. "That they which see might be made blind" (John 4:39c). All critics of Christ belong to this group. "And some of the Pharisees which were with him heard these words and said unto him,

Are we blind also? Jesus said unto them, If ye were blind, ye should have no sin: but now ye say, We see; therefore your sin remaineth" (John 9:40-41).

The Father of a Demon-Possessed Boy

I. The victims
   A. The helpless father—"And, behold, a man of the company cried out, saying, Master, I beseech thee, look upon my son: for he is mine only child" (Luke 9:38).
   B. The hopeless son
      1. The source of his problem—The boy was controlled by a demon (Mark 9:17; Luke 9:39).
      2. The symptoms of his problem
         a. The evil spirit would throw him down (Luke 9:42).
         b. It would throw him into fire and water (Mark 9:22).
         c. It caused him to foam at the mouth and grind his teeth (Mark 9:18).
         d. It tore at him (Luke 9:39).
         e. It bruised him (Luke 9:39).
         f. It was slowly killing him (Mark 9:18).
      3. The span of his problem—"And he asked his father, How long is it ago since this came unto him? And he said, Of a child" (Mark 9:21).
   C. The hapless disciples—"And I brought him to thy disciples, and they could not cure him" (Matt. 17:16).
II. The victor
   A. Jesus encouraged the father.
      1. The strength of faith—"Jesus said unto him, If thou canst believe, all things are possible to him that believeth" (Mark 9:23).
      2. The struggle for faith—"And straightway the father of the child cried out, and said with tears, Lord, I believe; help thou mine unbelief" (Mark 9:24).
   B. Jesus excoriated the demon.
      1. The rebuke—"When Jesus saw that the people came running together, he rebuked the foul spirit, saying unto him, Thou dumb and deaf spirit, I charge thee, come out of him, and enter no more into him" (Mark 9:25).
      2. The results—"And the spirit cried, and rent him sore, and came out of him: and he was as one dead; insomuch that many said, He is dead" (Mark 9:26).
   C. Jesus emancipated the son—"But Jesus took him by the hand, and lifted him up; and he arose" (Mark 9:27).
   D. Jesus enlightened the disciples.
      1. Their confusion—"And when he was come into the house, his disciples asked him privately, Why could not we cast him out?" (Mark 9:28).
      2. His clarification—"And he said unto them, This kind can come forth by nothing, but by prayer and fasting" (Mark 9:29).

The Ten Lepers

I. The request of the ten
   A. Their cry—"And as he entered into a certain village, there met him ten men that were lepers, which stood afar off: And they lifted up their voices, and said, Jesus, Master, have mercy on us" (Luke 17:12-13).
   B. Their command—"And when he saw them, he said unto them, Go shew yourselves unto the priests" (Luke 17:14a).
   C. Their cleansing—"And it came to pass, that, as they went, they were cleansed" (Luke 17:14b).
II. The return of the one
   A. Who he was—"He was a Samaritan" (Luke 17:16b).
   B. Why he came—"And one of them, when he saw that he was healed, turned back, and with a loud voice glorified God" (Luke 17:15). "And fell down on his face at his feet, giving him thanks" (Luke 17:16).
   C. What he experienced
      1. The sadness of Jesus—"And Jesus answering said, Were there not ten

cleansed? but where are the nine? There are not found that returned to give glory to God, save this stranger" (Luke 17:17-18).
2. The salvation from Jesus—"And he said unto him, Arise, go thy way: thy faith hath made thee whole" (Luke 17:19).

The Sinful Woman Who Washed Jesus' Feet

I. The sinner—"And, behold, a woman in the city, which was a sinner, when she knew that Jesus sat at meat in the Pharisee's house, brought an alabaster box of ointment" (Luke 7:37).
II. The sorrowful—"And stood at his feet behind him weeping" (Luke 7:38a).
III. The servant—"And began to wash his feet with tears, and did wipe them with the hairs of her head, and kissed his feet, and anointed them with the ointment" (Luke 7:38b).
IV. The saved—"And he said unto her, Thy sins are forgiven" (Luke 7:48).

The Sower, The Wheat, and the Tares

I. The diligence of the sower—"Another parable put he forth unto them, saying, The kingdom of heaven is likened unto a man which sowed good seed in his field" (Matt. 13:24).
II. The discovery of the sower
  A. The revenge by his enemy—"But while men slept, his enemy came and sowed tares among the wheat, and went his way. But when the blade was sprung up, and brought forth fruit, then appeared the tares also" (Matt. 13:25-26).
  B. The report by his servants—"So the servants of the householder came and said unto him, Sir, didst not thou sow good seed in thy field? from whence then hath it tares?" (Matt. 13:27).
III. The discernment of the sower—"He said unto them, An enemy hath done this. The servants said unto him, Wilt thou then that we go and gather them up?" (Matt. 13:28).
IV. The dilemma of the sower—"But he said, Nay; lest while ye gather up the tares, ye root up also the wheat with them" (Matt. 13:29).
V. The decision of the sower—"Let both grow together until the harvest: and in the time of harvest I will say to the reapers, Gather ye together first the tares, and bind them in bundles to burn them: but gather the wheat into my barn" (Matt. 13:30).

The Forgiven Servant Who Wouldn't Forgive

I. Scene 1: The servant and his master (first meeting)
  A. The debt he owed—"Therefore is the kingdom of heaven likened unto a certain king, which would take account of his servants. And when he had begun to reckon, one was brought unto him, which owed him ten thousand talents" (Matt. 18:23-24).
  B. The disaster he faced—"But forasmuch as he had not to pay, his lord commanded him to be sold, and his wife, and children, and all that he had, and payment to be made" (Matt. 18:25).
  C. The desperation he showed—"The servant therefore fell down, and worshipped him, saying, Lord, have patience with me, and I will pay thee all" (Matt. 18:26).
  D. The deliverance he gained—"Then the lord of that servant was moved with compassion, and loosed him, and forgave him the debt" (Matt. 18:27).
II. Scene 2: The servant and his servant—"But the same servant went out, and found one of his fellowservants, which owed him an hundred pence: and he laid hands on him, and took him by the throat, saying, Pay me that thou owest" (Matt. 18:28).
  A. The pitiful request of the lesser servant—"And his fellowservant fell down at his feet, and besought him, saying, Have patience with me, and I will pay thee all" (Matt. 18:29).
  B. The pitiless response of the greater servant—"And he would not: but went and cast him into prison, till he should pay the debt" (Matt. 18:30).

III. Scene 3: The servant and his master (final meeting). "So when his fellowservants saw what was done, they were very sorry, and came and told unto their lord all that was done" (Matt. 18:31).
   A. The outrage over this injustice
      1. Reminding the wicked servant—"Then his lord, after that he had called him, said unto him, O thou wicked servant, I forgave thee all that debt, because thou desiredst me" (Matt. 18:32).
      2. Rebuking the wicked servant—"Shouldest not thou also have had compassion on thy fellowservant, even as I had pity on thee?" (Matt. 18:33).
   B. The outcome of the injustice—"And his lord was wroth, and delivered him to the tormentors, till he should pay all that was due unto him" (Matt. 18:34).

The Good Samaritan

I. The actors—A traveler, some robbers, a priest, a Levite, and a Samaritan
II. The action
   A. The trip—"A certain man went down from Jerusalem to Jericho" (Luke 10:30a).
   B. The trouble—"And fell among thieves, which stripped him of his raiment, and wounded him, and departed, leaving him half dead" (Luke 10:30b).
   C. The test
      1. Failed by the priest—"And by chance there came down a certain priest that way: and when he saw him, he passed by on the other side" (Luke 10:31).
      2. Failed by the Levite—"And likewise a Levite, when he was at the place, came and looked on him, and passed by on the other side" (Luke 10:32).
      3. Passed by the Samaritan
         a. His compassion upon the traveler—"But a certain Samaritan, as he journeyed, came where he was: and when he saw him, he had compassion on him" (Luke 10:33).
         b. His care for the traveler—"And went to him, and bound up his wounds, pouring in oil and wine, and set him on his own beast, and brought him to an inn, and took care of him" (Luke 10:34).
         c. His commitment to the traveler—"And on the morrow when he departed, he took out two pence, and gave them to the host, and said unto him, Take care of him; and whatsoever thou spendest more, when I come again, I will repay thee" (Luke 10:35).
III. The attitudes
   A. That of the robbers: "What is thine is mine."
   B. That of the priest and Levite: "What is mine is mine."
   C. That of the Samaritan: "What is mine is thine."

The Rich Fool

I. His dilemma—"And he spake a parable unto them, saying, The ground of a certain rich man brought forth plentifully: and he thought within himself, saying, What shall I do, because I have no room where to bestow my fruits?" (Luke 12:16-17).
II. His decision—"And he said, This will I do: I will pull down my barns, and build greater; and there will I bestow all my fruits and my goods" (Luke 12:18).
III. His delusion—"And I will say to my soul, Soul, thou hast much goods laid up for many years; take thine ease, eat, drink, and be merry" (Luke 12:19).
IV. His destruction—"But God said unto him, Thou fool, this night thy soul shall be required of thee: then whose shall those things be, which thou hast provided?" (Luke 12:20).

The Rich Man Who Prepared a Great Supper

I. The invitation—"Then said he unto him, A certain man made a great supper, and bade many: and sent his servant at supper time to say to them that were bidden, Come; for all things are now ready" (Luke 14:16-17).

II. The invited—"And they all with one consent began to make excuse" (Luke 14:18a).
  A. First excuse—"The first said unto him, I have bought a piece of ground, and I must needs go and see it: I pray thee have me excused" (Luke 14:18b).
  B. Second excuse—"And another said, I have bought five yoke of oxen, and I go to prove them: I pray thee have me excused" (Luke 14:19).
  C. Third excuse—"And another said, I have married a wife, and therefore I cannot come" (Luke 14:20).

III. The invitation
  A. The revised guest list
    1. Consisting of suffering people—"So that servant came, and shewed his lord these things. Then the master of the house being angry said to his servant, Go out quickly into the streets and lanes of the city, and bring in hither the poor, and the maimed, and the halt, and the blind. And the servant said, Lord, it is done as thou hast commanded, and yet there is room" (Luke 14:21-22).
    2. Consisting of scattered people—"And the lord said unto the servant, Go out into the highways and hedges, and compel them to come in, that my house may be filled" (Luke 14:23).
  B. The rejected guest list—"For I say unto you, That none of those men which were bidden shall taste of my supper" (Luke 14:24).

The Prodigal Son

I. His rebellion
  A. The foolishness he exhibited
    1. In seeking his inheritance— "And he said, A certain man had two sons: And the younger of them said to his father, Father, give me the portion of goods that falleth to me. And he divided unto them his living" (Luke 15:11-12).
    2. In squandering his inheritance—"And not many days after the younger son gathered all together, and took his journey into a far country, and there wasted his substance with riotous living" (Luke 15:13).
  B. The famine he endured—"And when he had spent all, there arose a mighty famine in that land; and he began to be in want. And he went and joined himself to a citizen of that country; and he sent him into his fields to feed swine. And he would fain have filled his belly with the husks that the swine did eat: and no man gave unto him" (Luke 15:14-16).

II. His realization—"And when he came to himself, he said, How many hired servants of my father's have bread enough and to spare, and I perish with hunger!" (Luke 15:17).

III. His repentance—"I will arise and go to my father, and will say unto him, Father, I have sinned against heaven, and before thee, And am no more worthy to be called thy son: make me as one of thy hired servants" (Luke 15:18-19).

IV. His reunion
  A. The father's compassion—"And he arose, and came to his father. But when he was yet a great way off, his father saw him, and had compassion, and ran, and fell on his neck, and kissed him" (Luke 15:20).
  B. The son's confession—"And the son said unto him, Father, I have sinned against heaven, and in thy sight, and am no more worthy to be called thy son" (Luke 15:21).

V. His restoration
  A. The father's proposal (what he did)—"But the father said to his servants, Bring forth the best robe, and put it on him; and put a ring on his hand, and shoes on his feet: And bring hither the fatted calf, and kill it; and let us eat, and be merry" (Luke 15:22-23).
  B. The father's purpose (why he did it)—"For this my son was dead, and is alive

again; he was lost, and is found. And they began to be merry" (Luke 15:24).

The Prodigal Son's Brother

I. The resentment of this brother
  A. The basis—"Now his elder son was in the field: and as he came and drew nigh to the house, he heard musick and dancing. And he called one of the servants, and asked what these things meant. And he said unto him, Thy brother is come; and thy father hath killed the fatted calf, because he hath received him safe and sound" (Luke 15:25-27).
  B. The boycott—"And he was angry, and would not go in: therefore came his father out, and intreated him" (Luke 15:28).
  C. The bitterness
    1. My service to you has never been rewarded—"And he answering said to his father, Lo, these many years do I serve thee, neither transgressed I at any time thy commandment: and yet thou never gavest me a kid, that I might make merry with my friends" (Luke 15:29).
    2. His sin against you is now being rewarded—"But as soon as this thy son was come, which hath devoured thy living with harlots, thou hast killed for him the fatted calf" (Luke 15:30).

II. The reassurance of this brother—"And he said unto him, Son, thou art ever with me, and all that I have is thine. It was meet that we should make merry, and be glad: for this thy brother was dead, and is alive again; and was lost, and is found" (Luke 15:31-32).

The Unjust Steward

I. The crisis
  A. The dishonesty of this steward—"And he said also unto his disciples, There was a certain rich man, which had a steward; and the same was accused unto him that he had wasted his goods" (Luke 16:1).
  B. The dismissal of this steward—"And he called him, and said unto him, How is it that I hear this of thee? give an account of thy stewardship; for thou mayest be no longer steward" (Luke 16:2).

II. The concern—"Then the steward said within himself, What shall I do? for my lord taketh away from me the stewardship: I cannot dig; to beg I am ashamed" (Luke 16:3).

III. The craftiness
  A. The plan—"I am resolved what to do, that, when I am put out of the stewardship, they may receive me into their houses" (Luke 16:4).
  B. The performance—"So he called every one of his lord's debtors unto him, and said unto the first, How much owest thou unto my lord? And he said, An hundred measures of oil. And he said unto him, Take thy bill, and sit down quickly, and write fifty. Then said he to another, And how much owest thou? And he said, An hundred measures of wheat. And he said unto him, Take thy bill, and write fourscore" (Luke 16:5-7).

IV. The commendation—"And the lord commended the unjust steward, because he had done wisely: for the children of this world are in their generation wiser than the children of light" (Luke 16:8).

V. The conclusion
  A. The what of the matter—"And I say unto you, Make to yourselves friends of the mammon of unrighteousness; that, when ye fail, they may receive you into everlasting habitations. He that is faithful in that which is least is faithful also in much: and he that is unjust in the least is unjust also in much" (Luke 16:9-10).
  B. The why of the matter—"If therefore ye have not been faithful in the unrighteous mammon, who will commit to your trust the true riches? And if ye have not been faithful in that which is another man's, who shall give you that which is your own? No servant can serve two masters:

for either he will hate the one, and love the other; or else he will hold to the one, and despise the other. Ye cannot serve God and mammon" (Luke 16:11-13).

VI. The convicted—"And the Pharisees also, who were covetous, heard all these things: and they derided him" (Luke 16:14).

The Rich Man in Hell

I. His position—"There was a certain rich man, which was clothed in purple and fine linen, and fared sumptuously every day" (Luke 16:19).
II. His passing—"The rich man . . . died, and was buried" (Luke 16:22b).
III. His predicament—"And in hell he lift up his eyes, being in torments, and seeth Abraham afar off, and Lazarus in his bosom" (Luke 16:23).
IV. His prayers
   A. He prayed concerning relief for his body.
      1. The request—"And he cried and said, Father Abraham, have mercy on me, and send Lazarus, that he may dip the tip of his finger in water, and cool my tongue; for I am tormented in this flame" (Luke 16:24).
      2. The refusal—"But Abraham said, Son, remember that thou in thy lifetime receivedst thy good things, and likewise Lazarus evil things: but now he is comforted, and thou art tormented" (Luke 16:25).
      3. The reason—"And beside all this, between us and you there is a great gulf fixed: so that they which would pass from hence to you cannot; neither can they pass to us, that would come from thence" (Luke 16:26).
   B. He prayed concerning redemption for his brothers.
      1. The request—"Then he said, I pray thee therefore, father, that thou wouldest send him to my father's house: For I have five brethren; that he may testify unto them, lest they also come into this place of torment" (Luke 16:27-28).
      2. The refusal—"Abraham saith unto him, They have Moses and the prophets; let them hear them" (Luke 16:29).
      3. The reason—"And he said, Nay, father Abraham: but if one went unto them from the dead, they will repent. And he said unto him, If they hear not Moses and the prophets, neither will they be persuaded, though one rose from the dead" (Luke 16:30-31).

The Man Who Hired Workers for His Vineyard

I. The agreement
   A. The workers—"For the kingdom of heaven is like unto a man that is an householder, which went out early in the morning to hire labourers into his vineyard" (Matt. 20:1).
   B. The wages—"And when he had agreed with the labourers for a penny a day, he sent them into his vineyard" (Matt. 20:2).
   C. The work schedule
      1. Some worked from 6:00 A.M. to 6:00 P.M. (Matt. 20:1-2).
      2. Some worked from 9:00 A.M. to 6:00 P.M. (Matt. 20:3-4).
      3. Some worked from noon to 6:00 P.M. (Matt. 20:5).
      4. Some worked from 3:00 P.M. to 6:00 P.M. (Matt. 20:5).
      5. Some worked from 5:00 P.M. to 6:00 P.M. (Matt. 20:6-7).
II. The argument
   A. The payment—"So when even was come, the lord of the vineyard saith unto his steward, Call the labourers, and give them their hire, beginning from the last unto the first. And when they came that were hired about the eleventh hour, they received every man a penny" (Matt. 20:8-9).
   B. The protest
      1. Their resentment—"But when the first came, they supposed that they

should have received more; and they likewise received every man a penny. And when they had received it, they murmured against the goodman of the house, saying, These last have wrought but one hour, and thou hast made them equal unto us, which have borne the burden and heat of the day" (Matt. 20:10-12).

2. His reminder—"But he answered one of them, and said, Friend, I do thee no wrong: didst not thou agree with me for a penny? Take that thine is, and go thy way: I will give unto this last, even as unto thee. Is it not lawful for me to do what I will with mine own? Is thine eye evil, because I am good?" (Matt. 20:13-15).

The King Who Prepared a Marriage Feast for His Son

I. The invitations to the wedding—"The kingdom of heaven is like unto a certain king, which made a marriage for his son" (Matt. 22:2).
  A. The exclusive guest list
    1. First invitation
      a. The request—"And sent forth his servants to call them that were bidden to the wedding" (Matt. 22:3a).
      b. The refusal—"And they would not come" (Matt. 23:3b).
    2. Final invitation
      a. The request—"Again, he sent forth other servants, saying, Tell them which are bidden, Behold, I have prepared my dinner: my oxen and my fatlings are killed, and all things are ready: come unto the marriage" (Matt. 22:4).
      b. The ridicule—"But they made light of it, and went their ways, one to his farm, another to his merchandise" (Matt. 22:5).
      c. The ruthlessness—"And the remnant took his servants, and entreated them spitefully, and slew them" (Matt. 22:6).
      d. The reprisal—"But when the king heard thereof, he was wroth: and he sent forth his armies, and destroyed those murderers, and burned up their city" (Matt. 22:7).
  B. The expanded guest list—"Then saith he to his servants, The wedding is ready, but they which were bidden were not worthy" (Matt. 22:8).
    1. The invitation—"Go ye therefore into the highways, and as many as ye shall find, bid to the marriage" (Matt. 22:9).
    2. The ingathering—"So those servants went out into the highways, and gathered together all as many as they found, both bad and good: and the wedding was furnished with guests" (Matt. 22:10).

II. The incident at the wedding
  A. The problem
    1. The guest without a robe—"And when the king came in to see the guests, he saw there a man which had not on a wedding garment" (Matt. 22:11).
    2. The guest without a reply—"And he saith unto him, Friend, how camest thou in hither not having a wedding garment? And he was speechless" (Matt. 22:12).
  B. The punishment—"Then said the king to the servants, Bind him hand and foot, and take him away, and cast him into outer darkness; there shall be weeping and gnashing of teeth" (Matt. 22:13).

The Nobleman and His Servants

I. The assignment to the servants—"He said therefore, A certain nobleman went into a far country to receive for himself a kingdom, and to return. And he called his ten servants, and delivered them ten pounds, and said unto them, Occupy till I come" (Luke 19:12-13).

II. The accounting by the servants—"And it came to pass, that when he was returned, having received the kingdom, then he commanded these servants to be called unto him, to whom he had given the money, that he might know how much every man had gained by trading" (Luke 19:15).

A. First servant
   1. His report—"Then came the first, saying, Lord, thy pound hath gained ten pounds" (Luke 19:16).
   2. His reward—"And he said unto him, Well, thou good servant: because thou hast been faithful in a very little, have thou authority over ten cities" (Luke 19:17).

B. Second servant
   1. His report—"And the second came, saying, Lord, thy pound hath gained five pounds" (Luke 19:18).
   2. His reward—"And he said likewise to him, Be thou also over five cities" (Luke 19:19).

C. Third servant
   1. His report—"And another came, saying, Lord, behold, here is thy pound, which I have kept laid up in a napkin: For I feared thee, because thou art an austere man: thou takest up that thou layedst not down, and reapest that thou didst not sow" (Luke 19:20-21).
   2. His rejection
      a. The man was rebuked—"And he saith unto him, Out of thine own mouth will I judge thee, thou wicked servant. Thou knewest that I was an austere man, taking up that I laid not down, and reaping that I did not sow: Wherefore then gavest not thou my money into the bank, that at my coming I might have required mine own with usury?" (Luke 19:22-23).
      b. The money was repossessed—"And he said unto them that stood by, Take from him the pound, and give it to him that hath ten pounds" (Luke 19:24).

The Lame Man at the Temple Gate Beautiful

I. His helplessness—"And a certain man lame from his mother's womb was carried, whom they laid daily at the gate of the temple which is called Beautiful, to ask alms of them that entered into the temple; who seeing Peter and John about to go into the temple asked an alms" (Acts 3:2-3).

II. His hopefulness
   A. The exhortation—"And Peter, fastening his eyes upon him with John, said, Look on us" (Acts 3:4).
   B. The expectation—"And he gave heed unto them, expecting to receive something of them" (Acts 3:5).

III. His happiness
   A. The name—"Then Peter said, Silver and gold have I none; but such as I have give I thee: In the name of Jesus Christ of Nazareth rise up and walk" (Acts 3:6).
   B. The nature of his happiness
      1. The ministry of Peter—"And he took him by the right hand, and lifted him up: and immediately his feet and ankle bones received strength" (Acts 3:7).
      2. The miracle of God—"And he leaping up stood, and walked, and entered with them into the temple, walking, and leaping, and praising God" (Acts 3:8).
      3. The marvel of the crowd—"And all the people saw him walking and praising God: And they knew that it was he which sat for alms at the Beautiful gate of the temple: and they were filled with wonder and amazement at that which had happened unto him" (Acts 3:9-10).

The Ethiopian Eunuch

I. The concern for the eunuch—"And the angel of the Lord spake unto Philip, saying, Arise, and go toward the south unto the way that goeth down from Jerusalem unto Gaza, which is desert" (Acts 8:26).

II. The charge of the eunuch—"And he arose and went: and, behold, a man of Ethiopia, an eunuch of great authority under Candace queen of the Ethiopians, who had the charge of all her treasure, and had come to Jerusalem for a worship" (Acts 8:27).

III. The confusion of the eunuch
   A. The passage—"Was returning, and sitting in his chariot read Esaias the prophet. . . . The place of the scripture which he read was this, He was led as a sheep to the slaughter; and like a lamb dumb before his shearer, so opened he not his mouth: In his humiliation his judgment was taken away: and who shall declare his generation? for his life is taken from the earth" (Acts 8:28, 32-33).
   B. The problem—"Then the Spirit said unto Philip, Go near, and join thyself to this chariot. And Philip ran thither to him, and heard him read the prophet Esaias, and said, Understandest thou what thou readest? . . . And the eunuch answered Philip, and said, I pray thee, of whom speaketh the prophet this? of himself, or of some other man?" (Acts 8:29-30, 34).

IV. The clarification to the eunuch—"Then Philip opened his mouth, and began at the same scripture, and preached unto him Jesus" (Acts 8:35).

V. The conversion of the eunuch—"And as they went on their way, they came unto a certain water: and the eunuch said, See, here is water; what doth hinder me to be baptized? And Philip said, If thou believest with all thine heart, thou mayest. And he answered and said, I believe that Jesus Christ is the Son of God" (Acts 8:36-37).

VI. The confession of the eunuch—"And he commanded the chariot to stand still: and they went down both into the water, both Philip and the eunuch; and he baptized him. And when they were come up out of the water, the Spirit of the Lord caught away Philip, that the eunuch saw him no more: and he went on his way rejoicing" (Acts 8:38-39).

The Cripple at Lystra

I. The misery of the cripple—"And there sat a certain man at Lystra, impotent in his feet, being a cripple from his mother's womb, who never had walked" (Acts 14:8).

II. The ministry of the apostle—"The same heard Paul speak: who stedfastly beholding him, and perceiving that he had faith to be healed" (Acts 14:9).

III. The miracle of the Lord—"Said with a loud voice, Stand upright on thy feet. And he leaped and walked" (Acts 14:10).

IV. The misconception of the people—"And when the people saw what Paul had done, they lifted up their voices, saying in the speech of Lycaonia, The gods are come down to us in the likeness of men" (Acts 14:11).

The Young Girl at Philippi

I. The demon in this girl
   A. The money it produced through this girl—"And it came to pass, as we went to prayer, a certain damsel possessed with a spirit of divination met us, which brought her masters much gain by soothsaying" (Acts 16:16).
   B. The message it proclaimed through this girl—"The same followed Paul and us, and cried, saying, These men are the servants of the most high God, which shew unto us the way of salvation" (Acts 16:17).

II. The deliverance of this girl
   A. The apostle in this deliverance—"And this did she many days. But Paul, being grieved, turned and said to the spirit" (Acts 16:18a).
   B. The authority for this deliverance—"I command thee in the name of Jesus Christ to come out of her. And he came out the same hour" (Acts 16:18b).

The Philippian Jailor

I. The charge—"And when they had laid many stripes upon them, they cast them into prison, charging the jailor to keep them safely: Who, having received such a charge, thrust them into the inner prison, and made their feet fast in the stocks" (Acts 16:23-24).

II. The consternation
   A. The singing—"And at midnight Paul and Silas prayed, and sang praises unto God: and the prisoners heard them" (Acts 16:25).
   B. The shaking—"And suddenly there was a great earthquake, so that the foundations of the prison were shaken: and immediately all the doors were opened, and every one's bands were loosed" (Acts 16:26).

III. The conclusion—"And the keeper of the prison awaking out of his sleep, and seeing the prison doors open, he drew out his sword, and would have killed himself, supposing that the prisoners had been fled" (Acts 16:27).

IV. The command—"But Paul cried with a loud voice, saying, Do thyself no harm: for we are all here" (Acts 16:28).

V. The call—"Then he called for a light, and sprang in, and came trembling, and fell down before Paul and Silas" (Acts 16:29).

VI. The confusion—"And brought them out, and said, Sirs, what must I do to be saved?" (Acts 16:30).

VII. The clarification—"And they said, Believe on the Lord Jesus Christ, and thou shalt be saved, and thy house" (Acts 16:31).

VIII. The conversion
   A. His belief in Christ—"And they spake unto him the word of the Lord, and to all that were in his house" (Acts 16:32).
   B. His baptism in Christ—"And he took them the same hour of the night, and washed their stripes; and was baptized, he and all his, straightway" (Acts 16:33).

IX. His celebration—"And when he had brought them into his house, he set meat before them, and rejoiced, believing in God with all his house" (Acts 16:34).

The Twelve Apostles of John the Baptist

I. These disciples and the baptism of John
   A. Paul questioned them concerning their belief.
      1. His concern—"He said unto them, Have ye received the Holy Ghost since ye believed?" (Acts 19:2a).
      2. Their confession—"And they said unto him, We have not so much as heard whether there be any Holy Ghost" (Acts 19:2b).
   B. Paul questioned them concerning their baptism.
      1. His concern—"And he said unto them, Unto what then were ye baptized?" (Acts 19:3a).
      2. Their confession—"And they said, Unto John's baptism" (Acts 19:3b).

II. These men and the baptism of Christ
   A. The review by the apostle—"Then said Paul, John verily baptized with the baptism of repentance, saying unto the people, that they should believe on him which should come after him, that is, on Christ Jesus" (Acts 19:4).
   B. The response by the disciples—"When they heard this, they were baptized in the name of the Lord Jesus" (Acts 19:5).

III. These men and the baptism of the Spirit—"And when Paul had laid his hands upon them, the Holy Ghost came on them; and they spake with tongues, and prophesied. And all the men were about twelve" (Acts 19:6-7).

The Town Clerk in Ephesus

I. His words of wisdom—He prevented a dangerous riot from developing when an Ephesian mob felt its goddess Diana had been attacked.
   A. His reassurance to the mob—"And when the townclerk had appeased the people, he said, Ye men of Ephesus, what man is there that knoweth not how that the city of the Ephesians is a worshipper of the great goddess Diana, and of the image which fell down from Jupiter?" (Acts 19:35).
   B. His recommendation to the mob—"Seeing then that these things cannot

be spoken against, ye ought to be quiet, and to do nothing rashly" (Acts 19:36).

II. He spoke concerning the honesty of the opponents—"For ye have brought hither these men, which are neither robbers of churches, nor yet blasphemers of your goddess" (Acts 19:37).

III. He spoke concerning the legality of the matter—"Wherefore if Demetrius, and the craftsmen which are with him, have a matter against any man, the law is open, and there are deputies: let them implead one another. But if ye enquire any thing concerning other matters, it shall be determined in a lawful assembly" (Acts 19:38-39).

IV. He spoke concerning the (possible) hostility of the Romans—"For we are in danger to be called in question for this day's uproar, there being no cause whereby we may give an account of this concourse" (Acts 19:40).

The Nephew of Paul

I. Overhearing the plot against his uncle—"And when it was day, certain of the Jews banded together, and bound themselves under a curse, saying that they would neither eat nor drink till they had killed Paul. And when Paul's sister's son heard of their lying in wait, he went and entered into the castle, and told Paul" (Acts 23:12, 16).

II. Overturning the plot against his uncle
   A. His report to the chief captain—"Then the chief captain took him by the hand, and went with him aside privately, and asked him, What is that thou hast to tell me? And he said, The Jews have agreed to desire thee that thou wouldest bring down Paul to morrow into the council, as though they would enquire somewhat of him more perfectly" (Acts 23:19-20).
   B. His recommendation to the chief captain—"But do not thou yield unto them: for there lie in wait for him of them more than forty men, which have bound themselves with an oath, that they will neither eat nor drink till they have killed him: and now are they ready, looking for a promise from thee" (Acts 23:21).

The Fornicator in the Corinthian Church

I. His sin and the lack of chastisement by the Corinthian church
   A. The report—"It is reported commonly that there is fornication among you, and such fornication as is not so much as named among the Gentiles, that one should have his father's wife" (1 Cor. 5:1).
   B. The reaction—"And ye are puffed up, and have not rather mourned, that he that hath done this deed might be taken away from among you" (1 Cor. 5:2).
   C. The rebuke—"For I verily, as absent in body, but present in spirit, have judged already, as though I were present, concerning him that hath so done this deed" (1 Cor. 5:3).
   D. The removal
      1. This removal was to take place for the man's sake—"In the name of our Lord Jesus Christ, when ye are gathered together, and my spirit, with the power of our Lord Jesus Christ, To deliver such an one unto Satan for the destruction of the flesh, that the spirit may be saved in the day of the Lord Jesus" (1 Cor. 5:4-5).
      2. This removal was to take place for the church's sake—"Your glorying is not good. Know ye not that a little leaven leaveneth the whole lump?" (1 Cor. 5:6).

II. His sorrow and the lack of compassion by the Corinthian church—As Paul had previously rebuked the church for not removing the unrepentant member, he again rebuked them for not restoring the repentant member.
   A. This restoration was to take place for the man's sake—"So that contrariwise ye ought rather to forgive him, and comfort him, lest perhaps such

a one should be swallowed up with overmuch sorrow" (2 Cor. 2:7).

B. This restoration was to take place for the church's sake—"Lest Satan should get an advantage of us: for we are not ignorant of his devices" (2 Cor. 2:11).

The Elect Lady of 2 John

I. She was commended by the apostle—"The elder unto the elect lady and her children, whom I love in the truth; and not I only, but also all they that have known the truth; I rejoiced greatly that I found of thy children walking in truth, as we have received a commandment from the Father" (2 John 1, 4).

II. She was commanded by the apostle

A. That she walk in love—"And now I beseech thee, lady, not as though I wrote a new commandment unto thee, but that which we had from the beginning, that we love one another" (2 John 5).

B. That she walk in truth—"And this is love, that we walk after his commandments. This is the commandment, That, as ye have heard from the beginning, ye should walk in it" (2 John 6).

III. She was cautioned by the apostle

A. Look out for Satan.

1. The deception of his ministers—"For many deceivers are entered into the world, who confess not that Jesus Christ is come in the flesh. This is a deceiver and an antichrist" (2 John 7).

2. The rejection of his ministers

a. What the elect lady was to do—"If there come any unto you, and bring not this doctrine, receive him not into your house, neither bid him God speed" (2 John 10).

b. Why she was to do it—"For he that biddeth him God speed is partaker of his evil deeds" (2 John 11).

B. Look out for self—"Look to yourselves, that we lose not those things which we have wrought, but that we receive a full reward" (2 John 8).

IV. She was comforted by the apostle—"Having many things to write unto you, I would not write with paper and ink: but I trust to come unto you, and speak face to face, that our joy may be full" (2 John 12).

The Two Witnesses in Revelation 11

I. The ministry of these two witnesses

A. Who they are—"And I will give power unto my two witnesses" (Rev. 11:3a). It is suggested that they will be Moses and Elijah (see Mal. 4:4-6; Matt. 17:3).

B. When they appear—"And they shall prophesy a thousand two hundred and threescore days, clothed in sackcloth" (Rev. 11:3b).

C. What they accomplish

1. In regard to their enemies—"And if any man will hurt them, fire proceedeth out of their mouth, and devoureth their enemies: and if any man will hurt them, he must in this manner be killed" (Rev. 11:5).

2. In regard to the earth—"These have power to shut heaven, that it rain not in the days of their prophecy: and have power over waters to turn them to blood, and to smite the earth with all plagues, as often as they will" (Rev. 11:6).

II. The martyrdom of these two witnesses

A. The creature that causes their deaths—"And when they shall have finished their testimony, the beast that ascendeth out of the bottomless pit shall make war against them, and shall overcome them, and kill them" (Rev. 11:7).

B. The celebration that follows their deaths

1. The place—"And their dead bodies shall lie in the street of the great city, which spiritually is called Sodom and Egypt, where also our Lord was crucified" (Rev. 11:8).

2. The perversion

a. Their dead bodies will be reviled—"And they of the people and kindreds and tongues and nations shall see their dead bodies three days and an half, and shall not suffer their dead bodies to be put in graves" (Rev. 11:9).

b. Their dead bodies will be rejoiced over—"And they that dwell upon the earth shall rejoice over them, and make merry, and shall send gifts one to another; because these two prophets tormented them that dwelt on the earth" (Rev. 11:10).

III. The metamorphosis of these witnesses

A. Their resurrection upon the earth—"And after three days and an half the Spirit of life from God entered into them, and they stood upon their feet; and great fear fell upon them which saw them" (Rev. 11:11).

B. Their removal from the earth—"And they heard a great voice from heaven saying unto them, Come up hither. And they ascended up to heaven in a cloud; and their enemies beheld them" (Rev. 11:12).

The 144,000 in Revelation 7 and 14

I. The selection of the 144,000

A. Their installation

1. The seal—"And I saw another angel ascending from the east, having the seal of the living God: and he cried with a loud voice to the four angels, to whom it was given to hurt the earth and the sea" (Rev. 7:2).

2. The sealing

a. The plan for this sealing—"Saying, Hurt not the earth, neither the sea, nor the trees, till we have sealed the servants of our God in their foreheads" (Rev. 7:3).

b. The place of this sealing—"And I looked, and, lo, a Lamb stood on the mount Sion, and with him an hundred forty and four thousand, having his Father's name written in their foreheads" (Rev. 14:1).

B. Their identification—"And I heard the number of them which were sealed: and there were sealed an hundred and forty and four thousand of all the tribes of the children of Israel" (Rev. 7:4).

II. The song of the 144,000—"And they sung as it were a new song before the throne, and before the four beasts, and the elders: and no man could learn that song but the hundred and forty and four thousand, which were redeemed from the earth" (Rev. 14:3).

III. The spirituality of the 144,000

A. The purity of their works—"These are they which were not defiled with women; for they are virgins. These are they which follow the Lamb whithersoever he goeth. These were redeemed from among men, being the firstfruits unto God and to the Lamb" (Rev. 14:4).

B. The purity of their words—"And in their mouth was found no guile: for they are without fault before the throne of God" (Rev. 14:5).

The Philosophers on Mars Hill

I. Their request to hear Paul—"And they took him, and brought him unto Areopagus, saying, May we know what this new doctrine, whereof thou speakest, is? For thou bringest certain strange things to our ears: we would know therefore what these things mean" (Acts 17:19-20).

A. The allegations of these philosophers—"Then certain philosophers of the Epicureans, and of the Stoicks, encountered him. And some said, What will this babbler say? other some, He seemeth to be a setter forth of strange gods: because he preached unto them Jesus, and the resurrection" (Acts 17:18).

B. The arrogance of these philosophers—"(For all the Athenians and strangers which were there spent their time in nothing else, but either to tell, or to hear some new thing)" (Acts 17:21).

II. Their response upon hearing Paul

A. Some passed judgment—"And when they heard of the resurrection of the dead, some mocked" (Acts 17:32a).

B. Some postponed judgment—"and others said, We will hear thee again of this matter" (Acts 17:32b).

C. Some believed—"Howbeit certain men clave unto him, and believed: among the which *was* Dionysius the Areopagite, and a woman named Damaris, and others with them" (Acts 17:34).

The Shepherds

I. Watching—"And there were in the same country shepherds abiding in the field, keeping watch over their flock by night" (Luke 2:8).

II. Wondering

A. The reassurance by the angel of the Lord—"And, lo, the angel of the Lord came upon them, and the glory of the Lord shone round about them: and they were sore afraid. And the angel said unto them, Fear not: for, behold, I bring you good tidings of great joy, which shall be to all people" (Luke 2:9-10).

B. The revelation by the angel of the Lord

1. Concerning the Son of God—"For unto you is born this day in the city of David a Saviour, which is Christ the Lord" (Luke 2:11).

2. Concerning the sign from God—"And this shall be a sign unto you; Ye shall find the babe wrapped in swaddling clothes, lying in a manger" (Luke 2:12).

C. The rejoicing by the angels of the Lord—"And suddenly there was with the angel a multitude of the heavenly host praising God, and saying, Glory to God in the highest, and on earth peace, good will toward men" (Luke 2:13-14).

III. Worshiping

A. The decision of the shepherds—"And it came to pass, as the angels were gone away from them into heaven, the shepherds said one to another, Let us now go even unto Bethlehem, and see this thing which is come to pass, which the Lord hath made known unto us" (Luke 2:15).

B. The devotion of the shepherds—"And they came with haste, and found Mary, and Joseph, and the babe lying in a manger" (Luke 2:16).

IV. Witnessing—"And when they had seen it, they made known abroad the saying which was told them concerning this child. And all they that heard it wondered at those things which were told them by the shepherds" (Luke 2:17-18).

The Wise Men

I. The wise men: Their frustration in Jerusalem

A. Their public meeting

1. The request of the Magi—"Now when Jesus was born in Beth-lehem of Judaea in the days of Herod the king, behold, there came wise men from the east to Jerusalem, Saying, Where is he that is born King of the Jews? for we have seen his star in the east, and are come to worship him" (Matt. 2:1-2).

2. The reaction of the monarch

a. His concern—"When Herod the king had heard these things, he was troubled, and all Jerusalem with him" (Matt. 2:3).

b. His command—"And when he had gathered all the chief priests and scribes of the people together, he demanded of them where Christ should be born" (Matt. 2:4).

3. The reply of the ministers— "And they said unto him, In Beth-lehem of Judaea: for thus it is written by the prophet, And thou Beth-lehem, in the land of Juda, art not least among the princes of Juda: for out of thee shall come a Governor, that shall rule my people Israel" (Matt. 2:5-6).

B. Their private meeting

1. The king's demand—"Then Herod, when he had privily called the wise men, enquired of them diligently what time the star appeared" (Matt. 2:7).

2. The king's deception—"And he sent them to Beth-lehem, and said, Go and search diligently for the young child; and when ye have found him,

bring me word again, that I may come and worship him also" (Matt. 2:8).

II. The wise men: Their celebration in Bethlehem
   A. The witness of the star—"When they had heard the king, they departed; and, lo, the star, which they saw in the east, went before them, till it came and stood over where the young child was" (Matt. 2:9).
   B. The worship of the magi
      1. Their gladness—"When they saw the star, they rejoiced with exceeding great joy" (Matt. 2:10).
      2. Their gifts—"And when they were come into the house, they saw the young child with Mary his mother, and fell down, and worshipped him: and when they had opened their treasures, they presented unto him gifts; gold, and frankincense, and myrrh" (Matt. 2:11).
   C. The warning from the Lord—"And being warned of God in a dream that they should not return to Herod, they departed into their own country another way" (Matt. 2:12).

The Samaritan Woman

I. The sinner of Sychar
   A. The contact—"Then cometh he to a city of Samaria, which is called Sychar, near to the parcel of ground that Jacob gave to his son Joseph. Now Jacob's well was there. Jesus therefore, being wearied with his journey, sat thus on the well: and it was about the sixth hour" (John 4:5-6).
      1. His request—"There cometh a woman of Samaria to draw water: Jesus saith unto her, Give me to drink" (John 4:7).
      2. Her response—"Then saith the woman of Samaria unto him, How is it that thou, being a Jew, askest drink of me, which am a woman of Samaria? for the Jews have no dealings with the Samaritans" (John 4:9).
   B. The contrasts
      1. Jesus contrasted living water with liquid water.
         a. Living water
            (1) His revelation—"Jesus answered and said unto her, If thou knewest the gift of God, and who it is that saith to thee, Give me to drink; thou wouldest have asked of him, and he would have given thee living water" (John 4:10).
            (2) Her response—"The woman saith unto him, Sir, thou hast nothing to draw with, and the well is deep: from whence then hast thou that living water? Art thou greater than our father Jacob, which gave us the well, and drank thereof himself, and his children, and his cattle?" (John 4:11-12).
         b. Liquid water
            (1) His revelation—"Jesus answered and said unto her, Whosoever drinketh of this water shall thirst again: But whosoever drinketh of the water that I shall give him shall never thirst; but the water that I shall give him shall be in him a well of water springing up into everlasting life" (John 4:13-14).
            (2) Her response—"The woman saith unto him, Sir, give me this water, that I thirst not, neither come hither to draw" (John 4:15).
      2. Jesus contrasted true worship with traditional worship.
         a. The command—"Jesus saith unto her, Go, call thy husband, and come hither" (John 4:16).
         b. The concealment—"The woman answered and said, I have no husband. Jesus said unto her, Thou hast well said, I have no husband: For thou hast had five

husbands; and he whom thou now hast is not thy husband: in that saidst thou truly" (John 4:17-18).

c. The cleverness—She attempted to change the subject by complimenting Jesus. "The woman saith unto him, Sir, I perceive that thou art a prophet" (John 4:19).

d. The confusion—"Our fathers worshipped in this mountain; and ye say, that in Jerusalem is the place where men ought to worship" (John 4:20).

e. The correction—"Jesus saith unto her, Woman, believe me, the hour cometh, when ye shall neither in this mountain, nor yet at Jerusalem, worship the Father. But the hour cometh, and now is, when the true worshippers shall worship the Father in spirit and in truth: for the Father seeketh such to worship him. God is a Spirit: and they that worship him must worship him in spirit and in truth" (John 4:21, 23-24).

f. The conversion—"The woman saith unto him, I know that Messias cometh, which is called Christ: when he is come, he will tell us all things. Jesus saith unto her, I that speak unto thee am he" (John 4:25-26).

II. The soul winner of Sychar

A. The faithfulness of the woman—"The woman then left her waterpot, and went her way into the city, and saith to the men, Come, see a man, which told me all things that ever I did: is not this the Christ? Then they went out of the city, and came unto him" (John 4:28-30).

B. The fruit of the woman—"And many of the Samaritans of that city believed on him for the saying of the woman, which testified, He told me all that ever I did" (John 4:39).

The Woman Taken in Adultery

I. The connivers—"And the scribes and Pharisees brought unto him a woman taken in adultery; and when they had set her in the midst, they say unto him, Master, this woman was taken in adultery, in the very act" (John 8:3-4).

II. The conniving

A. What they said—"Now Moses in the law commanded us, that such should be stoned: but what sayest thou?" (John 8:5).

B. Why they said it—"This they said, tempting him, that they might have to accuse him" (John 8:6a).

III. The conviction—"But Jesus stooped down, and with his finger wrote on the ground, as though he heard them not" (John 8:6b). "So when they continued asking him, he lifted up himself, and said unto them, He that is without sin among you, let him first cast a stone at her" (John 8:7).

IV. The convicted—"And they which heard it, being convicted by their own conscience, went out one by one . . . even unto the last: and Jesus was left alone, and the woman standing in the midst" (John 8:9).

V. The cleansed

A. No earthly condemnation—"When Jesus had lifted up himself, and saw none but the woman, he said unto her, Woman, where are those thine accusers? hath no man condemned thee?" (John 8:10).

B. No heavenly condemnation—"She said, No man, Lord. And Jesus said unto her, Neither do I condemn thee: go, and sin no more" (John 8:11).

The Rich Young Ruler

The rich young ruler was confused concerning four things. Jesus corrected all four errors.

I. First confusion and correction

A. The confusion: Concerning the deity of Christ. "And when he was gone forth into the way, there came one running, and kneeled to him, and asked him, Good Master, what shall I do that I may inherit eternal life?" (Mark 10:17).

B. The correction: "And Jesus said unto him, Why callest thou me good? there is none good but one, that is, God" (Mark 10:18).

II. Second confusion and correction
  A. The confusion: Concerning the vanity of works. "And, behold, one came and said unto him, Good Master, what good thing shall I do, that I may have eternal life?" (Matt. 19:16).
  B. The correction: "And he said unto him, Why callest thou me good? there is none good but one, that is, God: but if thou wilt enter into life, keep the commandments" (Matt. 19:17). Note: Christ then listed five of the ten commandments.
    1. Honor thy father and mother (fifth).
    2. Thou shalt do no murder (sixth).
    3. Thou shalt not commit adultery (seventh).
    4. Thou shalt not steal (eighth).
    5. Thou shalt not bear false witness (ninth). He did not, however, list the first commandment (Thou shalt have no other gods before me), nor the tenth (Thou shalt not covet), the very two already broken by the rich young ruler. Apparently Christ wanted him to come to this conclusion himself.

III. Third confusion and correction
  A. The confusion: Concerning the depravity of man. "The young man saith unto him, All these things have I kept from my youth up: what lack I yet?" (Matt. 19:20).
  B. The correction: "Jesus said unto him, If thou wilt be perfect, go and sell that thou hast, and give to the poor, and thou shalt have treasure in heaven: and come and follow me" (Matt. 19:21).

IV. Fourth confusion and correction
  A. The confusion: Concerning the captivity of riches. "But when the young man heard that saying, he went away sorrowful: for he had great possessions" (Matt. 19:22).
  B. The correction: "Then said Jesus unto his disciples, Verily I say unto you, that a rich man shall hardly enter into the kingdom of heaven. And again I say unto you, It is easier for a camel to go through the eye of a needle, than for a rich man to enter into the kingdom of God. When his disciples heard it, they were exceedingly amazed, saying, Who then can be saved? But Jesus beheld them, and said unto them, With men this is impossible; but with God all things are possible" (Matt. 19:23-26).

A Dying Thief

I. Reviling—"Let Christ the King of Israel descend now from the cross, that we may see and believe. And they that were crucified with him reviled him" (Mark 15:32).

II. Rebuking—After awhile, one thief changed his attitude toward the Savior and defended him before the other thief.
  A. The derision—"And one of the malefactors which were hanged railed on him, saying, If thou be Christ, save thyself and us" (Luke 23:39).
  B. The defense—"But the other answering rebuked him, saying, Dost not thou fear God, seeing thou art in the same condemnation? And we indeed justly; for we receive the due reward of our deeds: but this man hath done nothing amiss" (Luke 23:40-41).

III. Requesting—"And he said unto Jesus, Lord, remember me when thou comest into thy kingdom" (Luke 23:42).

IV. Receiving—"And Jesus said unto him, Verily I say unto thee, To day shalt thou be with me in paradise" (Luke 23:43).

PART TWO

OBSERVATIONS AND APPLICATIONS FROM THE LIVES OF CERTAIN NEW TESTAMENT PEOPLE

OBSERVATIONS FROM THE LIFE OF CHRIST

I. His early years in Nazareth—"And the child grew, and waxed strong in spirit, filled with wisdom: and the grace of God was upon him. . . . And Jesus increased in wisdom and stature, and in favour with God and man" (Luke 2:40, 52).

While most liberal theologians tend to deny the deity of Jesus, evangelicals often downplay his humanity. As has been often observed, while upon this planet, our Lord was as much God had he never been man, but also as much man had he never been God. The second part of this statement is vital in rightly understanding his earthly ministry, lest we think of him in terms of gliding about down here with angelic movements, always looking upwards at the golden halo which surrounded his head. All this of course is pious nonsense, as demonstrated by the two key words "grew" and "increased," as found in Luke 2. How, then, did Jesus develop as a human being?

A. He increased in wisdom (mental maturity). Nowhere are we told he possessed total knowledge, allowing him to instantly understand all things as a baby. In fact, to the contrary, most conservative theologians believe that while he indeed retained his divine attributes, such as his omniscience, he did not, however, use them, but depended completely upon the Holy Spirit. (See Phil. 2:5-8; Luke 4:18; John 3:34.)

Thus, later in his ministry Jesus employed the Scriptures in a very effective way indeed in dealing with both his friends (Luke 24:25-27) and his foes (Matt. 4:1-11; 22:29), but only because he had faithfully studied the Hebrew Bible as a lad.

B. He increased in stature (physical maturity). There is positive evidence in the Gospel accounts that our Lord was a strong and powerfully built man. An indication of this can be seen by his ability to intimidate on two separate occasions the greedy money changers in the temple. (See John 2:13-16; Matt. 21:12-13.)

We are told that Joseph was a carpenter (Matt. 13:55), and it is not unreasonable to conclude that Jesus also learned this trade as a boy. However, in New Testament times a carpenter probably worked more with stone than wood, due to the abundance of the first. Our Lord thus had the opportunity to build strong muscles by diligently moving and molding those stones.

C. He increased in favor with God (spiritual maturity). Even though he was the unique Son of God and had, before Bethlehem, enjoyed unparalleled fellowship with his Father (John 17:5), he nevertheless cultivated his quiet time with God during long hours of prayer upon the hills surrounding Nazareth. The time involved was probably early morning, as suggested by his adult prayer habit: "And in the morning, rising up a great while before day, he went out, and departed into a solitary place, and there prayed" (Mark 1:35).

Not only was he faithful in prayer but also in attending his Father's house to hear the Word of God expounded. "And he came to Nazareth, where he had been brought up: and, as his custom was, he went into the synagogue on the sabbath day, and stood up for to read" (Luke 4:16).

D. He increased in favor with man (social maturity). Although he was sinless, Jesus apparently did not display his righteousness in a way that turned people off. To the contrary, he seemed to be well received among the citizens of Nazareth. It is true that his younger half brothers would later turn against him (John 7:5). However, for the most part he was viewed in a positive light. This characteristic was carried over into his public ministry. We are told "the common people heard him gladly" (Mark 12:37). Crowds flocked to hear him (Luke 8:19; 19:3). Parents brought their children to him (Mark 10:13). Both the sick (Matt. 9:18) and needy sinners sought him out (Luke 19:1-4).

What is the primary lesson from all the above? Simply this: While on earth, as a human being, Jesus Christ carefully and consistently developed his mental, physical, spiritual, and social features in such a way as to bring the greatest possible amount of glory to his Father and the greatest possible good to his fellow man. As redeemed human beings, God desires for us to do the exact same thing.

II. His baptism by John—"And Jesus, when he was baptized, went up straightway out of the water: and, lo, the heavens were opened unto him, and he saw the Spirit of God descending like a dove, and lighting upon him: And lo a voice from heaven, saying, This is my beloved Son, in whom I am well pleased" (Matt. 3:16-17). This marks the first of three occasions where the Father orally expresses his approval of his Son. It is also the most significant because of when it took place. At this time our Lord had yet to perform one miracle or preach one sermon. Yet his life had already won the favor of the Father. We are prone to reverse this, assuming God awaits spectacular works before he can officially approve us. But to the contrary, divine sanction rests upon present day attitudes and not upon future achievements. In fact, the first is the root from which the second becomes the fruit.

An example of this principle can be seen in the life of Timothy, whom Paul praised in the most glowing manner: "I hope in the Lord Jesus to send Timothy to you soon, that I also may be cheered when I receive news about you. I have no one else like him, who takes a genuine interest in your welfare. For everyone looks out for his own interests, not those of Jesus Christ. But you know that Timothy has proved himself, because as a son with his father he has served with me in the work of the gospel (Phil. 2:19-22,NIV).

This, then, describes the fruit of Timothy's ministry. But what of the root? The apostle speaks of this during his final epistle: "But continue thou in the things which thou hast learned and hast been assured of, knowing of whom thou hast learned them; and that from a child thou hast known the holy scriptures, which are able to make thee wise unto salvation through faith which is in Christ Jesus" (2 Tim. 3:14-15).

III. His temptation by Satan—"Then was Jesus led up of the spirit into the wilderness to be tempted of the devil" (Matt. 4:1).

Question: Is it a sin to be tempted?

Answer: It all depends upon who has led us into the temptation itself.

A. If our guide has been the Holy Spirit (as was the case here in Matthew 4), then it can be said that not only is temptation not a sin, it is actually both an honor and an opportunity.

1. It is an honor because it demonstrates that God can trust us. He knows just how much we can withstand (Ps. 103:13, 14), and will not allow the temptation to go beyond that limit (1 Cor. 10:13). This is why both James and Peter could describe temptation in such a positive light. "My brethren, count it all joy when ye fall into divers temptations . . . . Blessed is the man that endureth temptation: for when he is tried, he shall receive the crown of life, which the Lord hath promised to them that love him" (James 1:2, 12). "Wherein ye greatly rejoice, though now for a season, if need be, ye are in heaviness through manifold temptations: That the trial of your faith, being much more precious than of gold that perisheth, though it be tried with fire, might be found unto praise and honour and glory at the appearing of Jesus Christ"(1 Pet. 1:6-7).
2. It is an opportunity because we can use it to grow spiritually and to strengthen our faith. Paul writes of this: "And lest I should be exalted above measure through the abundance of the revelations, there was given to me a thorn in the flesh, the messenger of Satan to buffet me, lest I should be exalted above measure. For this thing I besought the Lord thrice, that it might depart from me. And he said unto me, My grace is sufficient for thee: for my strength is made perfect in weakness. Most gladly therefore will I rather glory in my infirmities, that the power of Christ may rest upon me. Therefore I take pleasure in infirmities, in reproaches, in necessities, in persecutions, in distresses for Christ's sake: for when I am weak, then am I strong" (2 Cor. 12:7-10).

B. If, however, our guide has been the old nature (as is often the case with us), then the temptation will prove harmful and even disastrous. James had this kind of guide in mind when he warned: "Let no man say when he is tempted, I am tempted of God: for God cannot be tempted with evil, neither tempteth he any man: But every man is tempted, when he is drawn away of his own lust, and enticed. Then when lust hath conceived, it bringeth forth sin: and sin, when it is finished, bringeth forth death" (James 1:13-15).

James was saying that we should not "tempt" temptation. Note the admonition of Solomon: "Can a man take fire in his bosom, and his clothes not be burned? Can one go upon hot coals, and his feet not be burned? So he that goeth in to his neighbour's wife; whosoever toucheth her shall not be innocent" (Prov. 6:27-29).

It has been correctly observed that while a believer may find it impossible to control himself under certain circumstances, he or she can always control the circumstances themselves.

An airline captain who had flown gigantic Boeing 747 passenger jetliners for years was once asked to define what constituted a great pilot. He replied: "A great pilot is an expert flier who never allows his plane to encounter those flying conditions which would require all of his greatness and expertise."

IV. His promise to build the church—"And Simon Peter answered and said, Thou art the Christ, the Son of the living God. And Jesus answered and said unto him, Blessed art thou, Simon Bar-jona: for flesh and blood hath not revealed it unto thee, but my Father which is in heaven. And I say also unto thee, That thou art Peter, and upon this rock I will build my church; and the gates of hell shall not prevail against it (Matt. 16:16-18).

A. Matthew 16 can be contrasted with Genesis 11.

1. Genesis 11:1-9 records the origin of Satan's church. Archaeological evidence has proven the tower

of Babel was in reality a religious temple, probably given over to the worship of the stars.

2. Matthew 16:13-19 records the origin of Christ's church.
3. Satan's church will be destroyed by the Antichrist during the great tribulation. "And the ten horns which thou sawest upon the beast, these shall hate the whore, and shall make her desolate and naked, and shall eat her flesh, and burn her with fire" (Rev. 17:16).
4. Christ's church will be delivered from the great tribulation by the Savior. "For the Lord himself shall descend from heaven with a shout, with the voice of the archangel, and with the trump of God: and the dead in Christ shall rise first: Then we which are alive and remain shall be caught up together with them in the clouds, to meet the Lord in the air: and so shall we ever be with the Lord" (1 Thess. 4:16-17).

B. Matthew 16 can be contrasted with John 6.

1. Both chapters record the testimony of Simon Peter. "From that time many of his disciples went back, and walked no more with him. Then said Jesus unto the twelve, Will ye also go away? Then Simon Peter answered him, Lord, to whom shall we go? thou hast the words of eternal life. And we believe and are sure that thou art that Christ, the Son of the living God" (John 6:66-69). "And Simon Peter answered and said, Thou art the Christ, the Son of the living God" (Matt. 16:16).
2. Both chapters record the treachery of the devil. "Jesus answered them, Have not I chosen you twelve, and one of you is a devil? He spake of Judas Iscariot the son of Simon: for he it was that should betray him, being one of the twelve" (John 6:70-71). "From that time forth began Jesus to shew unto his disciples, how that he must go unto Jerusalem, and suffer many things of the elders and chief priests and scribes, and be killed, and be raised again the third day. Then Peter took him, and began to rebuke him, saying, Be it far from thee, Lord: this shall not be unto thee. But he turned, and said unto Peter, Get thee behind me, Satan: thou art an offence unto me: for thou savourest not the things that be of God, but those that be of men" (Matt. 16:21-23).

V. His transfiguration—"And after six days Jesus taketh Peter, James, and John his brother, and bringeth them up into an high mountain apart, and was transfigured before them: and his face did shine as the sun, and his raiment was white as the light. And, behold, there appeared unto them Moses and Elias talking with him" (Matt. 17:1-3).

A. Both Moses and Elijah are seen here together, the second of three biblical accounts.

1. The first account, as recorded by Malachi—"Remember ye the law of Moses my servant, which I commanded unto him in Horeb for all Israel, with the statutes and judgments. Behold, I will send you Elijah the prophet before the coming of the great and dreadful day of the Lord: And he shall turn the heart of the fathers to the children, and the heart of the children to their fathers, lest I come and smite the earth with a curse" (Mal. 4:4-6).
2. The second account, as recorded here by Matthew (Matt. 17:3)
3. The third account, as recorded by John (assuming these men are the two witnesses who appear during the great tribulation)—"And I will give power unto my two witnesses, and they shall prophesy a thousand two hundred and threescore days, clothed in sackcloth" (Rev. 11:3).

B. During the transfiguration they speak of Christ's death in the city of Jerusalem. "Who appeared in glory, and spake of his decease which he should accomplish at Jerusalem" (Luke 9:31).

C. During the tribulation they themselves will die in the city of Jerusalem. "And when they shall have finished their testimony, the beast that ascendeth out of the bottomless pit shall make war against them, and shall overcome them, and kill them. And their dead bodies shall lie in the street of the great city, which spiritually is called Sodom and Egypt, where also our Lord was crucified" (Rev. 11:7-8).

D. Both Peter and John would later refer to the transfiguration.

1. Peter's comments—"For we have not followed cunningly devised fables, when we made known unto you the power and coming of our Lord Jesus Christ, but were eyewitnesses of his majesty. For he received from God the Father honour and glory, when there came such a voice to him from the excellent glory, This is my beloved Son, in whom I am well pleased. And this voice which came from heaven we heard, when we were with him in the holy mount. We have also a more sure word of prophecy; whereunto ye do well that ye take heed, as unto a light that shineth in a dark place, until the day dawn, and the day star arise in your hearts: Knowing this first, that no prophecy of the scripture is of any private interpretation. For the prophecy came not in old time by the will of man: but holy men of God spake as they were moved by the Holy Ghost" (2 Pet. 1:16-21).

   At this point, an extremely important truth should be observed. What Peter is saying here in verse 19 that however glorious the transfiguration was, there is something even *more glorious*, and that is *the written Word of God.* This is true for several reasons:

   a. Only three believers viewed the transfiguration, but the Scriptures are available to all believers.
   b. The transfiguration was historical in nature, while the Bible is eternal.
   c. The transfiguration revealed only one glimpse of Christ, while the Word of God fully presents the vital aspects of his person and work.

2. John's comments—"And the Word was made flesh, and dwelt among us, (and we beheld his glory, the glory as of the only begotten of the Father,) full of grace and truth" (John 1:14). Out of all humanity John alone would view the manifested glory of Christ the Prophet, Christ the Priest, and Christ the King. Note:

   a. The glory of Christ the Prophet (as described here)
   b. The glory of Christ the Priest—"I was in the Spirit on the Lord's day, and heard behind me a great voice, as of a trumpet, s aying, I am Alpha and Omega, the first and the last: and, What thou seest, write in a book, and send it unto the seven churches which are in Asia; unto Ephesus, and unto Smyrna, and unto Pergamos, and unto Thyatira, and unto Sardis, and unto Philadelphia, and unto Laodicea. And I turned to see the voice that spake with me. And being turned, I saw seven golden candlesticks; and in the midst of the seven candlesticks one like unto the Son of man, clothed with a garment down to the foot, and girt about the paps with a golden girdle. His head and his hairs were white like wool, as white as snow; and his eyes were as a flame of fire; and

his feet like unto fine brass, as if they burned in a furnace; and his voice as the sound of many waters. And he had in his right hand seven stars: and out of his mouth went a sharp twoedged sword: and his countenance was as the sun shineth in his strength. And when I saw him, I fell at his feet as dead. And he laid his right hand upon me, saying unto me, Fear not; I am the first and the last: I am he that liveth, and was dead; and, behold, I am alive for evermore, Amen; and have the keys of hell and of death" (Rev. 1:10-18).

c. The glory of Christ the King—"And I saw heaven opened, and behold a white horse; and he that sat upon him was called Faithful and True, and in righteousness he doth judge and make war. His eyes were as a flame of fire, and on his head were many crowns; and he had a name written, that no man knew, but he himself. And he was clothed with a vesture dipped in blood: and his name is called The Word of God. And the armies which were in heaven followed him upon white horses, clothed in fine linen, white and clean. And out of his mouth goeth a sharp sword, that with it he should smite the nations: and he shall rule them with a rod of iron: and he treadeth the winepress of the fierceness and wrath of Almighty God. And he hath on his vesture and on his thigh a name written, KING OF KINGS, AND LORD OF LORDS" (Rev. 19:11-16).

VI. His soul-winning activities—Jesus was a master soul winner during his earthly ministry. We will consider five of the many individuals he witnessed to and won over to himself.

A. Nicodemus (John 3:1-21)—"There was a man of the Pharisees, named Nicodemus, a ruler of the Jews" (John 3:1). The following features can be noted in Jesus' dealings with Nicodemus:

1. He was accessible. We are told (3:2) that Nicodemus came "by night." All too often a busy and successful Christian leader is anything but accessible to those who may desperately need godly counsel.
2. He was single-minded. The only issue Jesus wanted to discuss was the born-again experience. He refused to be side-tracked by the opening flattery of Nicodemus. Note the first statement from each man:

   Nicodemus: "Rabbi, we know that thou art a teacher come from God; for no man can do these miracles that thou doest, except God be with him" (John 3:2).

   Jesus: "Verily, verily, I say unto thee, Except a man be born again, he cannot see the kingdom of God" (John 3:3).
3. He was clear and concise. Realizing Nicodemus's confusion, Jesus related three helpful illustrations to explain the new birth.
   a. A physical illustration—"Jesus answered, Verily, verily, I say unto thee, Except a man be born of water and of the Spirit, he cannot enter into the kingdom of God. That which is born of the flesh is flesh; and that which is born of the Spirit is spirit" (John 3:5-6).
   b. A natural illustration—"The wind bloweth where it listeth, and thou hearest the sound thereof, but canst not tell whence it cometh, and whither it goeth: so is every one that is born of the Spirit" (John 3:8).

c. A Scriptural illustration—"And as Moses lifted up the serpent in the wilderness, even so must the Son of man be lifted up" (John 3:14).

4. He was well-informed. He knew the background of Nicodemus. "Jesus answered and said unto him, Art thou a master of Israel, and knowest not these things?" (John 3:10)
5. He was impartial. Even though Nicodemus was no doubt well-known and successful in the political, financial, and religious world, our Lord dealt with him for what he was, a poor lost sinner.

B. The Samaritan woman (John 4:1-42)

1. He arranged to meet her. "He left Judaea, and departed again into Galilee. And he must needs go through Samaria" (John 4:3-4).
2. He opened the conversation in a nonthreatening, polite manner. "There cometh a woman of Samaria to draw water: Jesus saith unto her, Give me to drink" (John 4:7).
3. He refused to argue with her concerning the two burning issues of that day.
   a. The social problem—"Then s aith the woman of Samaria unto him, How is it that thou, being a Jew, askest drink of me, which am a woman of Samaria? for the Jews have no dealings with the Samaritans" (John 4:9).
   b. The theological problem—"Our fathers worshipped in this mountain; and ye say, that in Jerusalem is the place where men ought to worship" (John 4:20).
4. He never brow-beat or belittled her.
5. He repeatedly spoke of living water, contrasting it with regular water. "Jesus answered and said unto her, Whosoever drinketh of this water shall thirst again: But whosoever drinketh of the water that I shall give him shall never thirst; but the water that I shall give him shall be in him a well of water springing up into everlasting life" (John 4:13-14).
6. He gently reminded her of her sin nature. "Jesus saith unto her, Go, call thy husband, and come hither. The woman answered and said, I have no husband. Jesus said unto her, Thou hast well said, I have no husband: For thou hast had five husbands; and he whom thou now hast is not thy husband: in that saidst thou truly" (John 4:16-18).
7. He concluded by pointing her to himself. "The woman saith unto him, I know that Messias cometh, which is called Christ: when he is come, he will tell us all things. Jesus saith unto her, I that speak unto thee am he" (John 4:25-26).

C. The woman taken in adultery (John 8:1-11)

1. He was accessible—"And early in the morning he came again into the temple, and all the people came unto him; and he sat down, and taught them" (John 8:2). Note: In John 3, Nicodemus met Christ late at night. Here the woman taken in adultery would meet him "early in the morning."
2. He did not condemn her, nor did he permit the self-righteous Pharisees to condemn her. Our Lord did not come to damn sinners, but rather to deliver them. "A bruised reed shall he not break, and smoking flax shall he not quench, till he send forth judgment unto victory" (Matt. 12:20).
3. He both forgave and instructed her. "Neither do I condemn thee: go, and sin no more" (John 8:11).

D. Zacchaeus (Luke 19:1-10)—"And Jesus entered and passed through Jericho. And, behold, there was a man named Zacchaeus, which was the chief among the publicans, and he was rich" (Luke 19:1-2). Little children love to sing about this "wee little man" who climbed a sycamore tree to see Jesus.

Four facts may be derived from this meeting.

1. Jesus saw Zacchaeus. "And when Jesus came to the place, he looked up, and saw him" (Luke 19:5a).
2. Jesus knew Zacchaeus. "And said unto him, Zacchaeus" (Luke 19:5b).
3. Jesus loved Zacchaeus."Make haste, and come down; for today I must abide at thy house" (Luke 19:5c).
4. Jesus saved Zacchaeus. "And he made haste, and came down, and received him joyfully. . . . And Jesus said unto him, This day is salvation come to this house forasmuch as he also is a son of Abraham" (Luke 19:6, 9).

E. The dying thief (Luke 23:39-43)—During his time of agony the dying thief observed Jesus in a fourfold light.

1. He saw Jesus the submissive. The man in the middle did not lash out against the hostility coming from the foot of the cross or the criticism coming from either side. "And they that passed by reviled him, wagging their heads, and saying, Thou that destroyest the temple, and buildest it in three days, save thyself. If thou be the Son of God, come down from the cross. Likewise also the chief priests mocking him, with the scribes and elders, said, He saved others; himself he cannot save. If he be the King of Israel, let him now come down from the cross, and we will believe him" (Matt. 27:39-42).

   In fact, to the contrary, the one in the center was actually praying for his tormentors. "Then said Jesus, Father, forgive them; for they know not what they do. And they parted his raiment, and cast lots" (Luke 23:34).
2. He saw Jesus the sinless. "And one of the malefactors which were hanged railed on him, saying, If thou be Christ, save thyself and us. But the other answering rebuked him, saying, Dost not thou fear God, seeing thou art in the same condemnation? And we indeed justly; for we receive the due reward of our deeds: but this man hath done nothing amiss" (Luke 23:39-41).
3. He saw Jesus the Savior. "And he said unto Jesus, Lord, remember me"(Luke 23:42a).
4. He saw Jesus the Sovereign. "When thou comest into thy kingdom" (Luke 23:42b).

VII. His Preaching Activities: On five specific occasions Jesus went out on an extended preaching mission. On two specific occasions he sent his disciples out on an extended preaching mission.

A. The preaching tours of Jesus

1. First tour—"And Jesus returned in the power of the Spirit into Galilee: and there went out a fame of him through all the region round about. And he taught in their synagogues, being glorified of all" (Luke 4:14-15).
   a. This tour took place shortly after his temptation in the wilderness (Luke 4:1-13).
   b. All his preaching missions apparently were centered in the Galilean area and not in Judea and Jerusalem. The reason for this seemed to be the intense hostility he experienced whenever he was in Jerusalem (see John 10:31; 11:8).
2. Second tour—"And Jesus went about all Galilee, teaching in their synagogues, and preaching the gospel of the kingdom, and healing all manner of sickness and all manner of disease among the people. And his fame went throughout all Syria: and they brought unto him all sick people that were taken with divers diseases and torments, and those which were possessed with devils, and those which were lunatick, and those that had the

palsy; and he healed them. And there followed him great multitudes of people from Galilee, and from Decapolis, and from Jerusalem, and from Judaea, and from beyond Jordan" (Matt. 4:23-25). This was undoubtedly his most successful crusade, with people flocking to hear him from Galilee, Judea, Syria, and the surrounding country.

3. Third tour—"And Jesus went about all the cities and villages, teaching in their synagogues, and preaching the gospel of the kingdom, and healing every sickness and every disease among the people" (Matt. 9:35).
   a. Here we are told the motivation prompting all his tours. "But when he saw the multitudes, he was moved with compassion on them, because they fainted, and were scattered abroad, as sheep having no shepherd" (Matt. 9:36).
   b. This tour also has a command attached to it. "Then saith he unto his disciples, The harvest truly is plenteous, but the labourers are few; pray ye therefore the Lord of the harvest, that he will send forth labourers into his harvest" (Matt. 9:37-38).
4. Fourth tour—"And it came to pass, when Jesus had made an end of commanding his twelve disciples, he departed thence to teach and to preach in their cities" (Matt. 11:1).
   a. Just prior to this tour our Lord had sent out his twelve disciples (Matt. 10).
   b. During this tour he is visited by two messengers sent by the imprisoned John the Baptist (Matt. 11:2).
5. Fifth tour—"And it came to pass afterward, that he went throughout every city and village, preaching and shewing the glad tidings of the kingdom of God: and the twelve were with him, and certain women, which had been healed of evil spirits and infirmities, Mary called Magdalene, out of whom went seven devils, and Joanna the wife of Chuza Herod's steward, and Susanna, and many others, which ministered unto him of their substance" (Luke 8:1-3). These women, converted during his final preaching crusade, would later render fruitful service to their Savior.
   a. They were present at the crucifixion (Matt. 27:56; Mark 15:40-41; Luke 23:49, 55).
   b. They were present at the resurrection (Luke 24:1-11).
   c. Mary Magdalene was the first human being to see the risen Christ (John 20:11-18).

B. The preaching tours of Jesus' disciples—As has been previously noted, Jesus sent a group of his disciples out on two occasions. These events are described in Matthew 10 and in Luke 10. The following offers both a contrast and comparison between these two groups.

1. The group in Matthew 10
   a. The number involved was 12 (Matt. 10:1).
   b. All 12 are named (Matt. 10:2-4)
   c. They were to preach a specific message. "And as ye go, preach, saying, The kingdom of heaven is at hand" (Matt. 10:7).
   d. They were given power to "heal the sick, cleanse the lepers, raise the dead, and to cast out devils" (Matt. 10:8).
   e. They were to preach only to Jews. "These twelve Jesus sent forth, and commanded them, saying, Go not into the way of the Gentiles, and into any city of the Samaritans enter ye not: But go rather to the lost sheep of the house of Israel" (Matt. 10:5-6).
   f. They were to travel lightly. "Provide neither gold, nor silver, nor brass in your purses, nor scrip for your journey, neither two coats, neither shoes, nor yet

staves: for the workman is worthy of his meat" (Matt. 10:9-10).

g. They were to expect persecution. "Behold, I send you forth as sheep in the midst of wolves: be ye therefore wise as serpents, and harmless as doves. But beware of men: for they will deliver you up to the councils, and they will scourge you in their synagogues; and ye shall be brought before governors and kings for my sake, for a testimony against them and the Gentiles" (Matt. 10:16-18).

h. They were promised the anointing of the Holy Spirit. "But when they deliver you up, take no thought how or what ye shall speak: for it shall be given you in that same hour what ye shall speak. For it is not ye that speak, but the Spirit of your Father which speaketh in you" (Matt. 10:19-20).

i. The results of their preaching trip are not recorded.

2. The group in Luke 10

a. The number involved was 70 (Luke 10:1).

b. None of the 70 are named.

c. They were to preach a specific message. "Say unto them, the kingdom of God is come nigh unto you" (Luke 10:9).

d. They were given power to heal the sick and to cast out demons (Luke 10:9, 17).

e. They were not restricted to preach only to the Jews. "After these things the Lord appointed other seventy also, and sent them two and two before his face into every city and place, whither he himself would come" (Luke 10:1).

f. They were to travel lightly (Luke 10:4).

g. They were to expect persecution. "Go your ways: behold, I send you forth as lambs among wolves" (Luke 10:3).

h. They were promised the anointing of the Father (implied in Luke 10:21).

i. The results of their preaching trip are recorded. "And the seventy returned again with joy, saying, Lord, even the devils are subject unto us through thy name. And he said unto them, I beheld Satan as lightning fall from heaven. Behold, I give unto you power to tread on serpents and scorpions, and over all the power of the enemy: and nothing shall by any means hurt you. Notwithstanding in this rejoice not, that the spirits are subject unto you; but rather rejoice, because your names are written in heaven" (Luke 10:17-20).

VIII. His triumphal entry (Matt. 21:1-11; Mark 11:1-10; Luke 19:29-38; John 12:12-19) "And they brought him to Jesus: and they cast their garments upon the colt, and they set Jesus thereon. And as he went, they spread their clothes in the way. And when he was come nigh, even now at the descent of the mount of Olives, the whole multitude of the disciples began to rejoice and praise God with a loud voice for all the mighty works that they had seen; saying, Blessed be the King that cometh in the name of the Lord: peace in heaven, and glory in the highest" (Luke 19:35-38). "And a very great multitude spread their garments in the way; others cut down branches from the trees, and strawed them in the way" (Matt. 21:8).

A. This marks the only "ticker tape parade" our Lord would receive during his earthly ministry, and it was, to say the least, short-lived. The disciples were no doubt excited over all this attention, but Jesus was not, for he knew what the future held, realizing the Jewish cries of celebration would soon turn into those of condemnation. Note the contrast:

1. The cries on Palm Sunday—"Blessed is the King that cometh in the name of the Lord" (Luke 19:38). "Blessed is the King of Israel"(John 12:13).
2. The cries on Good Friday—"When Pilate therefore heard that saying, he brought Jesus forth, and sat down in the judgment seat in a place that is called the Pavement, but in the Hebrew, Gabbatha. And it was the preparation of the passover, and about the sixth hour: and he saith unto the Jews, Behold your King! But they cried out, Away with him, away with him, crucify him. Pilate saith unto them, Shall I crucify your King? The chief priests answered, We have no king but Caesar" (John 19:13-15). "And when they had platted a crown of thorns, they put it upon his head, and a reed in his right hand: and they bowed the knee before him, and mocked him, saying, Hail, King of the Jews!" (Matt. 27:29).

B. On this occasion Jesus chose to enter Jerusalem on the foal of an ass. "And it came to pass, when he was come nigh to Bethphage and Bethany, at the mount called the mount of Olives, he sent two of his disciples, saying, Go ye into the village over against you; in the which at your entering ye shall find a colt tied, whereon yet never man sat: loose him, and bring him hither. And if any man ask you, Why do ye loose him? thus shall ye say unto him, Because the Lord hath need of him. And they that were sent went their way, and found even as he had said unto them. And as they were loosing the colt, the owners thereof said unto them, Why loose ye the colt? And they said, The Lord hath need of him. And they brought him to Jesus: and they cast their garments upon the colt, and they set Jesus thereon" (Luke 19:29-35). He did this for two reasons:

1. To fulfill prophecy—"All this was done, that it might be fulfilled which was spoken by the prophet, saying, Tell ye the daughter of Sion, Behold, thy king cometh unto thee, meek, and sitting upon an ass, and a colt the foal of an ass" (Matt. 21:4-5). This act of Christ was thus a direct fulfillment of the Old Testament prophecy written by Zechariah: "Rejoice greatly, O daughter of Zion; shout, O daughter of Jerusalem: behold, thy King cometh unto thee: he is just, and having salvation; lowly, and riding upon an ass, and upon a colt the foal of an ass" (Zech. 9:9).
2. To demonstrate the value of little things—Jesus often used the insignificant things to accomplish his divine will.
   a. Here he used a small animal.
   b. He had once used a little boy's lunch (John 6:9-11), some empty pots (John 2:6-9), and some clay (John 9:6-7). With these he provided food for the multitudes, wine for a wedding, and healing for the sightless. Paul later expounds upon this: "But God hath chosen the foolish things of the world to confound the wise; and God hath chosen the weak things of the world to confound the things which are mighty; and base things of the world, and things which are despised, hath God chosen, yea, and things which are not, to bring to nought things that are: That no flesh should glory in his presence" (1 Cor. 1:27-29).

C. Note the word *hosanna* as used by the crowd (Matt. 21:9). This word is only found five times in the Bible and all but one occur during the triumphal entry event. W. E. Vine comments: "Hosanna in the Hebrew means, 'save, we pray.' The word seems to have become an utterance of praise rather than of prayer, though originally, probably a cry for help. The people's cry at the Lord's triumphal entry into Jerusalem (Matt. 21:9, 15; Mark 11:9, 10; John 12:13), was taken from Psalm 118, which was recited at the Feast of Tabernacles in the great Hallel Psalms (113-118) in responses with the priest, accompanied by the waving of palms and willow branches. The last day of the feast was called 'the great Hosanna,' and the boughs called hosannas." (*Vine's Expository Dictionary of New Testament Words*, p. 564).

IX. His first and second temple cleansings (John 2:13-22; Matt. 21:12-13; Mark 11:15-17; Luke 19:45-46) These two may be favorably compared:

A. Both occurred at Passover time.

B. The first introduced Jesus' public ministry, while the second concluded it.

C. His death and resurrection is predicted on both occasions.

1. First occasion—"Then answered the Jews and said unto him, What sign shewest thou unto us, seeing that thou doest these things? Jesus answered and said unto them, Destroy this temple, and in three days I will raise it up. Then said the Jews, Forty and six years was this temple in building, and wilt thou rear it up in three days? But he spake of the temple of his body" (John 2:18-21).

2. Second occasion—"Verily, verily, I say unto you, Except a corn of wheat fall into the ground and die, it abideth alone: but if it die, it bringeth forth much fruit. . . . Now is my soul troubled; and what shall I say? Father, save me from this hour: but for this cause came I unto this hour. . . . And I, if I be lifted up from the earth, will draw all men unto me. This he said, signifying what death he should die" (John 12:24, 27, 32-33).

D. His glory was revealed just prior to the first cleansing. "This beginning of miracles did Jesus in Cana of Galilee, and manifested forth his glory; and his disciples believed on him" (John 2:11).

E. His glory was revealed just after the second cleansing. "Father, glorify thy name. Then came there a voice from heaven, saying, I have both glorified it, and will glorify it again" (John 12:28).

F. The Father is associated with both events.

1. First cleansing—"And said unto them that sold doves, Take these things hence; make not my Father's house an house of merchandise. And his disciples remembered that it was written, The zeal of thine house hath eaten me up" (John 2:16-17).

2. Second cleansing—"And Jesus went into the temple of God, and cast out all them that sold and bought in the temple, and overthrew the tables of the moneychangers, and the seats of them that sold doves, and said unto them, It is written, My house shall be called the house of prayer; but ye have made it a den of thieves" (Matt. 21:12-13).

X. His crucifixion—"And after that they had mocked him, they took the robe off from him, and put his own raiment on him, and led him away to crucify him" (Matt. 27:31). At least 12 Old Testament predictions regarding Christ were directly fulfilled at Calvary.

A. That he would be scourged and spat upon

1. The foretelling—"I gave my back to the smiters, and my cheeks to them that plucked off the hair: I hid not my face from shame and spitting" (Isa. 50:6).

2. The fulfillment—"Then did they spit in his face, and buffeted him; and others smote him with the palms of their hands" (Matt. 26:67). "Then

released he Barabbas unto them: and when he had scourged Jesus, he delivered him to be crucified" (Matt. 27:26).

B. That he would suffer a violent death
   1. The foretelling—"And after . . . shall Messiah be cut off" (Dan. 9:26). The Hebrew word *karath*, here translated "cut off," literally means to "cut down, to destroy." The same word is used in the following passages:
      a. 1 Sam. 17:51, where David severed the head of Goliath.
      b. 1 Sam. 31:9, where the Philistines cut off the head of King Saul.
      c. Exod. 31:14, where Sabbath breakers were to be put to death.
   2. The fulfillment—"And he bearing his cross went forth into a place called the place of a skull, which is called in the Hebrew Golgotha" (John 19:17).

C. That this sudden and violent death would involve crucifixion
   1. The foretelling—"I am poured out like water, and all my bones are out of joint: my heart is like wax; it is melted in the midst of my bowels. My strength is dried up like a potsherd; and my tongue cleaveth to my jaws; and thou hast brought me into the dust of death. For dogs have compassed me: the assembly of the wicked have inclosed me: they pierced my hands and my feet. I may tell all my bones: they look and stare upon me" (Psa. 22:14-17). Note the frightful language here:
      a. "All my bones are out of joint." "I may count all my bones." One of the most painful aspects of crucifixion was the dislocation of the victim's bones.
      b. "My tongue cleaveth to my jaws." Another agony was the terrible thirst.
      c. "They pierced my hands and my feet." This can only refer to crucifixion. (See also Zech. 12:10.)
   2. The fulfillment—"And it was the third hour, and they crucified him" (Mark 15:25).

D. That the ultimate force and source behind this death would be the Father himself
   1. The foretelling—"Yet it pleased the Lord to bruise him; he hath put him to grief: when thou shalt make his soul an offering for sin, he shall see his seed, he shall prolong his days, and the pleasure of the Lord shall prosper in his hand" (Isa. 53:10). "My God, my God, why hast thou forsaken me? why art thou so far from helping me, and from the words of my roaring?" (Psa. 22:1).
   2. The fulfillment—"And about the ninth hour Jesus cried with a loud voice, saying, Eli, Eli, lama sabachthani? that is to say, My God, my God, why hast thou forsaken me?" (Matt. 27:46) "For he hath made him to be sin for us, who knew no sin; that we might be made the righteousness of God in him" (2 Cor. 5:21).

E. That he would die with lawbreakers
   1. The foretelling—"He was numbered with the transgressors" (Isa. 53:12).
   2. The fulfillment—"Then were there two thieves crucified with him, one on the right hand, and another on the left" (Matt. 27:38).

F. That he would be given vinegar to drink
   1. The foretelling—"They gave me also gall for my meat; and in my thirst they gave me vinegar to drink" (Psa. 69:21).
   2. The fulfillment—"They gave him vinegar to drink mingled with gall: and when he had tasted thereof, he would not drink" (Matt. 27:34).

G. That he would pray for his enemies
   1. The foretelling—"He . . . made intercession for the transgressors" (Isa. 53:12b).
   2. The fulfillment—"Then said Jesus, Father, forgive them; for they know not what they do" (Luke 23:34a).

H. That he would be surrounded by his enemies
   1. The foretelling—"But I am a worm, and no man; a reproach of men, and despised of the people. All they that see me laugh me to scorn: they shoot out the lip, they shake the head, saying, He trusted on the Lord that he would deliver him: let him deliver him, seeing he delighted in him" (Psa. 22:6-8).
   2. The fulfillment—"And they that passed by reviled him, wagging their heads, and saying, Thou that destroyest the temple, and buildest it in three days, save thyself. If thou be the Son of God, come down from the cross. Likewise also the chief priests mocking him, with the scribes and elders, said, He saved others; himself he cannot save. If he be the King of Israel, let him now come down from the cross, and we will believe him. He trusted in God; let him deliver him now, if he will have him: for he said, I am the Son of God" (Matt. 27:39-43).

I. That his garments would be parted and gambled for
   1. The foretelling—"They part my garments among them, and cast lots upon my vesture" (Psa. 22:18).
   2. The fulfillment—"And they crucified him, and parted his garments, casting lots: that it might be fulfilled which was spoken by the prophet, They parted my garments among them, and upon my vesture did they cast lots" (Matt. 27:35).

J. That not one of his bones would be broken
   1. The foretelling—God had previously instructed Israel during that first Passover night in Egypt that not one bone of the sacrificial lamb was to be broken (Exod. 12:46). This command was later repeated at Mount Sinai (Num. 9:12). David also wrote of this: "He keeps all his bones: not one of them is broken" (Ps. 34:20).
   2. The fulfillment—"Then came the soldiers, and brake the legs of the first, and of the other which was crucified with him. But when they came to Jesus, and saw that he was dead already, they brake not his legs: But one of the soldiers with a spear pierced his side, and forth-with came there out blood and water. . . . For these things were done, that the scripture should be fulfilled, A bone of him shall not be broken" (John 19:32-34, 36).

K. That he would be looked upon in death
   1. The foretelling—"They shall look upon me whom they have pierced" (Zech. 12:10).
   2. The fulfillment—"Now when the centurion, and they that were with him, watching Jesus, saw the earthquake, and those things that were done, they feared greatly, saying, Truly this was the Son of God. . . . And all the people that came together to that sight, beholding the things which were done, smote their breasts, and returned. . . . And again another scripture saith, They shall look on him whom they pierced" (Matt. 27:54; Luke 23:48; John 19:37).

L. That his death would be associated with the rich
   1. The foretelling—"And he made his grave with . . . the rich in his death" (Isa. 53:9).
   2. The fulfillment—"Now when the centurion, and they that were with him, watching Jesus, saw the earthquake, and those things that were done, they feared greatly, saying, Truly this was the Son of God. And many women were

there beholding afar off, which followed Jesus from Galilee, ministering unto him: Among which was Mary Magdalene, and Mary the mother of James and Joses, and the mother of Zebedee's children. When the even was come, there came a rich man of Arimathaea, named Joseph, who also himself was Jesus' disciple: He went to Pilate, and begged the body of Jesus. Then Pilate commanded the body to be delivered. And when Joseph had taken the body, he wrapped it in a clean linen cloth, and laid it in his own new tomb, which he had hewn out in the rock: and he rolled a great stone to the door of the sepulchre, and departed." (Matt. 27:54-60).

XI. His resurrection—"But now is Christ risen from the dead, and become the firstfruits of them that slept" (1 Cor. 15:20). "I am he that liveth, and was dead; and, behold, I am alive for evermore, Amen; and have the keys of hell and of death" (Rev. 1:18).

A. Following his glorious resurrection, our Lord made ten appearances before ascending back to heaven.
1. To Mary Magdalene in the Garden (John 20:11-18)
2. To some women returning from the tomb (Matt. 28:9-10)
3. To two disciples on the Emmaus Road (Luke 24:13-32)
4. To Peter in Jerusalem (Luke 24:34; 1 Cor. 15:5)
5. To ten of his apostles in the upper room (Luke 24:36-43; John 20:19-23)
6. To the eleven in the upper room (John 20:24-29)
7. To seven apostles by the Galilean Sea (John 21:1-24)
8. To the eleven and 500 believers on Mount Tabor (Matt. 28:16-20; 1 Cor. 15:6)
9. To the eleven and James his half brother in Jerusalem (Mark 16:14-18; Luke 24:44-49; 1 Cor. 15:7)
10. To the eleven on the Mount of Olives (Luke 24:50-53)

B. Facts concerning these appearances
1. Five were made during the first Easter Sunday (numbers 1–5), and the final five (numbers 6–10) during the remaining 39 days.
2. The first two were made before women.
3. Six of the appearances were made to the gathered apostles (numbers 5–10).
4. The most detailed appearance recorded was number 3.
5. The least detailed appearances recorded were before Peter (number 4) and before James (number 9).
6. Seven out of ten occurred in or near Jerusalem (numbers 1, 2, 4, 5, 6, 9, and 10).
7. Two took place on mountains (numbers 8 and 10)
8. Angels accompanied two appearances (numbers 1 and 2).
9. On three occasions Jesus expounded upon the Scriptures (numbers 3, 5, and 9).
10. On two occasions he instructed his apostles to expound upon the Scriptures (numbers 7 and 8).
11. Supernatural events accompanied five of his ten appearances.
    a. Number 3: He vanished out of their sight (Luke 24:31).
    b. Number 5: He suddenly appeared in a locked room (Luke 24:36; John 20:19).
    c. Number 6: He again appeared in a locked room (John 20:26).
    d. Number 7: He arranged for a supernatural catch of fish (John 21:6).
    e. Number 10: He was taken to heaven by the glory cloud (Acts 1:9).
12. He ate during three of the appearances.
    a. Number 3: At Emmaus (Luke 24:30)

b. Number 5: In the upper room (Luke 24:41-43)
c. Number 7: By the Galilean sea (John 21:12, 13)

XII. His ascension (Mark 16:19-20; Luke 24:51-53; Acts 1:9-11)
1. Jesus thus became the final of three to bodily ascend into heaven.
a. Enoch was the first (Gen. 5).
b. Elijah was the second (2 Kings 2).
2. Jesus became the only person who had been previously dead to ascend bodily into heaven.

Key Activities in Christ's Life and the Number of Verses Describing Them

I. Twenty of the most important events in the life of Christ
A. A chronological listing (according to their historical occurrence)
1. Birth (announcements to Zacharias, Mary, Joseph, shepherds and wisemen, etc.): 120 verses
2. Baptism: 11 verses
3. Temptation: 26 verses
4. First temple cleansing: 10 verses
5. Call of Peter, Andrew, James, and John: 21 verses
6. Sending forth of the Twelve: 55 verses
7. Sending forth of the Seventy: 12 verses
8. Promise to build the church: 23 verses
9. Transfiguration: 24 verses
10. Anointing by Mary: 22 verses
11. Triumphal entry: 43 verses
12. Second temple cleansing: 12 verses
13. Confrontation with the Pharisees (final week): 130 verses
14. Upper room events: 134 verses
15. Great High Priestly prayer: 26 verses
16. Garden of Gethsemane: 71 verses
17. Unfair trials: 170 verses
18. Crucifixion: 93 verses
19. Resurrection and appearances: 137 verses
20. Ascension: 12 verses

B. A content listing (according to the number of verses used in describing the event)
1. Unfair trials: 170 verses
2. Resurrection and appearances: 137 verses
3. Upper room events: 134 verses
4. Confrontation with the Pharisees (final week): 130 verses
5. Birth: 120 verses
6. Crucifixion: 93 verses
7. Garden of Gethsemane: 71 verses
8. Sending forth of the Twelve: 55 verses
9. Triumphal entry: 43 verses
10. Temptation: 26 verses
11. Great High Priestly prayer: 26 verses
12. Transfiguration: 24 verses
13. Promise to build the church: 23 verses
14. Anointing by Mary: 22 verses
15. Call of Peter, Andrew, James, and John: 21 verses
16. Sending forth of the Seventy: 12 verses
17. Second temple cleansing: 12 verses
18. Ascension: 12 verses
19. Baptism: 11 verses
20. First temple cleansing: 10 verses

II. Seven important dialogues of Christ (according to verse content)
A. With Pilate: as described by 78 verses
B. With the rich young ruler: as described by 32 verses
C. With Nicodemus: as described by 21 verses
D. With the Samaritan woman: as described by 21 verses
E. With Cleopas: as described by 21 verses
F. With the woman taken in adultery: as described by 11 verses
G. With Zacchaeus: as described by 10 verses

III. Ten important miracles of Christ (according to verse content)
   A. Feeding of the 5000: as described by 45 verses
   B. Raising of Lazarus: as described by 44 verses
   C. Restoring of the maniac of Gadara: as described by 41 verses
   D. Healing of the man born blind: as described by 41 verses
   E. Healing of the paralytic: as described by 30 verses
   F. Healing of the demonic boy: as described by 30 verses
   G. Walking on the water: as described by 22 verses
   H. Healing of blind Bartimaeus: as described by 22 verses
   I. Healing of the impotent man: as described by 16 verses
   J. Second draught of fishes: as described by 14 verses

IV. Three Important Parables of Christ (according to verse content)
   A. The mysteries of the kingdom: as described by 101 verses
   B. Some vicious vine keepers: as described by 37 verses
   C. The missing sheep, coin, and Prodigal Son: as described by 32 verses

V. Ten important sermons of Christ (according to verse content)
   A. The Olivet Discourse: as described by 168 verses
   B. The Sermon on the Mount: as described by 155 verses
   C. The Abundance of Life sermon: as described by 60 verses
   D. The Water of Life sermon: as described by 53 verses
   E. The Bread of Life sermon: as described by 50 verses
   F. The Light of Life sermon: as described by 48 verses
   G. The Shepherd of Life sermon: as described by 39 verses
   H. The Sermon on John the Baptist: as described by 35 verses
   I. The Source of Life sermon: as described by 31 verses
   J. The Way and the Truth and the Life sermon: as described by 31 verses

OBSERVATIONS FROM THE LIFE OF PAUL

I. He was a redeemed sinner.

A. Paul's testimony of his salvation (Acts 9:1-18)

1. As he related it to the Jewish leaders in Jerusalem (Acts 22:1-21)
2. As he related it to King Agrippa in Caesarea (Acts 26:1-29)

COMMENT

These testimonies can be both compared and contrasted.

- One was before an angry mob.
- The other was before an audience of three (Agrippa, Bernice, and Festus).
- Paul emphasized four key facts during each testimony.

    His birth and early religious training in Tarsus

    His preconversion persecution of Christians

    His heavenly vision en route to Damascus

    His call to the Gentiles

- Both testimonies were rejected by the listeners, but for different reasons.

    Those in Jerusalem rejected it because of his reference to Gentiles. "And he said unto me, Depart: for I will send thee far hence unto the Gentiles. And they gave him audience unto this word, and then lifted up their voices, and said, Away with such a fellow from the earth: for it is not fit that he should live" (Acts 22:21-22).

    Those in Caesarea rejected it because of his references to the resurrection. "Why should it be thought a thing incredible with you, that God should raise the dead? . . . That Christ should suffer, and that he should be the first that should rise from the dead, and should shew light unto the people, and to the Gentiles. And as he thus spake for himself, Festus said with a loud voice, Paul, thou art beside thyself; much learning doth make thee mad" (Acts 26:8, 23-24).

B. Paul's thanksgiving for his salvation—"But God forbid that I should glory, save in the cross of our Lord Jesus Christ, by whom the world is crucified unto me, and I unto the world" (Gal. 6:14). "For I am the least of the apostles, that am not meet to be called an apostle, because I persecuted the church of God. But by the grace of God I am what I am: and his grace which was bestowed upon me was not in vain; but I laboured more abundantly than they all: yet not I, but the grace of God which was with me" (1 Cor. 15:9-10). "This is a faithful saying, and worthy of all acceptation, that Christ Jesus came into the world to save sinners; of whom I am chief" (1 Tim. 1:15).

COMMENT

What made Paul the man he was? His two little statements here in these verses probably summarize and explain it best. "I am the least [among saints]." This was his *horizontal view.* "I am chief [among sinners]." This was his *vertical view.*

II. He was a chosen vessel—"But the Lord said unto him, Go thy way: for he is a chosen vessel unto me, to bear my name before the Gentiles, and kings, and the children of Israel" (Acts 9:15).
   A. Paul was a vessel of mercy.(Rom. 9:23).
   B. He was an earthen vessel (2 Cor. 4:7).
   C. He was a vessel of honor (Rom. 9:21).
   D. He was a sanctified and worthy vessel (2 Tim. 2:21).

COMMENT

Note the threefold audience this chosen vessel would witness to:

- Gentiles: Paul shared the gospel to both Gentile pagans (Acts 14:8-18; 19:10-20) and philosophers (Acts 17:16-34).
- Kings: In Caesarea he stood before two Roman governors (Felix and Festus) and a king (Agrippa). (See Acts 24:25; 25:24; 26:28.) Furthermore, there is a possibility he may have appeared before Caesar himself (see Acts 25:11; Phil. 4:22).
- The children of Israel: Paul accomplished this in three key locations:
  - Antioch in Pisidia (Acts 13:14-43)
  - Jerusalem
    - Speaking before the Jewish people (Acts 22:1-21)
    - Speaking before the Jewish priests (Acts 23:1-6)
  - Rome (Acts 28:16-31)

III. He was a missionary to the Gentiles (Acts 9:15; 13:46-47, 18:6; 22:21; 28:28; Rom. 11:13; Gal. 2:7, 9; Eph. 3:6-8; 2 Tim. 4:17). "For I speak to you Gentiles, inasmuch as I am the apostle of the Gentiles, I magnify mine office" (Rom. 11:13).

IV. He was a heartbroken Israelite—"I say the truth in Christ, I lie not, my conscience also bearing me witness in the Holy Ghost, that I have great heaviness and continual sorrow in my heart. For I could wish that myself were accursed from Christ for my brethren, my kinsmen according to the flesh" (Rom. 9:1-3). "Brethren, my heart's desire and prayer to God for Israel is, that they might be saved" (Rom. 10:1). "For many walk, of whom I have told you often, and now tell you even weeping, that they are the enemies of the cross of Christ" (Phil. 3:18).

COMMENT

Paul is the last of at least seven men in the Bible to weep over the sins of Israel.

- Moses—"And Moses returned unto the Lord, and said, Oh, this people have sinned a great sin, and have made them gods of gold. Yet now, if thou wilt forgive their sin—; and if not, blot me, I pray thee, out of thy book which thou hast written" (Exod. 32:31-32).
- Ezra—"And at the evening sacrifice I arose up from my heaviness; and having rent my garment and my mantle, I fell upon my knees, and spread out my hands unto the Lord my God, and said, O my God, I am ashamed and blush to lift up my face to thee, my God: for our iniquities are increased over our head, and our trespass is grown up unto the heavens. . . . Now when Ezra had prayed, and when he had confessed, weeping and casting himself down before the house of God, there assembled unto him out of Israel a very great congregation of men and women and children: for the people wept very sore" (Ezra 9:5-6; 10:1).
- Nehemiah—"And it came to pass, when I heard these words, that I sat down and wept, and mourned certain days, and fasted, and prayed before the God of heaven . . . . We have dealt very corruptly against thee, and have not kept the commandments, nor the statutes, nor the judgments, which thou commandedst thy servant Moses" (Neh. 1:4, 7).
- Jeremiah—"Oh that my head were waters, and mine eyes a fountain of tears, that I might weep day and night for the slain of the daughter of my people!" (Jer. 9:1).

- Daniel—"And I set my face unto the Lord God, to seek by prayer and supplications, with fasting, and sackcloth, and ashes . . . . We have sinned, and have committed iniquity, and have done wickedly, and have rebelled, even by departing from thy precepts and from thy judgments" (Dan. 9:3, 5).
- Jesus—"And when he was come near, he beheld the city, and wept over it . . . . O Jerusalem, Jerusalem, thou that killest the prophets, and stonest them which are sent unto thee, how often would I have gathered thy children together, even as a hen gathereth her chickens under her wings, and ye would not! Behold, your house is left unto you desolate. For I say unto you, Ye shall not see me henceforth, till ye shall say, Blessed is he that cometh in the name of the Lord" (Luke 19:41; Matt. 23: 37-39).
- Paul—"I say the truth in Christ, I lie not, my conscience also bearing me witness in the Holy Ghost, that I have great heaviness and continual sorrow in my heart. . . . (For many walk, of whom I have told you often, and now tell you even weeping, that they are the enemies of the cross of Christ)" (Rom. 9:1-2; Phil. 3:18).

V. He was a mighty prayer warrior.
  A. Paul began and ended his Christian life by prayer.
    1. The beginning—"And the Lord said unto him, Arise, and go into the street which is called Straight, and enquire in the house of Judas for one called Saul, of Tarsus: for, behold, he prayeth" (Acts 9:11).
    2. The ending—"At my first answer no man stood with me, but all men forsook me: I pray God that it may not be laid to their charge" (2 Tim. 4:16).
  B. Paul prayed everywhere he went.
    1. In a prison—"And at midnight Paul and Silas prayed, and sang praises unto God: and the prisoners heard them" (Acts 16:25).
    2. On a seashore
      a. At Miletus—"And when he had thus spoken, he kneeled down, and prayed with them all" (Acts 20:36).
      b. At Tyre—"And when we had accomplished those days, we departed and went our way; and they all brought us on our way, with wives and children, till we were out of the city: and we kneeled down on the shore, and prayed" (Acts 21:5).
    3. In Jerusalem (Acts 22:17)
    4. On an island—"And it came to pass, that the father of Publius lay sick of a fever and of a bloody flux: to whom Paul entered in, and prayed, and laid his hands on him, and healed him" (Acts 28:8).
  C. Paul prayed for almost everyone he met.
    1. For the churches (Rom. 1:9; 1 Cor. 1:4; 2 Cor 13:7; Eph. 1:16; 3:14; Phil. 1:4, 9; Col. 1:3, 9; 1 Thess. 1:2; 3:10; 5:23; 2 Thess. 1:3, 11; 2:13)
    2. For Philemon (Philem. 4)
    3. For Timothy (2 Tim. 1:3)
    4. For Onesiphorus (2 Tim. 1:16-18)
    5. For those who forsook him in Rome (2 Tim. 4:16)
    6. For Israel—"Brethren, my heart's desire and prayer to God for Israel is, that they might be saved" (Rom. 10:1)
    7. For all men (1 Tim. 2:1-3, 8; 4:4-5)
  D. Paul constantly asked others to pray for him (Rom. 15:30; Col. 4:31; Thess. 5:25; 2 Thess. 3:1; Philem. 22).

COMMENT

Paul requested prayer in four areas:

- For furtherance of the gospel—"That the word of the Lord may speed rapidly and be glorified" (2 Thess. 3:1, NASB) "That God may open up to us a door for the word" (Col. 4:3, NASB). "ThatI may make it clear in the way I ought to speak" (Col. 4:4, NASB).

- For personal safety—"That we may be delivered from perverse and evil men" (2 Thess. 3:2, NASB). "That I may be delivered from those who are disobedient in Judea." (Rom. 15:31a, NASB)
- For release from his first Roman imprisonment (Philem. 22)
- For acceptance among the believers in Jerusalem (Rom. 15:31b)

VI. He was an apostle of Christ. Paul refers to his office as an apostle on twenty specific occasions (Rom. 1:1; 11:13; 1 Cor. 1:1; 4:9; 9:1-2; 15:9; 2 Cor. 1:1; 11:5; 12:11, 12; Gal. 1:1; Eph. 1:1; Col. 1:1; 1 Thess. 2:6; 1 Tim. 1:1; 2:7; 2 Tim. 1:1, 11; Titus 1:1).

VII. He was a prophet of God. Paul wrote the following predictions:

A. Concerning the last days (1 Tim. 4:1-3; 2 Tim. 3:1-5, 13; 4:3-4)—According to Paul:

1. Some in the church will turn away from Christ and become eager followers of teachers who offer devil-inspired ideas.
2. These false teachers will claim it is wrong to be married and to eat meat.
3. In the last days it will be very difficult to be a Christian.
4. People will love only themselves and their money.
5. They will be hotheaded and hard-headed trouble-making liars.
6. They will be immoral, rough, and cruel, sneering at those who try to do good.
7. They will be conceited, lovers of pleasure rather than lovers of God.
8. They will display a form of godliness but deny the power of God.

B. Concerning the Rapture (1 Cor. 15:51-53; 1 Thess. 1:10; 2:19; 3:13; 4:13-17; 5:23; Heb. 9:28)—"Behold, I shew you a mystery; We shall not all sleep, but we shall all be changed, in a moment, in the twinkling of an eye, at the last trump: for the trumpet shall sound, and the dead shall be raised incorruptible, and we shall be changed. For this corruptible must put on incorruption, and this mortal must put on immortality" (1 Cor. 15:51-53). "For the Lord himself shall descend from heaven with a shout, with the voice of the archangel, and with the trump of God: and the dead in Christ shall rise first: Then we which are alive and remain shall be caught up together with them in the clouds to meet the Lord in the air: and so shall we ever be with the Lord" (1 Thess. 4:16-17).

C. Concerning the resurrection (Rom. 8:23; 1 Cor. 15:42-49; 2 Cor. 5:1; Phil. 3:20-21)—"So also is the resurrection of the dead. It is sown in corruption; it is raised in incorruption: It is sown in dishonour; it is raised in glory: it is sown in weakness; it is raised in power: it is sown a natural body; it is raised a spiritual body. There is a natural body, and there is a spiritual body" (1 Cor. 15:42-44). "For we know that if our earthly house of this tabernacle were dissolved, we have a building of God, an house not made with hands, eternal in the heavens" (2 Cor. 5:1). "Who shall change our vile body, that it may be fashioned like unto his glorious body, according to the working whereby he is able even to subdue all things unto himself" (Phil. 3:21).

D. Concerning the bema, the judgment seat of Christ—"But why dost thou judge thy brother? or why dost thou set at nought thy brother? for we shall all stand before the judgment seat of Christ. For it is written, As I live, saith the Lord, every knee shall bow to me, and every tongue shall confess to God. So then every one of us shall give account of himself to God" (Rom. 14:10-12) "For other foundation can no man lay than that is laid, which is Jesus Christ. Now if any man build upon this foundation gold, silver, precious stones, wood, hay, stubble; every man's work shall be made manifest: for the day shall declare it, because it shall be revealed by fire; and the fire shall try every man's work of what sort it is. If any man's work abide which he hath built thereupon, he shall receive a reward. If any man's work shall be burned, he shall suffer loss: but he himself shall be saved; yet so as by fire" (1 Cor. 3:11-15). "For we must all appear before the judgment seat of Christ; that every one may receive the things done in his body, according to that he hath done, whether it be good or bad" (2 Cor. 5:10).

E. Concerning future rewards (1 Cor. 9:25-27; 2 Thess. 2:19; 2 Tim. 4:8; Heb. 6:10)—"I have fought a good fight, I have finished my course, I have kept the faith: Henceforth there is laid up for me a crown of righteousness, which the Lord, the righteous judge, shall give me at that day: and not to me only, but unto all them also that love his appearing" (2 Tim. 4:7-8).

COMMENT

This is the final of three reward *crowns* referred to by Paul in his writings. A quick analysis of Paul's life shows he will doubtless receive all three at the judgment seat of Christ.

- The incorruptible crown: Given to those who master the old nature—"And every man that striveth for the mastery is temperate in all things. Now they do it to obtain a corruptible crown; but we an incorruptible. I therefore so run, not as uncertainly; so fight I, not as one that beateth the air: But I keep under my body, and bring it into subjection: lest that by any means, when I have preached to others, I myself should be a castaway" (1 Cor. 9:25-27)
- The crown of rejoicing: Given to soul winners (1 Thess. 2:19-20)
- The crown of righteousness: Given to those who live their lives in light of the Rapture

---

F. Concerning the marriage of the church to Christ (Eph. 5:25-32; 2 Cor. 11:2)—"Husbands, love your wives, even as Christ also loved the church, and gave himself for it; that he might sanctify and cleanse it with the washing of water by the word, that he might present it to himself a glorious church, not having spot, or wrinkle, or any such thing; but that it should be holy and without blemish" (Eph. 5:25-27). "For I am jealous over you with godly jealousy: for I have espoused you to one husband, that I may present you as a chaste virgin to Christ" (2 Cor. 11:2).

G. Concerning the coming man of sin (2 Thess. 2:3-12)—"Let no man deceive you by any means: for that day shall not come, except there come a falling away first, and that man of sin be revealed, the son of perdition; Who opposeth and exalteth himself above all that is called God, or that is worshipped; so that he as God sitteth in the temple of God, shewing himself that he is God. . . . And then shall that Wicked be revealed, whom the Lord shall consume with the spirit of his mouth, and shall destroy with the brightness of his coming: Even him, whose coming is after the working of Satan with all power and signs and lying wonders" (2 Thess. 2:3-4, 8-9).

H. Concerning the second coming of Christ (2 Thess. 1:7-8; 2:8)—"And to you who are troubled rest with us, when the Lord Jesus shall be revealed from heaven with his mighty angels, in flaming fire taking vengeance on them that know not God, and that obey not the gospel of our Lord Jesus Christ" (2 Thess. 1:7- 8).

I. Concerning the restoration of Israel (Rom. 11:15, 25-27; 2 Cor. 3:16)—"And so all Israel shall be saved: as it is written, There shall come out of Sion the Deliverer, and shall turn away ungodliness from Jacob" (Rom. 11:26).

J. Concerning the Millennium (Rom. 8:16-23; 1 Cor. 6:2-3; 2 Cor. 4:17-18) "The Spirit himself testifies with our spirit that we are God's children. Now if we are children, then we are heirs—

heirs of God and co-heirs with Christ, if indeed we share in his sufferings in order that we may also share in his glory. I consider that our present sufferings are not worth comparing with the glory that will be revealed in us. The creation waits in eager expectation for the sons of God to be revealed. For the creation was subjected to frustration, not by its own choice, but by the will of the one who subjected it, in hope that the creation itself will be liberated from its bondage to decay and brought into the glorious freedom of the children of God. We know that the whole creation has been groaning as in the pains of childbirth right up to the present time. Not only so, but we ourselves, who have the firstfruits of the Spirit, groan inwardly as we wait eagerly for our adoption as sons, the redemption of our bodies" (Rom. 8:16-23, NIV). "For our light affliction, which is but for a moment, worketh for us a far more exceeding and eternal weight of glory; while we look not at the things which are seen, but at the things which are not seen: for the things which are seen are temporal; but the things which are not seen are eternal" (2 Cor. 4:17-18)

K. Concerning the great white throne judgment (Acts 17:31; Rom. 2:3-6, 8-16) "Because he hath appointed a day, in the which he will judge the world in righteousness by that man whom he hath ordained; whereof he hath given assurance unto all men, in that he hath raised him from the dead" (Acts 17:31). "Who will render to every man according to his deeds . . . . Tribulation and anguish, upon every soul of man that doeth evil, of the Jew first, and also of the Gentile" (Rom. 2:6, 9).

L. Concerning eternity—"That in the ages to come he might shew the exceeding riches of his grace in his kindness toward us through Christ Jesus" (Eph. 2:7).

VIII. He was a miracle worker (Acts 15:12; Rom. 15:19; 2 Cor. 12:12)

A. Blinding of Elymas on Cyprus (Acts 13:11)

B. Various miracles at Iconium (Acts 14:3)

C. Healing of a cripple man at Lystra (Acts 14:10)

D. Demons cast out and sick healed at Ephesus (Acts 19:11-12)

E. Raising of Eutychus at Troas (Acts 20:10-12)

F. Healing of Publius's father and others on Melita (Acts 28:8-9)

COMMENT

God worked miracles through Paul to accomplish a threefold purpose:

- To validate the authority of Paul's message

To the Jews—"And it came to pass in Iconium, that they went both together into the synagogue of the Jews, and so spake, that a great multitude both of the Jews and also of the Greeks believed. . . . Long time therefore abode they speaking boldly in the Lord, which gave testimony unto the word of his grace, and granted signs and wonders to be done by their hands" (Acts 14:1, 3). "Truly the signs of an apostle were wrought among you in all patience, in signs, and wonders, and mighty deeds" (2 Cor. 12:12).

To the Gentiles—"For I will not dare to speak of any of those things which Christ hath not wrought by me, to make the Gentiles obedient, by word and deed, through mighty signs and wonders, by the power of the Spirit of God; so that from Jerusalem, and round about unto Illyricum, I have fully preached the gospel of Christ" (Rom. 15:18-19).

To demons—"And God wrought special miracles by the hands of Paul: "So that from his body were brought unto the sick handkerchiefs or aprons, and the diseases departed from them, and the evil spirits went out of them. Then certain of the vagabond Jews, exorcists, took upon them to call over them which had evil spirits the name of the Lord Jesus, saying, We adjure you by Jesus whom Paul preacheth. And there were seven sons of one Sceva, a Jew, and chief of the priests, which did so. And the evil spirit answered and said, Jesus I know, and Paul I know; but who are ye?" (Acts 19:11-15).

- To counteract the opposition of Satan—"And when they had gone through the isle unto Paphos, they found a certain sorcerer, a false prophet, a Jew, whose name was Bar-jesus: Which was with the deputy of the country, Sergius Paulus, a prudent man; who called for Barnabas and Saul, and desired to hear the word of God. But Elymas the sorcerer (for so is his name by interpretation) withstood them, seeking to turn away the deputy from the faith. Then Saul, (who also is called Paul,) filled with the Holy Ghost, set his eyes on him, and said, O full of all subtilty and all mischief, thou child of the devil, thou enemy of all righteousness, wilt thou not cease to pervert the right ways of the Lord? And now, behold, the hand of the Lord is upon thee, and thou shalt be blind, not seeing the sun for a season. And immediately there fell on him a mist and a darkness; and he went about seeking some to lead him by the hand. Then the deputy, when he saw what was done, believed, being astonished at the doctrine of the Lord" (Acts 13:6-12).
- To reveal the only true God—"And there sat a certain man at Lystra, impotent in his feet, being a cripple from his mother's womb, who never had walked: The same heard Paul speak: who sted-fastly beholding him, and perceiving that he had faith to be healed, said with a loud voice, Stand upright on thy feet. And he leaped and walked. . . . Who in times past suffered all nations to walk in their own ways. Never-theless he left not himself without witness, in that he did good, and gave us rain from heaven, and fruitful seasons, filling our hearts with food and gladness" (Acts 14:8-10, 16-17)

IX. He was a tactful Christian. This is illustrated by the following:

A. Speaking to the philosophers in Athens (Acts 17:22)
B. Using Hebrew before the Jews in Jerusalem (Acts 22:1-2)
C. Witnessing before Festus and Agrippa in Caesarea (Acts 26:24-29)
D. Dealing with two disputing ladies in Philippi (Phil. 4:1-3)
E. Writing Philemon, in Colosse, concerning Onesimus (Philem.)

COMMENT

An overview of his tact can be seen as follows:

- Concerning the philosophers in Athens—Paul begins by complimenting them. "And Paul stood in the midst of the Areopagus and said, "Men of Athens, I observe that you are very religious in all respects." (Acts 17:22, NASB) He then quotes from one of their own poets. "For in him we live, and move, and have our being; as certain also of your own poets have said, For we are also his offspring" (Acts 17:28).
- Concerning the Jewish leaders in Jerusalem—He immediately commands their attention by speaking to them in Hebrew rather than the normal language of Greek or Aramaic.
- Concerning Festus and Agrippa in Caesarea
  - He refuses to respond in kind to Festus's ridicule, but instead shows great respect. "And as he thus spake for himself, Festus said with a loud voice, Paul, thou art beside thyself; much learning doth make thee mad. But he said, I am not mad, most noble Festus; but speak forth the words of truth and soberness" (Acts 26:24-25).
  - He acknowledges the wisdom and abilities of King Agrippa. "I think myself happy, king Agrippa, because I shall answer for myself this day before thee touching

all the things whereof I am accused of the Jews: Especially because I know thee to be expert in all customs and questions which are among the Jews: wherefore I beseech thee to hear me patiently. . . . For the king knoweth of these things, before whom also I speak freely: for I am persuaded that none of these things are hidden from him; for this thing was not done in a corner" (Acts 26:2-3, 26).

- Concerning the two women in Philippi
  - He played down the sin of these women. "I beseech Euodias, and beseech Syntyche, that they be of the same mind in the Lord" (Phil. 4:2).
  - He played up the service of these women. "And I entreat thee also, true yokefellow, help those women which laboured with me in the gospel, with Clement also, and with other my fellowlabourers, whose names are in the book of life" (Phil. 4:3).
- Concerning Philemon in Colosse: Paul appeals to Philemon on the basis of their long friendship to favorably receive Onesimus, a newly converted and formerly runaway slave.

X. He was a powerful preacher. This is seen by his sermons:

A. At Damascus (Acts 9:20-22)
B. In Jerusalem (Acts 9:29)
C. At Antioch in Pisidia (Acts 13:16-41)
D. At Lystra (Acts 14:12)
E. At Athens on Mars Hill (Acts 17:22-34)
F. At Troas (Acts 20:7-12)

COMMENT

Note the following recorded facts concerning his preaching:

- The *theme* of his sermons was demonstrated at *Damascus.* "Saul . . . confounded the Jews which dwelt at Damascus, proving that this is very Christ" (Acts 9:22).
- The *boldness* was seen at *Jerusalem.* "And he spake boldly in the name of the Lord Jesus, and disputed against the Grecians" (Acts 9:29).
- The *common appeal* was seen at *Antioch of Pisidia* where the entire city assembled to hear him preach (Acts 13:44).
- The *style* was seen at *Lystra,* where he was called Mercurius by the pagans. They believed Mercurius was the messenger of the gods (Acts 14:12).
- The *uniqueness* was seen at *Athens.* "Certain philosophers of the Epicureans, and of the Stoicks, encountered him. And some said, What will this babbler say? other some, He seemeth to be a setter forth of strange gods: because he preached unto them Jesus, and the resurrection. And they took him, and brought him unto Areopagus, saying, May we know what this new doctrine, whereof thou speakest, is? For thou bringest certain strange things to our ears: we would know therefore what these things mean" (Acts 17:18-20).
- The *length* was seen at *Troas.* "And upon the first day of the week, when the disciples came together to break bread, Paul preached unto them, ready to depart on the morrow; and continued his speech until midnight. . . . And there sat in a window a certain young man named Eutychus, being fallen into a deep sleep: and as Paul was long preaching, he sunk down with sleep, and fell down from the third loft, and was taken up dead" (Acts 20:7, 9).

XI. He was an effective teacher. This is seen through his ministry of instruction:

A. In Antioch (Acts 11:26; 13:1)
B. In Corinth (Acts 18:11)
C. In Ephesus (Acts 19:10)

XII. He was a respected coworker. This is seen by the following statements concerning Paul:

A. "Our beloved Barnabas and Paul" (Acts 15:25b).
B. "And they all wept sore, and fell on Paul's neck, and kissed him" (Acts 20:37).
C. "If it had been possible, ye would have plucked our your own eyes, and have given them to me" (Gal. 4:15).
D. "Our beloved brother Paul" (2 Pet. 3:15).

XIII. He was a faithful steward. "Let a man so account of us, as of the ministers of Christ, and stewards of the mysteries of God" (1 Cor. 4:1). "For we are not as many, which corrupt the word of God: but as of sincerity, but as of God, in the sight of God speak we in Christ" (2 Cor. 2:17). "Therefore seeing we have this ministry, as we have received mercy, we faint not; but have renounced the hidden things of dishonesty, not walking in craftiness, nor handling the word of God deceitfully; but by manifestation of the truth commending ourselves to every man's conscience in the sight of God. . . . Giving no offence in any thing, that the ministry be not blamed" (2 Cor. 4:1-2; 6:3).

XIV. He was a consistent example (Acts 20:17-38; 1 Cor. 8:13; 9:1, 15, 19-22; 10:23, 33; Rom. 15:1-2) "For I have not shunned to declare unto you all the counsel of God. . . . I have coveted no man's silver, or gold, or apparel. Yea, ye yourselves know, that these hands have ministered unto my necessities, and to them that were with me. I have shewed you all things, how that so labouring ye ought to support the weak, and to remember the words of the Lord Jesus, how he said, It is more blessed to give than to receive" (Acts 20:27, 33-35).

Because of his Christlike and consistent life-style, Paul could—and did—exhort his readers on eight specific occasions to *follow his example.* "Wherefore I beseech you, be ye followers of me. . . . Be ye followers of me, even as I also am of Christ" (1 Cor. 4:16; 11:1). "Brethren, I beseech you, be as I am; for I am as ye are: ye have not injured me at all" (Gal. 4:12). "Brethren, be followers together of me, and mark them which walk so as ye have us for an ensample. . . . Those things, which ye have both learned, and received, and heard, and seen in me, do: and the God of peace shall be with you" (Phil. 3:17; 4:9). "For our gospel came not unto you in word only, but also in power, and in the Holy Ghost, and in much assurance; as ye know what manner of men we were among you for your sake. And ye became followers of us, and of the Lord, having received the word in much affliction, with joy of the Holy Ghost . . . . Ye are witnesses, and God also, how holily and justly and unblamably we behaved ourselves among you that believe" (1 Thess. 1:5-6; 2:10). "For yourselves know how ye ought to follow us: for we behaved not ourselves disorderly among you; neither did we eat any man's bread for nought; but wrought with labour and travail night and day, that we might not be chargeable to any of you: Not because we have not power, but to make ourselves an ensample unto you to follow us" (2 Thess. 3:7-9).

XV. He was a compassionate soul winner (1 Cor. 9:22; Acts 20:19-20, 31; Rom. 9:1-3) "And how I kept back nothing that was profitable unto you, but have shewed you, and have taught you publickly, and from house to house . . . . Therefore watch, and remember, that by the space of three years I ceased not to warn every one night and day with tears" (Acts 20:20, 31). "To the weak became I as weak, that I might gain the weak: I am made all things to all men, that I might by all means save some" (1 Cor. 9:22). "I say the truth in Christ, I lie not, my conscience also bearing me witness in the Holy Ghost, that I have great heaviness and continual sorrow in my heart. For I could wish that myself were accursed from Christ for my brethren, my kinsmen according to the flesh" (Rom. 9:1-3).

COMMENT

The apostle's personal soul-winning record is impressive indeed.

- Individuals he led to Christ:
  - Those named
    - Sergius Paulus (Acts 13:7, 12)
    - Timothy (Acts 16:1; 1 Tim. 1:2)
    - Lydia (Acts 16:14, 15, 40)
    - Jason (Acts 17:5-7)
    - Dionysius (Acts 17:34)

Damaris (Acts 17:34)
Crispus (Acts 18:8)
Sosthenes (Acts 18:17; 1 Cor. 1:1)
Publius and his father—implied (Acts 28:8-10)
Gaius (1 Cor. 1:14)
Stephanas (1 Cor. 1:16; 16:15)
Onesimus (Philem. 10)

Those unnamed
The cripple at Lystra (Acts 14:8-10)
A demon-possessed girl at Philippi (Acts 16:16-18)
The Philippian jailor (Acts 16:27-34)

- Groups he led to Christ:
  - Consisting of Jews and Gentiles
    - In Antioch of Pisidia (Acts 13:43, 48)
    - In Iconium (Acts 14:1)
    - In Thessalonica (Acts 17:1-4)
    - In Berea (Acts 17:10-12)
    - In Ephesus (Acts 19:10-12, 17-18)
  - Consisting of Jews only—At Rome (Acts 28:17, 23-24)
  - Consisting of Gentiles only
    - In Athens (Acts 17:34)
    - In Corinth (Acts 18:8)
    - In Rome (Phil. 4:22)

XVI. He was a spiritual parent
  A. Serving as a father (1 Thess. 2:11; 1 Tim. 1:2)—"As ye know how we exhorted and comforted and charged every one of you, as a father doth his children" (1 Thess. 2:11).
  B. Serving as a mother (1 Thess. 2:7-8)—"But we were gentle among you, even as a nurse cherisheth her children" (1 Thess. 2:7).

XVII. He was a fearless giant. "It seemed good unto us, being assembled with one accord, to send chosen men unto you with our beloved Barnabas and Paul, men that have hazarded their lives for the name of our Lord Jesus Christ" (Acts 15:25-26).
  A. As seen by his boldness in returning to the city of Lystra, where he had only recently been stoned and left for dead (Acts 14:19-21)
  B. As seen by his testimony to the Ephesian elders—"And now, behold, I go bound in the spirit unto Jerusalem, not knowing the things that shall befall me there . . . . But none of these things move me, neither count I my life dear unto myself, so that I might finish my course with joy, and the ministry, which I have received of the Lord Jesus, to testify the gospel of the grace of God" (Acts 20:22, 24).
  C. As seen by his testimony to Philip the evangelist (Acts 21:8-14)—"Then Paul answered, What mean ye to weep and to break mine heart? for I am ready not to be bound only, but also to die at Jerusalem for the name of the Lord Jesus" (Acts 21:13).
  D. As seen by his testimony to the church at Galatia—"From henceforth let no man trouble me: for I bear in my body the marks of the Lord Jesus" (Gal. 6:17).
  E. As seen by his testimony to the church at Corinth—"If after the manner of men I have fought with beasts at Ephesus, what advantageth it me, if the dead rise not? let us eat and drink; for tomorrow we die" (1 Cor. 15:32).
  F. As seen by his rebuke of Simon Peter—"But when Peter was come to Antioch, I withstood him to the face, because he was to be blamed. For before that certain came from James, he did eat with the Gentiles: but when they were come, he withdrew and separated himself, fearing them which were of the circumcision" (Gal. 2:11-12).

XVIII. He was a tireless athlete (1 Cor. 9:24-27; Eph. 6:12; Heb. 12:1; Phil. 3:14; 1 Tim. 6:12).
  A. He ran the race (1 Cor. 9:24).
  B. He fought the fight (2 Tim. 4:7).
    1. As a wrestler (Eph. 6:12)
    2. As a boxer (1 Cor. 9:26)

XIX. He was a lover of Scripture. "All scripture is given by inspiration of God, and is profitable for doctrine, for reproof, for correction, for instruction in righteousness: That the man of God may be perfect, throughly furnished unto all good works" (2 Tim 3:16-17). "For the word of God is quick, and powerful, and sharper than any two-edged sword, piercing even to the dividing asunder of soul and spirit, and of the joints and marrow, and is a discerner of the thoughts and intents of the heart" (Heb. 4:12).

Paul loved and revered the Word of God. By actual count he quoted from or alludes to no less than 752 Old Testament Scriptures in his epistles, taking these from 30 Old Testament books. This can be shown by the following:

N.T. Epistles	*O.T. Passages*	*O.T. Books*
A. Romans	167	22
B. 1 Corinthians	110	18
C. 2 Corinthians	60	14
D. Galatians	29	10
E. Ephesians	50	13
F. Philippians	15	9
G. Colossians	10	7
H. 1 Thessalonians	15	8
I. 2 Thessalonians	18	9
J. 1 Timothy	23	11
K. 2 Timothy	10	7
L. Titus	9	6
M. Hebrews	236	21

COMMENT

These 752 Old Testament scriptures as employed by the Apostle refer to at least 27 O.T. individuals and some 30 O.T. events. Note:

- Old Testament individuals mentioned by Paul
  - Adam (1 Cor. 15:22, 45; Rom. 5:14)
  - Eve (2 Cor. 11:3)
  - Cain and Abel (Heb. 11:4)
  - Noah (Heb. 11:7)
  - Enoch (Heb. 11:5)
  - Abraham (Acts 14:26; Rom. 4:3; Heb. 11:8)
  - Sarah (Rom. 4:19; 9:9; Heb. 11:11)
  - Melchizedek (Heb. 5:6)
  - Hagar (Gal. 4:24)
  - Isaac (Rom. 9:9; Heb. 11:20)
  - Rebekah (Rom. 9:10)
  - Esau (Rom. 9:13; Heb. 11:20)
  - Jacob (Rom. 9:13; Heb. 11:21)
  - Joseph (Heb. 11:22)
  - Moses (Acts 14:39; 26:22; Heb. 11:23-29)
  - Aaron (Heb. 5:4)
  - Pharaoh (Rom. 9:17)
  - Rahab (Heb. 11:31)
  - Samuel (Acts 14:20; Heb. 11:32)
  - Barak (Heb. 11:32)
  - Gideon (Heb. 11:32)
  - Jephthah (Heb. 11:32)
  - Samson (Heb. 11:32)
  - Elijah (Rom. 11:2)
  - Saul (Acts 14:21)
  - David (Acts 14:22)
- Old Testament events mentioned by Paul
  - Creation (Acts 17:24-28)
  - Fall of man (Rom. 8:20-22)
  - Offering of Cain and Abel (Heb. 11:4)
  - Translation of Enoch (Heb. 11:5)
  - The universal flood (Heb. 11:7)
  - Departure of Abraham from Ur to Canaan (Heb. 11:8-10)
  - Meeting of Abraham and Melchizedek (Heb. 7:1-4)
  - Circumcision of Abraham (Rom. 4:9-12)
  - Supernatural birth of Isaac (Rom. 4:17-21)
  - Selection of Isaac over Ishmael (Rom. 9:9-11)
  - Offering up of Isaac (Heb. 11:17-19)
  - Conflict between Hagar and Sarah (Gal. 4:22-31)
  - Selection of Jacob over Esau (Rom. 9:10-13)
  - The selling of the birthright by Esau (Heb. 12:16, 17)
  - The faith of Moses' parents (Heb. 11:23)
  - Moses' decision for God (Heb. 11:24-26)
  - Contest between Moses and the Egyptian magicians (2 Tim. 3:8)
  - God's judgment upon Egypt (Rom. 9:17-18)
  - The first Passover (Heb. 11:26-28)
  - The Exodus (Acts 14:17-18; 1 Cor. 10:1-5, 7-10)
  - The Red Sea crossing (Heb. 11:29)
  - God's mercy to Israel at Matt. Sinai (Rom. 9:15)
  - Moses' descent from Mount Sinai (2 Cor. 3:7-14)
  - Details of the Tabernacle (Heb. 9:1-5)

Sanctifying the Law and tabernacle by Moses (Heb. 9:19-21)
The conquest of Canaan (Acts 14:19)
Fall of Jericho's walls (Heb. 11:30)
The judges of Israel (Acts 14:20)
The United Kingdom of Israel (Acts 14:21-23)
Elijah and God at Horeb (Rom. 11:2-4)

- Names given to the Old Testament Scriptures—Note also the various names and titles Paul gives for the Old Testament scriptures:
  The word of God (Acts 13:46; Rom. 9:6; 10:17; 2 Cor. 2:17; 4:2; 1 Thess. 2:13; Heb. 4:12; 6:5)
  The counsel of God (Acts 20:27)
  The oracles of God (Rom. 3:2; Heb. 5:12)
  The wisdom of God (1 Cor. 2:7)
  The mysteries of God (1 Cor. 4:1)
  The Gospel of God (1 Thess. 2:2, 9)
  The word of his grace (Acts 14:3; 20:32)
  The word of salvation (Acts 13:26)
  The word of life (Phil. 2:16)
  The word of Christ (Col. 3:16)
  The word of truth (2 Tim. 2:15)
  The word of righteousness (Heb. 5:13)
  The faithful word (Titus 1:9)
  The Gospel of the grace of God (Acts 20:24)
  The Gospel of Christ (1 Cor. 9:12, 18; 2 Cor. 9:13)
  The glorious Gospel of the blessed God (1 Tim. 1:11)
  The law of the fathers (Acts 22:3)
  The scriptures (Rom. 4:3; 9:17; 10:11; 1 Cor. 15:3)
  The holy scriptures (Rom. 1:2; 2 Tim. 3:15)
  The sword of the Spirit (Eph. 6:17)
  The doctrine (1 Tim. 4:13, 16; 5:17; 6:1, 3)
  The parchments (2 Tim. 4:13)

XX. He was an author of Scripture. If the Apostle wrote the book of Hebrews, he authored fourteen of the twenty-seven New Testament epistles, some 52 percent of the total. The following offers a basic outline overview of these New Testament books.

A. Romans
1. The courthouse of law: God's Wrath (Condemnation and Justification)—Romans 1–5
   a. The court reporter (1:1-17)—"I am debtor both to the Greeks, and to the Barbarians; both to the wise, and to the unwise. . . . For I am not ashamed of the gospel of Christ: for it is the power of God unto salvation to every one that believeth; to the Jew first, and also to the Greek" (Rom. 1:14, 16).
   b. The court record (1:18–4:25)—"For the wrath of God is revealed from heaven against all ungodliness and unrighteousness of men, who hold the truth in unrighteousness . . . . As it is written, There is none righteous, no, not one: There is none that understandeth, there is none that seeketh after God . . . . But now the righteousness of God without the law is manifested, being witnessed by the law and the prophets . . . . Being justified freely by his grace through the redemption that is in Christ Jesus . . . . Who was delivered for our offences, and was raised again for our justification" (Rom. 1:18; 3:10-11, 21, 24; 4:25).
   c. The court review (5:1-21)—"Therefore being justified by faith, we have peace with God through our Lord Jesus Christ. . . . For as by one man's disobedience many were made sinners, so by the obedience of one shall many be made righteous" (Rom. 5:1, 19).
2. The power plant of grace: God's way (Sanctification and Preservation)—Romans 6–8
   a. The plan: first floor of sanctification (Rom. 6)—"Know ye not, that so many of us as were

baptized into Jesus Christ were baptized into his death? Therefore we are buried with him by baptism into death: that like as Christ was raised up from the dead by the glory of the Father, even so we also should walk in newness of life. For if we have been planted together in the likeness of his death, we shall be also in the likeness of his resurrection: Knowing this, that our old man is crucified with him, that the body of sin might be destroyed, that henceforth we should not serve sin" (Rom. 6:3-6).

   b. The pain: second floor of frustration (Rom. 7)—"I find then a law, that, when I would do good, evil is present with me. For I delight in the law of God after the inward man: But I see another law in my members, warring against the law of my mind, and bringing me into captivity to the law of sin which is in my members. O wretched man that I am! who shall deliver me from the body of this death?" (Rom. 7:21-24).
   c. The prize: third floor of preservation (Rom. 8)—"And we know that all things work together for good to them that love God, to them who are the called according to his purpose. For whom he did foreknow, he also did predestinate to be conformed to the image of his Son, that he might be the firstborn among many brethren. Moreover whom he did predestinate, them he also called: and whom he called, them he also justified: and whom he justified, them he also glorified" (Rom. 8:28-30).
3. The synagogue of Israel: God's wisdom (Explanation and Vindication)—Romans 9–11
   a. The sovereignty of God and Israel's selection in the past (Rom. 9)—"Who are Israelites; to whom pertaineth the adoption, and the glory, and the c ovenants, and the giving of the law, and the service of God, and the promises; whose are the fathers, and of whom as concerning the flesh Christ came, who is over all, God blessed for ever. Amen." (Rom. 9:4-5).
   b. The righteousness of God and Israel's rejection at the present (Rom. 10)—"For they being ignorant of God's righteousness, and going about to establish their own righteousness, have not submitted themselves unto the righteousness of God" (Rom. 10:3).
   c. The wisdom of God and Israel's restoration in the future (Rom. 11)—"And so all Israel shall be saved: as it is written, There shall come out of Sion the Deliverer, and shall turn away ungodliness from Jacob . . . . O the depth of the riches both of the wisdom and knowledge of God! how unsearchable are his judgments, and his ways past finding out!" (Rom. 11:26, 33).
4. The temple of God: God's will (Transformation and Exhortation)—Romans 12–16
   a. Personal responsibilities for all the redeemed (12:1–15:13)—"I beseech you therefore, brethren, by the mercies of God, that ye present your bodies a living sacrifice, holy, acceptable unto God, which is your reasonable service. And be not conformed to this world: but be ye transformed by the renewing of your mind, that ye may prove what is that good, and acceptable, and perfect, will of God" (Rom. 12:1-2).

b. Personal remarks to the Roman redeemed (15:14–16:27)—"Now I beseech you, brethren, for the Lord Jesus Christ's sake, and for the love of the Spirit, that ye strive together with me in your prayers to God for me" (Rom. 15:30).

B. First Corinthians

1. The seven corruptions committed by the Corinthian church (1 Cor. 1–6)
   a. First corruption: They were following human leaders (1:10-17)—"Now this I say, that every one of you saith, I am of Paul; and I of Apollos; and I of Cephas; and I of Christ. Is Christ divided? was Paul crucified for you? or were ye baptized in the name of Paul?" (1 Cor. 1:12-13).
   b. Second corruption: They were favoring earthly wisdom (1:18–2:13)—"For ye see your calling, brethren, how that not many wise men after the flesh, not many mighty, not many noble, are called: But God hath chosen the foolish things of the world to confound the wise; and God hath chosen the weak things of the world to confound the things which are mighty; and base things of the world, and things which are despised, hath God chosen, yea, and things which are not, to bring to nought things that are: That no flesh should glory in his presence" (1 Cor. 1:26-29).
   c. Third corruption: They were floundering in the flesh (2:14–3:7)—"And I, brethren, could not speak unto you as unto spiritual, but as unto carnal, even as unto babes in Christ. I have fed you with milk, and not with meat: for hitherto ye were not able to bear it, neither yet now are ye able. For ye are yet carnal: for whereas there is among you envying, and strife, and divisions, are ye not carnal, and walk as men? For while one saith, I am of Paul; and another, I am of Apollos; are ye not carnal?" (1 Cor. 3:1-4).
   d. Fourth corruption: They were forgetting future judgment (3:8-23)—"Every man's work shall be made manifest: for the day shall declare it, because it shall be revealed by fire; and the fire shall try every man's work of what sort it is" (1 Cor. 3:13).
   e. Fifth corruption: They were flattering themselves (4:1-21)—"For who maketh thee to differ from another? and what hast thou that thou didst not receive? now if thou didst receive it, why dost thou glory, as if thou hadst not received it?" (1 Cor. 4:7).
   f. Sixth corruption: They were failing to discipline (5:1-13)—"It is reported commonly that there is fornication among you, and such fornication as is not so much as named among the Gentiles, that one should have his father's wife. And ye are puffed up, and have not rather mourned, that he that hath done this deed might be taken away from among you" (1 Cor. 5:1-2).
   g. Seventh corruption: They were fragmenting the body of Christ (6:1-20)—"Know ye not that your bodies are the members of Christ? . . . But he that is joined unto the Lord is one spirit" (1 Cor.6:16-17).
2. The six questions submitted by the Corinthian church (1 Cor. 7–16)
   a. First question: What about marriage? (1 Cor. 7) "Let the husband render unto the wife due benevolence: and likewise also the wife unto the husband" (1 Cor. 7:3).

b. Second question: What about Christian liberty? (1 Cor. 8–10) "But take heed lest by any means this liberty of yours become a stumbling block to them that are weak. . . . Wherefore, if meat make my brother to offend, I will eat no flesh while the world standeth, lest I make my brother to offend. . . . For though I be free from all men, yet have I made myself servant unto all, that I might gain the more. And unto the Jews I became as a Jew, that I might gain the Jews; to them that are under the law, as under the law, that I might gain them that are under the law; to them that are without law, as without law, (being not without law to God, but under the law to Christ,) that I might gain them that are without law. To the weak became I as weak, that I might gain the weak: I am made all things to all men, that I might by all means save some. . . . Whether therefore ye eat, or drink, or whatsoever ye do, do all to the glory of God. Give none offence, neither to the Jews, nor to the Gentiles, nor to the church of God" (1 Cor. 8:9, 13; 9:19-22; 10:31-32).

c. Third question: What about church conduct and communion? (1 Cor. 11) "For as often as ye eat this bread, and drink this cup, ye do shew the Lord's death till he come. Wherefore whosoever shall eat this bread, and drink this cup of the Lord, unworthily, shall be guilty of the body and blood of the Lord. But let a man examine himself, and so let him eat of that bread, and drink of that cup. For he that eateth and drinketh unworthily, eateth and drinketh damnation to himself, not discerning the Lord's body" (1 Cor. 11:26-29).

d. Fourth question: What about spiritual gifts? (1 Cor. 12–14) "Now concerning spiritual gifts, brethren, I would not have you ignorant. . . . For as the body is one, and hath many members, and all the members of that one body, being many, are one body: so also is Christ. For by one Spirit are we all baptized into one body, whether we be Jews or Gentiles, whether we be bond or free; and have been all made to drink into one Spirit. . . . Though I speak with the tongues of men and of angels, and have not charity, I am become as sounding brass, or a tinkling cymbal. . . . Let all things be done decently and in order" (1 Cor. 12:1, 12-13; 13:1; 14:40).

e. Fifth question: What about the resurrection? (1 Cor. 15) "Behold, I shew you a mystery; We shall not all sleep, but we shall all be changed, in a moment, in the twinkling of an eye, at the last trump: for the trumpet shall sound, and the dead shall be raised incorruptible, and we shall be changed. For this corruptible must put on incorruption, and this mortal must put on immortality" (1 Cor. 15:51-53).

f. Sixth question: What about Christian giving? (1 Cor. 16) "Upon the first day of the week let every one of you lay by him in store, as God hath prospered him, that there be no gatherings when I come" (1 Cor. 16:2).

C. Second Corinthians

1. Consolation (2 Cor. 1:1-7)—Here Paul discusses the person (God), purpose, and pattern concerning pain in the believer's life. "Blessed be God, even the Father of our Lord Jesus Christ, the Father of mercies,

and the God of all comfort; who comforteth us in all our tribulation, that we may be able to comfort them which are in any trouble, by the comfort wherewith we ourselves are comforted of God. For as the sufferings of Christ abound in us, so our consolation also aboundeth by Christ" (2 Cor. 1:3-5).

2. Explanation (1:8–2:13)—"For we would not, brethren, have you ignorant of our trouble which came to us in Asia, that we were pressed out of measure, above strength, insomuch that we despaired even of life" (2 Cor. 1:8).
3. Characterization (2:14–6:18)—Paul brings the church of Corinth up to date concerning his activities. In these chapters he lists fifteen desired characteristics of a successful Gospel ministry. "For we are not as many, which corrupt the word of God: but as of sincerity, but as of God, in the sight of God speak we in Christ. . . . Therefore seeing we have this ministry, as we have received mercy, we faint not; But have renounced the hidden things of dishonesty, not walking in craftiness, nor handling the word of God deceitfully; but by manifestation of the truth commending ourselves to every man's conscience in the sight of God. . . . Giving no offence in any thing, that the ministry be not blamed" (2 Cor. 2:17; 4:1-2; 6:3).
4. Gratification (7:1-16)—Paul expressed profound thanks to God for two things.
   a. Seeing Titus
   b. Hearing Titus—"Nevertheless God, that comforteth those that are cast down, comforted us by the coming of Titus; and not by his coming only, but by the consolation wherewith he was comforted in you, when he told us your earnest desire, your mourning, your fervent mind toward me; so that I rejoiced the more" (2 Cor. 7:6-7).
5. Solicitation (8:1–9:15)—This section is set aside in describing the godliness of giving. The apostle discusses:
   a. The example of giving—"Moreover, brethren, we do you to wit of the grace of God bestowed on the churches of Macedonia; how that in a great trial of affliction the abundance of their joy and their deep poverty abounded unto the riches of their liberality. . . . For ye know the grace of our Lord Jesus Christ, that, though he was rich, yet for your sakes he became poor, that ye through his poverty might be rich. . . . Thanks be unto God for his unspeakable gift" (2 Cor. 8:1-2, 9; 9:15).
   b. The characteristics of giving—"Every man according as he purposeth in his heart, so let him give; not grudgingly, or of necessity: for God loveth a cheerful giver" (2 Cor. 9:7).
   c. The results of giving—"But this I say, He which soweth sparingly shall reap also sparingly; and he which soweth bountifully shall reap also bountifully" (2 Cor. 9:6).
6. Vindication (10–13)—Paul writes these chapters to defend his name and ministry. Both were being undermined by his bitter enemies, the Judaizers. "For I suppose I was not a whit behind the very chiefest apostles. . . . Truly the signs of an apostle were wrought among you in all patience, in signs, and wonders, and mighty deeds" (2 Cor. 11:5; 12:12).

D. Galatians
   1. Justification by faith: The foundation (1:1-5)—"Paul, an apostle, (not of men, neither by man, but by

Jesus Christ, and God the Father, who raised him from the dead)" (Gal. 1:1).

2. Justification by faith: The aberration (1:6-9)—"I marvel that ye are so soon removed from him that called you into the grace of Christ unto another gospel" (Gal. 1:6).
3. Justification by faith: A revelation (1:10–2:10)—"But I certify you, brethren, that the gospel which was preached of me is not after man. For I neither received it of man, neither was I taught it, but by the revelation of Jesus Christ" (Gal. 1:11-12).
4. Justification by faith: A confrontation (2:11-14)—"But when Peter was come to Antioch, I withstood him to the face, because he was to be blamed. For before that certain came from James, he did eat with the Gentiles: but when they were come, he withdrew and separated himself, fearing them which were of the circumcision" (Gal. 2:11-12).
5. Justification by faith: The clarification (2:15-19)—"Knowing that a man is not justified by the works of the law, but by the faith of Jesus Christ, even we have believed in Jesus Christ, that we might be justified by the faith of Christ, and not by the works of the law: for by the works of the law shall no flesh be justified" (Gal. 2:16).
6. Justification by faith: The transformation (2:20-21)—"I am crucified with Christ: nevertheless I live; yet not I, but Christ liveth in me: and the life which I now live in the flesh I live by the faith of the Son of God, who loved me, and gave himself for me" (Gal. 2:20).
7. Justification by faith: An argumentation (3:1–4:20)—In these chapters Paul offers a series of arguments that prove the sufficiency of justification by faith alone. "Even as Abraham believed God, and it was accounted to him for righteousness. . . . Christ hath redeemed us from the curse of the law, being made a curse for us: for it is written, Cursed is every one that hangeth on a tree" (Gal. 3:6, 13).
8. Justification by faith: An allegorization (4:21-31)—Here Paul uses two Old Testament women, Hagar and Sarah, to allegorize the Law of Moses and the grace of God. "So then, brethren, we are not children of the bondwoman, but of the free" (Gal. 4:31).
9. Justification by faith: The application (5:1–6:18)—"Stand fast therefore in the liberty wherewith Christ hath made us free, and be not entangled again with the yoke of bondage. . . . This I say then, Walk in the Spirit, and ye shall not fulfil the lust of the flesh" (Gal. 5:1, 16).

E. Ephesians

1. The church is likened to a body (Eph. 1). "Which is his body, the fulness of him that filleth all in all" (Eph. 1:23).
   a. The creation of this body (1:1-14)
   b. The consecration of this body (1:15-23)
2. The church is likened to a temple (Eph. 2). "In whom all the building fitly framed together groweth unto an holy temple in the Lord" (Eph. 2:21).
3. The church is likened to a mystery (Eph. 3). "Whereby, when ye read, ye may understand my knowledge in the mystery of Christ" (Eph. 3:4).
4. The church is likened to a new man (Eph. 4). "And that ye put on the new man, which after God is created in righteousness and true holiness" (Eph. 4:24).
5. The church is likened to a bride (Eph. 5). "For the husband is the head of the wife, even as Christ is the head of the church: and he is the saviour of the body" (Eph. 5:23).

6. The church is likened to a soldier (Eph. 6). "Put on the whole armour of God, that ye may be able to stand against the wiles of the devil" (Eph. 6:11).
   a. Boot camp training (6:1-9)
   b. Front line fighting (6:10-24)

F. Philippians

1. Christ is life's purpose (Phil. 1). "For to me to live is Christ, and to die is gain" (Phil. 1:21).
   a. Knowing this, Paul could rest in God's security (1:1-12).
   b. Knowing this, Paul could rejoice in great suffering (1:13-20).
   c. Knowing this, Paul could remain in glad service (1:21-30).
2. Christ is life's pattern (Phil. 2). "Let this mind be in you, which was also in Christ Jesus" (Phil 2:5).
   a. The exhortation to this mind of Christ (2:1-4)—"Let nothing be done through strife or vainglory; but in lowliness of mind let each esteem other better than themselves" (Phil. 2:3).
   b. The examples of this mind of Christ (2:5-30)
3. Christ is life's prize (Phil. 3). "I press toward the mark for the prize of the high calling of God in Christ Jesus" (Phil. 3:14).
   a. The corrupters of this prize (3:1-3, 18-19)—"Beware of dogs, beware of evil workers, beware of the concision. . . . Whose end is destruction, whose God is their belly, and whose glory is in their shame, who mind earthly things" (Phil. 3:2, 19).
   b. The cost of this prize (3:4-6)—"Though I might also have confidence in the flesh. If any other man thinketh that he hath whereof he might trust in the flesh, I more" (Phil. 3:4).
   c. The crown of this prize (3:7-17, 20-21)—"But what things were gain to me, those I counted loss for Christ. Yea doubtless, and I count all things but loss for the excellency of the knowledge of Christ Jesus my Lord: for whom I have suffered the loss of all things, and do count them but dung, that I may win Christ . . . . That I may know him, and the power of his resurrection, and the fellowship of his sufferings, being made conformable unto his death . . . . Who shall change our vile body, that it may be fashioned like unto his glorious body, according to the working whereby he is able even to subdue all things unto himself" (Phil. 3:7-8, 10, 21).
4. Christ is life's power (Phil. 4). "I can do all things through Christ which strengtheneth me" (Phil. 4:13).

G. Colossians

1. The deity and preeminence of the Saviour (Col. 1)—"And he is before all things, and by him all things consist. And he is the head of the body, the church: who is the beginning, the firstborn from the dead; that in all things he might have the preeminence. For it pleased the Father that in him should all fulness dwell" (Col. 1:17-19).
2. The danger and perversion of the serpent (Col. 2)—"Beware lest any man spoil you through philosophy and vain deceit, after the tradition of men, after the rudiments of the world, and not after Christ" (Col. 2:8).
3. The duties and performance of the saints (Col. 3–4)—"If ye then be risen with Christ, seek those things which are above, where Christ sitteth on the right hand of God. Set your affection on things above, not on things on the earth. . . . Let the word of Christ dwell in you richly in all wisdom; teaching and admonishing one another in psalms and

hymns and spiritual songs, singing with grace in your hearts to the Lord. And whatsoever ye do in word or deed, do all in the name of the Lord Jesus, giving thanks to God and the Father by him" (Col. 3:1-2, 16-17).

H. First Thessalonians
   1. The reputation of the church (1 Thess. 1)—"For from you sounded out the word of the Lord not only in Macedonia and Achaia, but also in every place your faith to God-ward is spread abroad; so that we need not to speak any thing" (1 Thess. 1:8).
   2. The review of the church (1 Thess. 2–3)—In these chapters Paul review those circumstances involved in the founding of the Thessalonian church.
   3. The removal of the church (1 Thess. 4)—Here the apostle explains the nature of the rapture.
      a. The challenges in light of this removal (4:1-12)—"For this is the will of God, even your sanctification, that ye should abstain from fornication" (4:3).
      b. The chronology of this removal (4:13-18)—"For the Lord himself shall descend from heaven with a shout, with the voice of the archangel, and with the trump of God: and the dead in Christ shall rise first: Then we which are alive and remain shall be caught up together with them in the clouds to meet the Lord in the air: and so shall we ever be with the Lord" (1 Thess. 4:16-17).
   4. The Responsibility of the church (1 Thess. 5)
      a. The God of purpose: what he wills for us to do (5:1-22)—"Therefore let us not sleep, as do others; but let us watch and be sober" (1 Thess. 5:6).
      b. The God of peace: what he will do for us (5:23-28)—"And the very God of peace sanctify you wholly; and I pray God your whole spirit and soul and body be preserved blameless unto the coming of our Lord Jesus Christ" (1 Thess. 5:23).

I. Second Thessalonians
   1. Explanation—the way of the Lord: A pastoral encouragement (2 Thess. 1)—In this chapter Paul explains (in part) just why God often allows believers to suffer the persecution of men.
      a. God and the persecuted (1:4-6)
      b. God and the persecutors (1:7-9)—"In flaming fire taking vengeance on them that know not God, and that obey not the gospel of our Lord Jesus Christ" (2 Thess. 1:8).
   2. Tribulation—the wrath of the Lord: A prophetical enlightenment (2 Thess. 2)
      a. Facts concerning the day of the Lord (2:1-12)—"Let no man deceive you by any means: for that day shall not come, except there come a falling away first, and that man of sin be revealed, the son of perdition" (2 Thess. 2:3).
      b. Facts concerning the destined of the Lord (2:13-17)—"But we are bound to give thanks alway to God for you, brethren beloved of the Lord, because God hath from the beginning chosen you to salvation through sanctification of the Spirit and belief of the truth" (2 Thess. 2:13).
   3. Consecration—the will of the Lord: A practical exhortation (2 Thess. 3)—"But the Lord is faithful, who shall stablish you, and keep you from evil" (2 Thess. 3:3).

J. First Timothy—This epistle is, in essence, a personal letter to the family of God. "These things write I unto thee, hoping to come unto thee shortly: But if I tarry long, that thou mayest know how thou oughtest to behave thyself in the house of God, which is the church of the living God, the pillar and ground of the truth" (1 Tim. 3:14-15).

A topical summary reveals:

1. What Paul says about himself and the family of God—"And I thank Christ Jesus our Lord, who hath enabled me, for that he counted me faithful, putting me into the ministry; who was before a blasphemer, and a persecutor, and injurious: but I obtained mercy, because I did it ignorantly in unbelief. . . . Whereunto I am ordained a preacher, and an apostle, (I speak the truth in Christ, and lie not;) a teacher of the Gentiles in faith and verity" (1 Tim. 1:12-13; 2:7).
2. What Paul says about Timothy and the family of God—"Let no man despise thy youth; but be thou an example of the believers, in word, in conversation, in charity, in spirit, in faith, in purity. Till I come, give attendance to reading, to exhortation, to doctrine. Neglect not the gift that is in thee, which was given thee by prophecy, with the laying on of the hands of the presbytery. Meditate upon these things; give thyself wholly to them; that thy profiting may appear to all. Take heed unto thyself, and unto the doctrine; continue in them: for in doing this thou shalt both save thyself, and them that hear thee. . . . O Timothy, keep that which is committed to thy trust, avoiding profane and vain babblings, and oppositions of science falsely so called" (1 Tim. 4:12-16; 6:20).
3. What Paul says about church leaders and the family of God—"This is a true saying, If a man desire the office of a bishop, he desireth a good work. . . . Likewise must the deacons be grave, not doubletongued, not given to much wine, not greedy of filthy lucre" (1 Tim. 3:1, 8).
4. What Paul says about false teachers and the family of God—"Now the Spirit speaketh expressly, that in the latter times some shall depart from the faith, giving heed to seducing spirits, and doctrines of devils; speaking lies in hypocrisy; having their conscience seared with a hot iron" (1 Tim. 4:1-2).
5. What Paul says about the Saviour and the family of God—"For there is one God, and one mediator between God and men, the man Christ Jesus; who gave himself a ransom for all, to be testified in due time. . . . And without controversy great is the mystery of godliness: God was manifest in the flesh, justified in the Spirit, seen of angels, preached unto the Gentiles, believed on in the world, received up into glory" (1 Tim. 2:5-6: 3:16).

K. Second Timothy

1. Paul, the preacher (2 Tim. 1)—"Whereunto I am appointed a preacher, and an apostle, and a teacher of the Gentiles" (2 Tim. 1:11).
2. Paul, the pattern (2 Tim. 2)—"And the things that thou hast heard of me among many witnesses, the same commit thou to faithful men, who shall be able to teach others also" (2 Tim. 2:2).
3. Paul, the prophet (2 Tim. 3)—"This know also, that in the last days perilous times shall come" (2 Tim 3:1).
4. Paul, the pilgrim (2 Tim. 4)—"For I am now ready to be offered, and the time of my departure is at hand. I have fought a good fight, I have finished my course, I have kept the faith" (2 Tim. 4:6-7).

L. Titus

1. Titus and the apostle (Titus 1:1-4)—"To Titus, mine own son after the

common faith: Grace, mercy, and peace, from God the Father and the Lord Jesus Christ our Saviour" (Titus. 1:4).

2. Titus and the elders (Titus 1:5-16)—"For this cause left I thee in Crete, that thou shouldest set in order the things that are wanting, and ordain elders in every city, as I had appointed thee" (Titus 1:5).
3. Titus and the church (Titus 2:1–3:11)—"For the grace of God that bringeth salvation hath appeared to all men, teaching us that, denying ungodliness and worldly lusts, we should live soberly, righteously, and godly, in this present world; looking for that blessed hope, and the glorious appearing of the great God and our Saviour Jesus Christ" (Titus. 2:11-13).
4. Titus and the future (Titus 3:12-15)

M. Philemon
1. The appreciation and praise for Philemon (Philem. 1-7)
2. The appeal and plea for Onesimus (Philem. 8-17)—"I beseech thee for my son Onesimus, whom I have begotten in my bonds" (Philem. 10).
3. The assurance and pledge of Paul (Philem. 19-25)—"I Paul have written it with mine own hand, I will repay it: albeit I do not say to thee how thou owest unto me even thine own self besides" (Philem. 19).

N. Hebrews
1. Christ, the superior person (Heb. 1:1–5:10)
   a. He is better than the prophets (1:1-3).
   b. He is better than the angels (1:4–2:18).
   c. He is better than Moses (3:1–4:7, 9-16).
   d. He is better than Joshua (4:8-16).
   e. He is better than Aaron (5:1-10).
2. Perfection, the superior purpose (Heb. 5:11–6:20)
   a. The foes of this spiritual perfection (5:11–6:8)—"Of whom we have many things to say, and hard to be uttered, seeing ye are dull of hearing. For when for the time ye ought to be teachers, ye have need that one teach you again which be the first principles of the oracles of God; and are become such as have need of milk, and not of strong meat. For every one that useth milk is unskilful in the word of righteousness: for he is a babe" (Heb. 5:11-13).
   b. The friends of this spiritual perfection (6:9-20)—"That by two immutable things, in which it was impossible for God to lie, we might have a strong consolation, who have fled for refuge to lay hold upon the hope set before us: Which hope we have as an anchor of the soul, both sure and stedfast, and which entereth into that within the veil; Whither the forerunner is for us entered, even Jesus, made an high priest for ever after the order of Melchisedec" (Heb. 6:18-20).
3. Melchizedek, the superior priesthood (Heb. 7–10)
   a. It offers a better source: From Aaron to Melchizedek (Heb. 7)
   b. It offers a better script: From the old covenant to the new covenant (Heb. 8)
   c. It offers a better sanctuary: From the earthly to the heavenly (Heb. 9)
   d. It offers a better sacrifice: From animal lambs to God's Lamb (Heb. 10)
4. Faith, the superior principle (Heb. 11–13)
   a. The people of faith (Heb. 11)—"Now faith is the substance of things hoped for, the evidence of things not seen. For by it the elders obtained a good report" (Heb. 11:1-2).

b. The pattern of faith (Heb. 12)—"Wherefore seeing we also are compassed about with so great a cloud of witnesses, let us lay aside every weight, and the sin which doth so easily beset us, and let us run with patience the race that is set before us, looking unto Jesus the author and finisher of our faith; who for the joy that was set before him endured the cross, despising the shame, and is set down at the right hand of the throne of God" (Heb. 12:1-2).

c. The performance of faith (Heb. 13)—"Let brotherly love continue. . . . Let your conversation be without covetousness; and be content with such things as ye have: for he hath said, I will never leave thee, nor forsake thee" (Heb. 13:1, 5).

XXI. He was a separated servant. "Paul, a servant of Jesus Christ, called to be an apostle, separated unto the gospel of God" (Rom. 1:1). This divine separation of Paul by God is seen on three all-important occasions in his life.

A. At his birth—"But when it pleased God, who separated me from my mother's womb, and called me by his grace" (Gal. 1:15).

B. At his conversion—"But the Lord said unto him, Go thy way: for he is a chosen vessel unto me, to bear my name before the Gentiles, and kings, and the children of Israel" (Acts 9:15).

C. At his call to the mission field—"As they ministered to the Lord, and fasted, the Holy Ghost said, Separate me Barnabas and Saul for the work whereunto I have called them" (Acts 13:2).

COMMENT

It can be said the entire trinity was involved in this threefold separation:

- At Paul's birth in Tarsus it was the Father who set Paul apart.
- At Paul's conversion near Damascus it was the Son who set Paul apart.
- At Paul's missionary calling in Antioch it was the Holy Spirit who set Paul apart.

XXII. He was a suffering servant. Some five years after the ascension of Christ, the Lord spoke to a believer in the city of Damascus named Ananias, instructing him to call upon a new convert, a certain Saul of Tarsus. At first Ananias was extremely reluctant to do this, for Saul's previous attacks upon Christians were well-known. But God reassured his timid follower, saying:

"Go thy way: for he is a chosen vessel unto me, to bear my name before the Gentiles, and kings, and the children of Israel: For I will shew him how great things he must suffer for my name's sake" (Acts 9:15-16). In a nutshell, this last statement would perfectly summarize Saul's future life of service for Christ. He would indeed suffer great things for the Lord's name. In fact, years later in a Roman prison, Paul gave testimony to the accuracy of this prophecy: "But what things were gain to me, those I counted loss for Christ. Yea doubtless, and I count all things but loss for the excellency of the knowledge of Christ Jesus my Lord: for whom I have suffered the loss of all things, and do count them but dung, that I may win Christ" (Phil. 3:7-8). Many Bible students feel Paul was the greatest Christian of all time. His amazing life can be aptly summarized by four words: persecution, pain, performance, and praise. It can be concluded as one studies his life that the first two words provided the root that gave birth to the second two words, the fruit. No realm of suffering was foreign to him. Friend and foe alike on occasion added to his sorrow. He knew the travail of physical, mental, and satanic onslaughts.

A. An examination of Paul's sufferings (the record of his travail)
   1. He was plotted against on at least six occasions.
      a. In Damascus, after his salvation—"And after that many days were fulfilled, the Jews took counsel to kill him: But their laying await was known of Saul. And they watched the gates day and night to kill him. Then the disciples took him by night, and let him down by the wall in a basket" (Acts 9:23-25).
      b. In Jerusalem, during his first visit as a believer—"And he spake boldly in the name of the Lord Jesus, and disputed against the Grecians: but they went about to slay him" (Acts 9:29).
      c. In Greece, during his final missionary trip—"And there abode three months. And when the Jews laid wait for him, as he was about to sail into Syria, he purposed to return through Macedonia" (Acts 20:3).
      d. In Jerusalem, while speaking to the Jewish Sanhedrin—"And when there arose a great dissension, the chief captain, fearing lest Paul should have been pulled in pieces of them, commanded the soldiers to go down, and to take him by force from among them, and to bring him into the castle" (Acts 23:10).
      e. In Jerusalem, after his arrest—"And when it was day, certain of the Jews banded together, and bound themselves under a curse, saying that they would neither eat nor drink till they had killed Paul. And they were more than forty which had made this conspiracy. And they came to the chief priests and elders, and said, We have bound ourselves under a great curse, that we will eat nothing until we have slain Paul" (Acts 23:12-14).
      f. In Caesarea, during his imprisonment—"Then the high priest and the chief of the Jews informed him against Paul, and besought him, and desired favour against him, that he would send for him to Jerusalem, laying wait in the way to kill him" (Acts 25:2-3).
   2. He was at first mistrusted by believers. His former life had been so terrible that many leaders in the early church simply could not believe he was now one of them. "And when Saul was come to Jerusalem, he assayed to join himself to the disciples: but they were all afraid of him, and believed not that he was a disciple" (Acts 9:26).
   3. He was disliked by some disciples. This must have been particularly grievous to him, for he was suffering for Christ in a Roman prison at this time. "And many of the brethren in the Lord, waxing confident by my bonds, are much more bold to speak the word without fear. Some indeed preach Christ even of envy and strife; and some also of good will: The one preach Christ of contention, not sincerely, supposing to add affliction to my bonds" (Phil. 1:14-16).
   4. His work for God was constantly opposed by his own countrymen. This opposition occurred in at least five cities.
      a. In Antioch—"But when the Jews saw the multitudes, they were filled with envy, and spake against those things which were spoken by Paul, contradicting and blaspheming. . . . But the Jews stirred up the devout and honourable women, and the chief men of the city, and raised persecution against Paul and

Barnabas, and expelled them out of their coasts" (Acts 13:45, 50).

b. In Iconium—"But the unbelieving Jews stirred up the Gentiles, and made their minds evil affected against the brethren" (Acts 14:2).

c. In Thessalonica—"But the Jews which believed not, moved with envy, took unto them certain lewd fellows of the baser sort, and gathered a company, and set all the city on an uproar, and assaulted the house of Jason, and sought to bring them out to the people" (Acts 17:5).

d. In Berea—"But when the Jews of Thessalonica had knowledge that the word of God was preached of Paul at Berea, they came thither also, and stirred up the people" (Acts 17:13).

e. In Corinth—"And when they opposed themselves, and blasphemed, he shook his raiment, and said unto them, Your blood be upon your own heads; I am clean: from henceforth I will go unto the Gentiles" (Acts 18:6).

5. He was on one occasion stoned at Lystra and left for dead (Acts 14:19).
6. He suffered from repeated beatings. On five occasions he received 39 lashes (2 Cor. 11:24). Three times he was beaten with rods (2 Cor. 11:25). Small wonder that Paul could write: "I bear in my body the marks of the Lord Jesus" (Gal. 6:17).
7. He experienced four shipwrecks. The fourth happened after he had endured one of the most terrifying ocean storms in recorded ancient history (2 Cor. 11:25; Acts 27).
8. He was subjected to intense satanic pressure. He was confronted by a demonic sorcerer in Cyprus, and a witch at Philippi (Acts 13:8; 16:16-18). Satan prevented him from making a planned trip to the church in Thessalonica (1 Thess. 2:18). The most vicious, hellish onslaught, however, was a grievous thorn in the flesh, placed there by Satan himself (2 Cor. 12:7).
9. He was ridiculed. At Athens some philosophers concluded him to be a babbler and idiot (Acts 17:18, 32), while at Caesarea the Roman governor Festus interrupted his testimony, shouting out, "Paul, thou art beside thyself; much learning doth make thee mad" (Acts 26:24).
10. He was falsely accused on numerous occasions. At Corinth the Jewish leaders drug him to court, charging him with blasphemy (Acts 18:13). In Jerusalem later, James the half brother of Christ sadly informs Paul of the things the Jews of that city were saying about the apostle. "And they are informed of thee, that thou teachest all the Jews which are among the Gentiles to forsake Moses, saying that they ought not to circumcise their children, neither to walk after the customs" (Acts 21:21). When he was a political prisoner in Caesarea, Paul was charged by the high priest (who attended the trial) as follows: "For we have found this man a pestilent fellow, and a mover of sedition among all the Jews throughout the world, and a ringleader of the sect of the Nazarenes: Who also hath gone about to profane the temple: whom we took, and would have judged according to our law" (Acts 24:5-6).
11. He probably possessed a frail and unattractive body. There is little doubt that his eyes troubled him. Several passages in his Epistle to the Galatians bring this out. Note his words: "Ye know how through infirmity of the flesh I preached the gospel unto you at the first. And my temptation

which was in my flesh ye despised not, nor rejected; but received me as an angel of God, even as Christ Jesus" (Gal. 4:13-14). He then ends this epistle, "See with what large letters I am writing to you with my own hand" (Gal. 6:11, paraphrased) Some believe his ailment was chronic ophthalmia, a not extremely painful, but at times a very repulsive condition. In addition to his eyes, Paul seemed to suffer from a speech disability of some sort, as he indicates during his second letter to the church at Corinth. First, he quotes the charge levelled against him in that city by his enemies. "For his letters, say they, are weighty and powerful; but his bodily presence is weak, and his speech contemptible" (2 Cor. 10:10). He then responds to these accusations. "But though I be rude in speech, yet not in knowledge; but we have been throughly made manifest among you in all things" (2 Cor. 11:6).

12. He suffered the bite of a poisonous serpent (Acts 28:3-4).
13. He was often cast into prison. At Philippi, after being severely beaten, he was thrown into an inner prison, with his feet fastened in the stocks (Acts 16:24). In Caesarea he was unjustly imprisoned with no charges for two long years (Acts 24:27). After demanding his rights as a Roman citizen to appeal to Caesar, Paul was released from Caesarea, only to spend the next two years in house arrest as a political prisoner in Rome (Acts 28:30). He wrote of this imprisonment in Ephesians 6:20; Philippians 1;13; and Philemon 9. Finally, after a brief release, he was rearrested, condemned to death, and for the last time thrown into prison (2 Tim. 4:6-9).
14. He was well acquainted with physical hardships, such as sleeplessness, cold and exposure, hunger and thirst, and backbreaking labor (2 Cor. 6:4- 5; 11:27).
15. He was in constant danger, from rivers and robbers, Jews and Gentiles, in the cities and wilderness, on the sea, and among false brethren (2 Cor. 11:26).
16. He bore the awful pressure of concern over the various churches organized by him. "Beside those things that are without, that which cometh upon me daily, the care of all the churches" (2 Cor. 11:28). Note his intense concern about two churches in particular among the many:
    a. The church in Galatia—"Ye observe days, and months, and times, and years. I am afraid of you, lest I have bestowed upon you labour in vain. . . . My little children, of whom I travail in birth again until Christ be formed in you" (Gal. 4:10-11, 19).
    b. The church in Corinth—"For out of much affliction and anguish of heart I wrote unto you with many tears; not that ye should be grieved, but that ye might know the love which I have more abundantly unto you" (2 Cor. 2:4).

COMMENT

In fact, of the twenty-plus recorded churches in the New Testament, Paul founded and organized no less than 12 of them.

- The church in Antioch of Pisidia (Acts 13:14)—Where Paul preached his first recorded sermon (Acts 13:16)
- The church in Lystra (Acts 14:6)—Where Paul was stoned and left for dead (Acts 14:19)
- The church in Derbe (Acts 14:20-22)
- The church in Iconium (Acts 14:2)

- The church in Philippi (Acts 16:14-40)—Where the Philippian jailor was saved
- The church in Thessalonica (Acts 17:1)—Where Paul was accused of turning the world upside down (Acts 17:6)
- The church in Berea (Acts 17:11)—The church was made up of sound Bible students.
- The church in Athens (Acts 17:34)—It is entirely possible Paul established a church here following his sermon on Mars Hill.
- The church in Corinth (Acts 18:1)—Paul would later write two epistles to this church, First and Second Corinthians.
- The church in Ephesus (Acts 18:19)—This was the only church to receive letters from two New Testament writers. Paul wrote a letter to them (Ephesians), and the Apostle John would later direct a portion of his final book to them (Rev. 2:1-7).
- The church in Troas (Acts 20:7-12)—Here is the place where the last person recorded in history was raised from the dead.
- The church in Colosse (Col. 1:1-2)

17. He was slapped by orders of the Jewish high priest in the presence of his Pharisee peers (Acts 23:2).
18. He was nearly torn apart by an angry mob of his own countrymen in Jerusalem (Acts 21:30-32).
19. He knew the burden of internal pressure. He wrote this on two occasions: "For we would not, brethren, have you ignorant of our trouble which came to us in Asia, that we were pressed out of measure, above strength, insomuch that we despaired even of life" (2 Cor. 1:8). "For, when we were come into Macedonia, our flesh had no rest, but we were troubled on every side; without were fightings, within were fears" (2 Cor. 7:5).
20. During his final days on death row he was forsaken by his friends. "For Demas hath forsaken me, having loved this present world, and is departed unto Thessalonica" (2 Tim. 4:10). "At my first answer no man stood with me, but all men forsook me: I pray God that it may not be laid to their charge" (2 Tim. 4:16).

COMMENT

A comparison can be made between the sufferings and death of Paul with those experienced by Christ.

- Both were acquainted with hardships. "But in all things approving ourselves as the ministers of God, in much patience, in afflictions, in necessities, in distresses, in stripes, in imprisonments, in tumults, in labours, in watchings, in fastings . . . . In weariness and painfulness, in watchings often, in hunger and thirst, in fastings often, in cold and nakedness. . . . And Jesus saith unto him, The foxes have holes, and the birds of the air have nests; but the Son of man hath not where to lay his head" (2 Cor. 6:4-5; 11:27; Matt. 8:20).
- Both were accused of blasphemy. "Saying, This fellow persuadeth men to worship God contrary to the law. . . . Jesus saith unto him, Thou hast said: nevertheless I say unto you, Hereafter shall ye see the Son of man sitting on the right hand of power, and coming in the clouds of heaven. Then the high priest rent his clothes, saying, He hath spoken blasphemy; what further need have we of witnesses? behold, now ye have heard his blasphemy" (Acts 18:13; Matt. 26:64-65).
- Both experienced satanic oppression. "Wherefore we would have come unto you, even I Paul, once and again; but Satan hindered us. . . . And lest I should be exalted above measure through the abundance of the revelations, there was given to me a thorn in the flesh, the messenger of Satan to buffet me, lest I should be exalted above measure. . . . Then was Jesus led up of the Spirit into the wilderness to be tempted of the devil" (1 Thess. 2:18; 2 Cor. 12:7; Matt. 4:1).

- Both were rejected by their own people. "Then the high priest and the chief of the Jews informed him against Paul, and besought him, and desired favour against him, that he would send for him to Jerusalem, laying wait in the way to kill him. . . . He was in the world, and the world was made by him, and the world knew him not. He came unto his own, and his own received him not" (Acts 25:2-3; John 1:10-11).
- Both were often plotted against. "And when it was day, certain of the Jews banded together, and bound themselves under a curse, saying that they would neither eat nor drink till they had killed Paul. And they were more than forty which had made this conspiracy. And they came to the chief priests and elders, and said, We have bound ourselves under a great curse, that we will eat nothinguntil we have slain Paul. . . . Then gathered the chief priests and the Pharisees a council, and said, What do we? for this man doeth many miracles. . . . Then from that day forth they took counsel together for to put him to death" (Acts 23:12-14; John 11:47, 53).
- Both knew they would die violent deaths. "For I am now ready to be offered, and the time of my departure is at hand. . . . And Jesus going up to Jerusalem took the twelve disciples apart in the way, and said unto them, Behold, we go up to Jerusalem: and the Son of man shall be betrayed unto the chief priests and unto the scribes, and they shall condemn him to death, and shall deliver him to the Gentiles to mock, and to scourge, and to crucify him: and the third day he shall rise again" (2 Tim. 4:6; Matt. 20:17-19).
- Both anticipated a reward from the Father. "Henceforth there is laid up for me a crown of righteousness, which the Lord, the righteous judge, shall give me at that day: and not to me only, but unto all them also that love his appearing. . . . And now, O Father, glorify thou me with thine own self with the glory which I had with thee before the world was" (2 Tim. 4:8; John 17:5).
- Both would finish their assigned tasks. "I have fought a good fight, I have finished my course, I have kept the faith. . . . I have glorified thee on the earth: I have finished the work which thou gavest me to do" (2 Tim. 4:7; John 17:4).

B. An evaluation of Paul's sufferings—A reaction to his travail: What were the Apostle's thoughts concerning all the pain, pressure, and persecution he endured? Here is his personal evaluation, as given to:

1. The Ephesian elders—"But none of these things move me, neither count I my life dear unto myself, so that I might finish my course with joy, and the ministry, which I have received of the Lord Jesus, to testify the gospel of the grace of God" (Acts 20:24).
2. The church at Rome—"And not only so, but we glory in tribulations also: knowing that tribulation worketh patience; and patience, experience; and experience, hope" (Rom. 5:3-4). "For I reckon that the sufferings of this present time are not worthy to be compared with the glory which shall be revealed in us. . . . And we know that all things work together for good to them that love God, to them who are the called according to his purpose." (Rom. 8:18, 28).
3. The church at Corinth—"Who comforteth us in all our tribulation, that we may be able to comfort them which are in any trouble, by the comfort wherewith we ourselves are comforted of God. For as the sufferings of Christ abound in us, so our consolation also aboundeth by Christ" (2 Cor. 1:4-5). "We are troubled on every side, yet not distressed; we are perplexed, but not in despair; persecuted, but not forsaken; cast down, but not destroyed; always bearing about in the body

the dying of the Lord Jesus, that the life also of Jesus might be made manifest in our body. For we which live are alway delivered unto death for Jesus' sake, that the life also of Jesus might be made manifest in our mortal flesh. . . . For our light affliction, which is but for a moment, worketh for us a far more exceeding and eternal weight of glory" (2 Cor. 4:8-11, 17). "Therefore I take pleasure in infirmities, in reproaches, in necessities, in persecutions, in distresses for Christ's sake: for when I am weak, then am I strong" (2 Cor. 12:10).

4. The church at Thessalonica—"That no man should be moved by these afflictions: for yourselves know that we are appointed thereunto. For verily, when we were with you, we told you before that we should suffer tribulation; even as it came to pass, and ye know" (1 Thess. 3:3-4).
5. Timothy—"And the Lord shall deliver me from every evil work, and will preserve me unto his heavenly kingdom: to whom be glory for ever and ever. Amen" (2 Tim. 4:18).
6. The recipients of the book of Hebrews—"For whom the Lord loveth he chasteneth, and scourgeth every son whom he receiveth. . . . Now no chastening for the present seemeth to be joyous, but grievous: nevertheless afterward it yieldeth the peaceable fruit of righteousness unto them which are exercised thereby" (Heb. 12:6, 11).

XXIII. He was a viewer of heaven. On at least nine occasions Paul was allowed to see, hear, and be comforted by the resurrected Christ himself. These events occurred:

A. On the Damascus road—"And as he journeyed, he came near Damascus: and suddenly there shined round about him a light from heaven: And he fell to the earth, and heard a voice saying unto him, Saul, Saul, why persecutest thou me?" (Acts 9:3-4).

B. In Jerusalem
1. First occasion—"And it came to pass, that, when I was come again to Jerusalem, even while I prayed in the temple, I was in a trance; and saw him saying unto me, Make haste, and get thee quickly out of Jerusalem: for they will not receive thy testimony concerning me. . . . And he said unto me, Depart: for I will send thee far hence unto the Gentiles" (Acts 22:17-18, 21).
2. Second occasion—"And the night following the Lord stood by him, and said, Be of good cheer, Paul: for as thou hast testified of me in Jerusalem, so must thou bear witness also at Rome" (Acts 23:11).

C. During his stay in Arabia (Gal. 1:11-17)—"But I certify you, brethren, that the gospel which was preached of me is not after man. For I neither received it of man, neither was I taught it, but by the revelation of Jesus Christ" (Gal. 1:11-12).

D. In Troas—"And a vision appeared to Paul in the night; There stood a man of Macedonia, and prayed him, saying, Come over into Macedonia, and help us. And after he had seen the vision, immediately we endeavoured to go into Macedonia, assuredly gathering that the Lord had called us for to preach the gospel unto them" (Acts 16:9-10).

E. In Corinth—"Then spake the Lord to Paul in the night by a vision, Be not afraid, but speak, and hold not thy peace: For I am with thee, and no man shall set on thee to hurt thee: for I have much people in this city" (Acts 18:9-10).

F. On a ship—"For there stood by me this night the angel of God, whose I am, and whom I serve, saying, Fear not, Paul; thou must be brought before Caesar: and, lo, God hath given thee all them that sail with thee" (Acts 27:23-24).

G. At an undisclosed place—"I knew a man in Christ above fourteen years ago, (whether in the body, I cannot tell; or whether out of the body, I cannot tell: God knoweth;) such an one caught up to the third heaven. And I knew such a man, (whether i n the body, or out of the body, I cannot tell: God knoweth;) how that he was caught up into paradise, and heard unspeakable words, which it i s not lawful for a man to utter" (2 Cor. 12:2-4).

H. In Rome—"Notwithstanding the Lord stood with me, and strengthened me; that by me the preaching might be fully known, and that all the Gentiles might hear: and I was delivered out of the mouth of the lion" (2 Tim. 4:17).

XXIV. He was a willing martyr.

A. As told to the Ephesian elders—"And now, behold, I go bound in the spirit unto Jerusalem, not knowing the things that shall befall me there . . . . But none of these things move me, neither count I my life dear unto myself, so that I might finish my course with joy, and the ministry, which I have received of the Lord Jesus, to testify the gospel of the grace of God" (Acts 20:22, 24).

B. As told to Philip the Evangelist—"Then Paul answered, What mean ye to weep and to break mine heart? for I am ready not to be bound only, but also to die at Jerusalem for the name of the Lord Jesus" (Acts 21:13).

C. As told to Timothy—"For I am now ready to be offered, and the time of my departure is at hand" (2 Tim. 4:6).

XXV. He was a co-laborer with the Apostle Peter. Paul and Peter can be favorably compared in many areas.

A. Paul was the official messenger to the Gentiles, while Peter was God's spokesman to the Jews (Gal. 2:7-8).

B. Both played important roles in the Jerusalem Council (Acts 15).

C. Both healed lame men (Acts 3:1-8; 14:8-12).

D. Both dealt with satanic pretenders.

1. Peter confronted Simon the sorcerer at Samaria (Acts 8:9-24).
2. Paul confronted Bar-jesus the sorcerer at Salamis on the Isle of Cyprus (Acts 13:5-11).

E. Both were released from prison miraculously.

1. God sent an angel to free Peter (Acts 12:5-10).
2. God sent an earthquake to free Paul (Acts 16:25-29).

F. Both raised the dead.

1. Peter raised Dorcas from the dead (Acts 9:40).
2. Paul raised Eutychus from the dead (Acts 20:12).

G. Both received heavenly visions to minister to the lost.

1. Peter saw his vision at Joppa (Acts 10:9-23).
2. Paul saw his vision at Troas (Acts 16:8-10).

H. Both authored New Testament books.

1. Peter wrote two epistles.
2. Paul wrote 13 (possibly 14) epistles.

I. Both wrote key passages on the subjects of Biblical inspiration—"We have also a more sure word of prophecy; whereunto ye do well that ye take heed, as unto a light that shineth in a dark place, until the day dawn, and the day star arise in your hearts: Knowing this first, that no prophecy of the scripture is of any private interpretation. For the prophecy came not in old time by the will of man: but holy men of God spake as they were moved by the Holy Ghost. . . . All scripture is given by inspiration of God, and is profitable for doctrine, for reproof, for correction, for instruction in righteousness: That the man of God may be perfect, throughly furnished unto all good works" (2 Peter 1:19-21; 2 Tim. 3:16-17).

J. Both knew they would die as martyrs for Christ.

1. Peter's testimony—"Yea, I think it meet, as long as I am in this tabernacle, to stir you up by putting you in

remembrance; knowing that shortly I must put off this my tabernacle, even as our Lord Jesus Christ hath shewed me" (2 Peter 1:13-14).

2. Paul's testimony—"For I am now ready to be offered, and the time of my departure is at hand. I have fought a good fight, I have finished my course, I have kept the faith" (2 Tim. 4:6-7).

XXVI. He was a contrast to the Old Testament Saul.

A. Both were from the tribe of Benjamin (1 Sam. 9:1-2; Phil. 3:5).

B. One was tall and impressive and the other probably short and unimpressive (1 Sam. 9:2; Gal. 4:13-14; 2 Cor. 10:10).

C. One began as God's friend and the other as God's enemy (1 Sam. 9:16; 10:6-7; Acts 9:1).

D. One ended his life as God's enemy and the other as God's friend (1 Sam. 28:6; 2 Tim. 4:18).

E. One went to the witch in the hour of death (1 Sam. 28:7).

F. One went to the word in the hour of death (2 Tim. 4:6-8).

G. The life of one was characterized by disobedience (1 Sam. 13:13; 15:22-23). "And Samuel said, Hath the Lord as great delight in burnt offerings and sacrifices, as in obeying the voice of the Lord? Behold, to obey is better than sacrifice, and to hearken than the fat of rams. For rebellion is as the sin of witchcraft, and stubbornness is as iniquity and idolatry. Because thou hast rejected the word of the Lord, he hath also rejected thee from being king" (1 Sam. 15:22-23).

H. The life of one was characterized by obedience—"At midday, O king, I saw in the way a light from heaven, above the brightness of the sun, shining round about me and them which journeyed with me. . . . And I said, Who art thou, Lord? And he said, I am Jesus whom thou persecutest. But rise, and stand upon thy feet: for I have appeared unto thee for this purpose, to make thee a minister and a witness both of these things which thou hast seen, and of those things in the which I will appear unto thee . . . . Whereupon, O king Agrippa, I was not disobedient unto the heavenly vision" (Acts 26:13, 15-16, 19).

I. Physical death stripped the Old Testament Saul of his earthly crown.

J. Physical death presented the New Testament Saul with his eternal crown. "Henceforth there is laid up for me a crown of righteousness, which the Lord, the righteous judge, shall give me at that day: and not to me only, but unto all them also that love his appearing" (2 Tim 4:8).

OBSERVATIONS FROM THE LIFE OF PETER

I. Peter was a married man. We know this because of two things:

A. A miracle performed by Jesus—Our Lord healed Peter's mother-in-law (Matt. 8:14-17; Mark 1:29-34; Luke 4:38-41).

B. A statement made by Paul—"Have we not power to lead about a sister, a wife, as well as other apostles, and as the brethren of the Lord, and Cephas?" (1 Cor. 9:5). What was the status and nature of this marriage? Here at least three views have been offered:

1. View 1: He was divorced. This would seem highly unlikely on the basis of both the qualifications for the Old Testament priest and (later) the requirements laid down by Paul concerning pastors and deacons. "This is a true saying, If a man desire the office of a bishop, he desireth a good work. A bishop then must be blameless, the husband of one wife, vigilant, sober, of good behaviour, given to hospitality, apt to teach . . . . One that ruleth well his own house, having his children in subjection with all gravity; (For if a man know not how to rule his own house, how shall he take care of the church of God?) (1 Tim. 3:1-2, 4-5).

2. View 2: He was separated. This also is improbable based on the same arguments as listed above.

3. View 3: He was a widower. This would appear to be the most logical view in light of the fact that his wife's name is never mentioned. Note Peter's advice to both husbands and wives as found in his first epistle: "Likewise, ye wives, be in subjection to your own husbands; that, if any obey not the word, they also may without the word be won by the conversation of the wives; while they behold your chaste conversation coupled with fear. Whose adorning let it not be that outward adorning of plaiting the hair, and of wearing of gold, or of putting on of apparel; But let it be the hidden man of the heart, in that which is not corruptible, even the ornament of a meek and quiet spirit, which is in the sight of God of great price. For after this manner in the old time the holy women also, who trusted in God, adorned themselves, being in subjection unto their own husbands: Even as Sara obeyed Abraham, calling him lord: whose daughters ye are, as long as ye do well, and are not afraid with any amazement. Likewise, ye husbands, dwell with them according to knowledge, giving honour unto the wife, as unto the weaker vessel, and as being heirs together of the grace of life; that your prayers be not hindered" (1 Pet. 3:1-7).

II. Peter was a unique man.
   A. He was the only apostle to both see and write about the transfiguration of Christ (Matt. 17:1-8; 2 Pet. 1:16-18).
   B. He was the only apostle to declare the deity of Christ on two separate occasions. "From that time many of his disciples went back, and walked no more with him. Then said Jesus unto the twelve, Will ye also go away? Then Simon Peter answered him, Lord, to whom shall we go? thou hast the words of eternal life. And we believe and are sure that thou art that Christ, the Son of the living God" (John 6:66-69). "And Simon Peter answered and said, Thou art the Christ, the Son of the living God" (Matt. 16:16).
   C. He was the only apostle to argue with Christ. This he did on three occasions.
      1. Concerning the predicted sufferings and death of Christ—"From that time forth began Jesus to shew unto his disciples, how that he must go unto Jerusalem, and suffer many things of the elders and chief priests and scribes, and be killed, and be raised again the third day. Then Peter took him, and began to rebuke him, saying, Be it far from thee, Lord: this shall not be unto thee. But he turned, and said unto Peter, Get thee behind me, Satan: thou art an offence unto me: for thou savourest not the things that be of God, but those that be of men" (Matt. 16:21-23).
      2. Concerning the washing of his feet by Christ—"Jesus knowing that the Father had given all things into his hands, and that he was come from God, and went to God; he riseth from supper, and laid aside his garments; and took a towel, and girded himself. After that he poureth water into a basin, and began to wash the disciples' feet, and to wipe them with the towel wherewith he was girded. Then cometh he to Simon Peter: and Peter saith unto him, Lord, dost thou wash my feet? Jesus answered and said unto him, What I do thou knowest not now; but thou shalt know hereafter. Peter saith unto him, Thou shalt never wash my feet. Jesus answered him, If I wash thee not, thou hast no part with me" (John 13:3-8).
      3. Concerning the prophecy that he would betray Christ—"And Jesus saith unto them, All ye shall be offended because of me this night: for it is written, I will smite the shepherd, and the sheep shall be scattered. But after that I am risen, I will go before you into Galilee. But Peter said unto him, Although all shall be offended, yet will not I. And Jesus saith unto him, Verily I say unto thee, That this day, even in this night, before the cock crow twice, thou shalt deny me thrice. But he spake the more vehemently, If I should die with thee, I will not deny thee in any wise. Likewise also said they all" (Mark 14:27-31).
   D. He was the first apostle to have received a personal resurrection visit by Christ. "And they rose up the same hour, and returned to Jerusalem, and found the eleven gathered together, and them that were with them, Saying, The Lord is risen indeed, and hath appeared to Simon. . . . And that he was buried, and that he rose again the third day according to the scriptures: And that he was seen of Cephas, then of the twelve" (Luke 24:33-34; 1 Cor. 15:4-5).
   E. He was the only apostle to deny the Savior on three occasions. "Now Peter sat without in the palace: and a damsel came unto him, saying, Thou also wast with Jesus of Galilee. But he denied before them all, saying, I know not what thou sayest. And when he was gone out into the porch, another maid saw him, and said unto them that were there, This fellow was also with

Jesus of Nazareth. And again he denied with an oath, I do not know the man. And after a while came unto him they that stood by, and said to Peter, Surely thou also art one of them; for thy speech bewrayeth thee. Then began he to curse and to swear, saying, I know not the man. And immediately the cock crew" (Matt. 26:69-74).

F. He was the only apostle allowed to affirm his love for Christ on three occasions. "So when they had dined, Jesus saith to Simon Peter, Simon, son of Jonas, lovest thou me more than these? He saith unto him, Yea, Lord; thou knowest that I love thee. He saith unto him, Feed my lambs. He saith to him again the second time, Simon, son of Jonas, lovest thou me? He saith unto him, Yea, Lord; thou knowest that I love thee. He saith unto him, Feed my sheep. He saith unto him the third time, Simon, son of Jonas, lovest thou me? Peter was grieved because he said unto him the third time, Lovest thou me? And he said unto him, Lord, thou knowest all things; thou knowest that I love thee. Jesus saith unto him, Feed my sheep" (John 21:15-17).

G. He was the only apostle to be told he would die a martyr's death for Christ. "Verily, verily, I say unto thee, When thou wast young, thou girdedst thyself, and walkedst whither thou wouldest: but when thou shalt be old, thou shalt stretch forth thy hands, and another shall gird thee, and carry thee whither thou wouldest not. This spake he, signifying by what death he should glorify God. And when he had spoken this, he saith unto him, Follow me. . . . Yea, I think it meet, as long as I am in this tabernacle, to stir you up by putting you in remembrance; knowing that shortly I must put off this my tabernacle, even as our Lord Jesus Christ hath shewed me" (John 21:18-19; 2 Pet. 1:13-14).

H. He was the only apostle to be either directly or indirectly involved in at least eight of the recorded miracles of Christ.

1. His direct involvement
   a. Healing of his mother-in-law (Matt. 8:14-17; Mark 1:29-34; Luke 4:38-41)—"And when Jesus was come into Peter's house, he saw his wife's mother laid, and sick of a fever" (Matt. 8:14).
   b. The first great catch of fish (Matt. 4:18-22; Mark 1:16-20; Luke 5:1-11)—"And he entered into one of the ships, which was Simon's, and prayed him that he would thrust out a little from the land. And he sat down, and taught the people out of the ship. Now when he had left speaking, he said unto Simon, Launch out into the deep, and let down your nets for a draught. And Simon answering said unto him, Master, we have toiled all the night, and have taken nothing: nevertheless at thy word I will let down the net. And when they had this done, they enclosed a great multitude of fishes: and their net brake. And they beckoned unto their partners, which were in the other ship, that they should come and help them. And they came, and filled both the ships, so that they began to sink. When Simon Peter saw it, he fell down at Jesus' knees, saying, Depart from me; for I am a sinful man, O Lord" (Luke 5:3-8).
   c. Walking on the water (Matt. 14:24-33; Mark 6:47-52; John 6:16-21)—"And Peter answered him and said, Lord, if it be thou, bid me come unto thee on the water. And he said, Come. And when Peter was come down out of the ship, he walked on the water, to go to Jesus. But when he saw the wind boisterous, he was afraid; and beginning to sink, he cried, saying, Lord, save me. And immediately Jesus stretched forth his hand, and

caught him, and said unto him, O thou of little faith, wherefore didst thou doubt?" (Matt. 14:28-31)

d. The miracle of the tribute money (Matt. 17:24-27)—"And when they were come to Capernaum, they that received tribute money came to Peter, and said, Doth not your master pay tribute? He saith, Yes. And when he was come into the house, Jesus prevented him, saying, What thinkest thou, Simon? of whom do the kings of the earth take custom or tribute? of their own children, or of strangers? Peter saith unto him, Of strangers. Jesus saith unto him, Then are the children free. Notwithstanding, lest we should offend them, go thou to the sea, and cast an hook, and take up the fish that first cometh up; and when thou hast opened his mouth, thou shalt find a piece of money: that take, and give unto them for me and thee" (Matt. 17:24-27).

e. Restoring a severed ear (Luke 22:49-51)—"And one of them smote the servant of the high priest, and cut off his right ear. And Jesus answered and said, Suffer ye thus far. And he touched his ear, and healed him" (Luke 22:50-51). Then Simon Peter having a sword drew it, and smote the high priest's s ervant, and cut off his right ear. The servant's name was Malchus" (John 18:10).

2. His indirect involvement

a. Raising Jarius's daughter (Matt. 9:18-19, 23-26; Mark 5:22-24, 35-43; Luke 8:41-42, 49-56)—"While he yet spake, there came from the ruler of the synagogue's house certain which said, Thy daughter is dead: why troublest thou the Master any further? As soon as Jesus heard the word that was spoken, he saith unto the ruler of the synagogue, Be not afraid, only believe. And he suffered no man to follow him, save Peter, and James, and John the brother of James" (Mark 5:35-37).

b. Destroying a fig tree (Matt. 21:17-20, 43; Mark 11:12-14, 20-21)—"And in the morning, as they passed by, they saw the fig tree dried up from the roots. And Peter calling to remembrance saith unto him, Master, behold, the fig tree which thou cursedst is withered away" (Mark 11:20-21).

c. The second great catch of fish (John 21:1-14)—"Simon Peter went up, and drew the net to land full of great fishes, an hundred and fifty and three: and for all there were so many, yet was not the net broken" (John 21:11).

III. Peter was a leader in the early church. This fact is often played down to counteract the unscriptural position that he was the first pope. He, of course, was not; but as the record shows, Peter exerted great influence in the Christian community, especially in Jerusalem. Note these six examples.

A. In the selection of a man to replace Judas—"And in those days Peter stood up in the midst of the disciples, and said, (the number of names together were about an hundred and twenty,) Men and brethren, this scripture must needs have been fulfilled, which the Holy Ghost by the mouth of David spake before concerning Judas, which was guide to them that took Jesus. . . . For it is written in the book of Psalms, Let his habitation be desolate, and let no man dwell therein: and his bishoprick let another take. Wherefore of these men which have companied with us all the time that the Lord Jesus went in and out among us, beginning from the baptism of John, unto that same day that he was taken up from us, must one be ordained to be a witness with us of his resurrection" (Acts 1:15-16, 20-22).

B. At Pentecost—"But Peter, standing up with the eleven, lifted up his voice, and said unto them, Ye men of Judaea, and all ye that dwell at Jerusalem, be this known unto you, and hearken to my words" (Acts 2:14).

C. Near the Temple's Beautiful Gate—"And a certain man lame from his mother's womb was carried, whom they laid daily at the gate of the temple which is called Beautiful, to ask alms of them that entered into the temple . . . . Then Peter said, Silver and gold have I none; but such as I have give I thee: In the name of Jesus Christ of Nazareth rise up and walk. And he took him by the right hand, and lifted him up: and immediately his feet and ankle bones received strength. . . . And all the people saw him walking and praising God . . . . And when Peter saw it, he answered unto the people, Ye men of Israel, why marvel ye at this? or why look ye so earnestly on us, as though by our own power or holiness we had made this man to walk?" (Acts 3:2, 6-7, 9, 12).

D. Before the Jewish leaders—"And when they had set them in the midst, they asked, By what power, or by what name, have ye done this? Then Peter, filled with the Holy Ghost, said unto them, Ye rulers of the people, and elders of Israel, If we this day be examined of the good deed done to the impotent man, by what means he is made whole; be it known unto you all, and to all the people of Israel, that by the name of Jesus Christ of Nazareth, whom ye crucified, whom God raised from the dead, even by him doth this man stand here before you whole. This is the stone which was set at nought of you builders, which is become the head of the corner. Neither is there salvation in any other: for there is none other name under heaven given among men, whereby we must be saved" (Acts 4:7-12).

E. Concerning church discipline—"But a certain man named Ananias, with Sapphira his wife, sold a possession, and kept back part of the price, his wife also being privy to it, and brought a certain part, and laid it at the apostles' feet. But Peter said, Ananias, why hath Satan filled thine heart to lie to the Holy Ghost, and to keep back part of the price of the land? Whiles it remained, was it not thine own? and after it was sold, was it not in thine own power? why hast thou conceived this thing in thine heart? thou hast not lied unto men, but unto God. And Ananias hearing these words fell down, and gave up the ghost: and great fear came on all them that heard these things" (Acts 5:1-5).

F. In defending his actions before the Jewish Christian legalists—"And the apostles and brethren that were in Judaea heard that the Gentiles had also received the word of God. And when Peter was come up to Jerusalem, they that were of the circumcision contended with him, saying, Thou wentest in to men uncircumcised, and didst eat with them. But Peter rehearsed the matter from the beginning, and expounded it by order unto them, saying, I was in the city of Joppa praying: and in a trance I saw a vision, A certain vessel descend, as it had been a great sheet, let down from heaven by four corners; and it came even to me . . . . When they heard these things, they held their peace, and glorified God, saying, Then hath God also to the Gentiles granted repentance unto life" (Acts 11:1-5, 18). Consider his advice as a leader to other leaders: "The elders which are among you I exhort, who am also an elder, and a witness of the sufferings of Christ, and also a partaker of the glory that shall be revealed: Feed the flock of God which is among you, taking the oversight thereof, not by constraint, but willingly; not for filthy lucre, but of a ready mind; Neither as being lords over God's heritage, but being ensamples to the flock. And when the chief Shepherd shall appear, ye shall receive a crown of glory that fadeth not away" (1 Peter 5:1-4).

IV. Peter was a one-on-one kind of individual. Note his personal encounters.
   A. With the lame man (Acts 3:6)
   B. With Ananias and Sapphira (Acts 5:1-9)
   C. With Simon the sorcerer (Acts 8:20)
   D. With Aeneas (Acts 9:33)
   E. With Dorcas (Acts 9:36-41)
   F. With Cornelius (Acts 10:23-48)

V. Peter was a powerful preacher and communicator. At least six examples can be cited to illustrate this.
   A. In the upper room, prior to Pentecost (Acts 1:15-21)
      1. He aptly summarized the situation concerning the defection of Judas.
      2. He supported his summary with the proper scripture.
      3. He called attention to the need for and requirements of a replacement for Judas.
   B. At Pentecost (Acts 2:14-36)
      1. He defended and explained from the scriptures the phenomenon of tongues—"But Peter, standing up with the eleven, lifted up his voice, and said unto them, Ye men of Judaea, and all ye that dwell at Jerusalem, be this known unto you, and hearken to my words: For these are not drunken, as ye suppose, seeing it is but the third hour of the day. But this is that which was spoken by the prophet Joel" (Acts 2:14-16).
      2. He identified Jesus Christ as Israel's Messiah—"Ye men of Israel, hear these words; Jesus of Nazareth, a man approved of God among you by miracles and wonders and signs, which God did by him in the midst of you, as ye yourselves also know .... Therefore let all the house of Israel know assuredly, that God hath made that same Jesus, whom ye have crucified, both Lord and Christ" (Acts 2:22, 36).
      3. He convicted Israel of killing their Messiah—"Him, being delivered by the determinate counsel and foreknowledge of God, ye have taken, and by wicked hands have crucified and slain .... Now when they heard this, they were pricked in their heart, and said unto Peter and to the rest of the apostles, Men and brethren, what shall we do?" (Acts 2:23, 37).
      4. He extended an invitation to accept Christ as Savior—"Then Peter said unto them, Repent, and be baptized every one of you in the name of Jesus Christ for the remission of sins, and ye shall receive the gift of the Holy Ghost. For the promise is unto you, and to your children, and to all that are afar off, even as many as the Lord our God shall call. And with many other words did he testify and exhort, saying, Save yourselves from this untoward generation" (Acts 2:38-40).
   C. On Solomon's porch (Acts 3:11-26)
      1. Peter again convicted Israel of killing their Messiah—"But ye denied the Holy One and the Just, and desired a murderer to be granted unto you; and killed the Prince of life, whom God hath raised from the dead; whereof we are witnesses" (Acts 3:14-15).
      2. He again extended an invitation to accept Christ—"Repent ye therefore, and be converted, that your sins may be blotted out, when the times of refreshing shall come from the presence of the Lord" (Acts 3:19).
   D. Before the Sanhedrin (Acts 4:8-12, 14, 20)

1. For the third time Peter indicted Israel for crucifying their Messiah—"Be it known unto you all, and to all the people of Israel, that by the name of Jesus Christ of Nazareth, whom ye crucified, whom God raised from the dead, even by him doth this man stand here before you whole" (Acts 4:10).
2. For the third time he extends an invitation—"Neither is there salvation in any other: for there is none other name under heaven given among men, whereby we must be saved" (Acts 4:12).

E. In the house of Cornelius (Acts 10:34-48)—Peter's approach was somewhat different on this occasion for he was preaching to Gentiles. In essence, his sermon consisted of four key points.

1. The earthly ministry of Christ—"How God anointed Jesus of Nazareth with the Holy Ghost and with power: who went about doing good, and healing all that were oppressed of the devil; for God was with him " (Acts 10:38).
2. The death and resurrection of Christ—"And we are witnesses of all things which he did both in the land of the Jews, and in Jerusalem; whom they slew and hanged on a tree: Him God raised up the third day, and shewed him openly" (Acts 10:39-40).
3. The command of Christ—"And he commanded us to preach unto the people, and to testify that it is he which was ordained of God to be the Judge of quick and dead" (Acts 10:42).
4. The salvation offered by Christ—"To him give all the prophets witness, that through his name whosoever believeth in him shall receive remission of sins" (Acts 10:43).

F. Before the legalistic Jewish Christian leaders (Acts 11:1-17)—Here Peter defended his previous actions in ministering to the Gentiles (Cornelius and his friends). Peter justified this through a personal and scriptural argument.

1. The personal argument (Acts 11:4-15)—He related and explained the vision of the great sheet God had given him.
2. The scriptural argument—"Then remembered I the word of the Lord, how that he said, John indeed baptized with water; but ye shall be baptized with the Holy Ghost" (Acts 11:16).

OBSERVATIONS FROM THE LIFE OF JOHN THE BAPTIST

I. Introduction

A. Some 15 months before the birth of Christ in Bethlehem, the angel Gabriel appeared to an old priest named Zacharias in the Jerusalem temple and issued the following predictions (Luke 1:11-17).

1. That he and his barren wife Elisabeth would have a son
2. That he would be called John
3. That he would become a Spirit-filled Nazarite
4. That he would prepare the way for the Messiah

B. All these things happened, just as the angel said. At the dedication of his son, Zacharias acknowledged Gabriel's previous prophecy by the following testimony: "And thou, child, shalt be called the prophet of the Highest: for thou shalt go before the face of the Lord to prepare his ways; to give knowledge of salvation unto his people by the remission of their sins, through the tender mercy of our God; whereby the dayspring from on high hath visited us, to give light to them that sit in darkness and in the shadow of death, to guide our feet into the way of peace" (Luke 1:76-79).

C. Characteristics of John's that made him a champion of faith.

II. His official office

A. According to Gabriel's prophecy (Luke 1:15), John would be a Nazarite, which was different from a Nazarene.

1. A Nazarene was one who lived in the city of Nazareth. Jesus was a Nazarene because he lived some 28 years in Nazareth, but was not a Nazarite. He doubtless did have his hair cut. He drank of the fruit of the vine (John 2; Matt. 26), and he did come in contact with dead bodies (John 11).
2. A Nazarite was one who had a special calling or *vocation.* According to Numbers 6, a Nazarite took a holy vow in three areas.
   a. He would not have his hair cut.
   b. He would abstain from the fruit of the vine.
   c. He would avoid all contact with a dead body.

B. John the Baptist was a Nazarite. Here we see his first characteristic as a champion of the faith. John had taken a sacred vow to serve God and had totally dedicated himself to the work of the Lord. Note:

1. His preparation—"And the child grew, and waxed strong in spirit, and was in the deserts till the day of his shewing unto Israel" (Luke 1:80). He "waxed strong in spirit" through prayer (see Luke 11:1) and Bible study (compare Isa. 40:3-5 with Matt. 3:2-3).
2. His simple life-style—"And the same John had his raiment of camel's hair, and a leathern girdle about his loins; and his meat was locusts and wild honey" (Matt. 3:4). Jesus himself would later comment

on this: "And as they departed, Jesus began to say unto the multitudes concerning John, What went ye out into the wilderness to see? A reed shaken with the wind? But what went ye out for to see? A man clothed in soft raiment? behold, they that wear soft clothing are in kings' houses. But what went ye out for to see? A prophet? yea, I say unto you, and more than a prophet" (Matt. 11:7-9). Like Paul, John was a one-issue man, and that issue was glorifying Christ. As a student of the Hebrew Bible and a preacher who proclaimed God's kingdom, John undoubtedly had been impressed with David's prayer offered at the gathering of the materials to construct the temple. "Wherefore David blessed the LORD before all the congregation: and David said, Blessed be thou, LORD God of Israel our father, for ever and ever. Thine, O LORD, is the greatness, and the power, and the glory, and the victory, and the majesty: for all that is in the heaven and in the earth is thine; thine is the kingdom, O LORD, and thou art exalted as head above all. Both riches and honour come of thee, and thou reignest over all; and in thine hand is power and might; and in thine hand it is to make great, and to give strength unto all. Now therefore, our God, we thank thee, and praise thy glorious name" (1 Chron. 29:10-13).

III. His prayer life—"And it came to pass, that, as he was praying in a certain place, when he ceased, one of his disciples said unto him, Lord, teach us to pray, as John also taught his disciples" (Luke 11:1).
   A. According to Luke here, John not only was a great prayer warrior himself, but apparently conducted classes for his disciples on how to pray.
   B. D. L. Moody said shortly before his death that had he to live his life over, he would spend less time preaching and more time praying. By this he did not suggest that preaching was unimportant, but rather that praying was all-important.

IV. His unselfishness
   A. During the height of John the Baptist's ministry, two of his most devoted followers, the Apostle John and Andrew, leave the evangelist to join up with the Savior (John 1:35-40).
   B. This is the acid test for any preacher. But John encouraged them to follow Jesus.

V. His fearlessness—John truly preached without fear or favor.
   A. He rebuked the religious community because of its sins. "But when he saw many of the Pharisees and Sadducees come to his baptism, he said unto them, O generation of vipers, who hath warned you to flee from the wrath to come? Bring forth therefore fruits meet for repentance: And think not to say within yourselves, We have Abraham as our father: for I say unto you, that God is able of these stones to raise up children unto Abraham. And now also the axe is laid unto the root of the trees: therefore every tree which bringeth not forth good fruit is hewn down, and cast into the fire" (Matt. 3:7-10).
   B. He rebuked the political leader of that time for his sin. "For Herod himself had sent forth and laid hold upon John, and bound him in prison for Herodias' sake, his brother Philip's wife: for he had married her. For John had said unto Herod, It is not lawful for thee to have thy brother's wife" (Mark 6:17-18). How John would have thundered out against abortion, homosexuality, etc. had he lived in our day.

VI. His clear-cut message—John had but one message and kept it as simple as he could. The message was, Repent of your sins, and be baptized as evidence of your faith, for the coming of the Lord is at hand. John, of course, here referred to the first coming of

Christ. Our sin-sick world today desperately needs bold men of God to proclaim the same message in light of his second coming.

VII. His absolute devotion to the Lord Jesus Christ

A. He constantly honored his Savior. "And this is the record of John, when the Jews sent priests and Levites from Jerusalem to ask him, Who art thou? And he confessed, and denied not; but confessed, I am not the Christ. And they asked him, What then? Art thou Elias? And he saith, I am not. Art thou that prophet? And he answered, No. Then said they unto him, Who art thou? that we may give an answer to them that sent us. What sayest thou of thyself? He said, I am the voice of one crying in the wilderness, Make straight the way of the Lord, as said the prophet Esaias" (John 1:19-23). We note here John didn't even tell the Pharisees his name. He felt the nature of the message was *far more* important than the name of the messenger. John's final testimony concerning Christ is one of the greatest in the entire Bible. "John answered and said, A man can receive nothing, except it be given him from heaven. Ye yourselves bear me witness, that I said, I am not the Christ, but that I am sent before him. He that hath the bride is the bridegroom: but the friend of the bridegroom, which standeth and heareth him, rejoiceth greatly because of the bridegroom's voice: this my joy therefore is fulfilled. He must increase, but I must decrease" (John 3:27-30).

B. He faithfully served his Savior.

1. It was John's great privilege to baptize Jesus. "Then cometh Jesus from Galilee to Jordan unto John, to be baptized of him. But John forbad him, saying, I have need to be baptized of thee, and comest thou to me? And Jesus answering said unto him, Suffer it to be so now: for thus it becometh us to fulfil all righteousness. Then he suffered him. And Jesus, when he was baptized, went up straightway out of the water: and, lo, the heavens were opened unto him, and he saw the Spirit of God descending like a dove, and lighting upon him: And lo a voice from heaven, saying, This is my beloved Son, in whom I am well pleased" (Matt. 3:13-17).
2. It was John's joy to introduce Jesus. "The next day John seeth Jesus coming unto him, and saith, Behold the Lamb of God, which taketh away the sin of the world" (John 1:29).

C. He willingly died for his Savior. Because of his stand for righteousness, John is imprisoned and later beheaded by King Herod.

D. Jesus himself eulogized this great champion of the faith. "Verily I say unto you, Among them that are born of women there hath not risen a greater than John the Baptist: notwithstanding he that is least in the kingdom of heaven is greater than he." (Matt. 11:11).

VIII. His Old Testament counterpart—John the Baptist and Elijah the prophet can be favorably compared.

A. Both were familiar with the rugged outdoor life.

1. Elijah—"And they answered him, He was an hairy man, and girt with a girdle of leather about his loins. And he said, It is Elijah the Tishbite" (2 Kings 1:8).
2. John—"And the child grew, and waxed strong in spirit, and was in the deserts till the day of his shewing unto Israel. . . . And the same John had his raiment of camel's hair, and a leathern girdle about his loins; and his meat was locusts and wild honey " (Luke 1:80; Matt. 3:4).

B. Both attempted to call the people of Israel back to God.

1. Elijah—"And Elijah came unto all the people, and said, How long halt

ye between two opinions? if the Lord be God, follow him: but if Baal, then follow him. And the people answered him not a word" (1 Kings 18:21).

2. John—"In those days came John the Baptist, preaching in the wilderness of Judaea, and saying, Repent ye: for the kingdom of heaven is at hand" (Matt. 3:1-2).

C. Both condemned sinful kings.

1. Elijah condemned both Ahab and Ahaziah. "And Elijah the Tishbite, who was of the inhabitants of Gilead, said unto Ahab, As the LORD God of Israel liveth, before whom I stand, there shall not be dew nor rain these years, but according to my word. . . . And it came to pass, when Ahab saw Elijah, that Ahab said unto him, Art thou he that troubleth Israel? And he answered, I have not troubled Israel; but thou, and thy father's house, in that ye have forsaken the commandments of the LORD, and thou hast followed Baalim. . . . And Ahaziah fell down through a lattice in his upper chamber that was in Samaria, and was sick: and he sent messengers, and said unto them, Go, inquire of Baal-zebub the god of Ekron whether I shall recover of this disease. But the angel of the LORD said to Elijah the Tishbite, Arise, go up to meet the messengers of the king of Samaria, and say unto them, Is it not because there is not a God in Israel, that ye go to inquire of Baal-zebub the god of Ekron? Now therefore thus saith the LORD, Thou shalt not come down from that bed on which thou art gone up, but shalt surely die. And Elijah departed" (1 Kings 17:1; 18:17-18; 2 Kings 1:2-4).

2. John condemned Herod. "For John had said unto Herod, It is not lawful for thee to have thy brother's wife" (Mark 6:18).

D. Both were hated and hounded by godless women.

1. Elijah's foe—"And Ahab told Jezebel all that Elijah had done, and withal how he had slain all the prophets with the sword. Then Jezebel sent a messenger unto Elijah, saying, So let the gods do to me, and more also, if I make not thy life as the life of one of them by to morrow about this time. And when he saw that, he arose, and went for his life, and came to Beer-sheba, which belongeth to Judah, and left his servant there" (1 Kings 19:1-3).

2. John's foe—"Therefore Herodias had a quarrel against him, and would have killed him; but she could not" (Mark 6:19).

E. Both became discouraged.

1. Elijah—"But he himself went a day's journey into the wilderness, and came and sat down under a juniper tree: and he requested for himself that he might die; and said, It is enough; now, O LORD, take away my life; for I am not better than my fathers" (1 Kings 19:4).

2. John—"Now when John had heard in the prison the works of Christ, he sent two of his disciples, and said unto him, Art thou he that should come, or do we look for another?" (Matt. 11:2-3).

F. Both were comforted by Christ himself.

1. Elijah—"And as he lay and slept under a juniper tree, behold, then an angel touched him, and said unto him, Arise and eat. And he looked, and, behold, there was a cake baken on the coals, and a cruse of water at his head. And he did eat and drink, and laid him down again. And the angel of the LORD came again the second time, and touched him, and said, Arise and eat; because the journey is too great for thee" (1 Kings 19:5-7). Note: Most Bible students believe the angel of the

Lord title, when found in the Old Testament, is a reference to Jesus himself, that is, a preincarnate appearance of the Son of God.

2. John—"And in that same hour he cured many of their infirmities and plagues, and of evil spirits; and unto many that were blind he gave sight. Then Jesus answering said unto them, Go your way, and tell John what things ye have seen and heard; how that the blind see, the lame walk, the lepers are cleansed, the deaf hear, the dead are raised, to the poor the gospel is preached " (Luke 7:21-22).

G. Both were often associated with each other.

1. By Christ—"And as they came down from the mountain, Jesus charged them, saying, Tell the vision to no man, until the Son of man be risen again from the dead. And his disciples asked him, saying, Why then say the scribes that Elias must first come? And Jesus answered and said unto them, Elias truly shall first come, and restore all things. But I say unto you, That Elias is come already, and they knew him not, but have done unto him whatsoever they listed. Likewise shall also the Son of man suffer of them. Then the disciples understood that he spake unto them of John the Baptist" (Matt. 17:9-13).
2. By the Jewish leaders—"And this is the record of John, when the Jews sent priests and Levites from Jerusalem to ask him, Who art thou? And he confessed, and denied not; but confessed, I am not the Christ. And they asked him, What then? Art thou Elias? And he saith, I am not. Art thou that prophet? And he answered, No" (John 1:19-21).
3. By the crowds—"When Jesus came into the coasts of Caesarea Philippi, he asked his disciples, saying, Whom do men say that I the Son of man am? And they said, Some say that thou art John the Baptist: some, Elias; and others, Jeremias, or one of the prophets" (Matt. 16:13-14).

H. Both were widely acknowledged men of God.

1. Elijah—"And it came to pass after these things, that the son of the woman, the mistress of the house, fell sick; and his sickness was so sore, that there was no breath left in him. And she said unto Elijah, What have I to do with thee, O thou man of God? art thou come unto me to call my sin to remembrance, and to slay my son?" (1 Kings 17:17-18).
2. John—"For Herod feared John, knowing that he was a just man and an holy, and observed him; and when he heard him, he did many things, and heard him gladly" (Mark 6:20).

OBSERVATIONS FROM THE LIVES OF THE TWELVE APOSTLES

I. Basic Observations
   A. Several may have been married. "Have we not power to lead about a sister, a wife, as well as other apostles, and as the brethren of the Lord, and Cephas?" (1 Cor. 9:5).
   B. At least six of the apostles were brothers.
      1. Andrew and Peter (John 1:40)
      2. James and John (Matt. 4:21)
      3. James the Less and Thaddaeus (Matt. 10:3)
   C. Two were originally disciples of John the Baptist. These were Andrew and John (John 1:35).
   D. Two led another apostle to Christ.
      1. Andrew brought Peter to Jesus (John 1:40-42).
      2. Philip brought Nathanael to Jesus (John 1:45-51).
   E. The occupation of at least five apostles is given.
      1. Andrew, Peter, James, and John were fishermen (Matt. 4:18-22).
      2. Matthew was a tax collector (Luke 5:27).
   F. Tradition says 11 of the 12 (Judas excepted) died as martyrs for Christ. Scripture states specifically that two of them did.
      1. James—"Now about that time Herod the king stretched forth his hands to vex certain of the church. And he killed James the brother of John with the sword" (Acts 12:1-2).
      2. Peter—"Verily, verily, I say unto thee, When thou wast young, thou girdedst thyself, and walkedst whither thou wouldest: but when thou shalt be old, thou shalt stretch forth thy hands, and another shall gird thee, and carry thee whither thou wouldest not. This spake he, signifying by what death he should glorify God. And when he had spoken this, he saith unto him, Follow me. . . . Knowing that shortly I must put off this my tabernacle, even as our Lord Jesus Christ hath shewed me" (John 21:18-19; 2 Pet. 1:14).
   G. Three wrote New Testament books.
      1. Matthew (the Gospel of Matthew)
      2. Peter (1 and 2 Peter)
      3. John (the Gospel of John, 1, 2, 3 John, Revelation)
   H. According to scripture, James was the first to die. According to tradition, John was the last to die.
   I. The postresurrection activities of two apostles are described in the book of Acts, those of Peter and John.

II. Basic Applications
   A. All 12 apostles seemed to be busily engaged in their work when Christ called them. There are manifold examples in the scripture where Jesus touched the *lawless* and made them spiritual giants. There are no examples where He did the same for the *lazy*.
   B. The *extraordinary* fact about the Twelve is that they all seemed to be quite *ordinary*. Jesus did not choose them

for their intellectual or financial achievements. Instead, he selected ordinary men to later do extraordinary things. As Paul would later write: "For ye see your calling, brethren, how that not many wise men after the flesh, not many mighty, not many noble, are called: But God hath chosen the foolish things of the world to confound the wise; and God hath chosen the weak things of the world to confound the things which are mighty; and base things of the world, and things which are despised, hath God chosen, yea, and things which are not, to bring to nought things that are: That no flesh should glory in his presence" (1 Cor. 1:26-29).

C. According to reliable tradition all the apostles (Judas being excepted) would endure great hardships and eventually die as martyrs for Christ. Their stories totally refute and condemn that selfish and greedy false doctrine today known as prosperity theology, which teaches it is God's will for all his people to enjoy abundant health and great wealth.

OBSERVATIONS FROM THE LIVES OF OTHER NEW TESTAMENT PEOPLE

I. Apostles: Some observations and applications from the lives of the 12 apostles have already been considered. The following is a list of the actual 12 plus a number of others who are designated as apostles.
   A. Simon Peter, fisherman, the brother of Andrew (John 1:40)
   B. Andrew, fisherman, the brother of Simon Peter (John 1:40)
   C. John, fisherman, the brother of James (Matt. 4:21)
   D. James, fisherman, the brother of John (Matt. 4:21)
   E. Philip, who introduced his friend Nathaniel to Jesus (John 1:43)
   F. Nathanael, also called Bartholomew (John 1:45)
   G. Matthew, tax collector, also called Levi (Luke 5:27)
   H. Thaddaeus, also called Judas or Jude (Matt. 10:3)
   I. James the Less, son of Alphaeus, possibly the brother of Thaddaeus (Matt. 10:3)
   J. Simon the Zealot, member of a radical Jewish party (Matt. 10:4)
   K. Thomas, a twin (John 11:16)
   L. Judas Iscariot, the traitor (John 6:70)
   M. Matthias, elected to take Judas Iscariot's place (Acts 1:26)
   N. Paul, apostle to the Gentiles (Rom. 11:13)
   O. Barnabas, Paul's first missionary companion (Acts 13:2)
   P. Silas, Paul's second missionary companion (1 Thess. 2:7)
   Q. James, half brother of Christ and head of the Jerusalem church (Gal. 1:19)

II. Authors: There are at least eight (and possibly nine) individuals used by God in the writing of the New Testament.
   A. Identity of these authors
      1. Matthew (the Gospel of Matthew)
      2. Mark (the Gospel of Mark)
      3. Luke (the Gospel of Luke and Acts)
      4. John (the Gospel of John, 1, 2, and 3 John, and Revelation)
      5. Peter (books of 1 and 2 Peter)
      6. Paul (books of Romans, 1 and 2 Corinthians, Galatians, Ephesians, Philippians, Colossians, 1 and 2 Thessalonians, 1 and 2 Timothy, Titus, Philemon, and (possibly) Hebrews.
      7. James (book of James)
      8. Jude (book of Jude)
   B. Observations concerning these authors
      1. Two were the half brothers of Christ (James and Jude)—"Is not this the carpenter's son? is not his mother called Mary? and his brethren, James, and Joses, and Simon, and Judas?" (Matt. 13:55). "James, a servant of God and of the Lord Jesus Christ, to the twelve tribes which are scattered abroad, greeting" (Jas. 1:1). "Jude, the servant of Jesus Christ, and brother of James, to them that are sanctified by God the Father, and preserved in Jesus Christ, and called" (Jude 1).

2. Three were among the original 12 apostles called by Christ (Matthew, John, Peter).
3. Three had shown hostility to Jesus prior to their conversion (James, Jude, and Paul)—"His brethren therefore said unto him, Depart hence, and go into Judaea, that thy disciples also may see the works that thou doest. . . . For neither did his brethren believe in him" (John 7:3, 5). "And I persecuted this way unto the death, binding and delivering into prisons both men and women. As also the high priest doth bear me witness, and all the estate of the elders: from whom also I received letters unto the brethren, and went to Damascus, to bring them which were there bound unto Jerusalem, for to be punished" (Acts 22:4-5).
4. Four received a personal postresurrection visit by Christ (Peter, James, Paul, and John).
   a. During the 40-day period
      (1) Peter (Luke 24:34; 1 Cor. 15:5)
      (2) James (1 Cor. 15:7)
   b. Following his ascension
      (1) Paul (Acts 9:1-8)
      (2) John (Rev. 1:9-20)

III. Evangelists and Missionaries
   A. John the Baptist, great Nazarite New Testament evangelist and forerunner of Christ (Matt. 3:1-6)
   B. Philip, one of the original seven deacons, who later led the Ethiopian eunuch to Christ (Acts 8:5; 21:8)
   C. Paul, history's greatest missionary and evangelist and author of much of the New Testament (Acts 13–28; 1 Tim. 1:12)
   D. Barnabas, Paul's companion during the first missionary journey (Acts 9:26-31; 11:19-31: 13–14)
   E. John Mark, nephew of Barnabas, author of the Gospel of Mark, and traveling companion of Paul, though he failed Paul during the first missionary journey (Acts 12:25; 13:5; 15:36-39; 2 Tim. 4:11)
   F. Silas, Paul's companion during the second missionary journey (Acts 15:40–17:15)
   G. Timothy, Paul's companion during the second journey (Acts 16:1-5; 1 Tim. 1:3)
   H. Luke, Paul's traveling companion and author of the Gospel of Luke and Acts (Luke 1:1-4; Col. 4:14; 2 Tim. 4:11)
   I. Epaphras, an evangelist from Colosse trained by Paul (Col 1:7; 4:12-13)
   J. Apollos, powerful teacher from Alexandria (Acts 18:24-28)
   K. Titus, Paul's companion, appointed to oversee the church in Crete (Titus 1:5).

IV. Governors
   A. Identity of these governors
      1. Pilate (Matt. 27:1-2)
      2. Sergius Paulus (Acts 13:7)
      3. Felix (Acts 24:24)
      4. Festus (Acts 25:1)
      5. Publius (Acts 28:7)
   B. Observations concerning these governors
      1. Paul was associated with four of these men (Sergius Paulus, Felix, Festus, Publius).
      2. Three out of the five were godless (Pilate, Felix, Festus).
      3. All three of these godless governors had unique opportunities to accept Christ.
         a. Pilate—"Then Pilate entered into the judgment hall again, and called Jesus, and said unto him, Art thou the King of the Jews? Jesus answered him, Sayest t hou this thing of thyself, or did others tell it thee of me? Pilate answered, Am I a Jew? Thine own nation and the chief priests have delivered thee unto me: what hast thou done? Jesus answered, My kingdom is not of this world: if my kingdom were of this world, then would my servants fight, that I should

not be delivered to the Jews: but now is my kingdom not from hence. Pilate therefore said unto him, Art thou a king then? Jesus answered, Thou sayest that I am a king. To this end was I born, and for this cause came I into the world, that I should bear witness unto the truth. Every one that is of the truth heareth my voice. Pilate saith unto him, What is truth? And when he had said this, he went out again unto the Jews, and saith unto them, I find in him no fault at all" (John 18:33-38).

b. Felix—"And after certain days, when Felix came with his wife Drusilla, which was a Jewess, he sent for Paul, and heard him concerning the faith in Christ. And as he reasoned of righteousness, temperance, and judgment to come, Felix trembled, and answered, Go thy way for this time; when I have a convenient season, I will call for thee" (Acts 24:24-25).

c. Festus—"That Christ should suffer, and that he should be the first that should rise from the dead, and should shew light unto the people, and to the Gentiles. And as he thus spake for himself, Festus said with a loud voice, Paul, thou art beside thyself; much learning doth make thee mad. But he said, I am not mad, most noble Fetus; but speak forth the words of truth and soberness" (Acts 26:23-25).

V. Kings and Queens

A. Herodian

1. Herod the Great, ruler over Judah at the time of Jesus' birth (Matt. 2:1-20)
2. Herod Archelaus, oldest son of Herod the Great; king when Joseph, Mary, and Jesus left Egypt (Matt. 2:22)
3. Herod Philip, another son of Herod the Great and first husband of Herodias, who left him for Antipas, his brother (Matt. 14:3)
4. Herod Antipas, youngest son of Herod the Great and the king who killed John the Baptist (Matt. 14:1-11)
5. Herod Agrippa, grandson of Herod the Great and killer of the apostle James; an angel of the Lord killed him for accepting the people's worship (Acts 12).
6. Herod Agrippa II, great-grandson of Herod the Great and the king Paul spoke to about becoming a Christian (Acts 25:13–26:32)

B. Roman

1. Augustus Caesar, emperor when Jesus was born (Luke 2:1)
2. Tiberius Caesar, emperor during Jesus' earthly ministry (Luke 3:1; 20:22-25)

C. Queens

1. Herodias, Herod Antipas's vicious wife who plotted John the Baptist's death (Matt. 14:1-11)
2. Candace, Ethiopian queen who allowed her servant, the eunuch, to visit Judea (Acts 8:27-28)
3. Bernice, the sister and wife of King Agrippa (Acts 25:13, 23; 26:30)

VI. Martyrs

A. Stephen, the church's first martyr, stoned by the Jews (Acts 7:59)

B. James, the first of the 12 apostles to be martyred (Acts 12:1-2)

C. Paul, believed to have been beheaded by emperor Nero (2 Tim. 4:6)

D. Peter, believed to have been crucified upside down by Nero (John 21: 18-19; 2 Peter 1:14)

E. Antipas, martyred in the city of Pergamos (Rev. 2:13)

VII. Military Men

A. The identity of these men

1. Claudius Lysias, Roman commander (Greek: *chiliarchos:* officer in charge of 1,000 men) who sent Paul from Jerusalem to Felix, the

Roman governor in Caesarea (Acts 23:12-33)
2. The centurion (an officer in charge of 100 men) at Capernaum who asked and received from Jesus healing for his dying servant (Luke 7:1-10)
3. The officer (*chiliarchos*) present at the arrest of Jesus (John 18:12)
4. The centurion at Calvary who recognized Jesus as the Son of God (Matt. 27:54)
5. Cornelius, led to Christ by Peter at Caesarea (Acts 10)
6. The officer (*chiliarchos*) at Antonia fortress who rescued Paul from the Jews in Jerusalem (Acts 21:32; 22:24)
7. Julius, who treated Paul kindly during his fateful voyage to Rome (Acts 27:1-44)

B. Observations concerning these men
1. Four out of seven were centurions, that is, they commanded at least 100 soldiers. Three were officers, translated "chief captain," and were in charge of 1,000 men.
2. All but one, the officer present at the arrest of Christ, were presented in a very favorable light.
3. The salvation of one centurion (Cornelius) is recorded, and there is strong evidence that at least two more accepted Christ. Note their testimonies:
   a. The centurion at Capernaum—"And a certain centurion's servant, who was dear unto him, was sick, and ready to die. And when he heard of Jesus, he sent unto him the elders of the Jews, beseeching him that he would come and heal his servant. And when they came to Jesus, they besought him instantly, saying, That he was worthy for whom he should do this: For he loveth our nation, and he hath built us a synagogue. Then Jesus went with them. And when he was now not far from the house, the centurion sent friends to him, saying unto him, Lord, trouble not thyself: for I am not worthy that thou shouldest enter under my roof: Wherefore neither thought I myself worthy to come unto thee: but say in a word, and my servant shall be healed. For I also am a man set under authority, having under me soldiers, and I say unto one, Go, and he goeth; and to another, Come, and he cometh; and to my servant, Do this, and he doeth it. When Jesus heard these things, he marvelled at him, and turned him about, and said unto the people that followed him, I say unto you, I have not found so great faith, no, not in Israel" (Luke 7:2-9).
   b. The centurion at Calvary—"And Jesus cried with a loud voice, and gave up the ghost. And the veil of the temple was rent in twain from the top to the bottom. And when the centurion, which stood over against him, saw that he so cried out, and gave up the ghost, he said, Truly this man was the Son of God" (Mark 15:37-39).

VIII. Pharisees
A. The identity of these men: At least seven separate Pharisees are referred to in the New Testament.
1. Simon, the Pharisee with whom Jesus dined, who criticized Jesus for allowing an immoral woman to wash his feet (Luke 7:36, 40)
2. Another Pharisee with whom Jesus dined, who criticized the Savior for not observing the rite of cleansing before eating (Luke 11:37)
3. Another Pharisee with whom Jesus dined, whose home was the scene for Jesus healing a man with dropsy (Luke 14:1)

4. Hypocritical Pharisee whom Jesus contrasted with the humble publican (Luke 18:10-14)
5. Nicodemus, the sincere Pharisee who came to Jesus by night (John 3:1-20)
6. Gamaliel, famous Jewish teacher who cautioned the Sanhedrin against persecuting the apostles (Acts 5:34-40)
7. Paul, Scripture's greatest theologian and missionary (Acts 23:6)

B. Observations concerning these men
1. Four out of the seven were ungodly.
2. One (although probably unsaved) demonstrated much wisdom (Gamaliel).
3. Two were greatly used by God (Nicodemus and Paul).
4. Three of the four recorded biblical instances where Jesus dined in a private home were in Pharisees' homes. (For the non-Pharisee's home, see John 12:1-8; Matt. 26:6-13.)

IX. Priests

A. The identity of these men
1. Zacharias, father of John the Baptist (Luke 1:5-23, 59-64)
2. Annas, wicked former high priest during the time of Jesus (John 18:13; Acts 4:6)
3. Caiaphas, son-in-law of Annas and wicked high priest during the time of Jesus (Matt. 26:3; Luke 3:2; John 11:47-53; 18:13-14)
4. Ananias, president of the Sanhedrin when Paul was brought before it (Acts 23:2; 24:1)
5. Sceva, false Jewish priest living in Ephesus (Acts 19:14)

B. Observations concerning these men
1. Four out of five were godless priests.
2. Two persecuted both Jesus and his 12 apostles (Annas and Caiaphas). "Then the band and the captain and officers of the Jews took Jesus, and bound him, And led him away to Annas first; for he was father-in-law to Caiaphas, which was the high priest that same year. . . . Now Annas had sent him bound unto Caiaphas the high priest" (John 18:12-13, 24). "And Annas the high priest, and Caiaphas, and John, and Alexander, and as many as were of the kindred of the high priest, were gathered together at Jerusalem. And when they had set them in the midst, they asked, By what power, or by what name, have ye done this? Then Peter, filled with the Holy Ghost, said unto them, Ye rulers of the people, and elders of Israel . . . . Be it known unto you all, and to all the people of Israel, that by the name of Jesus Christ of Nazareth, whom ye crucified, whom God raised from the dead, even by him doth this man stand here before you whole" (Acts 4:6-8, 10).
3. One gave the first recorded messianic prophecy in the New Testament while another gave the last.
   a. The prophecy of Zacharias—"And his father Zacharias was filled with the Holy Ghost, and prophesied, saying, Blessed be the Lord God of Israel; for he hath visited and redeemed his people . . . . And thou, child, shalt be called the prophet of the Highest: for thou shalt go before the face of the Lord to prepare his ways" (Luke 1:67-68, 76).
   b. The prophecy of Caiaphas—"Then gathered the chief priests and the Pharisees a council, and said, What do we? for this man doeth many miracles. If we let him thus alone, all men will believe on him: and the Romans shall come and take away both our place and nation. And one of them, named Caiaphas, being the high priest that same year, said unto them, Ye know nothing at all, Nor consider that it is expedient for us, that one man should die for the people, and

that the whole nation perish not. And this spake he not of himself: but being high priest that year, he prophesied that Jesus should die for that nation; And not for that nation only, but that also he should gather together in one the children of God that were scattered abroad" (John 11:47-52).

X. Prophets and Prophetesses: Peter, Paul, the Apostle John, and John the Baptist were, of course, prophets. However, there were others less known but equally inspired prophets and prophetesses mentioned in the New Testament.

A. Simeon, who predicted the future ministry of Christ (Luke 2:25-35)—"Lord, now lettest thou thy servant depart in peace, according to thy word: For mine eyes have seen thy salvation, which thou hast prepared before the face of all people; a light to lighten the Gentiles, and the glory of thy people Israel. . . . And Simeon blessed them, and said unto Mary his mother, Behold, this child is set for the fall and rising again of many in Israel; and for a sign which shall be spoken against" (Luke 2:29-32, 34).

B. Anna—"And there was one Anna, a prophetess, the daughter of Phanuel, of the tribe of Aser: she was of a great age, and had lived with an husband seven years from her virginity; and she was a widow of about fourscore and four years, which departed not from the temple, but served God with fastings and prayers night and day. And she coming in that instant gave thanks likewise unto the Lord, and spake of him to all them that looked for redemption in Jerusalem" (Luke 2:36-38).

C. Agabus

1. First recorded prediction—"And in these days came prophets from Jerusalem unto Antioch. And there stood up one of them named Agabus, and signified by the spirit that there should be great dearth throughout all the world: which came to pass in the days of Claudius Caesar" (Acts 11:27-28).

2. Second recorded prediction—"And as we tarried there many days, there came down from Judaea a certain prophet, named Agabus. And when he was come unto us, he took Paul's girdle, and bound his own hands and feet, and said, Thus saith the Holy Ghost, So shall the Jews at Jerusalem bind the man that owneth this girdle, and shall deliver him into the hands of the Gentiles" (Acts 21:10-11).

D. Judas and Silas—"And Judas and Silas, being prophets also themselves, exhorted the brethren with many words, and confirmed them" (Acts 15:32).

E. Philip's four unmarried daughters (Acts 21:8-9)

F. Elymas, a false prophet and sorcerer who confronted Paul on Cyprus (Acts 13:6, 8)

G. Jezebel, a self-appointed prophetess in the church at Thyatira (Rev. 2:20)

XI. Recipients of New Testament Books

A. The identity of these individuals

1. Theophilus—"It seemed good to me also, having had perfect understanding of all things from the very first, to write unto thee in order, most excellent Theophilus" (Luke 1:3). "The former treatise have I made, O Theophilus, of all that Jesus began both to do and teach" (Acts 1:1).

2. Titus—"To Titus, mine own son after the common faith: Grace, mercy, and peace, from God the Father and the Lord Jesus Christ our Saviour" (Titus 1:4).

3. Timothy—"Unto Timothy, my own son in the faith: Grace, mercy, and peace, from God our Father and Jesus Christ our Lord" (1 Tim. 1:2). "To Timothy, my dearly beloved son: Grace, mercy, and peace, from

God the Father and Christ Jesus our Lord" (2 Tim. 1:2).

4. Philemon—"Paul, a prisoner of Jesus Christ, and Timothy our brother, unto Philemon our dearly beloved, and fellowlabourer" (Philem. 1).
5. Elect lady—"The elder unto the elect lady and her children, whom I love in the truth; and not I only, but also all they that have known the truth" (2 John 1).
6. Gaius—"The elder unto the wellbeloved Gaius, whom I love in the truth" (3 John 1).

B. Observations concerning these individuals
1. Only one was a Gentile (Theophilus).
2. Two were pastors (Titus and Timothy).
3. These eight books were written by three authors:
   a. Luke: author of the Gospel of Luke and Acts
   b. Paul: author of First and Second Timothy, Titus, and Philemon
   c. John: author of Second and Third John

XII. Restored to health and life: A great number of New Testament individuals were healed of various sicknesses and infirmities, including death.

A. The identity of these individuals
1. The lepers
   a. The leper in Capernaum (Matt. 8:2-4; Mark 1:20-25; Luke 5:12-16)
   b. The ten lepers in Samaria (Luke 17:11-19)
2. The blind
   a. Two blind men (Matt. 9:27-31)
   b. The blind man in Bethsaida (Mark 8:22-26)
   c. The man born blind in Jerusalem (John 9:1-41)
   d. Bartimaeus (Matt. 20:29-34; Mark 10:46-52; Luke 18:35-43)
3. The deaf—The deaf man with a speech impediment (Mark 7:31-37)
4. The crippled
   a. The cripple of 38 years by the pool of Bethesda (John 5:1-16)
   b. The lame man by the temple gate (Acts 3:6-7)
   c. The crippled man in Lystra (Acts 14:8-10)
5. The fever-ridden
   a. The nobleman's son in Capernaum (John 4:43-54)
   b. Peter's mother-in-law (Matt. 8:14-17; Mark 1:29-34; Luke 4:38-41)
   c. The centurion's servant (Matt. 8:5-13; Luke 7:1-10)
6. Those with internal ailments
   a. The woman with the bloody flux (Matt. 9:20-22; Mark 5:25-34; Luke 8:43-48)
   b. Publius's father (Acts 28:7-8)
7. The deformed: The man with a withered hand (Matt. 12:9-14; Mark 3:1-6; Luke 6:6-11)
8. A paralytic (Matt. 9:1-8; Mark 2:1-12; Luke 5:17-26)
9. Those with heart problems—The man with dropsy (Luke 14:1-6)
10. The maimed—The high priest's servant whose ear was severed (Luke 22:49-51)
11. The demon-possessed
    a. A man in Capernaum (Mark 1:24; Luke 4:35)
    b. Maniac of Gadara (Matt. 8:28-32; Mark 5:2-13; Luke 8:33)
    c. A mute man (Matt. 9:32-33)
    d. A girl from Tyre and Sidon (Matt. 15:28; Mark 7:29)
    e. A boy at the base of Mount Hermon (Matt. 17:18; Mark 9:25; Luke 9:42)
    f. A blind and deaf man (Matt. 12:22; Luke 11:14)
    g. A woman with an 18-year infirmity (Luke 13:10-13)
    h. Mary Magdalene (Mark 16:9; Luke 8:2)
    i. A slave girl at Philippi (Acts 16:16-18)

12. The dead: Five New Testament people were raised from the dead.
    a. A little daughter (Matt. 9:18-19, 23-26; Mark 5:22-24, 35-43; Luke 8:41-42, 49-56)
    b. A young son (Luke 7:11-17)
    c. A brother (John 11:1-46)
    d. Dorcas (Acts 9:36-41)
    e. Eutychus (Acts 20:7-12)

B. Observations concerning these individuals
1. Out of the 45 or so recorded miracles in the New Testament (not counting those occurring in the great tribulation as found in the book of Revelation), no less than 34 involve healing or resurrection.
2. Only six individuals are referred to by name (Lazarus, Bartimaeus, Malchus, Aeneas, Dorcas, and Eutychus).
3. Nine of the miracles involved Gentiles.
4. Twenty-three involved men; five, women; three, boys; and three, girls.
5. The duration of suffering is given in at least seven instances.
    a. The woman with the bloody flux—12 years (Matt. 9:20)
    b. The cripple beside Bethesda—38 years (John 5:5)
    c. The crippled woman—18 years (Luke 13:11)
    d. The crippled man beside the temple gate—40 years (Acts 3:2; 4:22)
    e. The cripple at Lystra—from his mother's womb (Acts 14:8)
    f. The man with palsy—eight years (Acts 9:33)
    g. The blind man in Jerusalem—from his mother's womb (John 9:1)

XIII. Twenty individuals who are referred to most in the New Testament, excepting Jesus

A. The identification of these people
1. Peter, referred to 183 times
2. Paul, referred to 180 times
3. John the Baptist, referred to 90 times
4. Pilate, referred to 53 times
5. John the apostle, referred to 42 times
6. Luke, referred to 41 times
7. Barnabas, referred to 30 times
8. Herod Antipas, referred to 27 times
9. Timothy, referred to 24 times
10. Judas Iscariot, referred to 22 times
11. James the apostle, referred to 19 times
12. Mary, mother of Jesus, referred to 19 times
13. Joseph, husband of mary, referred to 16 times
14. Philip the apostle, referred to 16 times
15. Philip the evangelist, referred to 16 times
16. Thomas, referred to 15 times
17. Mary Magdalene, referred to 14 times
18. Festus, referred to 13 times
19. Silas, referred to 13 times
20. Titus, referred to 12 times

B. Observations concerning these people
1. The top three (Peter, Paul, and John the Baptist) are mentioned more times than the remaining 17 individuals combined.
    a. The first three are mentioned 482 times.
    b. The final 17 are mentioned 363 times.
2. Only two women are listed in the top 20, Mary, mother of Jesus and Mary Magdalene.
3. Five apostles are listed (Peter, John, James, Philip, and Thomas).
4. Four godless individuals are included (Pilate, Herod Antipas, Judas, and Festus).

NOTES

N O T E S

NOTES

NOTES

NOTES

NOTES

NOTES

NOTES

NOTES

NOTES